A logo is a flag, a signature, an escutcheon.
A logo doesn't sell (directly), it identifies.
A logo is rarely a description of a business.
A logo derives its meaning from the quality of the
thing it symbolizes, not the other way around.
A logo is less important than the product it
signifies; what it means is more important than
what it looks like.
Paul Rand

Jens Müller
Julius Wiedemann (Ed.)

LOGO BEGINNINGS
LOGO MODERNISM

TASCHEN

Contents

LOGO
BEGINNINGS

B

The Beginnings of Branding
Jens Müller

It is said that in nineteenth-century China, an ousted minister would sometimes take his official seal with him out of spite. Without a seal, it was virtually impossible for the minister's successor to issue new decrees, because the impression of an official stamp was the only trusted form of authentication in China at the time. Thus, an invented symbol was given more credence than a person's signature. This anecdote is a particularly striking example of the historical power of marks. Over the course of industrialization in the past 150 years, however, marks have primarily been used by companies. With their own individually designed marks, even everyday consumer goods, such as toilet paper and matches, have become distinct brand-name products. The logo has become an established fixture in all aspects of human activity. These days, it is almost impossible to imagine a university, band, medical practice, community initiative, or app without a custom-designed source identifier composed of shapes and letters.

While the background and current state of this evolution have been the subject of extensive research and publication, many works pay surprisingly little attention to the early days of the modern logo; instead, these works often reference the same examples over and over again. Leaving out Ford's wordmark, which has only been marginally altered over the past 100 years, is as unheard of as omitting an evolution of trademarks from awkwardly figurative marks to minimalist abstract logos. But so far, a detailed examination of the formal language of early logos has been lacking. At first glance, a simple examination of trademarks from before 1945 indeed seems challenging. The inconsistencies that emerged even in the early days of registered trademarks seem too great: The first registered logo in the United States, a design for the paint manufacturer Averill from 1870, for example, shows an eagle holding a paintbrush in its beak against the skyline of Chicago. Rippling above the paintbrush is a banderole bearing the words "Durable, Beautiful, Economical." The first registered trademark in Europe in 1875, on the other hand, consists merely of a red triangle representing the English Bass Brewery [→ 01].

But before we devote ourselves to the contemporaneity of abstraction and representationalism in early logos, it is worth first examining the general circumstances under which trademarks originally developed. It is, after all, no coincidence that around 1870, both the United States and western European countries, such as Great Britain, introduced the first trademark laws. A brief mention of the beginnings of the history of industrialization can provide more context. In certain countries in the mid nineteenth century, the trade of products such as food and furnishings initially developed exclusively through regional distribution. This gave rise to new competitive situations, making it necessary for businesses to identify and distinguish themselves from providers of similar products. The first consciously designed packaging was created, which, besides a description of the contents, indicated, for example, whether a manufacturer was a purveyor to the court or had received a national quality award for its product. However, what truly set a business apart from the competition was the condensed depiction of its name in the form of a logo. Although numerous earlier examples of related marks exist, it was at this time that brands and trademarks as they are understood today emerged.

Even at the beginning of this development, various and sometimes contrary design concepts for logos emerged, including wordmarks, acronym marks, figurative drawings, and abstract forms. By and large, these main categories established more than 170 years ago form the basis of logo design to this day. Despite the continued development toward systematically applicable corporate design solutions, it is astonishing that many of the marks designed in the early days still work so well—in an entirely different media landscape—as the core element of numerous brands. Ultimately, big companies such as General Electric, Mitsubishi, and Lufthansa, which have been using their logos essentially unchanged for more than a century, do not only hold on to the original designs out of nostalgia. At the same time, there are just as many examples of radical evolutions in brand representation. The logo history of the German calculator manufacturer Brunsviga [→ 02] is almost paradigmatic for the continuous development toward the modern logo in the first half of the 20th century. There is no conclusive answer as to why—contrary to the logic of this development—abstract logos already existed in the early days. However, a closer look at the history makes it plausible that abstraction emerged in early goldsmith, mason, and potter marks, because production processes at the time simply did not allow for the application of more complex marks. Thus, early abstract marks may have developed not so much out of an understanding that they were more eye-catching as in response to purely practical constraints. By contrast, 16th-century European printers used complex representational illustrations of people and animals for their marks. The reason for this was probably that printing techniques had finally made wood and steel engraving suitable for this kind of artistic expression. These are likely the conflicting historical origins that allowed representationalism and abstraction to emerge as equivalent design options at the beginning of the development of the modern logo.

On the other hand, reduction was not used deliberately as a design principle to facilitate effective communication until the beginning of the 20th century. Some limited treatments of the topic often attribute this innovation to, above all, the avant-garde around the Bauhaus, which manifested and propagated this principle from the school's founding in 1919. However, a look at European or Russian graphic design from the 1910s reveals that print material with deliberately reduced designs had become established even beyond avant-garde circles early on—possibly as a counterargument to the ornateness of Art Nouveau or in response to the changing conditions of consumption in the modern big city. In the field of trademarks, this change manifested in a shift toward basic geometric shapes and a dramatic increase in technically constructed solutions. The *Blickfang-Serie* [→ 06] ("Eye-catcher series"), a collection of logo-like design templates for printers published in 1927, is proof of this development and its entry into everyday design. By then, reduction and simplicity had been established as optimal requirements for recognizable logos. As designer Kurt Wiedemann later once said: a good logo is one you can draw from memory in the sand with your big toe.

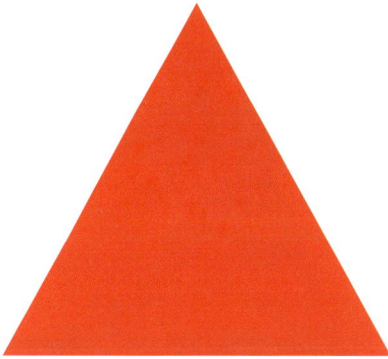

01

The first registered logo in the
United States for the paint manufacturer Averill (above) from 1870
and the first registered logo in
Europe for the British brewery Bass
(below) from 1875

Das erste in den USA registrierte
Logo für den Farbenhersteller Averill
(oben) von 1870 und das erste in
Europa registrierte Logo für die
britische Brauerei Bass (unten) aus
dem Jahr 1875

Le premier logo enregistré aux USA,
celui du fabricant de peintures
Averill (en haut), en 1870, et le
premier logo enregistré en Europe,
celui de la brasserie britannique
Bass (en bas), de 1875

1892

1900s

1900s

1912

1929

1929

1947

1960

1964

02
The development of the logo of
a German calculating machine
producer between 1892 and 1964

Die Logoentwicklung eines deutschen Rechenmaschinenherstellers
zwischen 1892 und 1964

L'évolution du logo d'un fabricant
allemand de machines à calculer,
de 1892 à 1964

In the early 1910s, over 150,000 trademarks had already been registered and legally protected in Germany alone. This enormous sum clearly demonstrates the incalculable number of different logos at that time. Distinguishing a business from the competition solely through a mark was challenging even in the early days of branding. Even though companies such as the Coca-Cola Company successfully sued competitors with similar names and wordmarks, (→ 09) businesses developed brand attributes beyond their trademarks, such as company colors or unique forms of packaging. In the first decades of the 20th century, manufacturers with particularly innovative products of outstanding quality, creative advertising, and good distribution successfully rose to become global brands. Businesses such as Kodak, Olivetti, Heinz, and Singer became international corporations. That precisely these brands established eye-catching, consistently applied designs early on may be a significant contributing factor to their long-term and global success.

Over the years, certain conventions have developed in the field of logos. Construction companies use particularly "sturdily" designed marks, while sporting goods manufacturers communicate dynamism and movement in their marks. In many early logos, these kinds of perceived rules of modern-day communication design were entirely ignored. Thus, from today's perspective, some marks are characterized by a certain naiveté and simplicity, without exhibiting any deficiencies in craftsmanship. Until the 1930s, illustrations of people and animals, for example, were completely natural elements in pictorial marks across all industries. In contemporary logo design, however, comparable examples are rare. Other categories long thought to be extinct, such as the emblem, a usually circular stamp-like arrangement of pictorial and textual elements, experienced a renaissance a few years ago. Small owner-operated cafés and shops used this at first unusual and anachronistic-looking logo style as a visual countermodel to the branding of big chains.

Although the aspect of timelessness regarding logos is—in contrast to many other forms of media in graphic design—of prominent importance, every design is inevitably a child of its time. The early logos discussed here are also characterized by the trends and styles of the eras in which they were created. Even marks consisting of only a few elements reveal the influence of Art Nouveau, Futurism, and Art Deco. However, a factor that speaks against the purely chronological ordering of logos is the far more interesting examination of common design parameters that, beyond any short-lived trend, still dictate the design principles of trademarks today.

This book is based on the principle of an equally qualitative and quantitative collection of marks and their systematic categorization. It is through the selection and subsequent classification of thousands of logos into various categories and sub-groups that universal design principles and those typical for their time come into view. The idea behind the famous logo of the pharmaceutical manufacturer Bayer, with the horizontally and vertically intersecting company name, for example, is shown to have been a popular and frequently used design concept. Especially in the United States, hundreds of script logotypes existed—of which only those of Kellogg's, Ford, and Coca-Cola are familiar to us today. The collection presented here shows how many famous trademarks are still used, essentially unchanged, today. At the same time, the collection shines a light on countless forgotten designs. In an age when, thanks to social media, developments in logo design are globally circulated almost in real time, a look at long-forgotten design ideas reveals entirely different influences. It is impossible to predict exactly what marks will look like in the future. What is certain, however, is that the original fundamental principles used in such a variety of ways over one hundred years ago will continue to play a role.

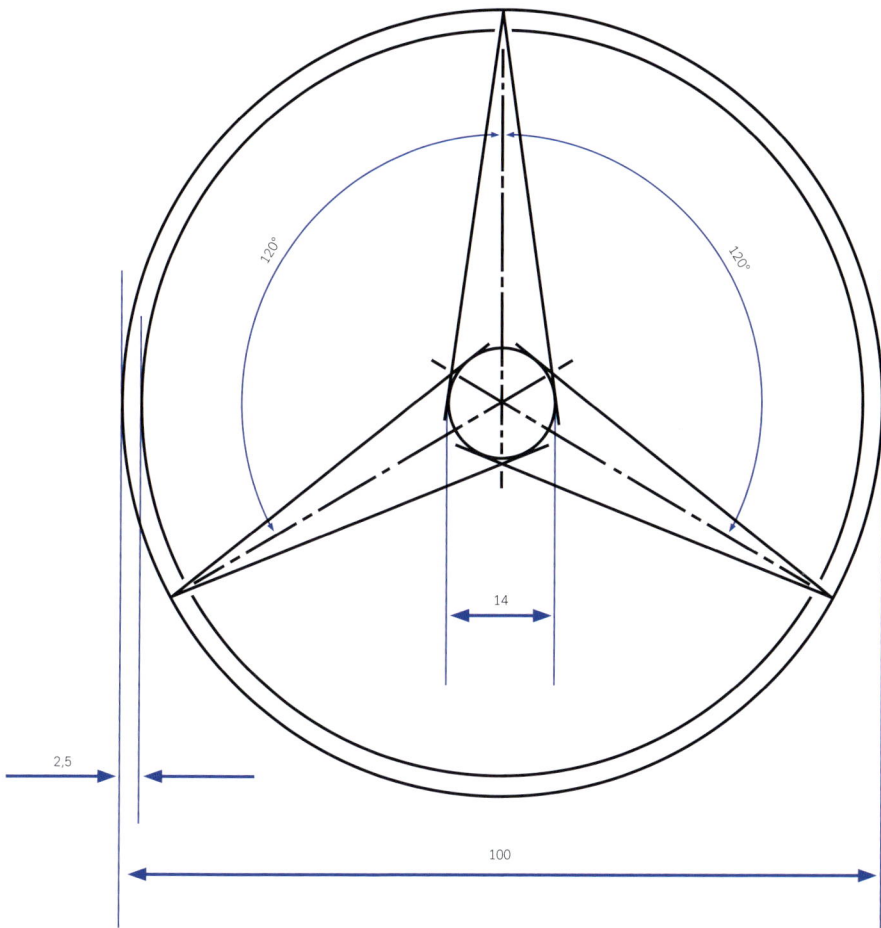

120°

120°

14

2,5

100

03
Design drawing of the logo for the
German automobile manufacturer
Daimler from 1933

Konstruktionszeichnung für das
Logo des deutschen Automobilherstellers Daimler aus dem Jahr
1933

Croquis de conception du logo du
constructeur automobile allemand
Daimler de 1933

04
Dutch marketing magazine with a constructivist design by the graphic artist Machiel Wilmink, 1927

Niederländische Werbezeitschrift mit einem konstruktivistischen Entwurf des Grafikers Machiel Wilmink, 1927

Revue publicitaire néerlandaise à la conception constructiviste par le graphiste Machiel Wilmink, 1927

Die Anfänge der Marken
Jens Müller

Im China des 19. Jahrhunderts soll es manchmal vorgekommen sein, dass ein abgesetzter Minister aus Trotz sein Amtssiegel mitnahm. Das fehlende Siegel machte es seinem Nachfolger praktisch unmöglich, neue Verordnungen zu erlassen, da nur der Abdruck eines offiziellen Stempels im damaligen China als vertrauenswürdige Legitimation galt. Menschen vertrauten einem gestalteten Zeichen also mehr als der Unterschrift einer Person. Dies ist ein Beispiel, das die historische Wirkungsmacht von Zeichen besonders eindrucksvoll belegt. Im Zuge der Industrialisierung waren es in den vergangenen 150 Jahren jedoch vor allem Firmen, die sich Marken zunutze machten. Mit individuell gestalteten Absenderkennungen wurden selbst banale Verbrauchsgüter wie Toilettenpapier oder Streichhölzer zu unterscheidbaren Markenprodukten. Inzwischen hat sich das Logo in sämtlichen Ausprägungen menschlichen Handelns etabliert. Universitäten, Bands, Arztpraxen, Bürgerinitiativen oder Apps sind heutzutage ohne eine gestaltete Absenderkennung aus Formen und Buchstaben kaum mehr denkbar.

Während die Vorgeschichte und Gegenwart dieser Entwicklung ausgiebig erforscht und publiziert sind, kommt die Anfangszeit des modernen Logos in vielen Abhandlungen erstaunlich kurz, und es werden immer wieder die gleichen Beispiele herangezogen. Der Ford-Schriftzug, der sich in den vergangenen 100 Jahren nur marginal verändert hat, darf da genauso wenig fehlen wie eine Markenentwicklung vom unbeholfenen gegenständlichen Zeichen hin zum abstrakt-minimalistischen Logo. Eine detaillierte Untersuchung der Formensprache früher Logos fehlte allerdings bislang. Auf den ersten Blick ist eine einfache Betrachtung von Zeichen aus der Zeit vor 1945 auch tatsächlich schwierig. Zu groß erscheinen die Widersprüche, die bereits in den Anfangstagen registrierter Markenzeichen zutage traten: So zeigt das erste in den USA registrierte Logo für den Farbenhersteller Averill aus dem Jahr 1870 die Silhouette der Stadt Chicago in Verbindung mit einem Adler, der einen Pinsel im Schnabel hält und von einer Banderole mit den Begriffen „Durable, Beautiful, Economical" umrahmt wird. Das erste in Europa registrierte Zeichen war 1875 dagegen schlicht ein rotes Dreieck, das für die britische Brauerei Bass stand [→ 01].

Bevor wir uns jedoch der Gleichzeitigkeit von Abstraktion und Gegenständlichkeit im frühen Logo widmen, lohnt zunächst der Blick auf die generellen Rahmenbedingungen früher Markenentwicklung. Es ist schließlich kein Zufall, dass um das Jahr 1870 sowohl die USA als auch westeuropäische Länder wie Großbritannien erste Gesetze zum Schutz von Markenzeichen einführten. Ohne die vollständige Entwicklungsgeschichte der Industrialisierung aufzurollen, kann man festhalten, dass sich in bestimmten Staaten Mitte des 19. Jahrhunderts der Handel mit Produkten wie Lebensmitteln oder Einrichtungsgegenständen erstmals über eine ausschließlich regionale Verbreitung hinaus entwickelt hatte. Daraus erwuchsen neuartige Konkurrenzsituationen, die eine Kennzeichnung und Unterscheidbarkeit von anderen Anbietern gleicher Produkte notwendig machten. Erste bewusst gestaltete Verpackungen entstanden, die neben der Beschreibung des Inhalts auch darauf hinwiesen, ob ein Hersteller beispielsweise Hoflieferant war oder für ein Produkt eine staatliche Qualitätsmedaille erhalten hatte. Die wesentliche Abgrenzung zur Konkurrenz war aber die eigene

Firmierung, die konzentriert in einem Logo verbildlicht wurde. Auch wenn zahlreiche frühere Beispiele für artverwandte Absenderkennungen existieren, entstanden Marken und Markenzeichen im heutigen Verständnis zu jener Zeit.

Bereits am Anfang dieser Entwicklung standen unterschiedliche und teils konträre Gestaltungskonzepte für Logos: Wortmarken, Buchstabenkürzel, gegenständliche Zeichnungen sowie abstrakte Formen. Im Grunde bilden diese vor mehr als 170 Jahren etablierten Hauptkategorien bis heute die Basis des Logodesigns. Bei aller Weiterentwicklung hin zu systematisch anwendbaren Corporate-Design-Lösungen ist es erstaunlich, dass viele der damals entworfenen Zeichen noch heute – in einem medial völlig veränderten Alltag – bestens als Kernelement vieler Marken funktionieren. Große Unternehmen wie General Electric, Mitsubishi oder Lufthansa, die ihre Logos seit über einem Jahrhundert weitgehend unverändert einsetzen, halten schließlich nicht nur aus nostalgischen Gründen an den ursprünglichen Entwürfen fest. Gleichzeitig gibt es ebenso viele Beispiele für radikale Evolutionen der Markendarstellung. Die Logohistorie des deutschen Rechenmaschinenherstellers Brunsviga [→ 02] ist geradezu exemplarisch für die kontinuierliche Weiterentwicklung zum modernen Logo in der ersten Hälfte des 20. Jahrhunderts. Die Frage, warum es entgegen der Logik dieser Entwicklung bereits in der Frühzeit abstrakte Logos gab, lässt sich nicht ganz abschließend klären. Beschäftigt man sich jedoch ausführlicher mit der Historie, erscheint es einleuchtend, dass Abstraktion bei frühen Goldschmiede-, Steinmetz- oder Töpferzeichen entstand, da der damalige Produktionsprozess die Anbringung komplexerer Zeichen schlichtweg nicht zuließ. Frühe abstrakte Zeichen könnten sich also weniger aus der Erkenntnis um bessere Prägnanz heraus entwickelt haben als vielmehr aus rein praktischen Zwängen. Europäische Buchdrucker des 16. Jahrhunderts nutzten für ihre Zeichen hingegen komplexe gegenständliche Darstellungen von Menschen oder Tieren – wahrscheinlich, weil es die damalige Drucktechnik nun erstmals ermöglichte, im Holz- oder Stahlstich entsprechend künstlerisch expressiv zu arbeiten. Es sind wohl diese beiden gegensätzlichen historischen Ursprünge, die zu Beginn der modernen Logoentwicklung sowohl Gegenständlichkeit als auch Abstraktion als gleichwertige Gestaltungsoptionen erscheinen ließen.

GEG (Fritz Rosen, Germany, 1927), Yacco (France, 1929), and Spratt's (Max Field-Bush, Great Britain, 1936) were among the first companies to work with modular logo systems.

GEG (Fritz Rosen, Deutschland, 1927), Yacco (Frankreich, 1929) und Spratt's (Max Field-Bush, Großbritannien, 1936) gehörten zu den ersten Unternehmen, die mit modularen Logosystemen arbeiteten.

GEG (Fritz Rosen, Allemagne, 1927), Yacco (France, 1929) et Spratt's (Max Field-Bush, Grande-Bretagne, 1936) font partie des premières entreprises à avoir travaillé avec des systèmes de logos modulables.

Reduktion wurde hingegen erst zu Anfang des 20. Jahrhunderts gezielt als Gestaltungsprinzip effektiver Kommunikation eingesetzt. In manch verkürzter Darstellung wird diese Innovation gerne vor allem der Avantgarde rund um das Bauhaus zugeschrieben, die dieses Prinzip seit Gründung der Schule im Jahr 1919 manifestierte und propagierte. Schaut man sich europäisches oder russisches Grafikdesign aus den 1910er-Jahren an, zeigt sich allerdings, dass sich bewusst reduziert gestaltete Drucksachen sehr früh auch jenseits avantgardistischer Kreise etablierten – möglicherweise als Gegenthese zum verschnörkelten Jugendstil oder als Reaktion auf die veränderten Konsumbedingungen in der modernen Großstadt. Im Bereich des Markenzeichens zeigte sich diese Veränderung in einer Hinwendung zu geometrischen Grundformen und in einer starken Zunahme technisch-konstruierter Lösungen. Die 1927 veröffentlichte „Blickfang-Serie" (→ 06), eine Sammlung logoähnlicher Gestaltungsvorlagen für Druckereien, belegt diese Entwicklung und ihren Einzug ins alltägliche Design. Zu dieser Zeit hatte sich bereits die allgemeine Erkenntnis durchgesetzt, dass Reduktion und Einfachheit optimale Voraussetzungen für wiedererkennbare Logos sind – oder wie es der Gestalter Kurt Weidemann später einmal formulierte: dass man ein gutes Logo aus der Erinnerung heraus mit dem Fuß in den Sand zeichnen können muss.

Allein in Deutschland waren Anfang der 1910er-Jahre bereits über 150 000 Warenzeichen eingetragen und gesetzlich geschützt. Diese riesige Zahl belegt sehr eindrücklich die schon damals unüberschaubare Zahl unterschiedlicher Logos. Sich ausschließlich über ein Zeichen von der Konkurrenz abzugrenzen war also bereits in der Frühzeit des Markenwesens schwierig. Auch wenn Unternehmen wie die Coca-Cola Company gegen Konkurrenten mit ähnlichen Namen und Schriftzügen erfolgreich gerichtlich vorgingen (→ 09), entwickelten Firmen über ihr Zeichen hinaus weitere Markeneigenschaften wie die Unternehmensfarbe oder spezielle Verpackungsformen. Herstellern mit besonders innovativen Produkten, einer herausragenden Qualität, einfallsreicher Werbung und einem guten Vertrieb gelang es in den ersten Jahrzehnten des 20. Jahrhunderts zu Weltmarken aufzusteigen. Unternehmen wie Kodak, Olivetti, Heinz oder Singer wurden zu international agierenden Konzernen. Dass genau diese Marken besonders früh prägnante Designkonstanten etablierten, dürfte ein wesentlicher Baustein ihres langfristigen und globalen Erfolgs gewesen sein.

Über die Jahre hinweg entwickelten sich gewisse Konventionen im Bereich des Logos. Bauunternehmen setzen besonders „stabil" konstruierte Zeichen ein, während Sportartikelhersteller bereits in ihrer Absenderkennung Dynamik und Bewegung vermitteln. In vielen frühen Logos wurden solche scheinbaren Gesetzmäßigkeiten des heutigen Kommunikationsdesigns völlig ignoriert. Aus dem Blickwinkel der Gegenwart sind manche Zeichen daher durch eine gewisse Naivität und Arglosigkeit geprägt – ohne dabei handwerkliche Defizite zu offenbaren. So war die Abbildung von Menschen oder Tieren in Bildmarken sämtlicher Branchen bis in die 1930er-Jahre völlig selbstverständlich. Im aktuellen Logodesign finden sich hingegen kaum vergleichbare Beispiele. Andere längst tot geglaubte Kategorien wie die Plakette, eine stempelartige Anordnung von Bild- und Textelementen in einer meist runden Form, erlebten vor wenigen Jahren eine Renaissance. Kleine inhabergeführte Cafés und Läden nutzen diese zunächst ungewöhnliche und anachronistisch anmutende Logoform als visuelles Gegenmodell zum Branding großer Ketten.

BLICKFANG-SERIE

a (1)

▲
Zeichnung von
**KUNSTMALER
K. H. SCHAEFER**
Hagen, Westf.
▼

b (1)

d (2)

c (1)

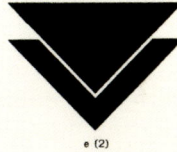

e (2)

g (2)

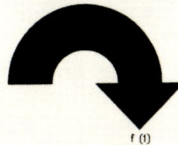

f (1)

h (2)

j (2)

i (2)

k (2)

06
The "Blickfang-Serie" ("Eyecatcher series"), a shape library for printers published in 1927, harnessed the impact of geometric constructions.

Die „Blickfang-Serie", eine 1927 herausgegebene Formenbibliothek für Druckereien, nutzte die Wirkungskraft geometrischer Konstruktionen.

La «Blickfang-Serie», une bibliothèque de formes pour l'imprimerie publiée en 1927, tire parti des constructions géométriques.

07

The front page of a catalog for
building materials from the late
1920s, the design of which is
centered around the modernist logo

Titelseite eines Katalogs für
Baumaterialien aus den späten
1920er-Jahren, deren Gestaltung
vollständig auf das modernistische
Logo zugeschnitten ist

Page de garde d'un catalogue de
matériaux de construction de la fin
des années 1920 dont la conception
tourne autour du logo moderniste

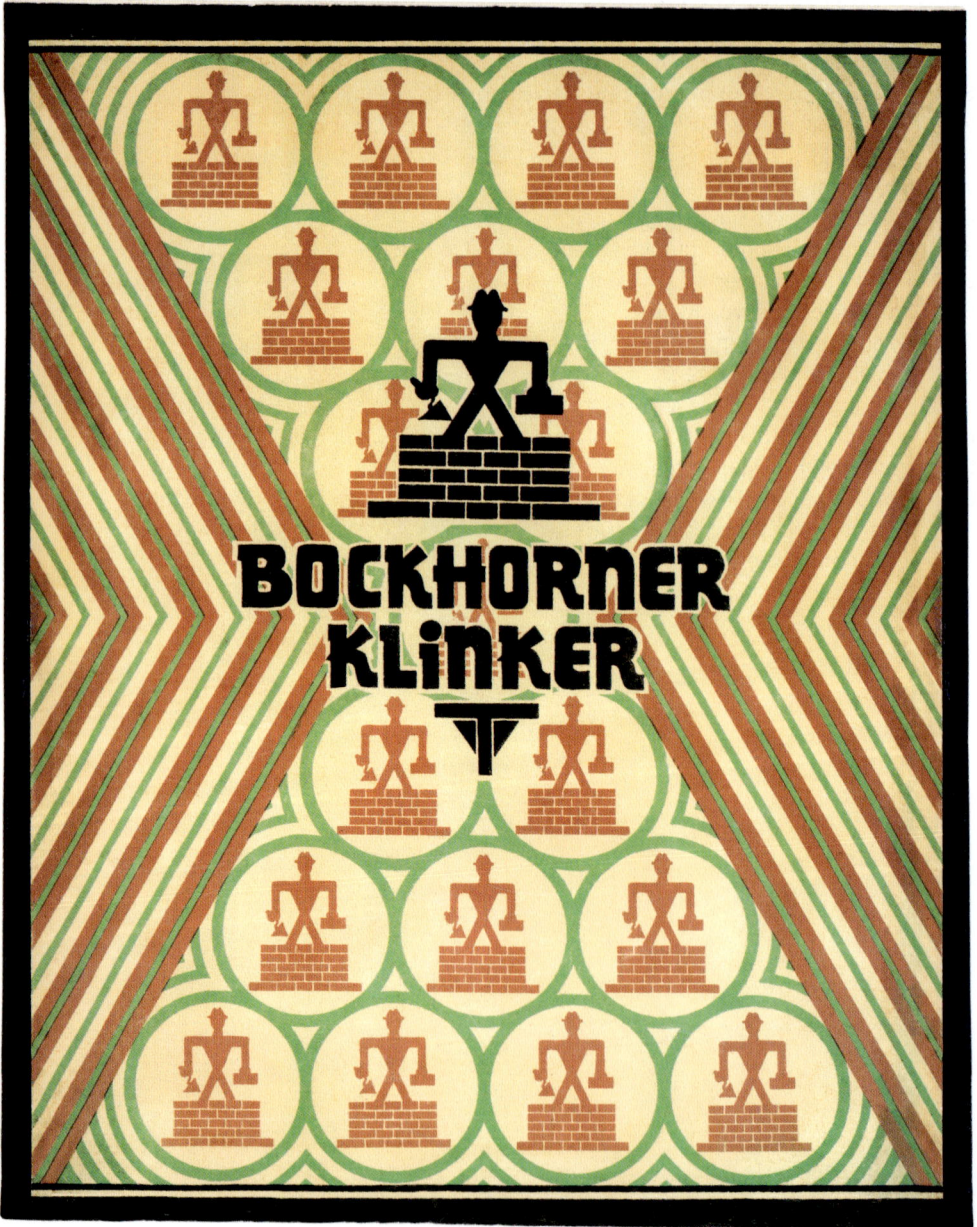

Obwohl der Aspekt der Zeitlosigkeit bei Logos – im Gegensatz zu manch anderen Medien aus dem Feld des Grafikdesigns – eine herausgehobene Bedeutung hat, ist jeder Entwurf doch zwangsläufig ein Kind seiner Entstehungszeit. Auch die hier behandelten frühen Logos sind durch Trends und Stilrichtungen ihrer Zeit geprägt. Selbst Zeichen, die nur aus wenigen Elementen bestehen, lassen den Einfluss von Jugendstil, Futurismus oder Art déco erkennen. Gegen eine rein chronologische Sortierung der Logos spricht aber die wesentlich interessantere Untersuchung verbindender Gestaltungsparameter, die über jeden kurzlebigen Trend hinaus bis heute die Entwurfsprinzipien von Markenzeichen bestimmen.

Diesem Buch liegt das Prinzip einer gleichermaßen qualitativen wie quantitativen Sammlung von Zeichen und deren systematischer Kategorisierung zugrunde. Die Auswahl und anschließende Einteilung Tausender Logos in verschiedene Haupt- und Untergruppen lassen universelle sowie zeittypische Gestaltungsprinzipien sichtbar werden. So lässt sich beispielsweise belegen, dass die Idee hinter dem berühmten Logo des Pharmaherstellers Bayer mit dem horizontal und vertikal gekreuzten Firmennamen ein damals populäres und häufig eingesetztes Designkonzept war. Oder dass es vor allem in den USA Hunderte Firmenschriftzügen in Schreibschrift gab – von denen wir heute nur noch die von Kellogg's, Ford oder Coca-Cola kennen. Die vorliegende Sammlung zeigt zum einen, wie viele bekannte Zeichen noch immer weitgehend unverändert im Einsatz sind. Gleichzeitig holt sie unzählige in Vergessenheit geratene Entwürfe wieder ans Tageslicht. In einer Zeit, in der sich Entwicklungen im Logodesign dank Social Media nahezu in Echtzeit global verbreiten, offenbart der Blick auf längst vergessene Gestaltungsideen völlig andere Einflüsse. Es lässt sich zwar nicht prognostizieren, wie genau die Zeichen der Zukunft aussehen werden; die ursprünglichen Grundprinzipien, die bereits vor mehr als einhundert Jahren in vielfältiger Weise eingesetzt wurden, werden aber mit Sicherheit weiter eine Rolle dabei spielen.

La naissance des marques

Jens Müller

Dans la Chine du XIXᵉ siècle, on raconte qu'un ministre déchu conservait parfois par dépit le sceau officiel de sa fonction. L'absence de sceau rendait en pratique toute nouvelle promulgation impossible pour son successeur car, à cette époque en Chine, seul un tampon officiel constituait alors une légitimation authentique – la confiance envers un signe composé était plus grande que celle envers une signature. Cet exemple est particulièrement révélateur de la force historique des signes. Avec l'industrialisation, l'utilisation de marques est cependant restée essentiellement le fait d'entreprises au cours des 150 dernières années. L'identification personnalisée a transformé en produits de marque les biens de consommation courante les plus ordinaires, du papier-toilette aux allumettes. Le logo est aujourd'hui bien établi dans la vie commerciale sous toutes ses formes, tandis qu'universités, groupes de musique, cabinets médicaux, initiatives citoyennes ou applis ne sont désormais plus imaginables sans un signe distinctif composé de formes et de lettres.

Si les origines et l'actualité de cette évolution font l'objet de recherches et de publications abondantes, bon nombre ne traitent les débuts des logos modernes qu'avec une étonnante brièveté, et en alléguant toujours les mêmes exemples. Si on fait abstraction de l'inscription Ford, qui n'a connu que des modifications mineures depuis 100 ans, l'évolution des marques, passées des signes figuratifs maladroits aux logos minimalistes abstraits, brille par son absence. Nous ne disposons en effet encore d'aucune étude détaillée du langage formel des anciens logos. Il faut dire aussi qu'il est difficile, à première vue, de se pencher sur les signes d'avant 1945. Les contradictions déjà apparues aux débuts des marques déposées paraissent de taille : le premier logo enregistré aux USA, celui du fabricant de peintures Averill en 1870, représente la silhouette de la ville de Chicago associée à un aigle qui tient un pinceau dans son bec, encadré d'une bannière portant les adjectifs «Durable, Beautiful, Economical», tandis que la première image de marque enregistrée en Europe en 1875 est un simple triangle rouge pour symboliser la brasserie britannique Bass [→ 01].

Avant de nous intéresser à l'étonnante concomitance entre l'abstraction et la figuration dans les premiers logos, un regard sur les conditions générales du développement des premières marques s'impose. Car ce n'est pas un hasard si, dans les années 1870, les USA et certains pays d'Europe occidentale comme la Grande-Bretagne ont adopté les premières lois pour protéger les images de marques. Sans passer en revue toute l'histoire de l'industrialisation, on constate que dans certains États, au milieu du XIXᵉ siècle, le commerce de certains produits, notamment les produits alimentaires ou le mobilier, se développe pour la première fois au-delà des seules frontières régionales. Il en résulte de nouvelles situations de concurrence qui rendent nécessaires une identification et une différenciation des autres fournisseurs de produits semblables. On voit apparaître les premiers emballages conçus avec intention qui, en plus du contenu, indiquent aussi qu'un fabricant est par exemple fournisseur de la cour ou qu'il a obtenu une médaille de qualité nationale pour un produit donné. C'est cependant la raison sociale, illustrée et pour ainsi dire concentrée dans un logo, qui opère la distinction fondamentale par rapport à la concurrence. Et même si ne manquent pas des exemples antérieurs semblables, les marques et images de marques qui apparaissent alors correspondent déjà aux critères actuels.

Dès le début de cette évolution, on trouve parmi les logos des concepts et configurations variés, et parfois contradictoires : marques verbales, sigles, illustrations figuratives ou formes abstraites. Ces catégories principales, établies il y a plus de 170 ans, continuent aujourd'hui de former la base de la conception des logos. Les multiples progrès techniques et la systématisation des chartes graphiques ou identités visuelles n'y ont rien changé, et il reste surprenant de voir que bon nombre des emblèmes conçus autrefois fonctionnent encore aujourd'hui – dans un panorama médiatique radicalement différent – comme l'essence de nombreuses marques. Car ce n'est pas seulement par nostalgie que de grandes entreprises comme General Electric, Mitsubishi ou Lufthansa, qui utilisent des logos quasiment inchangés depuis plus d'un siècle, s'en tiennent aux modèles d'origine. Les exemples sont néanmoins tout aussi nombreux de transformations radicales de l'image de marque. L'histoire du logo du fabricant allemand de machines à calculer Brunsviga ⁽→ 02⁾ est notamment paradigmatique, avec une évolution constante la première moitié du XXᵉ siècle jusqu'au logo moderne. Aucune raison véritablement convaincante ne peut non plus expliquer pourquoi des logos abstraits ont existé dès le début, à l'encontre de cette logique de perfectionnement. Mais en examinant de plus près l'histoire, il apparaît clairement que l'abstraction a été adoptée par les premiers orfèvres, tailleurs de pierre ou potiers pour la simple raison que les processus de production de l'époque ne permettaient pas d'utiliser des signes trop complexes. Les premiers logos abstraits pourraient donc bien être le fruit moins de la conscience d'un plus grand impact que de contraintes purement pratiques. Là encore pourtant, les imprimeurs européens du XVIᵉ siècle utilisaient des représentations figuratives complexes de personnages ou d'animaux comme marques – il est probable que les techniques d'impression de l'époque permettaient alors pour la première fois de graver le bois ou l'acier pour un travail expressif et artistique. Ce sont ces deux histoires opposées qui ont fait de la figuration et de l'abstraction des options valables pour la conception des premiers logos modernes.

09

In 1923, the Coca-Cola Company published a nearly 700-page collection of court decisions against competitors who had used similar names and logos on their products.

1923 veröffentlichte die Coca-Cola Company ein rund 700 Seiten umfassendes Buch mit gesammelten Gerichtsurteilen gegen Konkurrenten, die ähnliche Namen und Logos auf ihren Produkten verwendet hatten.

En 1923, The Coca-Cola Company publie un recueil de près de 700 pages de tous les jugements rendus contre des concurrents ayant utilisé des noms et des logos semblables pour leurs produits.

La tendance minimaliste n'a débuté de manière ciblée qu'au début du XXᵉ siècle en quête d'une communication plus efficace. Certaines études succinctes attribuent parfois trop rapidement cette innovation à l'avant-garde du Bauhaus qui a exprimé et diffusé ce principe dès l'ouverture de l'école en 1919. Or, en examinant des graphismes européens ou russes des années 1910, on s'aperçoit que des imprimés de conception délibérément réduite se sont aussi imposés très tôt hors des cercles avant-gardistes – peut-être en opposition aux fioritures chargées de l'Art nouveau ou en réaction aux nouvelles conditions de consommation dans les grandes villes modernes. En ce qui concerne les images de marques, cette évolution s'est manifestée par un intérêt nouveau pour les formes géométriques de base et par la prolifération de solutions techniquement élaborées. La « Blickfang Serie » (série « Accroche-regards ») publiée en 1927 [→ 06], une collection de modèles de logos pour l'imprimerie, témoigne notamment de cette tendance et de son application aux objets quotidiens. Le principe général que la réduction et la simplicité sont les conditions optimales d'un logo facilement reconnaissable s'est alors imposé – le créateur Kurt Weidemann le formulera plus tard en expliquant qu'un logo est bon dès lors qu'il peut être tracé de mémoire dans le sable avec le gros orteil.

Rien qu'en Allemagne au début des années 1910, plus de 150 000 marques de fabrique avaient déjà été déposées et étaient protégées par la loi. Ce chiffre très élevé atteste du nombre incalculable de logos déjà existants. Le signe seul ne suffisait donc déjà plus à se distinguer de ses concurrents aux premiers temps des marques. Et si des entreprises comme Coca-Cola Company ont intenté et remporté des procès contre des concurrents aux noms et inscriptions similaires [→ 09], les sociétés ont appris à développer, au-delà du signe distinctif, d'autres qualités de leurs marques, telles qu'une couleur maison ou des formes d'emballages spécifiques. Les fabricants de produits particulièrement innovants, de qualité exceptionnelle, se sont ainsi hissés au rang de marques mondiales grâce à une publicité créative et à une bonne distribution pendant les premières décennies du XXᵉ siècle. Des entreprises comme Kodak, Olivetti, Heinz ou Singer se sont converties en groupes internationaux. Or, ce sont justement ces marques qui ont adopté très tôt des constantes en matière de design original, ce qui constitue sans doute l'une des bases essentielles de leur durable succès mondial.

10
The logo image "His Master's Voice," in use since 1899, is still used by various record companies today (above) as is the heraldic figure of the French automobile manufacturer Peugeot (below).

Das ab 1899 verwendete Logobild „His Master's Voice" wird bis heute von verschiedenen Plattenfirmen verwendet (oben), ebenso wie das Wappentier des französischen Autoherstellers Peugeot (unten).

L'image-logo « La voix de son maître » utilisée à partir de 1899 l'est encore aujourd'hui par plusieurs maisons de disque (en haut), de même que le lion façon blason du fabricant automobile français Peugeot (en bas).

An advertisement from 1930 shows how deliberately the company has utilized the logo with the interlocking letters created in 1890.

Eine Anzeige aus dem Jahr 1930 zeigt, wie gezielt das Unternehmen das bereits 1890 entstandene Logo mit den verzahnten Buchstaben einsetzte.

On voit sur cette publicité de 1930 comment l'entreprise a tiré parti du logo aux lettres emboîtées les unes dans les autres, créé dès 1890.

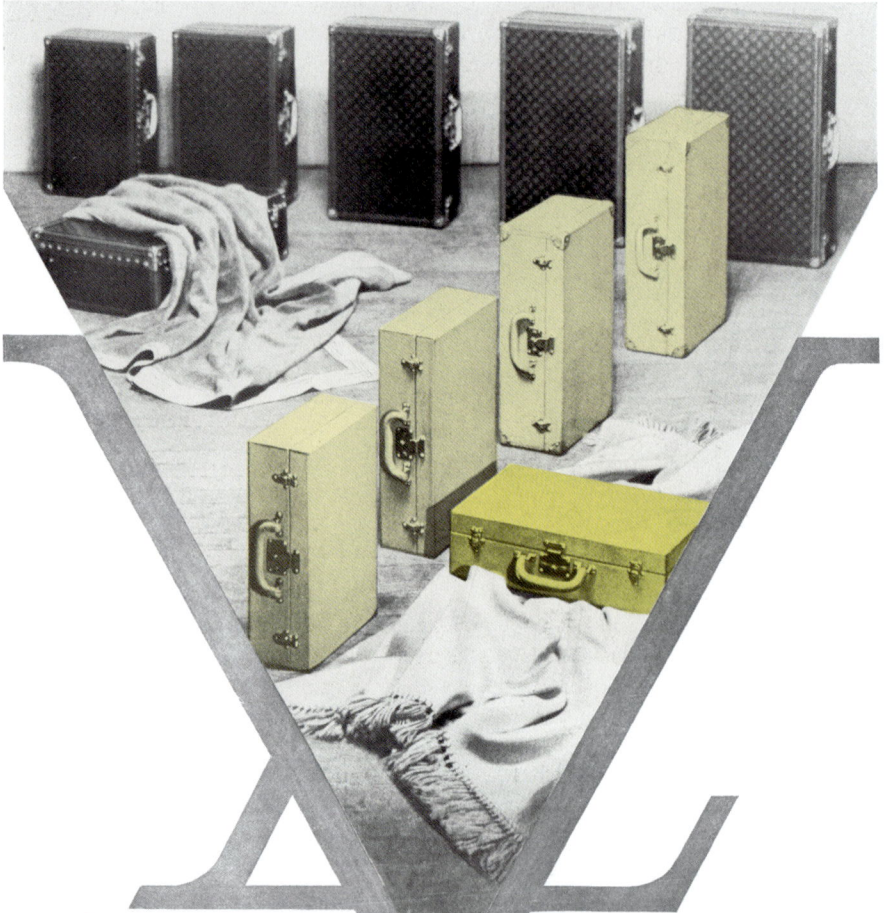

Avec le temps, certaines conventions ont évolué en matière de logos. Les entreprises de construction optent généralement pour des signes de configuration particulièrement « stable », tandis que les fournisseurs d'articles de sport s'identifient d'emblée en donnant une impression de dynamisme et de mouvement. Beaucoup de logos plus anciens ne tiennent aucun compte de ces lois apparentes de communication et de conception. C'est ce qui, du point de vue actuel, leur confère une certaine naïveté et candeur, sans qu'ils présentent pour autant le moindre déficit créatif. La représentation d'hommes et d'animaux pour les marques figuratives allait par exemple de soi dans tous les secteurs jusque dans les années 1930, alors qu'on n'en trouve guère d'exemples comparables parmi les logos créés aujourd'hui. En revanche, d'autres catégories considérées depuis longtemps comme définitivement enterrées ont connu une renaissance il y a quelques années – c'est le cas de l'emblème, qui combine texte et illustration de forme généralement ronde à la manière d'un tampon. Les propriétaires de petits cafés et magasins ont opté pour ce format de logo d'allure inhabituelle et anachronique comme contre-modèle aux marques de grandes chaînes.

La question de l'intemporalité a beau être privilégiée dans les logos, contrairement à d'autres médias graphiques, ils sont toujours nécessairement un reflet de l'époque où ils ont été créés. Les logos anciens étudiés ici sont, eux aussi, marqués par les tendances et les styles de leur temps. Même lorsqu'ils ne sont composés que d'un petit nombre d'éléments, ils témoignent de l'influence de l'Art nouveau, du futurisme ou de l'Art déco. C'est pourquoi, plus qu'un classement purement chronologique, il est certainement plus intéressant de se pencher sur les paramètres de création communs qui déterminent encore aujourd'hui les principes de conception des images de marques, au-delà de toute tendance passagère.

Ce livre repose sur une collection tant qualitative que quantitative de logos et classement systématique. La sélection et le classement de milliers de logos dans différentes catégories principales et secondaires permettent de mettre en évidence des principes universels de conception et ceux caractéristiques de leur époque. On peut ainsi attester, par exemple, que l'idée du célèbre logo du laboratoire pharmaceutique Bayer, le nom de l'entreprise écrit horizontalement et verticalement en croix, était alors un concept fréquent et très populaire. Ou qu'on trouvait surtout aux USA des centaines d'inscriptions cursives de noms de société, dont nous ne connaissons plus que Kellogg's, Ford ou Coca-Cola. La compilation de logos qui suit montre, d'une part, combien de logos connus sont encore utilisés presque sans aucune modification et dévoile, d'autre part, d'innombrables designs tombés dans l'oubli. À une époque où l'évolution de la conception de logos est diffusée par les médias sociaux presque en temps réel, un regard jeté sur des idées perdues de vue depuis longtemps révèle de tout autres influences. S'il est impossible de prédire à quoi ressembleront les logos de demain, il est certain qu'ils seront encore conçus selon les principes fondamentaux d'origine, déjà utilisés de diverses manières il y a plus d'un siècle.

P

Figuratif

Figürlich

Pictorial

When today's constant flood of images still seemed unimaginable, a pictorial image as a logo paved the way to a high level of recognizability. Companies used drawings of people, animals, landscapes, and objects to graphically represent their brands on letterheads, factory signs, and catalogs. It was not uncommon for these representational solutions to have a clear affinity with early insignia such as seals and coats of arms. This context also explains the frequent use of decorative ornaments in early company logos. But logos did not always depict products and services directly.

In einer Zeit, in der die tägliche Bilderflut des heutigen Alltags noch unvorstellbar erschien, ermöglichte die Verwendung einer figürlichen Abbildung als Logo durchaus eine hohe Wiedererkennbarkeit. Auf Briefköpfen, Fabrikschildern oder Katalogen nutzten Unternehmen Zeichnungen von Menschen, Tieren, Landschaften oder Objekten als grafische Repräsentation ihrer Marke. Nicht selten zeigte sich bei diesen gegenständlichen Lösungen noch eine deutliche Verwandtschaft mit frühen Hoheitszeichen wie Siegeln oder Wappen. Vor diesem Hintergrund ist auch die häufige Verwendung dekorativer Zierelemente bei frühen Firmenzeichen zu verstehen. Nicht immer wurden jedoch Produkte oder Dienstleistungen direkt abgebildet.

À une époque où le flux d'images qui nous inonde aujourd'hui au quotidien semblait encore inimaginable, le recours à une illustration figurative en guise de logo garantissait un degré élevé de reconnaissance. Les entreprises plaçaient sur leurs en-têtes de lettres, leurs enseignes ou leurs catalogues des dessins de personnages, d'animaux, de paysages ou d'objets qui constituaient une représentation graphique de leur marque. Ces signes figuratifs étaient encore souvent apparentés à d'anciens emblèmes de souveraineté, tels un cachet ou des armoiries. C'est dans ce contexte qu'il faut comprendre la fréquente présence d'éléments décoratifs dans les premières marques de fabrique.

The Brainerd and Armstrong Company
Yarns
1868 · US

Small & Parkes, Manchester
Textiles
1885 · UK

Transit Cycles
1888 · US

Fabrikken Oppositionen
Beer
1885 · DK

Schirmherr Regenschirme
Umbrellas
1908 · DE

Active Stoves
1880 · US

Union Carbide Company
1908 · US

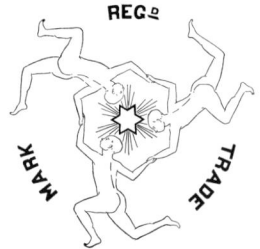

Alois Schwiger & Co.
Metal goods
1909 · AT

César
Canned foods
1911 · FR

Quaker Oats
(The American Cereal Company)
1895 · US

Josef Feinhals Zigaretten
Cigarettes
1912 · F. H. Ehmcke · DE

Euréka
Writing inks
1913 · FR

Burberrys
Clothes
1901 · UK

Chocolat François-Meunier
Chocolates
1911 · FR

Vogue
Fashion magazine
1914 · US

Electra Brutau
Chemicals
1915 · ES

Highland Shaker Sweater Company
Clothes
1914 · US

Fennir Skotøjsfabrikken
Footwear
1923 · DK

Friedrich Wilhelm Beckmann
Cutlery and knives
1882 · DE

Volharding Drukkerij
Printing
1917 · NL

Southern Oak Flooring Industries
1913 · US

Atelier voor Reclamekunst
Design studio
1916 · NL

Mergenthaler Linotype
Typesetting machines
1930 · Clarence P. Hornung · US

Constantin Cigaretten
Cigarettes
1923 · DE

Der Organisator
Magazine
1924 · CH

Niederdeutsche Zeitung
Newspaper
1923 · DE

Mablo-Werke
Foods
1924 · DE

Promonta
Sewing machines
1924 · Max Hertwig · DE

Meuble de famille
Cabinet work
1933 · FR

American Soccer Society
1932 ·Sascha A. Maurer · US

Sikkens Lakfabrieken
Paints
1934 · NL

Nîmoise de lingerie Etex
Lingerie
1936 · FR

JC
Photographer
1935 · R. Lloyd Jones · UK

Marcel Dhorme
Sport clothes
1937 · FR

Edmonton's Gas Company
1938 · CA

Columbia Ribbon & Carbon Manufacturing Company
1939 · UK

Cajac
Textiles
1940 · DK

Kohorn Teppiche
Carpets
1926 · DE

Ludwig Gräf Likörfabrik
Liquors
1920 · DE

A. A. Zimmer
Office supply
1923 · DE

Weber & Heilbronner
Clothes
1920 · Hans Schleger Zero · DE

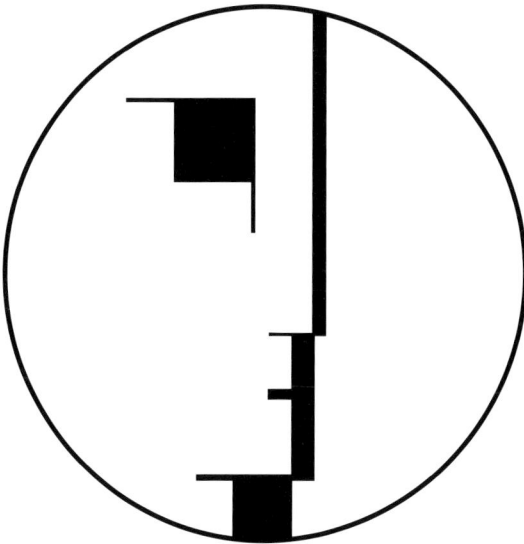

Staatliches Bauhaus Weimar
Design school
1922 · Oskar Schlemmer · DE

Gollnow & Sohn
Steel production
1921 · Karl Schulpig · DE

Meierei C. Bolle
Dairy products
1922 · Karl Schulpig · DE

Edvard V. F. Storr
Toys
1927 · DK

Wilhelm Eilers jr.
Leahter products
1923 · DE

De Tabak
Cigarettes
1926 · Machiel Wilmink · NL

Carfo
Charcoal
1931 · FR

Läufer Gummi
Rubber products
1925 · DE

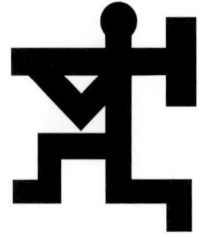

Wintershall
Metal products
1938 · Wilhelm Deffke · DE

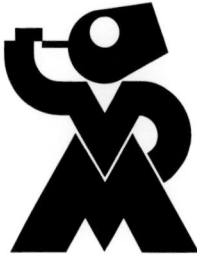

VM
Personal mark
1931 · Sascha A. Maurer · US

American Murex Company
Welding
1935 · US

G. H. Bührmann's Papiergrothandel
Paper products
1932 · NL

Ideał
Paper products
1932 · PL

Metalmen
Metal tools
1938 · US

Keiser
Music instruments
1943 · Ernst Keiser · CH

Gnom
1921 · H.W. Hahn · DE

Moturba
Motor oils
1921 · Karl Schulpig · DE

Melodium
Record label
1927 · FR

Azda
Paper tissues
1929 · FR

Michelin & Cie
Tires
1898 · FR

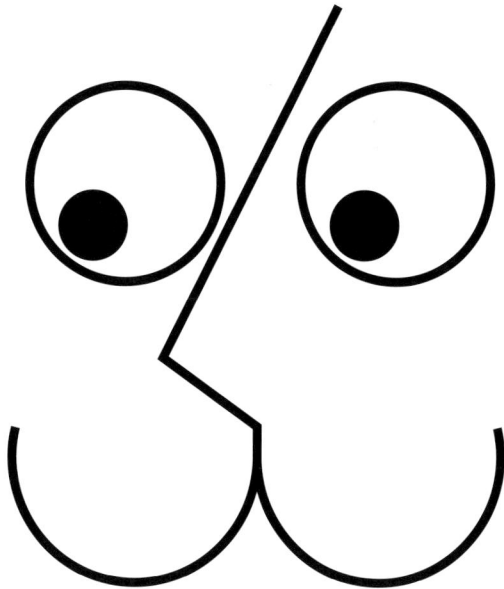

Esquire Magazine
1938 · Paul Rand · US

Socialist Labor Party of America
1877 · US

Thos. Samuel & Son
Fabrics
1896 · CA

Rudge-Whitworth
Tires
1903 · UK

PÅHLMANSKA VARUMÄRKET.

Gottlieb Ernst Clausen Gad
Bookshop
1888 · DK

Herkules
Whips
1914 · DK

Lovos
Cleanser
1912 · DK

Alba
Chalks
1909 · NL

Ozenina
Pharmaceuticals
1908 · ES

Vulcain
Machinery
1899 · CH

Martin-Senour
Paints
1920 · CA

EV
Personal mark
1920 · Georg Hoffmann · DE

Holtite Manufacturing Company
Clothes
1921 · US

Moraff, Twinning & Co.
Fabrics
1922 · US

Barbour
Irish Flax Thread
1896 · CA

Mi-ki
Soaps
1931 · FR

J. Pick & Sons
Working clothes
1918 · UK

HAND
BRAND

John Dewsbury & Son
China ware
1912 · UK

Tefag
Radios
1924 · DE

Eulan
Pesticides
1932 · Karl Schulpig · DE

S. Feuer
Painter
1933 · AT

Tempo
Publishing
1930 · Clarence P. Hornung · US

Hirsch
Machinery
1926 · Ernst Rössner · DE

Böhme Fettchemie
Chemicals
1940 · DE

Bowers Bros.
Foods
1914 · US

Herbig-Haarhaus Farben
Paints
1933 · DE

E3
Electronics
1932 · Franz Timm · DE

H. Viney & Company
Paper products
1938 · UK

Rudge-Whitworth
Bicycles
1941 · UK

Optimol Motorenöle
Motor oils
1929 · Atelier Senger · DE

Wella
Cosmetics
1930 · DE

Ad. Müller & Söhne
Prostheses
1928 · DE

Fernseh AG
Television technology
1937 · Wilhelm Deffke · DE

M. Hurst & Company
Music instruments
1944 · UK

J. Legge and Company
Locks
1931 · UK

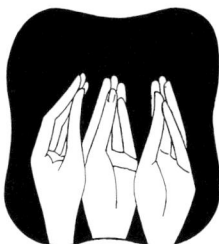

Ourivesaria aliança
Goldsmiths association
1941 · PT

Pedykur
Cosmetics
1928 · ES

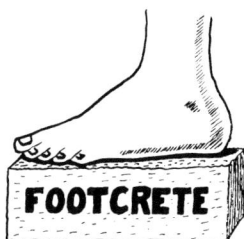

Planters' Stores & Agency Company
Cement
1932 · UK

Solvolith-Erzeugung
Dr. med. Karl Hermann
Dental products
1934 · CZ

Varno
Chemicals
1947 · DK

J & J. Baldwin
Wool
1876 · UK

Deutsche Kabelwerke
Cables
1920 · DE

Hektor Schlatter & Co.
Carpenter
1921 · CH

Chrystal Gin
Liquors
1899 · NL

Farbenfabriken Otto Baer
Printing colors
1923 · DE

Fællesforeningen for
Danmarks Brugsforeninger
Foods
1929 · DK

Compania Ron Barcardi
Liquors
1930 · CU

Papilio
Cosmetics
1904 · JP

Berolina Film
Film production
1924 · Kupfer-Sachs · DE

"BUNNY"

Donaldson Manufacturing Glasgow
Toys
1925 · UK

Ryff & Co.
Textiles
1914 · CH

Glasurit-Werke
Paints
1923 · DE

NESTLÉ'S

Nestlé
Foods
1911 · CH

S. Minder-Weinhagen
Iron products
1911 · CH

Papierfabrik Scheufelen
Paper products
1930 · DE

HERON

Heron
Cosmetics
1936 · US

Fukusaya
Cakes
1890 · JP

Deutsche Luft Reederei
Airline
1918 · Otto Firle · DE

R. Silcock & Sons
Trading
1931 · UK

FABRICATION FRANÇAISE

IBIS

MARQUE DÉPOSÉE

IBIS
Razors
1929 · FR

Chantecler
Rubber heels
1910 · AT

ESTABLISHED 1818.

Brooks Brothers
Men's clothes
1850 · US

Challenge Brand
Foods
1880 · US

Aristo Eiercognac
Beverages
1930 · CH

The Texas Company
Petroleum
1910 · US

Oud
Liquors
1926 · NL

Club Old Tom Gin
1902 · CA

Pudse-Fabriken
Shoe polish
1920 · DK

Vaca Roja
Dairy products
1923 · DK

Rothkirk
Footwear
1927 · US

New Home
Sewing Machine Company
1899 · US

National Dairy
1932 · Frederick E. Kliem · US

Spratt's
Pet shop
1936 · Max Field-Bush · UK

Allwood Lime Company
Construction materials
1924 · US

His Master's Voice
Record label
1901 · Francis Barraud · UK

Rollo
Clothes
1928 · DK

Ermopiev Film Factory
Film production
1916 · RU

Wadi
1921 · Fritz Ahlers · DE

Alfred R. Knopf
Publishing
1910 · Rudolph Ruzicka · US

Galgo
Restaurant
1943 · PT

Mampe Spirituosen
Liquors
1920 · DE

Clark & Company
Yarns
1876 · UK

Dr. C. Wolf & Sohn
Printing
1929 · DE

Kaspar Creme
Cosmetics
1909 · DK

Boston Belting Company
1895 · US

A. Clavel & Fritz Lindenmeyer
Textiles
1931 · CH

Fluin
Flours
1913 · DK

Adlerwerke
Bicycles
1898 · DE

Edoardo Bianchi
Cars
1901 · IT

The American Printer
1910 · Edmund G. Gress · US

Condor
Tanning
1910 · DE

Glory Skocrem
Shoe polish
1920 · DK

Union Trust Company
Bank
1915 · US

Karl W. Hiersemann Verlag
Publishing
1922 · Erich Gruner · DE

Sefi
Film production
1937 · CH

Phoenixbrouwerij Amersfoort
Beer
1926 · N.P. de Koo · NL

Deutsche Bank
1930 · Hans Schleger Zero · DE

Brandt & Co.
Printing
1927 · DE

Reconstruction Finance Corporation
1930 · Clarence P. Hornung · US

Preservitas
Food preservation
1887 · UK

Johnson & Sons
Sea foods
1920 · UK

Ferdinand Flinsch
Paper products
1922 · DE

Reichs-Rundfunk-Gesellschaft
Broadcasting
1932 · DE

Strøm & Poulsens
Soaps
1922 · DK

M. Amieux & Cie
Canned foods
1910 · FR

Muth's Bread
Foods
1881 · US

Eduard Kipp Randers Humleforretning
Foods
1895 · DK

Hänsel & Co.
Textiles
1927 · DE

Air France
Airline
1933 · FR

Pegasus
Needles
1928 · DE

Cigarettenfabrikken Norden
Cigarettes
1914 · DK

Amazon Wilhelm Hering
Stockings
1938 · UK

Lawina
Ice cream
1938 · PL

Levi Strauss & Co.
Clothes
1890 · US

Remy's Royal Rice Starch
1894 · CA

Wiener Øl
Beer
1891 · DK

Eminenta
Import-export
1911 · DK

Harry Grant Burke
Pharmaceuticals
1915 · US

Metro Goldwyn Mayer
Film production
1924 · US

Société Anonyme de Usines Remy
Foods
1920 · BE

Société Anonyme des Automobiles &
Cycles Peugeot
Automobiles
1920 · FR

El León
Cement
1933 · ES

The Owls
Social organisation
1904 · US

Neenah
Paper products
1920 · UK

Master Lock Company
Door locks
1923 · US

Stadt Düsseldorf
City
1908 · DE

Brotherton & Co.
Fabrics
1932 · UK

J. & W. N. Hutchings
Tannery
1922 · UK

Pilsworth
Fabrics
1931 · UK

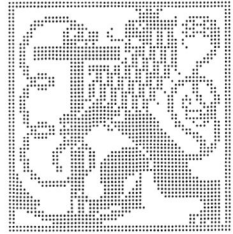

Paon Royal
Copper carbonate
1911 · BE

A. Apahko
Film production
1916 · RU

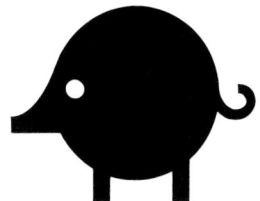

Fleischerei München
Foods
1929 · Max Hertwig · DE

Travise
Fabrics
1928 · DE

Pelikan
Pens
1936 · O.H.W. Hadank · DE

Schaeffer & Cie
Textiles
1931 · FR

Salamander
Footwear
1903 · DE

Rider Safety Razor Company
1938 · US

Salamander
Footwear
1920 · DE

Dubied
Refrigeration equipment
1933 · FR

Bernhards und Stroever
Shellac
1919 · Ida C. Stoever · DE

D. M. C. Reimers
Pharmacy
1890 · DK

Tiger
Metal products
1910 · DE

Bargola Werkzeuggesellschaft
Machine tools
1914 · DE

Dr. Kurt Ruelke
1914 · Julius Gipkens · DE

Cholekinaza
Chemicals
1927 · PL

Saturn
Footwear
1920 · CZ

Schildkröte
Electronics
1924 · DE

Dansk Sæbeindustri
Soaps
1921 · DK

New Devices Limited
Car parts
1932 · UK

Penguin Books
Publishing
1935 · Edward Young · UK

Gorham Manufacturing Company
Silver polish
1869 · US

Walter Kersting
Graphic designer
1920 · Walter M. Kersting · DE

Clark & Co.
Fabrics
1884 · UK

Christian Olsen
Department store
1929 · DK

Heidsieck & Co.
Champagne
1910 · FR

Delmenhorster Anker-Linoleumfabrik
Floorings
1906 · Peter Behrens · DE

Wester Bros.
Trading
1910 · US

HAPAG
Ocean line
1920 · Albert Fuss · DE

Kra-Krie
Bread
1910 · AT

Moteurs Ballot
Motors
1915 · FR

Aktiebolaget Järnförädling
Pipes
1918 · SE

Société Suisse de Tissage
de Soies à Bluter
Textiles
1910 · CH

Internationale Ausstellung für Binnen-
schiffahrt und Wasserkraftnutzung
Maritime trade fair
1925 · Robert Stöcklin · CH

Boustead & Co.
Axeheads
1938 · UK

American Telephone & Telegraph Company
1877 · US

Majer Sztal
Steel products
1925 · PL

Kaiser's Kaffee
Supermarket chain
1938 · DE

Dorrinck & Co.
Machine oils
1884 · DE

Crown
Petroleum
1908 · NL

Bakken Braden Koken
Promotion for gas
1926 · NL

H.S. Salomon
Liquors
1887 · DK

J. P. Coats
Cottons
1885 · UK

Samos
Coffee
1933 · FR

Kanegafuchi Spinning Company
1894 · JP

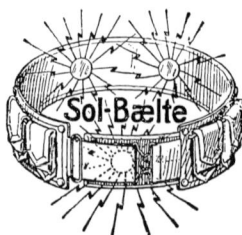

Sol-Bælte
Electronics
1911 · DK

Lancia & Co.
Cars
1911 · IT

C. M. Schmidt
Pesticides
1891 · US

Planeta
Printing machines
1925 · ES

Kjøbenhavvns Talsgsmelteri
Trading
1892 · DK

Fairbanks Standard Company
Scales
1893 · CA

Electrolux
Electronics
1936 · US

Peter Cailler
Chocolates
1912 · CH

Grosschweimachina
Sewing machines
1930 · RU

Douglas Aircraft Company
1937 · US

Pol Registrator Compagnie
Trading
1920 · DE

Górniczo-Hutnicze
Mining
1939 · PL

Continental Aviation
1946 · US

Excelsior
Construction materials
1904 · IT

Guinness
Beer
1862 · IE

Peter Valdemar Nielsen
Department store
1892 · DK

Thorvald Petersens
Elektrotekniske Forretning
Electronics
1912 · DK

Schweizerischer Bankverein
Swiss Banking Association
1930 · CH

EAST SIDE
WEST SIDE
WANTS
SMITH

Alfred E. Smith
Political campaign
1928 · US

Bug Death
Fertilizer
1909 · US

J. Weck & Co.
Glass products
1919 · DE

Huntonit
Wood trade
1936 · Gumaelius Reklame · NO

John Meier
Footwear
1889 · US

Beet-Sugar
Foods
1934 · C.W. Bacon · UK

Insel Verlag
Publishing
1899 · Peter Behrens · DE

Goodyear
Tires
1898 · US

Lacôme
Cosmetics
1942 · FR

Erwin, Wasey & Company
Advertising agency
1910 · US

Uffe
Asphalt factory
1882 · DK

E.L. Mustee & Sons
Heating systems
1945 · US

Tania Titan Co.
Paints
1933 · NO

Aspor
Sporting goods
1909 · AT

Apollo Auto Werke
Automobiles
1924 · Gerhard Marggraff · DE

Air Flow
China ware
1938 · US

Charles A. Scott
Tissue papers
1924 · US

Royal
Motor oils
1925 · IT

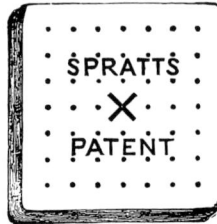

Spratts
Biscuits
1886 · UK

**Lecco Loggers Equipment &
Car Company**
1924 · US

Lin-O-Let (Helly J. Hansen)
Textiles
1931 · NO

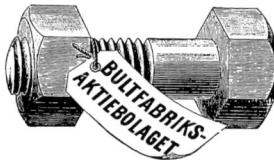

Bultfabriks
Machine tools
1887 · DK

Burmol
Chemicals
1925 · DE

The Torpedo
Yarns
1938 · UK

Union Braunkohlen-Verkaufsverein
Coals
1901 · DE

Blue Band Margarine
Foods
1925 · NL

Otto Walser Optiker
Optician
1945 · Erwin Zimmerli · CH

Rotex
Construction materials
1930 · US

Adao
Men's clothes
1943 · PT

Husqvarna
Sewing machines
1926 · DK

Nivea Creme
Cosmetics
1930 · DE

Jingle Bell
Ice cream
1938 · US

Molkerei Osthafen
Dairy products
1929 · DE

Flamfix
Matchboxes
1930 · NL

**Pacific Safety
Equipment Company**
1926 · US

The Baynard Press
Design studio
1935 · UK

Destileria de Aguardientes
Distillery
1902 · ES

Kurshaus
Transportation
1929 · NL

Christen Marinus Thomsen
Gloves
1896 · DK

Brown Dexter Company
Fabrics
1911 · US

Bardon, Clere & Cie.
Cables
1906 · FR

Ostindisk Kaffelager K. Godtfredsen
Coffee trading
1932 · DK

Pitcairn Varnish Company
1905 · US

The West-Indian Trading Company
1927 · UK/IN

Verband Schweizerischer
Konsumvereine
Trade union
1908 · CH

Gustav Najork Papierfabrik
Paper products
1928 · DE

Electro Purator
Electronics
1929 · FR

M. Markiewicz
Wine trading
1906 · DE

Froebel, Zurich
Gardening
1925 · CH

Ka-Ri-Bi
Fabrics
1938 · PL

Paramount Pictures
Film production
1914 · US

Fujisawa
Pharmaceuticals
1940 · JP

Palmin
Foods
1910 · DE

The Magadi Soda Company
1913 · UK

Por Los Pirineos
Publishing
1903 · ES

Popocatepil Pictures
Film production
1921 · MX

Fuji Film
Photographic products
1934 · JP

PLM
Railways
1937 · FR

Suvesco
Trading
1931 · UK

Japan Travel Bureau
1916 · JP

Navyug Chitrapat
Investments
1939 · IN

American Oil Company
1925 · US

Capitol Comedies
Film production
1918 · US

Sigurd Stenhøf
Machinery
1919 · DK

National Water-Proofing Company
Paper products
1914 · US

Patriot
Shoe cream
1910 · AT

High Rock Knitting Company
1909 · US

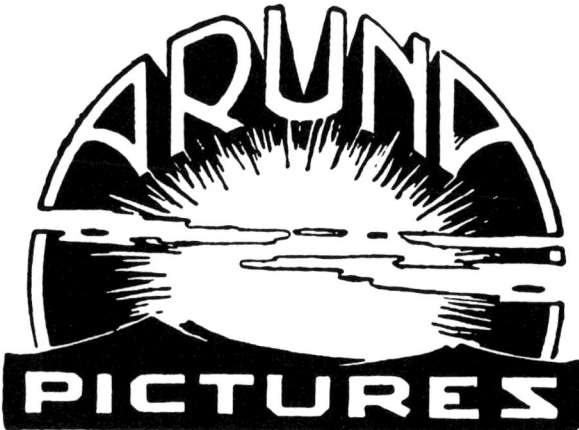

Aruna Pictures
Film production
1938 · IN

GHB Holland
Paper products
1930 · NL

Milson Limited
Foods
1931 · UK

Canadian Pacific Railways
1896 · CA

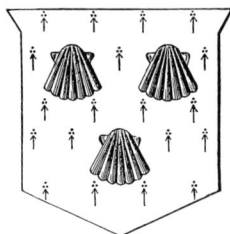

John Dewhurst & Sons
Yarns
1876 · UK

**Louis Peter Mitteldeutsche
Gummiwarenfabrik**
Rubber products
1907 · DE

T. M. Werner
Ice trading
1883 · DK

Falcon
Varnishes
1907 · CA

C. Koch
Photography
1914 · CH

The Salvation Army
1918 · UK

W. Girardet Verlag
Publishing
1925 · Karl Möhler · DE

Paul Steiger
Umbrellas
1918 · P. Kammüller · CH

Carl Lunds Fabrikker
Metal goods
1915 · DK

HAPAG
Ocean liner
1926 · DE

Gabriel Sedlmayr
Beer
1884 · Otto Hupp · DE

British Petroleum
Gasoline
1920 · A.R. Saunders · UK

Warner Bros.
Film production
1935 · US

DKW
Cars
1930 · DE

Rex
Refrigerators
1933 · IT

Vacuum Oil Company
1932 · US

F.B. Flint
Trading
1936 · DK

Beck's
Beer
1929 · DE

The Beaver Products Company
1920 · US

Mitteldeutsche Fahrradwerke
Bicycles
1928 · DE

Philips
Electronics
1929 · NL

Eastside Brewery
Beer
1922 · US

Dassler
Sport shoes
1924 · DE

Craftex Company
Paints
1931 · Joseph Sinel · US

Super
Machine tools
1938 · DE

THE DELIVERY SYSTEM
FOR STORES OF QUALITY

SINCE 1907

United Parcel Service
1937 · US

Guth Lighting
1923 · US

Ignacy Roman Ska
Sporting goods
1937 · PL

Richard Haworth and Company
Fabrics
1932 · UK

Nos Vins
Wines
1933 · FR

Royal Nitro
Chemicals
1929 · BE

Dessau & Küster
Butcher
1885 · DK

Apolinaris
Table water
1876 · UK

Henry Campbell & Co.
Sewing machines
1883 · UK

Anatole Descamps
Yarns
1882 · FR

Pfister & McKey Dundee Creamery
1888 · US

Kao
Cosmetics
1890 · JP

Viggo C. Eberth
Trading
1891 · DK

M. Naef & Cie
Pharmaceuticals
1910 · CH

American Express Axle Grease
1895 · US

P & S Corsets
1898 · CA

American Telephone and Telegraph Company
1910 · T. N. Vail · US

W. Rosskopf & Co.
Watches
1907 · CH

Brüder Wurm
Insulating materials
1911 · CZ/AT

Braw Laddie Golf Company
1910 · E.L. Hubbard · US

Crème de Camembert
Cheese
1911 · FR

Tobaccos
Cigarettes
1920 · DK

Maschinenfabrik Sürth
Machinery
1928 · DE

Semeuse
Bicycles
1914 · FR

Mundus Labore Crescit
Research lab
1920 · Hentschel · NL

Deutsches Kunstdruckpapier
Paper products
1931 · DE

**Schnellpressenfabrik
Frankenthal Albert & Cie**
Printing machines
1923 · DE

Kaminwerk Allschwil
Stoves
1927 · CH

Los Tres Peintures
Paints
1931 · US

Columbia Records
1914 · US

Midnight Sun
Nutritional oils
1927 · NO

Badplaats Noordwijk
Tourism
1932 · NL

Wytwórnia wyrobów territowych
Tadeusz Rychłowski
Territ products
1932 · PL

Radio Corporation of America
Sound system
1940 · US

ABC Film
Film production
1917 · US

Mercedes Benz
Automobiles
1935 · DE

Færøsk Fisk
Fish trading
1932 · DK

Otto van Tussenbroek
Graphic designer
1918 · Otto van Tussenbroek · NL

Vereeniging Voor Reclame
Advertising union
1936 · A. Visser · NL

Birdseye Electric Company
1935 · US

The National Automobile Association
1909 · US

Natraj Films
Film production
1937 · IN

Kaisers Kaffeegeschäft
Supermarket chain
1910 · DE

Ragis Kartoffelzucht GmbH
Foods
1925 · DE

Douwe Egberts
Coffee
1930 · NL

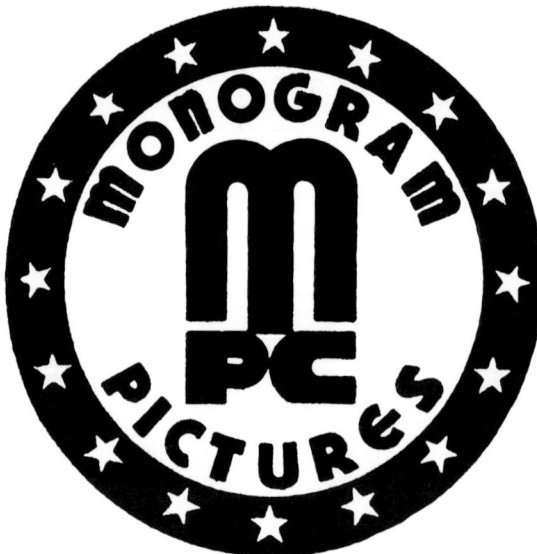

Engrais
Chemicals
1929 · FR

National Benzole
Gasoline
1934 · UK

Yorkshire
Foods
1935 · PL

Monogram Pictures
Film distribution
1938 · US

Franz Scherrer Buchdruckerei
Printing
1926 · H.G. Reinstein · DE

Leyens & Levenbach
Department store
1926 · Fritz Lewy · DE

Neue Element Werke
Electronics
1926 · DE

De Mutator
Business services
1936 · NL

Bell & Zoller
Coals
1948 · US

Charles Ewald
Perfumes
1899 · CH

Vittorio Rossi
Bicycles
1910 · IT

Graham Brothers
Automobiles
1927 · US

Val de Travers Etat
Construction materials
1911 · CH

Albina
Bicycles
1906 · DE

J. P. Bloch
Wools
1887 · DK

**The Black & Decker
Manufacturing Company**
1926 · US

Faust
Bicycles
1920 · IT

No. 4711
Perfumes
1894 · DE

Bentley
Automobiles
1921 · UK

Raybaut, Riva & Cie
Olive products
1911 · FR

Tapetenhaus C. Heckendorn-Bertuch
Wallpapers
1919 · CH

Anheuser-Busch
Brewing Association
1880 · US

Boekdrukkerij Industrie Amsterdam
Printing
1916 · NL

Usines Contonniéres Gand-Zele-Tubize
Cotton pillows
1910 · BE

Nederlandsche Ijzerhandel
Construction materials
1917 · NL

KBV
Jewellery
1920 · C. de Haas · NL

KLM
Airline
1919 · NL

Sanaye Pashm
Wool
1935 · IR

Eerste Nederlandsche Rijwielen Machinefabriek
Machinery
1922 · NL

T. Krauss
Personal mark
1919 · Alfons Niemann · DE

Képérer
Chocolates
1934 · FR

Vakschool voor de Typografie
Design school
1919 · R.W.P. de Vries Jr. · NL

Lotus Limited
Footwear
1920 · UK

BTA Verlag
Publishing
1910 · Hanns Thaddäus Hoyer · DE

W. Stoeden
Personal mark
1919 · R.W.P. de Vries Jr. · NL

The Mautner Blanket Company
1929 · UK

Brusse
Publishing
1927 · H.P. Berlage · NL

Christian Nielsen & Company
Socks
1923 · DK

Emery & Beers Company
Hosiery
1905 · US

Le Bresilienne
Coffee
1910 · NL

SD & V
Personal mark
1919 · Wybo Meijer · NL

Mouilbau, Fayaud, Laurain & Cie
Bracelets
1910 · FR

Bee Hive Knitting Wools
1898 · CA

Leiter Nijpels Maastricht
Publishing
1927 · S.H. de Roos · NL

Amazon Insurance Company
1870 · US

MAN Druck München
Printing
1922 · DE

Golden Sun Pictures
Film production
1921 · US

Best British Bicycle
1930 · UK

Red Men Corduroy
Trousers
1912 · US

The Advertiser Job
Advertising services
1913 · CA

Vitagraph Pictures
Film production
1918 · US

Mosch Film
Film production
1919 · DE

Tipografia La Academica
Printing
1917 · ES

QS
Personal mark
1918 · Heukelom · NL

The Times
Newspaper
1919 · UK

Forme

Form

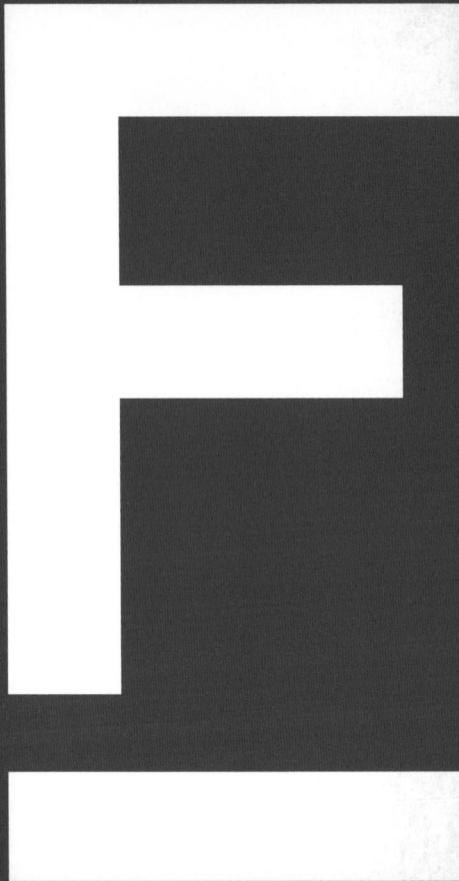

Form

The idea that abstraction is a modern invention is one of the biggest misconceptions in visual communications. The cave paintings of Lascaux or ancient Egyptian hieroglyphics dispute this misconception readily. Even in the field of logos, there have always been abstract solutions. However, it is also true that logos with simplified designs did not gain acceptance until the 1920s. In view of more complex communication tasks and the progressive technologizing of today's world, logo designs based on geometric shapes such as circles, squares, triangles, and lines suddenly seemed optimal. This development was preceded by the realization that overly complex marks are not as easily retained in viewers' minds—a belief still held today.

Dass Abstraktion eine Erfindung der Moderne sei, gehört zu den größten Fehlannahmen im Bereich der visuellen Kommunikation. Man denke nur an die Höhlenzeichnungen von Lascaux oder die Zeichensysteme der alten Ägypter. Selbst im Bereich der Logos gab es schon immer auch abstrahierte Lösungen. Richtig ist aber ebenso, dass sich reduziert gestaltete Logos erst in den 1920er-Jahren durchsetzten. Vor dem Hintergrund komplexerer Kommunikationsaufgaben und einer fortschreitenden Technisierung der Gegenwart erschienen Logokonstruktionen auf Basis geometrischer Formen wie Kreis, Quadrat, Dreieck oder Linie auf einmal als optimal. Dieser Entwicklung ging die bis heute akzeptierte Erkenntnis voran, dass zu komplexe Zeichen nicht so leicht in den Köpfen der Betrachtenden haften bleiben.

L'abstraction n'a pas été inventée à l'époque moderne, c'est l'une des plus grandes erreurs de la communication visuelle que de le croire : il suffit de penser aux peintures rupestres de Lascaux ou aux hiéroglyphes de l'Égypte antique. De la même façon, on a toujours vu des options abstraites parmi les logos. Il n'en est pas moins vrai que les logos de conception simplifiée ne se sont pas imposés avant les années 1920. Face à la complexité croissante de la communication et aux progrès technologiques, les logos basés sur des formes géométriques (cercle, carré, triangle ou ligne) sont brusquement apparus comme les plus appropriés. Cette évolution devance le principe en vigueur aujourd'hui encore que des signes trop complexes sont moins faciles à mémoriser.

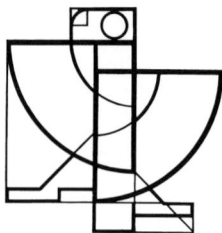

Frankfurt am Main
City
1929 · Hans Leistikow · DE

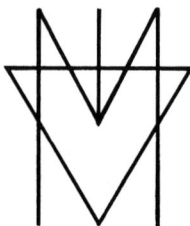

Noveltex
Fabrics
1929 · FR

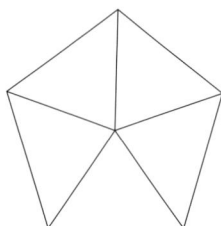

P. R. Madsen
Bricklayer
1943 · DK

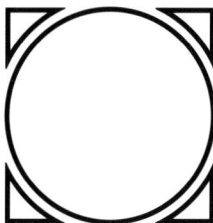

Aktieselskabet Ny Kalbrænderi
Cement
1907 · DK

Jenaer Glaswerk Schott & Gen
Glass products
1917 · DE

Carl Schenk
Printing
1920 · Hartmuth Pfeil · DE

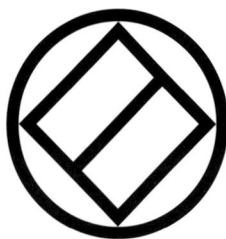

**Bayerische Flaschen-Glashüttenwerke
Wiegand & Söhne**
Glass bottles
1931 · DE

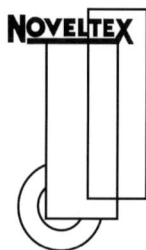

Bang & Olufsen
Radios
1936 · DK

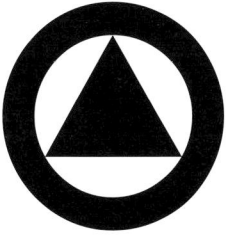

Monmouth County Farmers Exchange
Foods
1908 · US

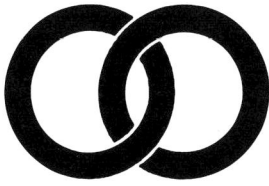

Vibe-Hastrup
Chemicals
1908 · DK

R. Heusser
Wallpapers
1930 · CH

All Information Film Service
Film distribution
1920 · US

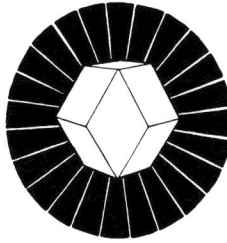

Chemische Fabriken Kunheim & Co.
Chemicals
1924 · DE

Natronag
Paper products
1930 · PL

Pyramid Shoe
Footwear
1925 · AT

Pronova
Design agency
1929 · Sascha A. Maurer · DE/US

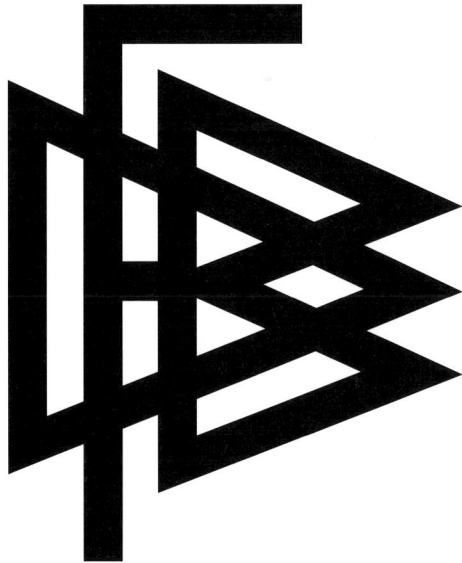

Deutscher Fußball Bund
German Soccer Association
1926 · DE

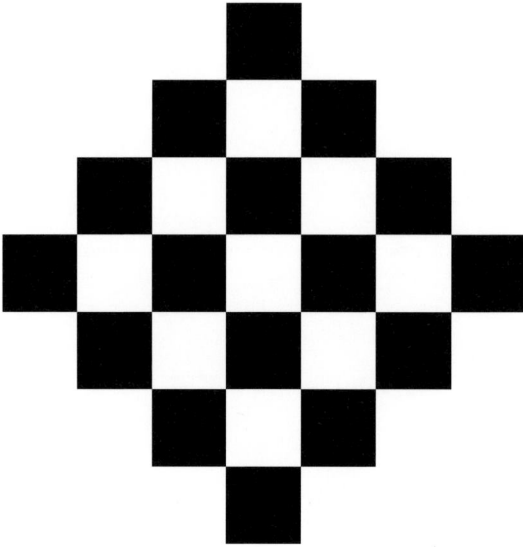

Ekkol Sæbefabrik
Soaps
1937 · DK

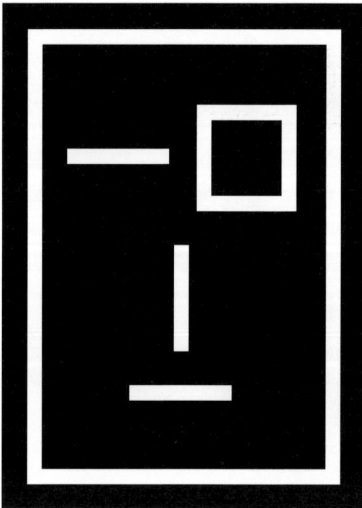

Morister Radio
Radios
1931 · FR

Shoesmith & Shoesmith
Cosmetics
1929 · UK

Ophinag
Lamps
1935 · DE

Muster-Schmidt Verlagsgesellschaft
Publishing
1905 · Christian Hansen-Schmidt · DE

Hotpoint Electric Appliance
Household appliances
1921 · UK

VDS Spiegelglas
Glass
1922 · Hans Raithel · DE

Olza
Furniture
1932 · PL

Padova
Footwear
1933 · FR

Pelikan
Pens
1924 · Kurt Schwitters · DE

Polydor
Record company
1928 · DE

Foti
Textiles
1933 · George Bonta · HU

Werner Quack Verlag
Publishing
1926 · DE

Cercle et Carré
Art magazine
1930 · FR

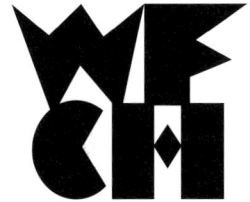

Wytwórnia Fotochemiczna
Photographic products
1931 · PL

Compagnie des Arts Français
Interior design
1928 · FR

Neola
Lubricants
1930 · FR

Maison Damour
Interior design
1930 · FR

Kreis

Les Couronnes
Beer
1883 · BE

Valdemar Ludvigsen
Trading
1921 · DK

Nobel-Diesel
Machinery
1910 · SE

Kuraray
Chemicals
1926 · Kurashiki Kenshoku · JP

Saturn
Rubber products
1894 · US

Julius Brilles
Electronics
1927 · PL

The Absorbent Cotton
Company of America
1918 · US

Ditto
Photocopiers
1919 · US

Super Radio
Radios
1926 · IT

FOBA
Measuring instruments
1932 · CH

Daimler-Benz
Automobiles
1938 · DE

Austro Daimler
Cars
1928 · AT

Lajzer-Wolf Toporek
Stockings
1932 · PL

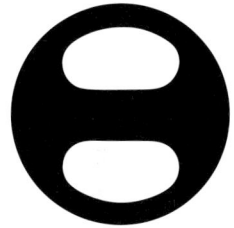

Nippon Metal Industry
1932 · JP

Electroacustic-Gesellschaft
Electronics
1928 · DE

Reinforced Glass Company
1932 · UK

Auto Union
Automobiles
1934 · DE

Lumen
Shoe polish
1929 · FR

Trüb Taüber & Cie
Electronics
1933 · CH

Die Linse
Photo magazine
1933 · DE

Hans Cassel & Co.
Clothes
1935 · AT

Beogradski Izdavačko Grafički Zavod
Publishing
1941 · Miloš Ćirić · YU

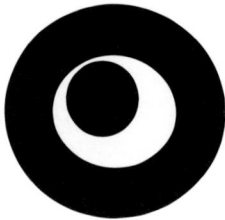

Gruschwitz Textilwerke
Textiles
1928 · DE

Kumagai Gumi
Construction company
1938 · Jinichi Makita,
Tasuburo Kumagai · JP

Daiei
Film production
1942 · JP

Popea Kosmetik
Cosmetics
1945 · Rudolf Bircher · CH

Norddeutsche Hefeindustrie
Foods
1939 · Wilhelm Deffke · DE

Tokai Bank
1941 · JP

Werkzeugmaschinen Bührle & Co.
Machine tools
1944 · Balthasar Rauch · CH

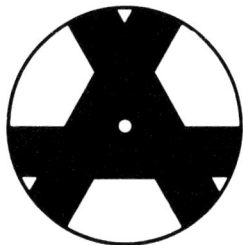

Alpine Eisengiesserei
Iron works
1948 · DE

Uitgever D. Coene
Publishing
1927 · Chris Lebeau · NL

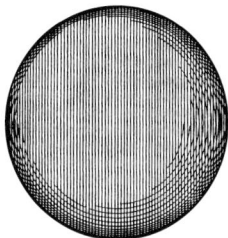

Stilling Anderson
Foods
1923 · DK

Normal Company
Foods
1886 · UK

Ad Astra Aero
Airline
1920 · CH

Rudge-Whitworth
Motorcycles
1924 · UK

Mishawaka Rubber and Woolen Manufacturing Company
1898 · US

Matthias Bäuerle Rechenmaschinen
Calculating machines
1920 · Karl Schulpig · DE

Plodoeksport USSR
Fruit export
1930 · RU

Gaumont
Film production
1908 · FR

Kluppell & Ebeling
Printing
1918 · NL

The Barrit Company
Motor oils
1930 · US

C.A.V.-Bosch
Machinery
1931 · UK

Clearso
Soda silicates
1937 · US

Le Men Tonnais
Toys
1933 · FR

Thomas Chimiques
Chemicals
1931 · BE

Rose Pictures
Film production
1941 · IN

Peppy Boy
Noodles
1934 · US

Addiator
Calculating machines
1922 · Karl Schulpig · DE

H. B. Lochner Spielwaren
Toys
1945 · Albert Leemann · CH

Purlap
Fur imitations
1937 · FR

Hydrawerk Berlin
Radios
1934 · DE

Heberlein
Publishing
1943 · Walter Käch · CH

Philis
Clothes
1931 · UK

Grand Hotel, New York
1930 · US

Albesco
Construction materials
1931 · CZ

G-Berlin
Publishing
1933 · Ernst Böhm · DE

Olma
Sewing machines
1918 · CH

**The Jewett Radio &
Phonograph Company**
1924 · US

Agip
Gas stations
1926 · IT

United States Rubber Company
1914 · US

AJP
Personal mark
1926 · Franz Wilck · DE

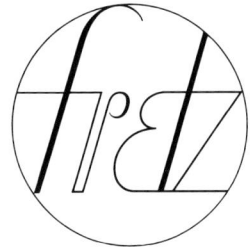

Gebrüder Fretz
Printing
1930 · CH

J. E. Schmalfeld
Tobacco
1880 · DK

L'Oreal
Cosmetics
1909 · FR

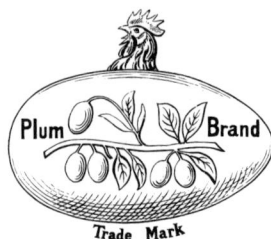

N. M. & F. Plum
Department store
1907 · DK

Ford
Automobiles
1912 · US

Fiat
Cars
1904 · Carlo Biscaretti · IT

Double Palmtree
Distillery
1901 · NL

Méran Fréres
Heating devices
1909 · FR

Waist Craft
Clothes
1920 · US

F.J. Schirmer & Co.
Paper products
1924 · DE

Officine Meccaniche
Automobiles
1915 · IT

C. Lorenz
Telecommunication
1922 · DE

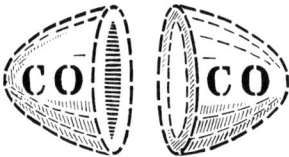

Coco Margarinefabrikken
Foods
1919 · DK

Sangamo Electric Company
1915 · US

Perl
Automobiles
1924 · AT

Typographic Service New York
Typesetting
1923 · US

Du Pont
Paints
1917 · US

Ernal Mydla (Szymon Munk)
Soaps
1926 · PL

American Automobile Association
American Automobile Association
1922 · US

Esso
Gas stations
1934 · US

Karl Petersen & Co.
Tobacco
1925 · DK

Luterma
Machinery
1931 · EE

Dr. August Oetker
Foods
1936 · DE

NRC
Publishing
1928 · NL

Uovo
Foods
1932 · UK

Henkel
Chemicals
1927 · DE

Gebroeders Slaets
Household goods
1929 · BE

Arli
Textiles
1933 · DK

Dr. Erich F. Huth
Radios
1925 · DE

Ragnar Carlstedt
Machinery
1931 · SE

The Mitchell Vance Company
Lamps
1916 · US

Simmons Paper Company
1939 · UK

Franz Gutmann & Weinberg
Gloves
1932 · O.H.W. Hadank · DE

The Ohio Brass Company
Machinery
1907 · US

Linton's Bristols
Paper products
1935 · US

Fairchild Aviation
1929 · US

Pope's Metaaldraatlampenfabriek
Lamps
1923 · NL

Isuzu
Automobiles
1935 · JP

AEG
Electric products
1908 · Peter Behrens · DE

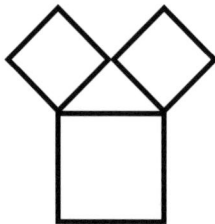

Elise Imhauser
Watches
1882 · US

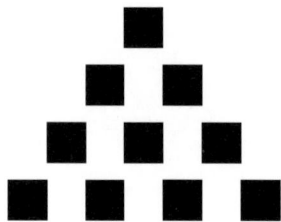

The American Sugar Refining Company
1876 · US

Banwell Wire Fence Company
1906 · CA

National Electric Novelty Company
1921 · US

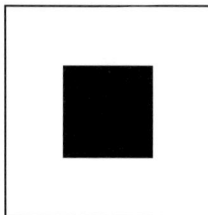

Stilles Försäljnings Aktiebolag
Paints
1936 · SE

Galerie Miethke
Art gallery
1905 · Koloman Moser · AT

Joh. Backhausen & Söhne
Furniture
1900 · Koloman Moser · AT

Harcourt, Brace and Company
Publishing
1910 · Charles K. Stevens · US

Winold Reiss Decorating Company
1910 · Winold Reiss · US

Onoma
Paper products
1912 · Julius Gipkens · DE

Meubelfabriek Lovoosterbeek
Furniture
1928 · NL

Primula
Canned foods
1918 · NL

Arnold Print Works
1887 · US

Moe
Machinery
1930 · Carl Keidel · DE

Telefunken
Electronics
1920 · DE

Schubert & Zacher
Isolated wires
1923 · DE

Walter Fritz Elektrotechnik
Electronics
1930 · Carl Keidel · DE

FT
Personal mark
1934 · IT

Pukocid
Chemicals
1928 · Max Körner · DE

Jag van der Steur
Constructions
1918 · J.G. Veldheer · NL

JH
Seafoods
1922 · UK

Ergasta
Chemicals
1925 · PL

Farbwerke Max Mühsam
Printing colors
1924 · DE

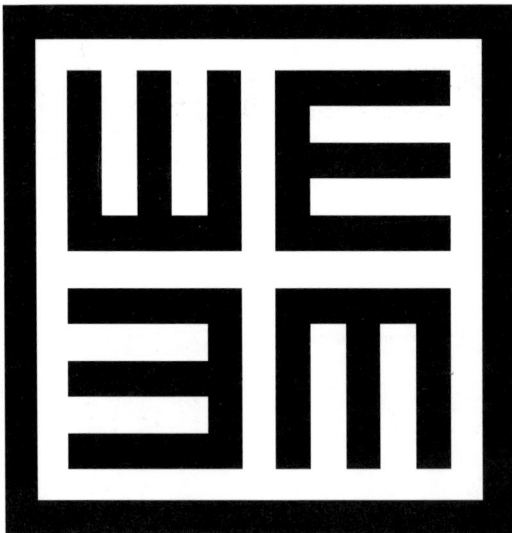

The Ellis Chemical Company
1931 · UK

Tigler Maschinenbau
Machinery
1924 · H.K. Schaefer · DE

Fritz Lang Film
Film production
1929 · DE

Merz
Magazines
1922 · Kurt Schwitters · DE

A. Brunnschweiler & Company
Fabrics
1932 · UK

PPP
Foods
1938 · FR

Gebrüder Mertens Gartenarchitekten
Garden architecture
1918 · CH

Arbo-Bähr & Co.
Paints
1937 · DK

Eiselsberg Rosmanit Koffer
Suitcases
1909 · AT

Lois Moniat
Furniture
1940 · Walter Herdeg · CH

Charles Churchill & Company
Machine tools
1931 · UK

Langbein-Pfanhauser Werker
Chrome plating
1929 · DE

Das Werbehaus
Advertising agency
1938 · Das Werbehaus · DE

Heinz Wurche
Graphic designer
1939 · Heinz Wurche · DE

Henkels Elektrizitätswerke
Electricity works
1931 · DE

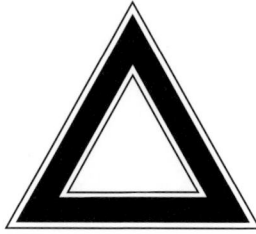

Triangle Overall Company
Work clothes
1914 · DE

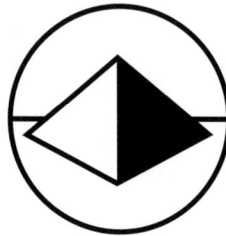

Fitema Technische Maatschappij
Machinery
1932 · NL

The Industrial Paint Company
1921 · US

Landmændens Andels Export Slagteri
Foods
1933 · DK

Viggo Valdemar Julius Andresen
Trading
1921 · DK

Trójkąt w Kole
Yarns
1934 · PL

Dr. Albert Lessing
Electronics
1922 · DE

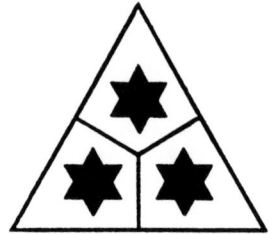

Townsend Plan Party
Political party
1936 · US

The Salt Union Limited
Salts
1899 · UK

Gloria
Heating technology
1932 · IT

Aage Havemann København
Radios ·
1925 · DK

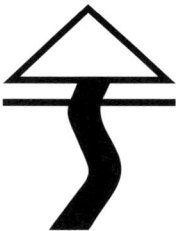

Theodor Schlatter & Cie
Carpenter
1932 · CH

Viktoria Yegyészeti Művek
Paints
1929 · HU

Raglan Cycle
Bicycles
1910 · UK

Normal-Zeit
Watches
1925 · DE

Mende & Co.
Radios
1928 · DE

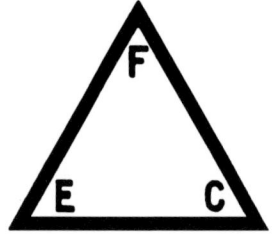

Federal Export Corporation
1916 · US

Angerer, Koch & Co
Leather products
1922 · DE

Alls
Dental products
1929 · PL

Statens Plateavls-Laboratorium
Research laboratories
1925 · DK

Wegmann & Co.
Wagons
1924 · DE

War Savings Stamps
1918 · CA

DBS
Personal mark
1926 · Josef Dominicus · DE

Vitachrom
Advertising services
1927 · DK

Auto-Betriebs-Compagnie
Car repair
1919 · AT

Jil
Textiles
1927 · FR

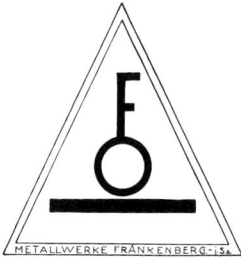

Metallwerke Frankenberg
Metal works
1929 · DE

Haus der Elektrotechnik
Trade union
1927 · DE

Kola Dallmann
Pharmaceuticals
1925 · DE

Markt & Co.
Cleaning fluids
1932 · DK

Ingold Christian Jensen
Electronics
1919 · DK

Ostar Radio
Radios
1929 · AT

JAP Markt & Co.
Sporting goods
1933 · DK

Watt Elektrizitäts-AG
Radios
1923 · DE

North American Aviation
Airplanes
1934 · US

Organpol
Music instruments
1929 · PL

Selekod
Fabrics
1928 · FR

Latexo Nederlandsche Elastiekfabrik
Rubber products
1933 · NL

Finska Pappersbruksforeningen
Paper products
1922 · FI

Delta Airlines
1929 · US

CBS Radio
Broadcasting
1935 · US

Argenta
Light bulbs
1922 · NL

Nederlandse Ind. Genootschap
voor Reclame
Advertising union
1930 · NL

New York Tire Company
1888 · US

Labor
Design studio
1923 · Jos Leonard · NL

Vim
Cleaning powder
1926 · UK

Penman's Manufacturing Comapny
1905 · CA

Tiger
Motorcycles
1927 · DE

Efficia
Paper products
1934 · FR

Opal
Cosmetics
1909 · DK

The Triangel Ice Machine Company
1922 · DK

Adamic
Cosmetics
1931 · FR

Young Men's Christian Association
1897 · US

Stilling-Anderson
Foods
1922 · US

Cinelux
Film production
1929 · FR

Barwień
Varnishes
1935 · PL

Du ski
Ski equipment
1932 · FR

Amavet
Typewriter ribbons
1931 · FR

Au Bûcheron
Department store
1928 · FR

Tate & Co.
Yarns
1890 · US

Diamond H
Electrics
1905 · CA

J. S. Turner Manufacturing Company
Leather products
1918 · US

Bjur Bros.
Music instruments
1909 · US

Renault
Automobiles
1925 · FR

Peter J. Oestergaard
Publishing
1914 · DE

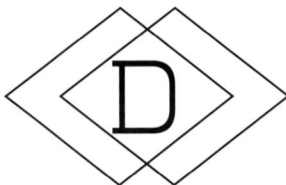

J. D. Koopmanns Svineslagteri
Butcher
1894 · DK

A. Braun & Co.
Printing
1919 · DE

Dynic
Paper products
1919 · JP

Audit Bureau of Circulations
1921 · US

Barber-Greene Company
Machinery
1920 · US

Gerstein Brothers
Construction materials
1921 · US

Ernst Meding
Electronics
1925 · DE

Van Staal & Co.
Publishing
1926 · NL

Julius Moser
Personal mark
1924 · Erwin Reusch · DE

Z Radziwillow Marja Skórzweska
Foods
1925 · PL

Stumpp & Kurz
Screws
1928 · DE

Sigismund Felix Lehmann
Graphic designer
1929 · Sigismund Felix Lehmann · DE

F. Guhl & Co.
Printing
1931 · DE

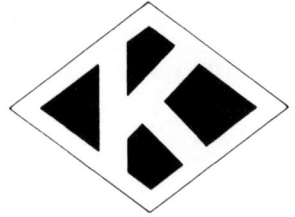

Kosuga
Sporting goods
1943 · JP

Froitzheim und Rudert
Machinery
1931 · DE

PTT
Dutch postal services
1935 · NL

ÖRA
Austrian radio journal
1930 · AT

United Artists
Film production
1919 · US

Umbro
Sporting goods
1930 · UK

Roxford Knitting Company
1907 · US

Agarase
Pharmaceuticals
1909 · FR

Cafola
Chocolates
1921 · CH

Bobby
Tobacco
1925 · UK

Empire Grain & Elevator Company
Foods
1912 · US

The Marion Line
Machinery
1921 · US

Aro Pedersen & Velfling
Foods
1926 · DK

Hääge
Metal works
1914 · CH

Gebrüder Jaeger Schalter
Switches
1923 · DE

Oligo
Car parts
1929 · AT

Sanpic
Pharmaceuticals
1920 · AT

Firefly Lighter
1925 · UK

Napa
Car repair
1930 · US

Meerkotter Amsterdam
Advertising services
1932 · NL

Agfa
Photographic products
1924 · DE

5 Reclame-Ontwerpers
Design exhibition
1926 · NL

Siris
Hygiene products
1937 · FR

AWB
Metal products
1932 · UK

Sociéte L'Air Liquide
Gasoline
1929 · FR

Erroll Engineering Company
1946 · UK

Belplastic
Plastics
1932 · UK

Diana Films
Film production
1935 · ES

Yacco
Motor oils
1929 · FR

Vertex
Stockings
1933 · FR

Enamolin
Floor finish
1916 · US

Afri Cola
Beverages
1930 · DE

Mekaniske Net- & Garnfabrik
N. P. Utzon
Fishing nets
1915 · DK

Gaba
Pharmaceuticals
1930 · CH

**Skandinavisk ABC Sports- &
Læderindustri**
Sporting goods
1934 · DK

Iseki
Agricultural machines
1936 · JP

Diplopol
Plastic products
1938 · PL

115

Falsa Prodo
Paper products
1885 · DK

Pipe
Automobiles
1911 · BE

Vilhelm Emilius Raben
Instruments
1894 · DK

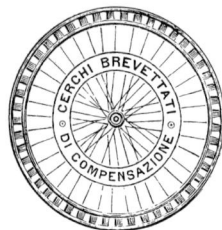

E. Kloss
Bicycles
1897 · IT

Wolo
Pharmaceuticals
1909 · CH

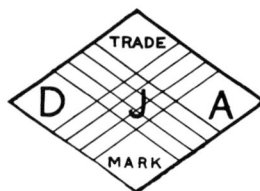

David & Joh Anderson
Fabrics
1910 · UK

Federal
Car parts
1911 · CH

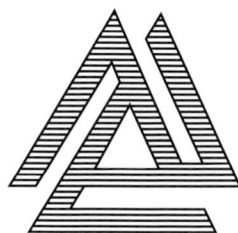

Finska Handelskompagniet
Trading
1918 · FI

Camenbert
Cheese quality seal
1925 · FR

Fango di Battaglia
Pharmaceuticals
1929 · CH

Julius Schmid
Canned foods
1938 · US

ATM
Yarns
1920 · FR

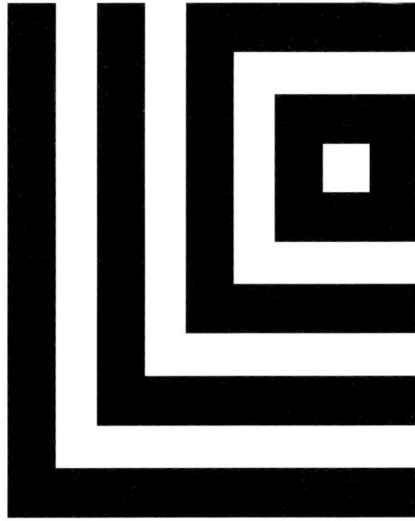

Ludwig Loewe & Co.
Machinery
1926 · DE

Ulrika
Safety matches
1923 · FI

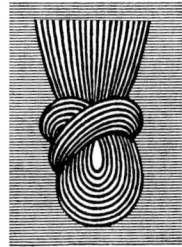

National Carbon Company
1930 · US

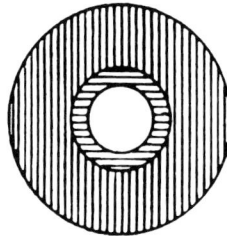

Davistan
Carpets
1928 · DE

Carat
Cigarettes
1924 · DK

Kol Yisrael
Broadcasting
1936 · IL

Atelier Buchstein
Graphic design
1929 · Atelier Buchstein · DE

Baum & Co.
Paints
1889 · US

Orgos
Household products
1929 · PL

Catalana de Gas y Electricidad
Energy supplier
1912 · ES

Goodyear
Tires
1918 · CA

Osram
Light bulbs
1921 · DE

Perrier
Table water
1917 · FR

Sinclair Refining Company
Gasoline
1920 · US

OK Alart & Mc Guire Company
Foods
1916 · US

Oxo
Foods
1910 · UK

Prince Paint Company
1915 · US

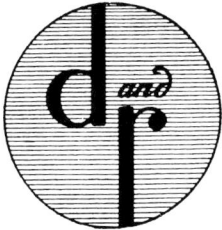

Daggett & Ramsdell
Cosmetics
1929 · US

Union Metallic Cartridge Company
1887 · US

P. C. Olsen
Soaps
1923 · DK

Munktells Mekaniska Verkstads
Machinery
1915 · SE

S. Danelius & Co.
Metal products
1887 · US

Asbern
Machinery
1923 · DE

Ago
Machinery
1910 · AT

Gewerkschaft Leuchtenburg
Quarry
1911 · DE

Shanks Insul Boards
1930 · UK

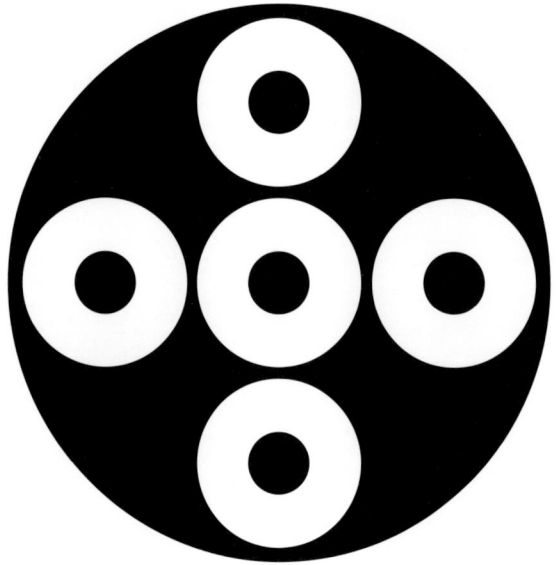

Tanabe Seiyaku
Pharmaceuticals
1942 · JP

Volta-Kors
Pharmaceuticals
1890 · DK

Aalborg Export Akvarit
Liqours
1914 · DK

Angostura
Liquors
1885 · DK

Birmo
Pharmaceuticals
1930 · CH

White Cross
Anti-Liquor society
1912 · US

O. Roth & Co.
Foods
1928 · CH

Bayer
Pharmaceuticals
1904 · Hans Schneider · DE

Theodor Møller
Trading
1893 · DK

Suchard
Chocolates
1922 · CH

Weiß & Lingmann
Printing
1926 · CH

Maggi
Food extract
1895 · DE

Moll-Werke
Machinery
1923 · DE

William Turner
Foods
1931 · UK

Union Smelting & Refining Company
Metal castings
1903 · US

L. J. Akker
Chemicals
1914 · NL

Diosal
Pharmaceuticals
1918 · US

Chevrolet
Automobiles
1914 · Anonymous

The Mason Regulator Company
Machinery
1905 · US

Aalborg Exportkompagni
Food trading
1919 · DK

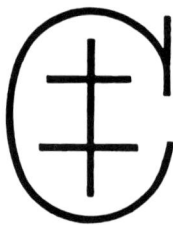

Sociéte Le Carbone-Lorraine
Electric products
1937 · FR

Kalasiris
Underwear
1907 · DE

Halpaus
Cigarettes
1920 · DE

The Willey Company
Washing machines
1920 · US

The William M. Eisen Company
Medical products
1924 · US

Der Weg
Art school
1930 · DE

**Sociedad Española de
Construcciones Electricas**
Electronics
1921 · ES

Naxos-Film
Film distribution
1928 · DE

Durex Abrasives Corporation
1929 · US

Koholyt
Paper products
1924 · DE

Pyrozon
Motor oils
1929 · FR

Lamson Paragon Supply Company
Office materials
1937 · UK

Totalbau
Construction company
1924 · DE

Vimro
Fruit imports
1929 · NL

Fezfabriken
Textiles
1941 · AT

Wrigley's Chewing Sweet
1924 · US

Matsushita Electric Industrial
1937 · JP

Usine Genevoise de Degrossiage D'or
Wheels for watches
1889 · CH

Klotz, Wunderlich & Co.
Beverages
1932 · DE

Gillette
Razor blades
1901 · US

Volvo
Automobiles
1930 · SE

Škoda
Automobiles
1925 · CZ

DEFU
Film production
1928 · Kupfer-Sachs · DE

Joseph Robinson
Heating systems
1915 · US

Bofors
Iron works
1925 · SE

Nowea Messegesellschaft Düsseldorf
Trade fair
1947 · Walter Müller · DE

Vesta
Electrics
1919 · DK

Anton Nielsen Troelstrup
Department store
1912 · DK

Georg Printz & Co.
Electronics
1895 · DE

125

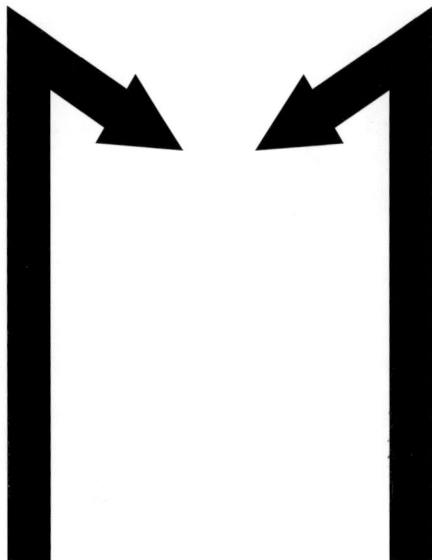

RKO Radio Pictures
Film production
1928 · US

H. E. Gosch & Co.
Matchboxes
1914 · DK

Volta
Electrochemicals
1929 · PL

Radiateur
Electronics
1895 · FR

Stockholms Superfosfat Fabriks
Chemicals
1927 · SE

RAM
Radios
1929 · IT

Acerboni
Electric lights
1910 · IT

Ellinger & Geißler
Electronics
1928 · DE

Laboradium
Pharmaceuticals
1929 · FR

Tabozon
Canned foods
1930 · CH

Antilaamsiekte Hartig
Cattle Remedy
1926 · Hans Schleger Zero · DE/UK

Imprex Gustav Ruth
Chemicals
1926 · DE

Rheinische Elektro-Industrie Josef Abels
Electronics
1925 · DE

The Chase Brass & Copper Company
Copper products
1929 · F.G. Cooper · US

Paul Schlesinger
Graphic designer
1924 · Paul Schlesinger · DE

Stormbull Oslo
Construction materials
1936 · Fabritius Reklamebyrå · NO

Rudolf Boye Elektrizitätsgesellschaft
Motors
1922 · DE

WB
Personal mark
1923 · Christian Prelle · DE

Osram-Philips Neon
Neon signs
1931 · DE

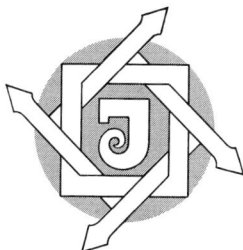

Jaroslaw Mikant
Insulators
1922 · DE

Emag
Electronics
1925 · DE

Stern

Carlsberg Beer
1880 · DK

North Star Wollen Mill Company
1870 · US

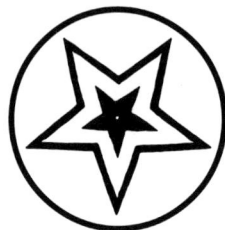

JCT Krogh
Leather products
1882 · DK

Star Shirt
Clothes
1898 · CA

Buffalo Printing Ink Corporation
1886 · US

Star

Canadian Rubber Company
1892 · CA

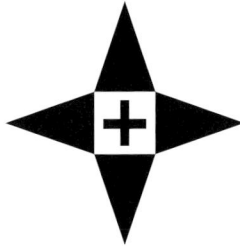

Maggi
Foods
1899 · DE

The East Asiatic Company
Foods
1932 · UK

Star Manufacturers
Flours
1890 · US

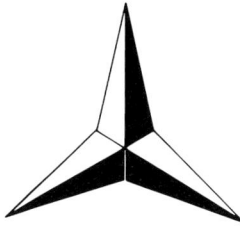

Daimler
Automobiles
1909 · DE

Deutsche Polizei
German police
1926 · Ernst Böhm · DE

Astral
Sanitary articles
1893 · DE

Pirelli & Co.
Tires
1920 · IT

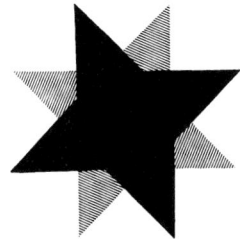

Alfred Olsen & Co.
Oils
1929 · DK

Englebert & Co.
Tires
1934 · BE

Star Motors
Automobiles
1922 · US

Randers
Milk bottles
1936 · UK

129

Stella
Phonographs
1932 · FR

Dodge Brothers
Automobiles
1914 · US

Procter & Gamble
Cosmetics
1918 · US

Orion
Chemicals
1923 · DK

F. Farge
Fabrics
1911 · ES

PTT
Dutch postal services
1932 · N.P. de Koo · NL

Skiltefabrikken Reflex
Signs
1923 · DK

**Manhattan Electrical
Supply Company**
1907 · US

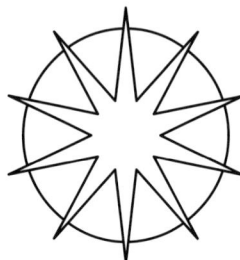

Astra
Chemicals
1936 · SE

Azur
Gasoline
1920 · NL

Piles Mazda Cipel
Accumulators
1930 · FR

C.H. Meyer & Son
Beer
1896 · DK

Continental Petroleum Company
1912 · BE

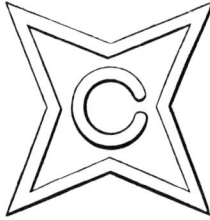

Cookson & Company
Steel products
1910 · UK

The Star Whitewear
Manufacturing company
1900 · CA

Green River Lumber Company
1911 · US

Aalborg Eksportkompagni
Foods
1940 · DK

Wilhelm Wippermann
Car parts
1905 · DE

Sterna
Foods
1909 · CH

Niels Christian Christensen
Soaps
1880 · DK

**American Association of
Passenger Traffic Operations**
1915 · US

Axios
Liquors
1924 · DK

Heinrich Thiele & Companie
Printing machines
1923 · DE

Star Fuse Company
Electronics
1914 · US

Effekt

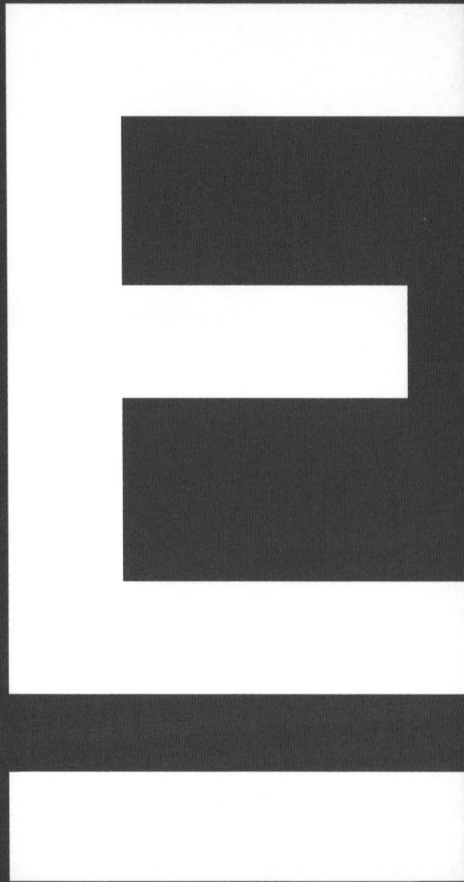

Sketches from the first phase of the history of design are often attributed a certain artistic arbitrariness due to their hand-drawn origins. However, a closer look and quantitative examination reveal that the designs of early logos also followed particular compositional principles. Many of these concepts, such as rotation, reflection, and overlay, remain popular methods used in the search for the optimal form. It is also worth noting that many marks do not use just one design parameter; rather, it is precisely the combination of several effects that leads to exciting and unique logo designs. Particularly in the context of a highly optimized digital design process, the often naïve joy in graphic experimentation apparent in many of the logos pictured here serves as an inspiring model.

Entwürfen aus der Anfangsphase der Designgeschichte wird aufgrund ihrer händischen Entstehungsweise gern eine gewisse künstlerische Willkür zugeschrieben. Der genauere Blick und eine quantitative Untersuchung zeigen jedoch, dass auch der Entwurf früher Logos ganz bestimmten Gestaltungsprinzipien folgte. Viele dieser Schemata, wie Rotation, Spiegelung oder Überlagerung, sind bis heute gängige Methoden bei der Suche nach der optimalen Form. Beachtenswert ist dabei auch, dass in vielen Zeichen nicht nur ein einzelner Gestaltungsparameter Anwendung findet, sondern gerade die Kombination mehrerer Effekte zu besonders spannungsreichen und individuellen Logoentwürfen führt. Die oft naive Freude am grafischen Experiment, die in vielen der abgebildeten Logos erkennbar wird, ist gerade im Kontext eines durchoptimierten digitalen Entwurfsprozesses ein anregendes Vorbild.

Les esquisses des premiers temps du design sont volontiers taxées d'un certain arbitraire artistique du fait de leur tracé à la main. Or, un regard plus minutieux et une analyse quantitative montrent que la conception des premiers logos obéissait à des principes formels précis. Bon nombre de ces concepts, notamment la rotation, la réflexion ou la superposition, sont encore aujourd'hui des approches courantes pour la recherche de la forme idéale. On remarque aussi que de nombreux signes ne se limitent pas à un seul paramètre conceptuel, et c'est justement la combinaison de plusieurs effets qui produit des logos uniques et attrayants. Le plaisir souvent naïf de la quête graphique qui transparaît dans beaucoup des logos représentés ici constitue un exemple particulièrement stimulant dans le contexte actuel de la conception numérique optimisée.

Württembergische Metallwarenfabrik
Metal products
1907 · DE

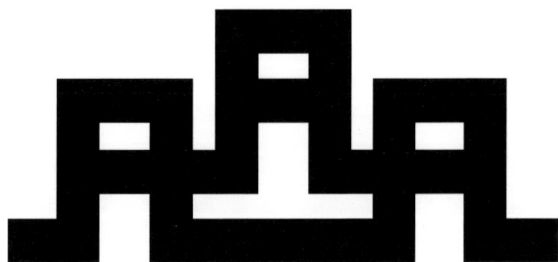

Axel & Albert Andersen
Bicycles
1919 · DK

Emil Heinicke
Interior design
1912 · DE

GF
Personal mark
1922 · UK

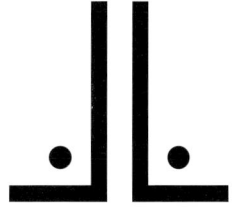

Lanooy
Glassware
1924 · NL

Nitsche & Günther
Opticals
1920 · DE

Accumulatorenfabrik Wilhelm Hagen
Accumulators
1923 · DE

**New York Hamburger Gummiwaren
Compagnie**
Rubber products
1924 · US/DE

Bouwassociatie
Architecture
1920 · C. de Haas · NL

Marie Teinitzerová
Personal mark
1923 · Jaroslav Benda · CZ

Moe
Machinery
1930 · Carl Keidel · DE

Niederrheinische Messe Wesel
Trade fair
1922 · DE

Kaufhaus Schocken
Department stores
1926 · E.P. Weise · DE

Eisen Heunert
Iron works
1926 · Johannes Molzahn · DE

August Jacobi
Electronics
1928 · DE

Inton
Radios
1931 · DK

Meyer
Fabrics
1929 · FR

Schmidt & Melmer
Household products
1929 · DE

Klei
Architectural magazine
1924 · NL

Miray
Watches
1929 · FR

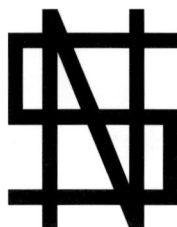

Schreiber & Neffen
Glass products
1929 · CZ

Sinpo
Newspaper
1925 · NL

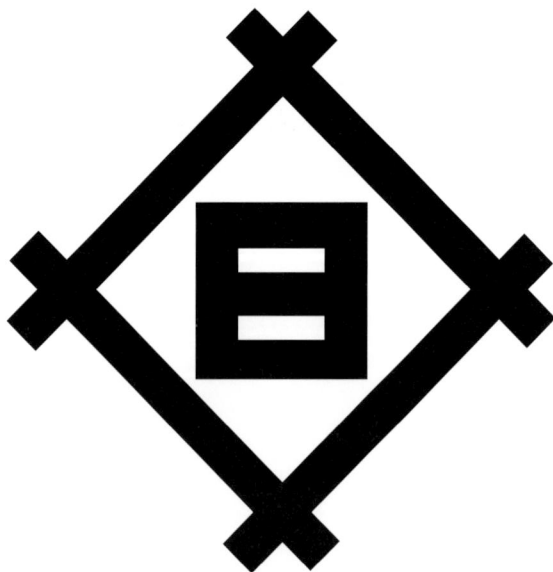

Mizuno
Sporting goods
1906 · JP

The Empire State Engraving Company
Prepress services
1912 · US

Wereldbibliotheek Amsterdam
Publishing
1932 · NL

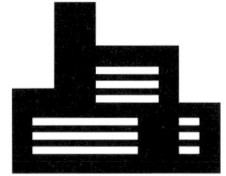

Burgolin Lack- und Farbenwerke
Paints
1932 · CH

Remaco
Advertising services
1928 · NL

Münchner Lehrwerkstätten
Craftmen school
1937 · DE

Smit
Printing
1931 · NL

Simmen Brugg
Furniture
1929 · CH

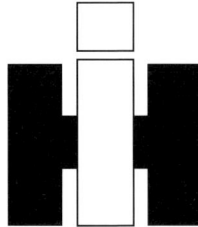

International Harvester Company
Harvesting machines
1944 · Raymond Loewy · US

Clysmic Spring Company
Table water
1915 · US

VAG
Industry
1928 · Kupfer-Sachs · DE

Karnak
Fabrics
1920 · US

British Petroleum
Gasoline
1920 · UK

P. Ballatine & Sons
Beer
1880 · US

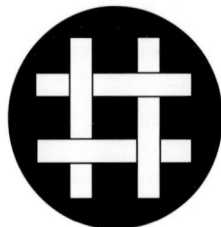

Sociéte Franço-Suisse de Brosserie
Brushes
1922 · FR-CH

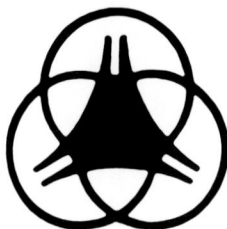

Zeiss Ikon
Opticals
1920 · DE

New York Yankees
Baseball team
1909 · US

The Munsingwear Corporation
Hosiery
1922 · US

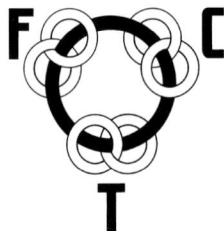

Federal Coordinator of Transportation
1930 · Clarence P. Hornung · US

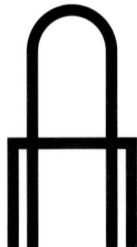

Thonet-Mundus Gesellschaft
Furniture
1929 · AT

Seven O Seven
Chemicals
1932 · UK

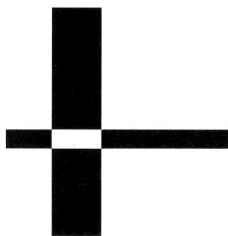

Burroughs Adding Machine Company
Calculating machines
1939 · US

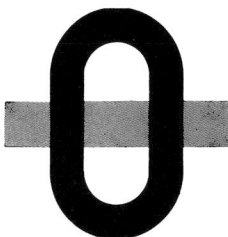

Det forenede Oljekompagni
Oils
1920 · DK

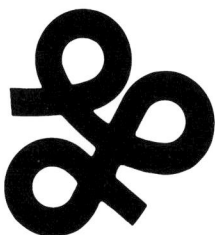

Asagaya College of Art and Design
1934 · Takashi Miwa · JP

Audi Auto-Union
Automobiles
1932 · DE

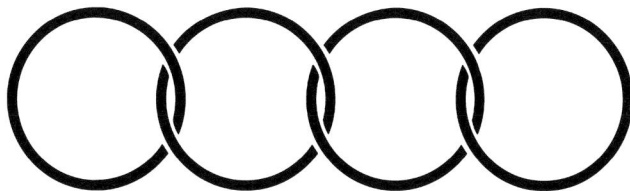

Ontario Agricultural College
1904 · CA

AEG
Electronics
1907 · Peter Behrens · DE

Siemens
Electronics
1899 · DE

Hammell Cracker Company
1906 · US

Hupmobile
Automobiles
1908 · US

Louis Vuitton
Clothes
1896 · FR

Redfield-Kendrick-Odell Company
Printing
1910 · Vance Goss · US

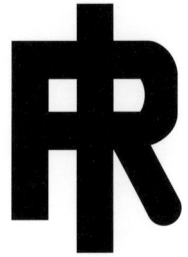

Ingersoll-Rand Company
Machine parts
1913 · US

Abercrombie & Fitch
Sporting goods store
1917 · US

Buick
Automobiles
1911 · US

The Traffic Club of New York
1913 · US

C.J. Hoffmann
Cigarettes
1909 · DK

Computing-Tabulating-Recording Company
1911 · US

Triumph Mills
Coffee
1913 · US

A. A. Wire Company
1910 · US

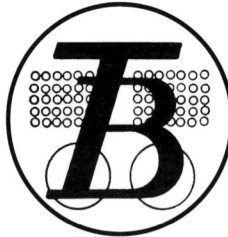

Temperatur-Balans
Machinery
1912 · SE

Sterling Bronze
Interior design
1917 · US

Mount Vernon Company
Medical products
1918 · US

**American Machine &
Foundry Company**
1924 · US

Gebrüder Wolf Zigarettenfabrik
Cigarettes
1926 · W. Wörner · DE

G. Schillemans
Personal mark
1919 · R.W.P. de Vries Jr. · NL

Związkowa Centrala Maszyn
Machinery
1925 · PL

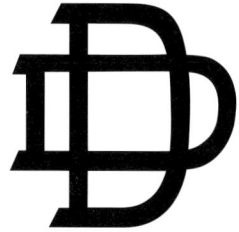

Deutz Diesel
Automobiles
1928 · DE

A. Molling & Company
Packaging
1920 · DE

Druckerei Hubert Hoch
Printing
1920 · DE

Rolls-Royce
Automobiles
1924 · UK

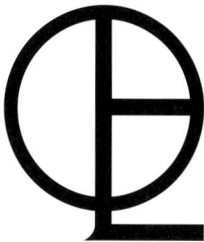

De Bazel
Glass products
1924 · NL

Hansa-Druckerei
Printing
1926 · Ernst Schmidt · DE

**Association des Manufactures de
Glaces d'l'Europe Continentale**
Glass products
1927 · BE

Match
Sporting goods
1928 · FR

Maybach
Automobiles
1929 · DE

Picking-Glas
Glass products
1930 · DE

Comptoir des Textiles Artificiels
Fabrics
1928 · FR

Union Artistes Décorateurs
Decorators union
1929 · FR

FN El Turista
Motorcycles
1931 · ES

Ganz & Comp.
Machinery
1928 · HU

Druckerei August Osterrieth
Printing
1929 · Henze-Dessau · DE

Schlesische Zellwolle
Fabrics
1936 · DE

Hartwig-Quelle
Table water
1928 · Walter Trias · DE

Handwerk Handel und Gewerbe Krankenversicherungsanstalt
Insurance
1930 · DE

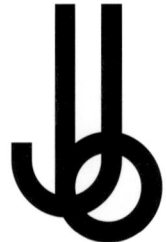

Jé-Bé Reclame
Advertising
1936 · NL

Laboratoire D'isothérapie Appliquée
Pharmaceuticals
1939 · FR

Kool
Cigarettes
1931 · US

Brooks
Bicycle saddles
1920 · UK

PEL
Steel furniture
1932 · UK

To-R Radio
Radios
1935 · DK

SNCF
French Railways
1937 · Maximilian Vox · FR

Franklin Field Illustrated
Magazine
1928 · US

Associated Growers of British Columbia
Fruits
1924 · CA

Intourist
Russian Tourism Office
1930 · RU

Tissages Gueny-Dupery et Fils
Fabrics
1931 · FR

Eagle Lye Works
Chemicals
1910 · US

Touring Club Ciclistico Italiano
Bicycle Club of Italy
1897 · IT

Ivorit
Construction materials
1929 · CZ

**Schweizerische
Landesausstellung Zürich**
Trade fair
1939 · CH

M. Jakobi
Gasoline
1923 · DE

A. Hagenbucher
Pharmaceuticals
1899 · CH

British Automobile Association
1932 · UK

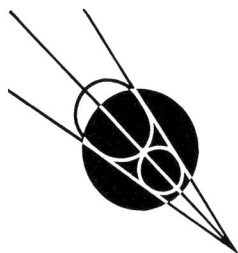

Ford V8
Automobiles
1935 · US

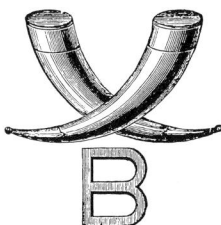

Herman Arnold Rothenborg
Machinery
1892 · DK

Sileo
Typewriters
1914 · IT

Otto Meyer
Furniture
1932 · DK

Triumph
Bicycles
1895 · UK

Castonite
Metal products
1912 · US

Tol
Art gallery
1929 · FR

H. Niemojewski
Medical products
1938 · PL

Zjednoczone Fabryki Związków Azotowych w Mościcach i Chorzowie
Chemicals
1935 · PL

Ratol
Gas
1935 · DK

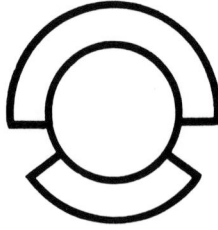

W. S. Rockwell Company
Electronics
1909 · US

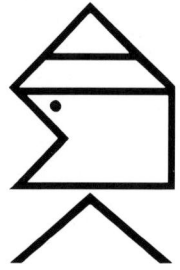

Malik Verlag
Publishing
1925 · Georg Grosz · DE

International Motor Company
1915 · US

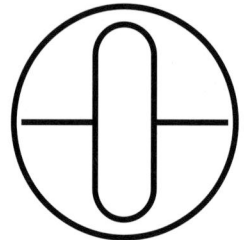

Anschütz & Co.
Scientific instruments
1931 · DE

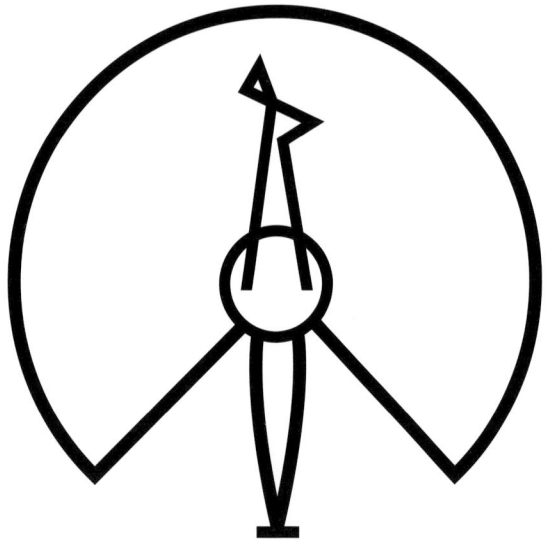

Pfau's America Instruments Company
1920 · US

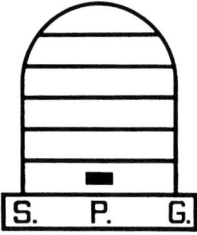

De Bijenkorf
Department stores
1930 · NL

Jules Grouvelle, H. Arquembourg & Cie
Engineering
1910 · FR

Harley-Davidson Motorcycles
1910 · US

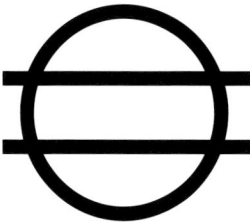

Varta
Accumulators
1937 · DE

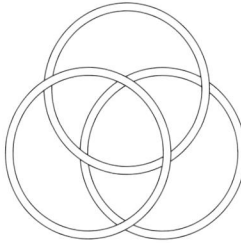

Friedrich Krupp
Steel products
1875 · DE

Nokia Suomen Gumitehdas Osakeyhtiö
Rubber products
1898 · FI

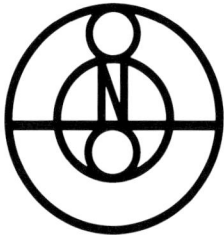

Neri
Drugstore
1943 · Carlo L. Vivarelli · CH

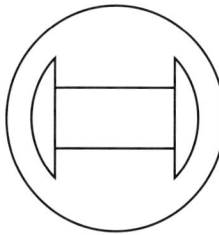

Robert Bosch
Car parts
1918 · DE

The Pyle National Company
Steam locomotives
1921 · US

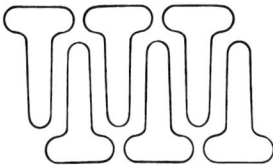

Telleborgs Gummifabriks
Rubbers
1914 · DK

Wondergrip Products
Packings
1938 · UK

**The Firestone Tire &
Rubber Company**
1922 · US

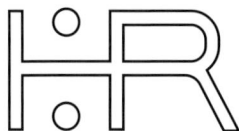

Hans Renold Manchester
Vehicles
1909 · UK

Doma
Hygiene products
1936 · SE

Birds Eye
Foods
1923 · US

Oscar Kohorn & Co.
Machinery
1928 · AT

Plexiglas
1940 · DE

Kerr Glass Manufacturing Company
1906 · US

Alpa
Pharmaceuticals
1929 · CZ

William Penn Hammond
Chemicals
1900 · US

Einar H. Petersen & Co.
Chemicals
1913 · DK

Nescafé
Instant coffee
1937 · CH

Greyhound Lines
Bus services
1914 · US

Tabak-Haus Philipp
Tobacco
1924 · Max Körner · DE

François Bossy
Soaps
1909 · FR

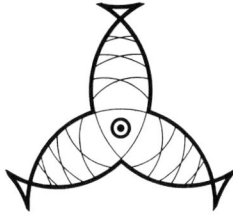

Tozaburo Suzuski
Fertilizers
1912 · JP

Fichtel & Sachs
Motors
1938 · Hartmuth Pfeil · DE

Greif Büromöbel
Office furniture
1918 · P. Hosch · CH

Florida
Foods
1884 · DK

Viscosity Oil Company
1911 · US

Kolster-Brandes Radio
1934 · C.W. Bacon · UK

Societe André Citroën
Automobiles
1932 · FR

Dormy
Footwear
1931 · UK

Positiv-
Negativ

Positive-
Negative

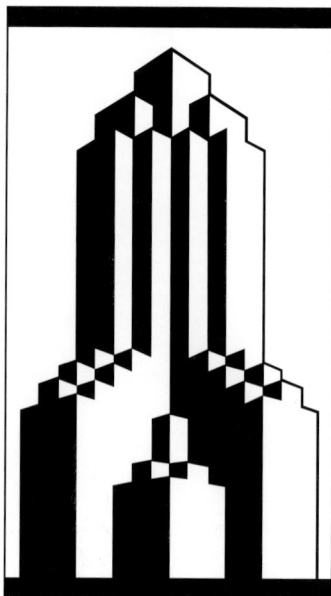

General Building Contractor
1930 · Clarence P. Hornung · US

Bayerische Motoren Werke
Automobiles
1916 · DE

Berliner Verkehrsbetriebe
Public transportation
1890 · DE

New Deal
Political party
1936 · US

Cletus Petersen & Co.
Trading
1921 · DK

Genesee Salt Company
1889 · US

Cresent Ice Cream
1918 · US

Victor-Auguste Deschiens
Yarns
1910 · FR

William Stannard & Co.
Fabrics
1900 · UK

Allan Christensen & Co.
Trading
1920 · DK

Films Artistiques
Film production
1921 · FR

Plants Plantoids
Fertilizers
1911 · UK

**New Era Spring &
Speciality Company**
1920 · H.C. Glidden · US

Vistra
Fabrics
1929 · DE

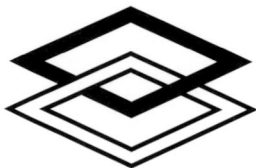

Automotive Gear Works
1916 · US

Mineira
Hoes
1923 · Alan C. Rogers · UK

Lubitsch Filmproduktion
Film production
1924 · Kupfer-Sachs · DE

Spezialbeton AG
Iron concrete
1921 · CH

Hans Schwarzkopf
Cosmetics
1922 · DE

IG Farbenindustrie
Chemicals
1926 · DE

HI Lichtdruk
Printing
1926 · Machiel Wilmink · NL

Wendum Maschinengesellschaft
Printing machines
1923 · DE

G. Wilmking
Engineering
1926 · Johannes Molzahn · DE

Hahn im Korb
Soap
1927 · Albert Trueb · DE

Tapetenwerk Berolina
Wallpapers
1926 · DE

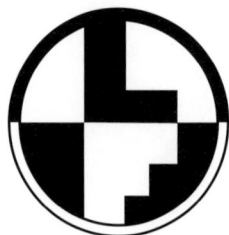

Willys
Automobiles
1930 · US

Farrar & Rinehart
Publishing
1930 · Clarence P. Hornung · US

IMH
1932 · Sascha A. Maurer · US

The Cleveland Gypsum Company
Plasters
1948 · US

Fotobel
Photographic products
1929 · BE

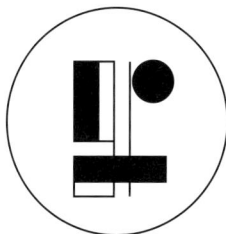

Graphischer Ring
Design association
1930 · Carl Keidel · DE

Club Espanol de Futbol Barcelona
Soccer club
1901 · ES

Linoleum AG
Floorings
1929 · Thoma · CH

Towarzystwo Chemiczne Yon
Chemicals
1934 · PL

Henri Weber
Stationary products
1929 · CH

**Vereinigte Glühlampen
und Elektrizitäts AG**
Electricity
1938 · HU

Kolin
City
1936 · Jaroslav Benda · CZ

Krupke & Oestreicher
Light bulbs
1930 · DE

Gajag
1930 · Dore Mönkemeyer-Corty · DE

Artstone Products
1930 · Clarence P. Hornung · US

Vada Drukkerij
Printing
1932 · NL

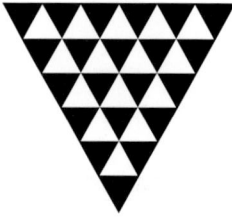

London Art School
1920 · G. M. Ellwood · UK

Nederl.-Indisch Genootschap
voor Reklame
Advertising association
1931 · Soepardi · IN/NL

Kayser
Clothes
1932 · UK

Degussa
Metal trading
1929 · Karl Schulpig · DE

Gebrüder Putzler Glashüttenwerke
Glass products
1932 · DE

Filmofono
Film production
1935 · ES

Berlin im Licht
Berlin Light Show
1930 · Erich Charall · DE

Proost-Drukwerk Ontwerp-Service
Design service
1932 · NL

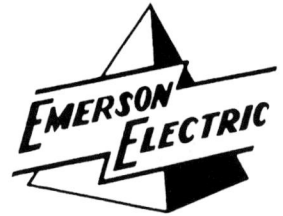

Emerson Electric Manufacturing
1940 · US

Deutsche Gasglühlicht AG
Gas lighting
1908 · DE

Machiel Wilmink
Graphic designer
1921 · Machiel Wilmink · NL

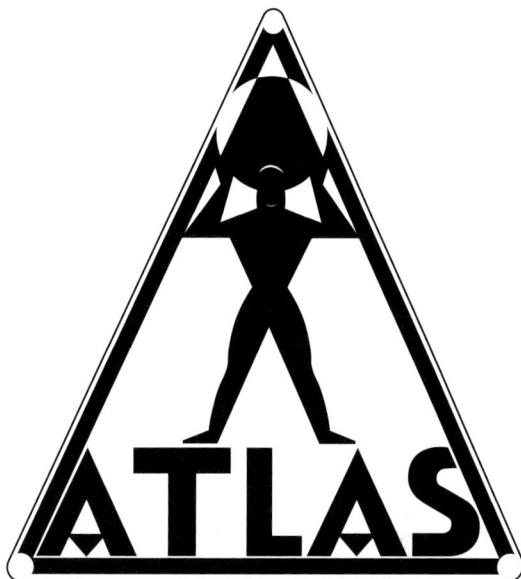

Aktieselskabet Atlas
Machinery
1932 · DK

Echo Radio
1931 · FR

Odin
Beverages
1933 · DK

Marmorit
Textiles
1934 · DK

Re-Na-Co Saalen
Footwear
1931 · DK

Citroen
Automobiles
1933 · FR

Stella
Plywood boards
1938 · US

Companhia Editoria Nacional
Publishing
1925 · BR

Blauenfeldt & Tvede
Chemicals
1913 · DK

The Sun
Newspaper
1894 · US

Juan Soler y Ca
Fabrics
1918 · ES

Henry Hughes & Son
Measuring instruments
1918 · UK

Juvito
Chemicals
1917 · US

Sol Habana
Cigars
1927 · CU

Asahi Nihontabi Kabushiki Kaisha
Footwear
1931 · JP

Amedee Huyghe
Pipes
1932 · BE

Codan
Rubber products
1925 · DK

Carl Schlieper
Music instruments
1939 · UK

Colson and Colson
Seeds
1922 · US

Solar
Industrial oils
1924 · TN

Home Counties Malt Vinegar Company
Foods
1932 · UK

Sunray
Foods
1925 · UK

Hoka
Automobiles
1930 · DK

De Forende Margarinefabriker
Foods
1938 · DK

**The Firestone Tire and
Rubber Company**
Rubber
1908 · US

Alexander Grammont
Light bulbs
1909 · FR

Rayon
Textiles
1926 · CH

Olfak
Oils
1920 · DK

Renu Manufacturing Company
Abrasives
1925 · US

Awel
Chocolates
1923 · CH

Aero
Heating systems
1910 · NL

**Vereinigte Carborundum-
und Elektrit-Werke**
Chemicals
1908 · AT

The Canton Cycle
Manufacturing company
1888 · US

California Optical Company
1925 · US

VEWAG
Electronics
1920 · DE

Lyonsilke
Fabrics
1935 · DK

Hexsun
Metal polish
1927 · DK

Dordtsche Glashandel
Glass
1939 · NL

Livets The
Teas
1896 · FR

Energi
Bicycles
1920 · DK

Victor Animatograph Company
Projecting lanterns
1912 · US

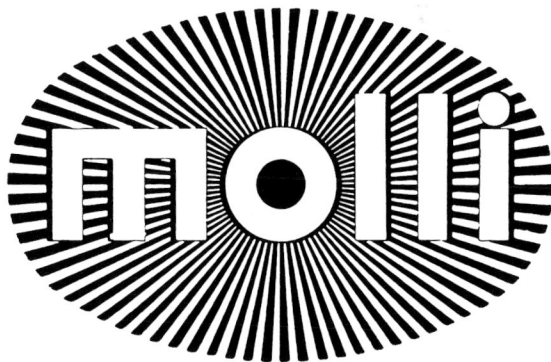

Molli
Heating technology
1945 · Werner Weiskönig · CH

159

General Electrics
1899 · A.L. Rich · US

The Phosphor-Bronze Company
1876 · UK

E. Grossenbacher & Co.
Electronics
1918 · CH

Borup Savværk
Sawmill
1883 · DK

Wittler-Werke
Bicycles
1930 · DE

Verlag Christian Friedrich Vieweg
Publishing
1930 · DE

John M. Hansen
Furniture
1916 · US

Deutsche Spiegelglas Gesellschaft
Mirrors
1923 · DE

Unus
Machinery
1930 · IT

Olexol
Motor oils
1920 · DE

General Mills
Foods
1928 · US

Ozo
Gas stations
1936 · FR

Johnson, Handley, Johnson Company
Furniture
1924 · US

G. Meidinger & Cie
Air conditioning
1930 · CH

Rexo
Gasoline
1938 · FR

Deutsche Huragan
Milling machines
1927 · DE

Verne Noll
Personal mark
1931 · US

Gruschwitz Textilwerke
Fabrics
1920 · DE

C.H. Funch
Vinegar
1888 · DK

Fritz Haastrup
Hoisery
1907 · DK

Bötzow
Beer
1920 · DE

F. V. Loehrs Efterfølger
Foods
1893 · DK

Jacarp
Foods
1910 · NL

Cinema du vieux colombier
Movie theater
1929 · FR

E. Zwietusch & Co.
Soldering irons
1931 · DE

Tokyo Shibaura Denki
Electronics
1943 · JP

Lanolin
Chemicals
1886 · DE

Standard Oil Corporation of California
1940 · US

J. R. Geigy
Pharmaceuticals
1939 · Ferdinand Schott · CH

Volkswagenwerk
Automobiles
1938 · DE

**Deutsch-Luxemburgische
Bergwerks- und Hütten-AG**
Mining
1923 · DE

Ryngraf
Construction materials
1922 · PL

Nora
Radios
1923 · DE

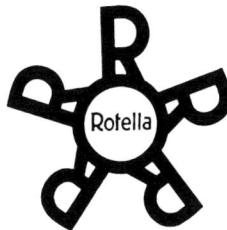

Rotella-Margarine
Foods
1932 · Louis Oppenheim · DE

Ruppert, Singer & Cie
Windows
1922 · CH

FABRICS

The Wiley-Bickford-Sweet Company
Fabrics
1921 · US

Dansk Elektromaskin-Aktieselskab
Electric machines
1921 · DK

Medizindienst Hannover
Medial services
1923 · Christian Prelle · DE

Paul Eberth & Co.
Lighting
1927 · CH

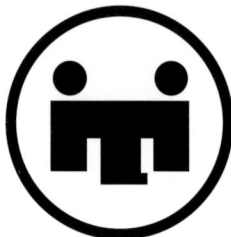

Nordisch Deutsche Woche Kiel
Folk festival
1929 · Alfred Mahlau · DE

Mannesmann Licht
Accumulators
1927 · DE

Ultrola
Record label
1930 · DE

Hyogo Bank
1944 · JP

Tigges & Co.
Magnets
1930 · DE

London Passenger Transport Board
1934 · C.W. Bacon · UK

Chemisch-Pharmazeutische Gesellschaft Bad Homburg
Chemicals
1928 · DE

Wilbur & Thomas Fertilizer Company
Chemicals
1930 · US

Böhme Fettchemie
Chemicals
1935 · DE

Delta Airlines
1934 · US

E-H Engineering
1932 · UK

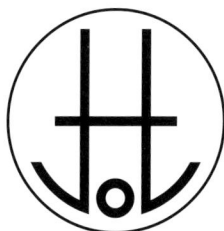

Johann Hartleib
Prepress services
1938 · DE

Schiele & Bruchsaler
Lightning protection
1924 · DE

Rigaud
Cigarettes
1934 · FR

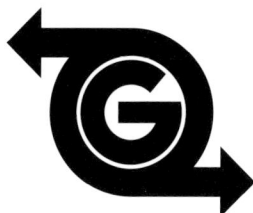

Carl Gabler Werbegesellschaft
Advertising agency
1949 · DE

Spille & von Lühmann
Men's clothes
1940 · DE

XIX Medicine Company
1889 · US

Mannesmannröhren-Werke
Pipes
1916 · DE

Zarifi Isfahan
Silk shirts
1927 · IR

Optiker Meier
Optician
1926 · Georg Wagner · DE

Phil Smith Parker
Clothes
1931 · UK

Tsuchiya Tabi kabushiki Kaisha
Footwear
1932 · JP

KAK Köhlerfeuer
Metal products
1926 · Wilhelm Metzig · DE

Denk & Duckwitz
Socks
1922 · DE

Otto Wolff
Metal products
1938 · DE

Gerhardt & Teltow
Printing
1930 · J. Heinz Böttcher · DE

Indische Tentoonstelling Zypendaal Arnhem
Trade fair
1928 · N.P. de Koo · NL

Lenko
Textiles
1938 · PL

United States War Assets Association
1946 · US

AGA
Automobiles
1924 · Karl Bültmann · DE

Kontex
Office machines
1930 · CZ

Reklame Ausführungs Gesellschaft
Advertising services
1921 · DE

Cox Fréres
Paper glue
1899 · BE

Agfa Repro
Photographic products
1935 · DE

Comptoir Suisse Lausanne
Trade fair
1932 · CH

Doppelhand Gutmann & Weinberg
Gloves
1921 · O.H.W. Hadank · DE

Alvis Limited
Aircraft engines
1938 · UK

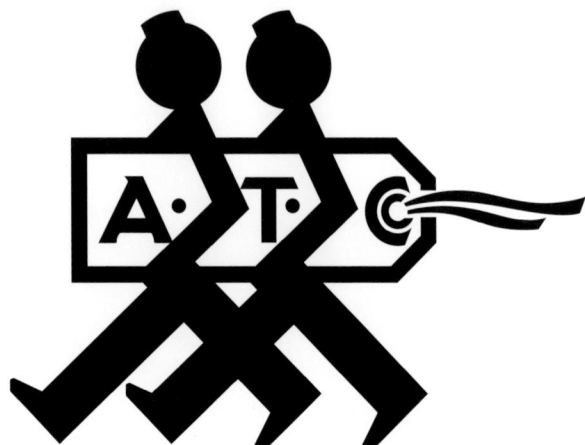

American Tag Company
1929 · Clarence P. Hornung · US

Spirax
Papers
1928 · FR

Brüder Dobesch
Hats
1930 · AT

Ziegelei Wolfshöhe
Brick factory
1929 · Max Körner · DE

Kali-Chemie
Chemicals
1931 · DE

Klein
Cosmetics
1932 · FR

H. Rost & Co.
Machine parts
1934 · DE

Breyers
Ice cream
1915 · US

Berlin
Tourism
1930 · Erich Charall · DE

Avalon leather Board Company
Leather products
1939 · UK

Brasil Oticica
Nutritional oils
1935 · BR

Gaba
Pharmaceuticals
1929 · CH

**Spółka Akcyjna Prze
mysłu Włókienniczego H. Dietel**
Chemicals
1927 · PL

The Crime Club
1929 · Joseph Sinel · US

Hirsch Lederwerke
Leather shoes
1933 · Josef Friedrich Gustav Binder · DE

Oertel & Spörer
Fire extinguisher
1924 · Max Hertwig · DE

Otag Einrichtungshaus
Furniture store
1928 · Georg Goedecker · DE

Triumphator
Machinery
1928 · CH

Urbinwerke
Chemicals
1930 · PL

J.D. Riedel
Chemicals
1925 · DE

G. Winiwarter
Steel pellets
1911 · AT

Riz Indochine
Rice
1931 · FR

Smelting Svenska Metallverken
Metal works
1931 · SE

Sarotti
Chocolates
1920 · DE

Diabol
Industrial chemicals
1931 · FR

Sphinx-Film
Film distribution
1942 · CH

Giant Umbrella Company
1910 · US

Café Kranzler
Café
1933 · DE

Sabroe's Pølser
Sausages
1907 · DK

Green Gate Inn
1910 · Harold von Schmidt · US

Nordens Gummiværk
Rubber products
1931 · DK

Tennessee Valley Authority
1933 · US

Quieta-Werke
Foods
1920 · DE

Hackerbräu München
Beer
1894 · DE

Binding Brauerei
Beer
1938 · Hartmuth Pfeil · DE

Yamaha
Music instruments
1936 · JP

**Krakowska Fabryka Wyrobów
Metalowych Spółka**
Screws
1936 · PL

Clinoto
Car wash
1934 · FR

Pillsbury's Best Flour
1870 · US

Zitol
Salts
1912 · DK

W. H. Burnet
Refined lard
1886 · US

Jose Sabater
Olive oil
1918 · ES

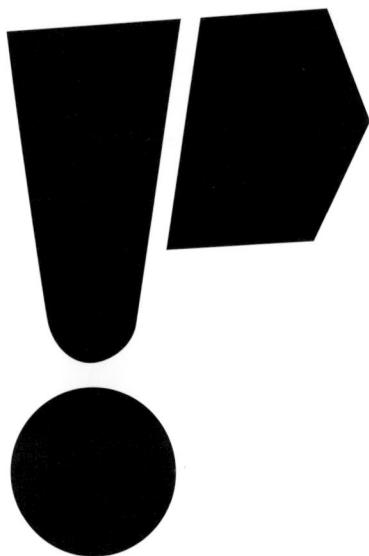

Propaganda Stuttgart
Advertising agency
1930 · DE

Pochoir

Schablone

Stencil

Hills Brothers
Foods
1887 · US

Fiske Brothers Refinining Company
1915 · US

Mather Brothers
Motor oils
1888 · US

G. Noak
Wholesales
1882 · DK

CC Holland
Foods
1929 · NL

John M. Brant Company
Oils
1915 · US

The Gripwell
Pharmaceuticals
1886 · UK

Wellington Sears & Co
Textiles
1916 · US

Vat 69
Whisky
1912 · UK

**Koninklijke Stearine
Kaarsenfabriek Gouda**
Cheese
1909 · NL

Frank Grutchfield Company
Fertilizers
1918 · US

Falconbridge
Metal industry
1932 · CA

Zellenbeton
Cement
1929 · CH

Feliks Tomkiewicz, Warszawa
Iron products
1934 · PL

James H. Rhodes & Company
Polishing materials
1914 · US

Detroit Brass & Malleable Works
1904 · US

Aspergren & Co.
Foods
1912 · US

Grefco
Electronics
1928 · FR

Standard Oil Company
1911 · US

The Russian Oil Company
1917 · US

American Malt Company
Beverages
1925 · US

Barrett Manufacturing Company
1889 · US

Lion Oil Company
Gasoline
1924 · US

Herborg
Machinery
1925 · DK

EVA

A.-S. Holbæk Dampmølle
Mills
1922 · UK

Covertex

Covertex
Textiles
1924 · US

KLEAN KLEEN

Dearson Chemical Company
1918 · US

HIM-JENSEN

H. I. M. Jensen
Photographic products
1934 · DK

CLIMAX

Wadhams Oil Company
1894 · US

NUOLENE

Nuolene
Oil tanks
1921 · US

TITAN

Mill and Mine Supply Company
Machinery
1908 · US

joyce

NOYO

Union Lumber Company
1918 · US

Joyce
Leather products
1940 · US

Twentieth Century Fox
Film production
1935 · US

Occo
Cigars
1907 · DK

Davistan
Carpets
1929 · DE

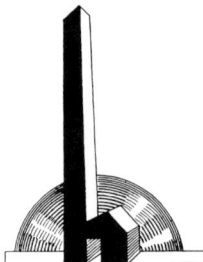

Homophon
Record label
1922 · DE

KM
Personal mark
1926 · E. Krause · DE

Velada
Aluminium
1932 · NL

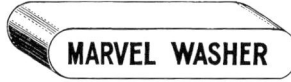

Hazlehurst & Sons
Soaps
1921 · UK

Sindhoo Productions
Film production
1939 · IN

Tamina
Insulated pipes
1934 · CH

Internationale Verbandstoff-Fabrik
Medical goods
1911 · CH

Dependabel
Furniture
1931 · UK

Viro
Leather products
1928 · DE

The Roth Coal Company
1921 · US

The Bowes-Field Steel Company
1932 · UK

Metallochemische Fabrik
Electronics
1928 · DE

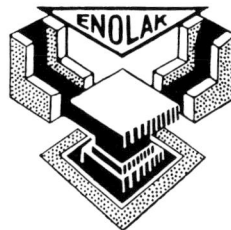

A. & S. Henry & Company
Imitation leather
1939 · UK

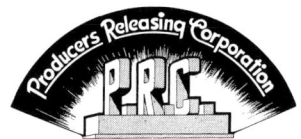

Producers Releasing Corporation
Film distribution
1940 · US

Arosa
Tourism
1930 · CH

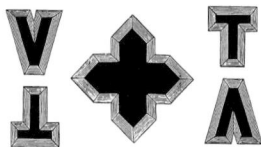

Val de Travers Etat
Asphalt
1911 · CH

Carl Josef Hoch Weinhandel
Wine trading
1926 · Fritz Rosen · DE

Knackstedt & Näther
Printing
1907 · DE

Ekko
Explosives
1915 · NO

Luna
Fabrics
1920 · UK

Charles S. Downing & Son
Cardboard boxes
1932 · UK

Odol
Mouth care
1897 · UK

Perrier
Table water
1907 · FR

Audi
Automobiles
1920 · Lucian Bernhard · DE

Paratao
Gas blowers
1932 · FR

Daimon Polska Fabryka Ogniw i Bateryj
Accumulators
1933 · PL

De Telegraaf
Newspaper
1922 · NL

Esso
Gas stations
1938 · UK

Reis & Co.
Machinery
1936 · DE

Gruen
Watches
1927 · CH

Luftschiffbau Zeppelin
Airships
1924 · Max Körner · DE

Holig Homogenholz-Werke
Construction materials
1941 · DE

Eduard Lingel
Footwear
1929 · DE

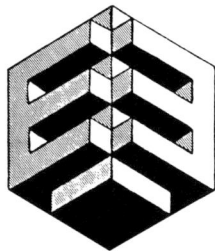

Eternit Emaille
Construction materials
1927 · BE

Robert Gair Company
Paper boxes
1947 · US

Blanc sur
noir

Weiß auf
Schwarz

White on
Black

National Biscuit Company
Foods
1898 · US

Inter Milan
Soccer club
1908 · IT

Borax
Soaps
1878 · UK

Le Fébre
Automobiles
1909 · FR

The Baker Bread Company
1914 · US

Delaware & Hudson R.R.
Transportation
1890 · US

Vesta Brikettenfabriek
Coals
1909 · NL

The Iceless Refrigeration Company
1914 · US

McTear and Co.
Roofing
1890 · US

Hero Conserven
Food
1910 · CH

Alfa Romeo
Automobiles
1916 · IT

Karl Düren
Personal mark
1907 · DE

Marco-Polo Tee
Tea
1910 · DE

Shine Bros. & Wilson Company
Foods
1917 · US

Druid Felt Company
1888 · US

Phono Phun
Records label
1920 · US

Aclement Lafarge
Construction materials
1923 · FR

The Boston Music Company
Music store
1917 · US

C. Wiemann & Co.
Precision tools
1922 · DE

Siemens
Electronics
1928 · DE

Gelber Verlag
Publishing
1919 · Rudolf Koch · DE

Rotapfel-Verlag
Publishing
1923 · CH

Mydło Kogut
Soaps
1926 · PL

Hooseiline
Pharmaceuticals
1920 · UK

Colloïd
Radios
1925 · FR

Haid & Neu Nähmaschinenfabrik
Sewing machines
1927 · Albert Trueb · DE

Plexiglas
Chemicals
1928 · DE

The Yale & Towne
Manufacturing Company
1930 · UK

Opel Blitz
Automobiles
1931 · DE

Reis
Underwear
1928 · US

Schmoll Pasta
Shoe polish
1930 · AT

Société Anonyme Voges
Foods
1931 · FR

Creatonal
Radios
1929 · CH

Hauff
Photography
1930 · FR

Schindler & Cie
Elevators
1926 · CH

Durinol
Chemicals
1932 · DE

Arthur Martin
Hotplates
1933 · FR

Colloidal Chemists
Toilet cream
1938 · UK

Lettergieterij Amsterdam
Type foundry
1931 · NL

Naval
Chemicals
1935 · DK

Tintas Vernizes
Paints
1941 · PT

Wardonia
Shavers
1932 · NL

Reo
Automobiles
1935 · US

Bethlehem Steel
Construction materials
1920 · US

John Cartmell & Sons
Wood products
1932 · UK

Przemysł Bieliźniany Asko
Chemicals
1936 · PL

Konkon
Bicycle parts
1932 · PL

Nina
Restaurant
1943 · PT

Slipsfabriken Pelo
Ties
1933 · DK

Flox
Fabrics
1937 · DE

Centro Nacional Suíço do Turismo
Tourism
1946 · PT

Danish Milk Condensing Company
Foods
1896 · DK

Saccharinfabrik List & Co.
Chemicals
1921 · US

Waldorf Paper Products
1946 · US

Aton Scheel Thomsen
Stucco
1907 · DK

Orion Radio
1924 · József Bottlík · HU

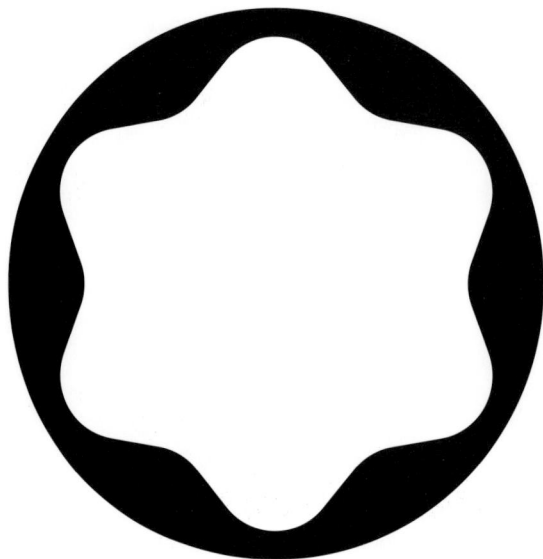

Montblanc
Pens
1921 · DE

Daimon
Accumulators
1931 · DE

Verband Deutscher Offiziere
Military association
1926 · Wilhelm Deffke · DE

Bagel Druck
Printing
1927 · DE

Fakir Handelsgesellschaft
Cleaning machines
1927 · DE

Radio Record
Radios
1928 · DE

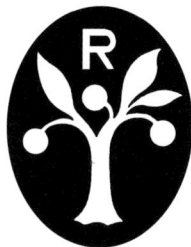

Brouwerij d'Oranjeboom te Rotterdam
Beer
1928 · Machiel Wilmink · NL

Kolmag
Photographic products
1929 · CH

Boys Clubs of America
Youth organization
1938 · Clarence P. Hornung · US

Solitaire
Shoe polish
1930 · DE

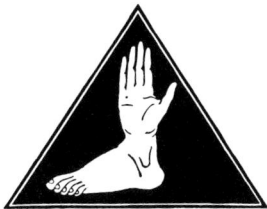

Kalor
Metal products
1929 · CZ

Panair do Brasil
Airline
1948 · BR

Citroën
Automobiles
1920 · FR

Ottesca
Textiles
1937 · IT

Brandt & Co.
Lettering
1923 · DE

Starrett Tools
1905 · CA

Gothaer Waggonfabrik
Wagons
1937 · DE

ICS
1931 · Georg Trump · DE

T

Typographique

Typografisch

Typographic

Typographie

Besides representational and abstract depictions, the typographic representation of a brand form the third main group of logos. In contrast to symbol-based marks, wordmarks are directly "readable" and, for literate consumers, a part of everyday life. In the age of early logos, company names in cursive constituted their own category. The origin can often be traced back to the founder's signature—such as the Ford and Kellogg's wordmarks, which are still used worldwide today. This kind of typographic logo, especially prevalent in the United States, has largely fallen out of favor in design today. By contrast, designs based on one or multiple individual letters and wordmarks featuring fonts specially created for companies' names are still among the most frequently chosen solutions for new and revised logos.

Neben der gegenständlichen und der abstrahierten Darstellung bildet die typografische Repräsentation einer Marke die dritte große Hauptgruppe unter den Logoarten. Im Gegensatz zu symbolbasierten Zeichen sind Wortmarken direkt „lesbar" und gehören für den alphabetisierten Menschen zum natürlichen Konsum. In der Epoche früher Logos bilden Firmennamen in Schreibschrift eine eigene Kategorie. Der Ursprung ist oft in der Signatur der Gründer zu finden – so auch in den bis heute weltweit verwendeten Schriftzügen von Ford oder Kellogg's. Diese besonders in den USA weitverbreitete Form des typografischen Logos ist bei Neuentwürfen heute weitgehend verschwunden. Entwürfe auf Basis eines oder mehrerer Einzelbuchstaben sowie Wortmarken aus einer speziell für den Firmennamen gezeichneten Schrift gehören hingegen noch immer zu den am häufigsten gewählten Lösungen für neue und überarbeitete Logos.

Avec les représentations figuratives et abstraites, l'illustration typographique d'une marque constitue le troisième grand groupe de logos. À la différence des signes basés sur des symboles, les marques verbales sont immédiatement « lisibles » et font partie de la consommation naturelle de tout individu alphabétisé. Du temps des premiers logos, les noms de sociétés en écriture cursive formaient une catégorie à part. Ils avaient souvent pour origine la signature du fondateur de l'entreprise – comme les inscriptions de Ford ou Kellogg's, toujours présentes dans le monde entier. Cette forme de logo typographique, particulièrement répandue aux États-Unis, a aujourd'hui presque totalement disparu des nouvelles conceptions. En revanche, les créations à partir d'une ou plusieurs lettres et les marques verbales dans une police d'écriture spécialement conçue pour une entreprise comptent encore parmi les options les plus fréquentes lorsqu'il s'agit de créer ou de modifier des logos.

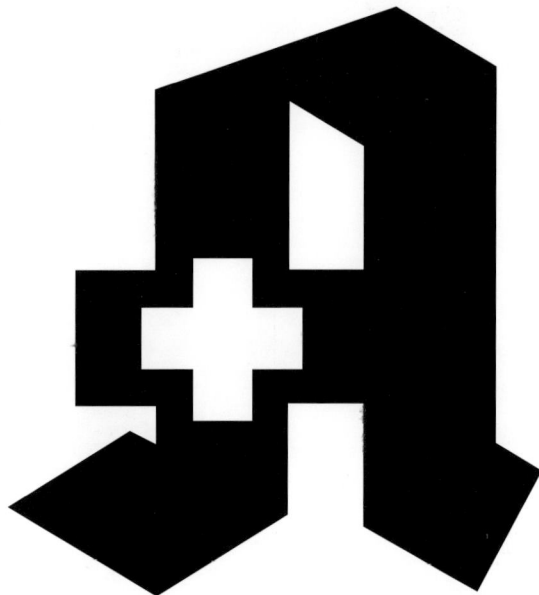

Deutsche Apotheken
German pharmacies
1936 · E. P. Weise · DE

Quicksilver Mining Company
1873 · US

American Film Company
Film production
1916 · US

Attleboro Silver Manufacturing
1898 · US

Accrington Observer & Times
Advertising services
1932 · UK

Atlas
Shipping boxes
1948 · US

Berliner Malerwerkstatt
Painter
1926 · Hans Lindenstaedt · DE

Crane and Company
Paper products
1875 · US

The Amalgamated Dental Company
1929 · UK

Bykmyrs
1935 · Hans Schleger Zero · DE/UK

Claude
Trading
1920 · FR

Aultman, Miller & Company
Harvesting machines
1888 · US

Rindsholm Mølle
Foods
1931 · DK

Chicago Cardinals
American football team
1920 · US

Behringer & Co.
Toys
1922 · Max Körner · DE

Bismarck Hotel, Chicago
1927 · August Trueb · US

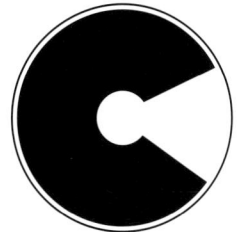

Continental Films
Film distribution
1942 · CH

Cellere & Co.
Road constructions
1945 · Werner Weiskönig · CH

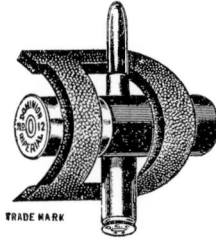

Dominion Ammnunition
1907 · CA

Elida
Cosmetics
1928 · CZ

Cyclax Limited
Cosmetics
1932 · UK

Deutsche Werke
Machinery
1924 · DE

Excelsior
Electronics
1927 · BE

Combina
Furniture
1933 · AT

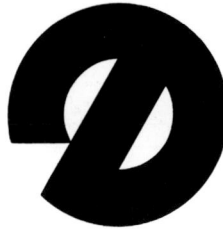

Dürkopp Nähmaschinen
Sewing machines
1940 · DE

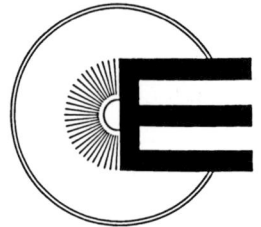

Antoni Wyporek
Electronics
1936 · PL

The Albert Dickinson Company
Grass seeds
1900 · US

Dürkopp
Bicycles
1927 · AT

Elektrowerke Berlin
Electronics
1929 · Wilhelm Berg · DE

Albert Frisch Druckerei
Printing
1927 · DE

Geveart
Film material
1932 · BE

H. van Gimborn
Printing colors
1930 · NL

GA Weinhandel
Wine trading
1926 · Hans Schreiber · DE

Banketbakkerij Geldermans
Bakery
1932 · NL

Glimar
Pharmaceuticals
1934 · PL

Gibbs
Cosmetics
1924 · FR

Gaumont
Film production
1910 · FR

Gustaw Ganz & Co.
Electronics
1929 · AT

RCH Corporation
Automobiles
1911 · US

Harefa
Trading
1941 · Philipp Seitz · DE

Horch
Automobiles
1926 · Ernst Böhm · DE

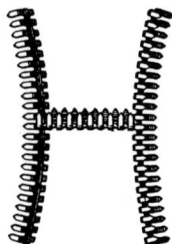

E. H. Hotchkiss Company
Household articles
1906 · US

Rudolf Hostettler
Graphic designer
1945 · Rudolf Hostettler · CH

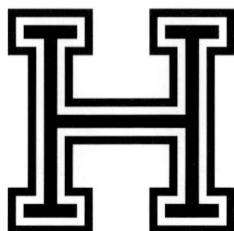

Hermes
Clothes
1927 · FR

Henkel & Cie
Adhesives
1925 · DE

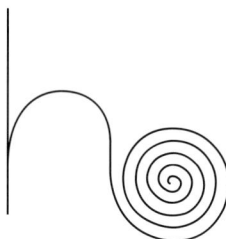

Helbros Watch Company
1943 · Paul Rand · US

Thica
Wallpapers
1926 · DE

Hermann Hienerwadel
Interior design
1927 · August Trueb · DE

Apollo Seidensiedergewerke
Cosmetics
1921 · AT

J. Wilhelm Hofmann
Metal products
1930 · DE

E. Knüsli
Heating systems
1925 · CH

Dr. Köhler & Co.
Printing
1929 · DE

Lignoza
Chemicals
1934 · PL

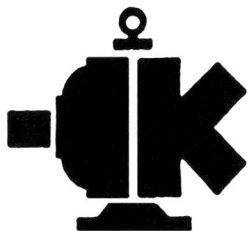

Kalliope
Music instruments
1923 · DE

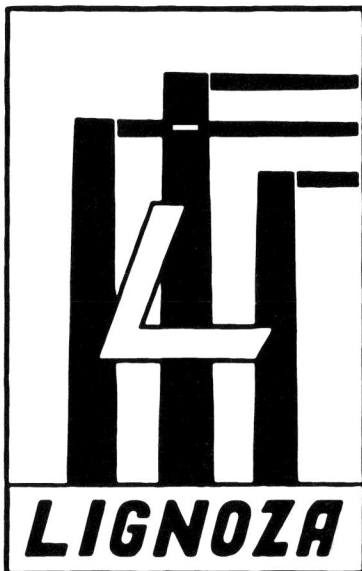

Laurentian Spring Water Company
1896 · CA

Stickerei Lühdemann
Textiles
1928 · Erich Krubeck · DE

Kicherer & Co. Elektromotorenwerke
Motors
1923 · DE

Holger Lyhne
Textiles
1933 · DK

Leonhard Papier
Paper products
1926 · Fritz Rosen, Atelier Bernhard · DE

Philipp Mühsam Benzinwerke
Gasoline
1923 · Louis Oppenheim · DE

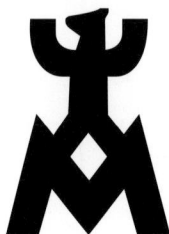

Berliner Messen
Berlin Trade Fair
1924 · DE

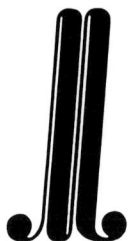

Berthold Menkel Innenarchitekt
Interior design
1925 · DE

Menasco Manufacturing Company
1939 · US

MICA
Social campaign
1935 · NL

Moscow Metro
Public transportation
1935 · RU

Märksch
Textile dyeing
1940 · DE

Saretz & Stümer
Bicycle tires
1921 · DE

Printype New York
Typesetting
1930 · US

Fabryka Dywanów Mayzel
Carpets
1932 · PL

Omega Watch Company
1911 · CH

Gütting
Heating technolgy
1938 · Hartmuth Pfeil · DE

Neckarkanal AG
Waterways
1924 · Max Körner · DE

Otte
Fabrics
1927 · AT

Deux Moutons
Fabrics
1930 · FR

Hermann Nadge
Wood trading
1928 · DE

Orchestrola Vocalion
Telephones
1928 · DE

Sun Press
Publishing
1932 · Sascha A. Maurer · US

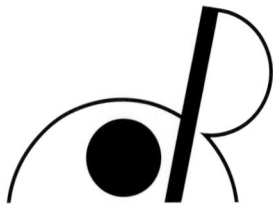

Reimann School and Studios, London
Design school
1936 · UK

Franz Sysel Klischee-Anstalt
Prepress services
1936 · DE

Torpedo
Bicycle parts
1936 · DE

Radium Gummiwerke
Rubber products
1928 · DE

Sulzer
Heating systems
1938 · CH

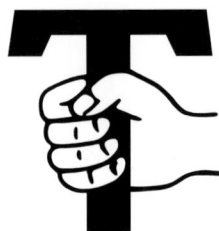

Sharp
Electronics
1921 · JP

Georg Schicht
Soaps
1919 · CZ

Chicago White Sox
Baseball
1912 · US

Schuchardt & Schütte
Machinery
1919 · DK

Perfumes M. Jorude Gaston
Cosmetics
1922 · FR

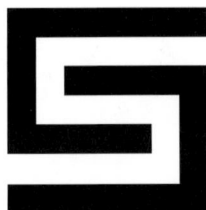

Schuchardt & Schütte
Machinery
1919 · DK

Uranol
Motor oils
1930 · DE

Vali
1941 · Philipp Seitz · DE

XEW-AM
Broadcasting
1930 · MX

G. Anzoni
Machinery
1920 · IT

Zenith Zement
Cement
1930 · DE

Westinghouse Electric & Manufacturing Company
1910 · US

Shibaura Electronic Works
1919 · JP

199

American Kinema
Film production
1910 · FR

General Electrics
1912 · US

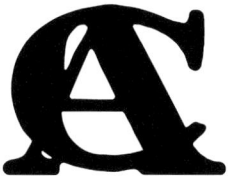

Mooney & Co.
Horseshoes
1877 · US

DuPont Motors
Automobiles
1910 · US

Nauta & Haagen
Advertising
1917 · NL

Antikamnia Chemical Company
Pharmaceuticals
1890 · US

Max Hertwig
Graphic designer
1914 · Max Hertwig · DE

Gustaf Dorén
Interior design
1917 · Wilhelm Deffke · DE

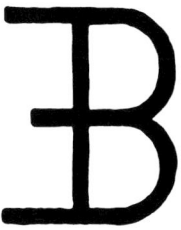

Bergmann Elektricitätswerke
Machinery
1906 · DE

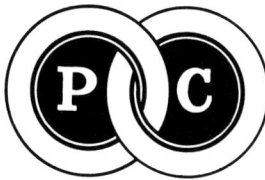

Paul Christensen
Car tires
1911 · DK

Canet y Sagalés
Wools
1918 · ES

Patent Medicines Company
Medical products
1908 · IT

Lauritz Peter Knudsen
Electronics
1913 · DK

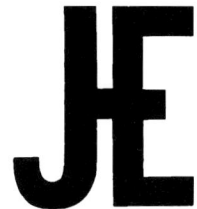

Robert Dinzl
Tires
1919 · PL

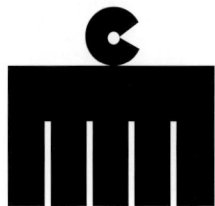

Capitol Kino
Movie theater
1920 · DE

Kühlstein Wagenbau
Automobiles
1922 · DE

Merian & Bader
Cement
1923 · Walter M. Kersting · DE

Møllerhøj & Berthelsen
Electrics
1920 · DK

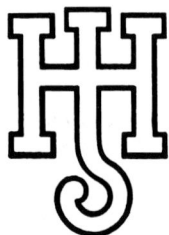

Heinrich Jessens Chokoladefabrik
Chocolates
1923 · DK

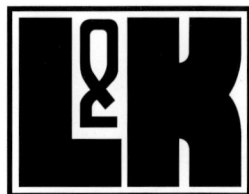

Leidenberg & Knick
Printing supplies
1924 · DE

Louis Oppenheim
Graphic designer
1920 · Louis Oppenheim · DE

Weltuniversität Wien
University
1923 · Julius Klinger · AT

The Eaton Axle and Spring Company
Car parts
1923 · US

Ernst Kummer
Tiles
1921 · CH

PB
Personal mark
1923 · Karel Maes · NL

Lange Film
Film distribution
1924 · Weil-Dassel · DE

Carl Schimpf Abziehbilderfabrik
Printing
1925 · DE

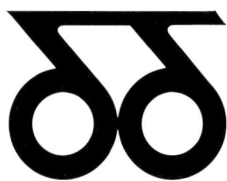

Druckerei Friedrich Dietz
Printing
1926 · W. Wörner · DE

ELTE Tapeten
Wallpapers
1928 · DE

HaKa
Liquors
1925 · DE

Carl Ruppert
Printing
1927 · DE

Villeroy & Boch Keramische Werke
Ceramics
1928 · DE

VILLEROY & BOCH

Jung & Co.
Isolating tape
1925 · DE

Kyodo
Printing
1927 · JP

Hermann Schött
Printing
1929 · DE

Volta-Werke
Electronics
1925 · DE

Albert Heijn
Supermarket chain
1927 · NL

Art Director's Club New York
1929 · US

Wohnung und Werkraum
Werkbundausstellung Breslau
Interior design exhibition
1929 · Johannes Molzahn · DE

The Berlitz Schools of Languages
1929 · FR

Dansk Gelatine Fabrik
Foods
1933 · DK

Etzold & Kiessling
Printing
1930 · DE

Horgen-Glarus
Furniture
1934 · CH

CK
Personal mark
1926 · Martin Weinberg · DE

Meissner & Buch
Printing
1930 · DE

Hazemeyer-Hengelo
Electronics
1932 · NL

Löwenstein & Meycke
1926 · Werner Brand · DE

M&S
Beverages
1930 · US

BW
Personal mark
1932 · Sascha A. Maurer · US

Szopen
Soft drinks
1934 · PL

A. C. Spark Plug Company
1933 · US

Kadra-Kajet
Paper products
1934 · PL

Zakłady Elektro Spółka Akcyjna
Electronics
1936 · PL

Druckerei Nöthen
Printing
1938 · Walter Breker · DE

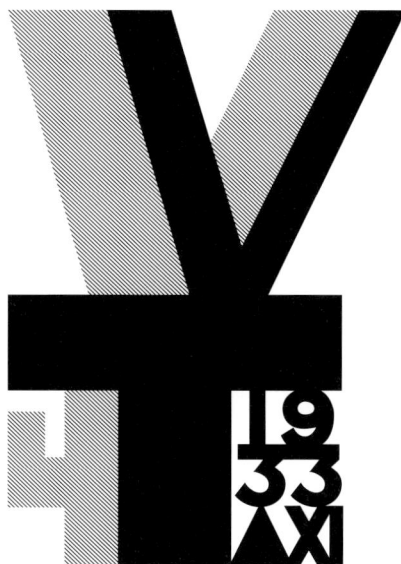

Fith Milan Triennial
Art exhibition
1932 · IT

Ronald Trist & Co.
Packing
1938 · UK

The Continental Sanitary Company
Cleaning products
1911 · BE

S+K
Heating technology
1943 · Ernst Keiser · CH

Toppan
Printing
1900 · JP

P. D. Corsets
1896 · CA

Keystone Watch Case Company
1900 · CA

Aktiebolaget Järnförädling
Pipes
1918 · SE

Augustiner Bräu
Beer
1920 · DE

**Brødrene Tychsens Etablissement
for Confecturer**
1882 · DK

Kantorowicz Liköre
Liqours
1923 · Louis Oppenheim · DE

E. Weyeh
Personal mark
1910 · Rockwell Kent · US

Léon Pichon
Publishing
1927 · FR

Van Ysendijk's Koffie
Coffee
1928 · Machiel Wilmink · NL

Georg Gengenbach
Paper products
1925 · DE

I. Dennison & Co.
Wine trading
1925 · UK

**Laboratorjum Chemiczno-
Farmaceutyczne M. Malinowskiego**
Pharmaceuticals
1931 · PL

T. Trautwein
Pianos
1923 · Karl Schulpig · DE

Pantser Beton
Concrete
1928 · I.L.C. Kalff · NL

ER
Personal mark
1932 · Sascha A. Maurer · US

H. Timmermann
Construction materials
1927 · DE

**Société Anonyme des Aéroplanes
Henry Potez**
Aviation
1929 · FR

WH Gartenbau
Gardening
1943 · Willy Simmler · CH

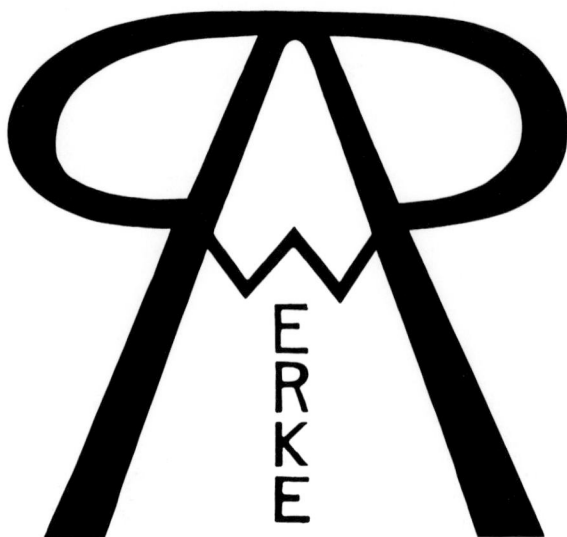

Mischmaschinen- und Kunstbackofenfabrik Werner & Pfleiderer
Baking machines
1910 · AT

Consolidated Fastener Company
1890 · US

Berliner Elektricitaetswerke
Electricity
1906 · Peter Behrens · DE

Andrea Pensotti
Machinery
1909 · IT

A. Batschari Cigaretten
Cigarettes
1910 · DE

ALA
Lamps
1911 · FR

The J. C. Hub Manufacturing Company
1910 · Chester Siebold · US

Gebrüder Heine Leipzig
Fabrics
1912 · DE

B. A. S.
Chemicals
1909 · FR

Orlystis M. Potterf
Clothes
1911 · US

A. B. Clippinger & Sons
Car parts
1912 · US

Verlag für Sozialpolitik
Publishing
1910 · DE

Zip
Cosmetics
1921 · US

Schweizer Werkbund
Design association
1918 · Otto Morach · CH

Robert Stewart Jr.
Chemicals
1912 · US

Hoevel Sandblast Machine Company
1914 · US

The Petroleum Iron Works Company
1917 · US

Verein Deutscher Ingenieure
Industrial trade organzation
1913 · DE

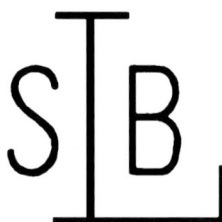

Logan Iron & Steel Company
1916 · US

Aktiebolaget Arvika-Verken
Harvesting machines
1918 · SE

Uba
Chemicals
1913 · DK

CIN Fábrica de Tintas e Vernizes
Paints
1917 · PT

Bauer & Black
Medical products
1918 · US

Deutsche Bierbrauerei AG
Beer
1914 · DE

The D. D. D. Company
Pharmaceuticals
1918 · UK

Allgemeine Werkzeugmaschinenfabrik
Machinery
1920 · DE

Deutsche Schleifmaschinen
Gesellschaft
Grinding machines
1920 · DE

SKF
Motors
1919 · SE

Wielkopolska Fabryka Farb
Paints
1921 · PL

Grimm & Triepel
Tobacco
1920 · DE

Styria-Fahrrad und Dürkopp-Werke
Bicycles
1923 · AT

Arbeiterwohlfahrt
Welfare organization
1921 · Karl Schulpig · DE

The Associated Equipment Company
Cars
1920 · UK

Köln-Rottweil AG
Chemicals
1921 · DE

Schweizerische Wagonsfabrik Schlieren
Elevators
1922 · CH

Ozo
Car polish
1922 · US

RAP
Radios
1938 · IN

Berlin-Neuroder Kunstanstalten
Printing
1939 · Heinz Becker · DE

PAN

Pan
Magazine
1922 · UK

Deutscher Metallhandel
Metal trading
1923 · DE

FIT

TRADE MARK

FIT
Tires
1923 · FR

Cece-Graphit-Werk
Electronics
1923 · CH

OXO

Oxo
Foods
1920 · UK

NUF

NUF
Abrasives
1925 · US

212

Editioni Noi
Publishing
1923 · IT

NFG Adolf Nissen
Electronics
1925 · DE

Radio Corporation of America
1922 · US

Ego
Cosmetics
1923 · US

Lab Company
Chemicals
1926 · US

Drahtwerk Joseph Linker
Wires
1926 · Werner Brand · DE

Colonia Elektrizitätsgesellschaft
Transformers
1925 · DE

Tar Products Corporation
Construction materials
1926 · US

H. W. Egli
Machinery
1927 · CH

Dornemann & Co.
Advertising services
1925 · DE

NRF
Publishing
1927 · FR

CKP
Electronics
1928 · AT

NSF
Radios
1929 · NL

Neuer Deutscher Verlag
Publishing
1928 · DE

Kramer & Löbl
Electronics
1928 · DE

Imperial Chemical Industries
1929 · UK

VDS
Glass
1928 · Karl Schulpig · DE

Magdeburger Werkzeugmaschinenfabrik
Machinery
1928 · DE

Gummi und Kabelwerke Josef Reithoffer
Cables
1929 · AT

Leuchter BAG Turgi
Lamps
1930 · CH

Fox
Soaps
1930 · UK

Obo
Socks
1932 · DK

Lih
Stoves
1930 · CZ

Rogers, Kellogg, Stillson Company
Advertising agency
1930 · US

International Ticket Service
1931 · US

**Oberländische
Gewerbeausstellung Frutigen**
Trade fair
1930 · CH

Verein Deutscher Tafelglashütten
Glass production
1931 · DE

O. F. Kutscher
Graphic designer
1929 · O.F. Kutscher · DE

OCÉ
Chemicals
1930 · NL

CIM
Insulating materials
1931 · FR

Rex Gardinstænger
Curtain rods
1932 · DK

Seven-Up
Beverages
1938 · US

Wagner, Muding & Co.
Iron production
1935 · DE

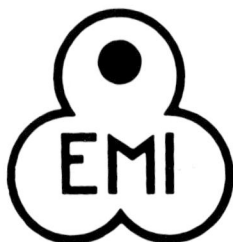

Fabryka Kabli Spółka Akcyjna
Cables
1932 · PL

C. H. F. Müller
Radios
1937 · DE

ABM
Transportation
1919 · Jan Rotgans · NL

OUA
Liquors
1932 · NL

British Industries Fair
1931 · Tom Purvis · UK

Fritz Claude Sägenfabrik
Saws
1920 · DE

Metalowe Zakłady Hutnicze
Metal products
1938 · PL

Heinrich Hatt-Haller
Construction company
1933 · CH

Vox-Schallplatten
Record label
1920 · Wilhelm Deffke · DE

Weiler-ter Meer Chemische Fabriken
Chemicals
1921 · DE

MWP
Personal mark
1926 · Carlos Tips · DE

Deutsche Röhrenwerke
Pipes
1938 · DE

IVV Ing. Vladislav Vlček
Engineering
1920 · Jaroslav Benda · CZ

Correios, Telégrafos e Telefones
Telecommunications
1936 · PT

Dea
Matresses
1939 · Pierre Gauchat · CH

VIK Zigaretten
Cigarettes
1923 · Walter M. Kersting · DE

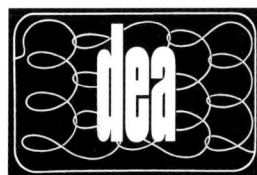

Deutsche Reichs-Korrespondenz
Publishing
1925 · DE

ICI
Film production
1943 · IT

C. F. Bally
Footwear
1907 · CH

Joseph Gahm & Son
Beer
1903 · US

Pepsi Cola Company
Beverages
1898 · US

Maggi
Foods
1897 · DE

Coca Cola Company
Beverages
1887 · US

Borsalino
Hats
1901 · IT

Ford Motor Company
Automobiles
1909 · US

Walgreen
Drugstore
1901 · US

Campbell's Soups
Foods
1906 · US

Lancia
Automobiles
1907 · IT

Renault
Automobiles
1909 · FR

C. F. Bally
Footwear
1907 · CH

Clark's
Foods
1909 · CA

Kohler
Chocolates
1910 · CH

Alpine Milk
1910 · US

Knorr
Foods
1915 · DE

Johnson & Johnson
Pharmaceuticals
1920 · US

Milka
Chocolates
1911 · CH

Thor
Washing machines
1918 · US

Capi
Photographic products
1923 · NL

Buick
Automobiles
1913 · US

Champion
Sporting goods
1919 · US

Guaraná
Beverages
1921 · BR

Sidway
Baby articles
1913 · US

Albert Heijn
Supermarket chain
1920 · NL

Melitta-Werke Bentz & Sohn
Instant coffee
1939 · DE

Harrods
Department store
1932 · UK

Ray Ban
Sunglasses
1937 · IT

Steinberg & Co. Pianofortefabrik
Pianos
1921 · Karl Schulpig · DE

Cartier
Jewellery
1932 · US

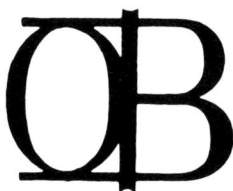

F. A. Ostrander
Construction materials
1889 · US

**N. Kjærgaard Jensen's
Teknisk-Kemiske-Fabrik**
Chemicals
1919 · DK

Kellogs Toasted Corn Flaks Company
Foods
1917 · US

General Railway Signal Company
1909 · US

Germania Linoleum Werke
Floorings
1925 · CH

Otis Elevator Company
1928 · US

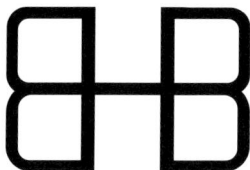

Büchner Werke
Toilets
1911 · DE

Kontakt
Construction materials
1929 · DE

**Ètablissements Lyonnais
Rochet-Schneider**
Automobiles
1929 · FR

Rex
Gas stations
1938 · FR

Alfred Teves Maschinenfabrik
Car parts
1940 · DE

Tolo Anton Loibl
Bicycle parts
1937 · DE

No. 4711
Perfumes
1890 · DE

Campari
Beverages
1918 · IT

H+N Bildgießerei
Prepress services
1940 · Ernst Böhm · DE

Vortex Manufacturing Corporation
Beverages
1914 · US

Buckeye
Beer
1920 · US

Theodor Laible
Wallpaper
1945 · Arthur Bayer · CH

**Yawman & Erbe
Manufacturing Company**
Furniture
1914 · US

Abloy Osakeyhtiö
Locks
1921 · FI

Daimler
Automobiles
1912 · DE

Aladdin
Foods
1915 · US

Conlove
Underwear
1936 · UK

Erdal
Shoe polish
1913 · AT

Union Truck Manufacturing Company
1916 · US

Facit
Calculating machines
1921 · SE

Norida
Cosmetics
1922 · US

Flury
Construction materials
1929 · CH

Cyber
Clothes
1929 · FR

Velvetone
Chemicals
1922 · US

Eternit
Cement
1929 · DE

Automobiles Peugeot
Automobiles
1930 · FR

Esso
Gas stations
1923 · US

Rollofon
Radios
1929 · DK

Gaba
Pharmaceuticals
1930 · CH

Radio Safar
1926 · IT

Castrol
Motor oil
1929 · FR

Dorndorf
Footwear
1930 · DE

Haribo
Foods
1930 · DE

Motorola
Electronics
1930 · US

Rhenser Mineralbrunnen
Table water
1931 · DE

Kofa
Furniture
1931 · NL

Essany
Film production
1912 · US

American Steel Export Company
1916 · US

Kandya
Furniture
1932 · UK

Steerease
Car parts
1911 · US

Federal
Automobiles
1915 · US

Pepsodent
Toothpaste
1918 · UK

Triumph
Motorcycles
1928 · UK

Zerk
Soaps
1938 · UK

Altesse Zigarettenhülsenfabrik
Cigarettes
1919 · AT

Lynite
Aluminium
1928 · US

Sursum
Switches
1927 · DE

Efluvia
Cosmetics
1920 · ES

M. Droz
Jewellery
1931 · FR

Aktiebolaget Durotapet
Wallpapers
1930 · SE

Pope
Lamps
1920 · NL

Bonko
Soaps
1932 · DK

Shaler
Fabrics
1931 · US

alba

Alba
Enamel products
1926 · PL

fifh

Fifh
1931 · Georg Trump · DE

CRiNOL

Crinol
Cosmetics
1934 · DK

Kappel

Kappel Drehbänke
Machinery
1938 · DE

FLEXO

Flexo
Lamps
1935 · CH

ROBOT

Robot
Photo cameras
1937 · DE

Dr Price's

Dr. Price Flavoring Extract Company
Foods
1871 · US

PEACOCK

The Ouerbacker Coffee Company
1905 · US

BONDS

Bond Envelopes
Paper products
1883 · US

VIMULETS

Vimulets
Foods
1912 · US

THERMOS

Thermos Bottle Company
1911 · CA

MOËT & CHANDON

Moët & Chandon
Champagne
1910 · FR

CAMEL

Heinz Tomato Ketchup
Foods
1909 · US

VALVO

Valvo
Radios
1929 · IT

LAVOPTIK

George W. Peavey
Chemicals
1912 · US

Chocolate Sponge

Chocolate Sponge
Foods
1901 · US

EDORO

Edward O'Rourke
Paints
1915 · US

LOZIER

Lozier
Automobiles
1902 · US

HEINZ

Heinz Tomato Ketchup
Foods
1909 · US

VALVOLINE TRADE MARK

Valvoline
Motor oils
1930 · US

A. Steinhäuser
Machinery
1928 · DE

Wavoil
Cosmetics
1924 · US

Lynx Knitting Mills
1921 · US

Dansk Skinke-Export
Foods
1928 · DK

Warner Bros.
Film production
1923 · US

Roto-Press
Printing machines
1926 · CH

Votis
Pharmaceuticals
1921 · US

Bluhill Cheese
1913 · US

Satam
Tank plants
1929 · CH

Antiba
Cosmetics
1929 · PL

Vittorio Volpato
Fertilizers
1916 · IT

Missouri Shoe Company
1912 · US

Magneti Marelli
Car parts
1919 · IT

Stringo Company
Trading
1922 · SE

Centric
Trading
1910 · UK

Moon Motor Car Company
Automobiles
1915 · US

Mennen's
Hygiene products
1907 · UK

Gants Aris
Gloves
1937 · FR

Queen City Specialty Company
Cleaning products
1913 · US

Pandetikon
Trading
1923 · DK

Balmer & Schwitter
Prepress services
1918 · CH

Universum Film
Film production
1918 · DE

Eclipse
Clothes
1887 · US

Aiouni
Pharmaceuticals
1910 · CH

Aeroplane
Aviation
1923 · Alan C. Rogers · UK

Conus
Machinery
1913 · SE

Prowoduik
Rubber products
1907 · RU

Buka Druckerei
Printing
1923 · DE

Dansk Agerbrugsforsyning
Foods
1882 · DK

Mascot
Motor oils
1924 · DK

Harex Werke
Construction materials
1923 · Hans Breidenstein · DE

W. & J. Sloane
Furniture
1896 · US

Filflex
Sporting goods
1930 · UK

Hedingham Radio Company
1932 · UK

Goldwing
Motor oils
1935 · UK

Bravo
Magazine
1929 · FR

Metropolitain Paris
Public transportation
1901 · Hector Guimard · FR

Seibt
Radios
1934 · DE

Tobis
Film production
1927 · Rudolf Bossek · DE

The Fisheries Products Comapny
1920 · US

Fregola
Furniture
1933 · E. Crous · ES

Polkodot
Foods
1924 · US

Purma
Photo cameras
1936 · UK

Ratag
Radios
1923 · DE

Akiz
Electronics
1929 · NL

Bourday
Perfumes
1924 · US

Dansk Staal Industri
Steel production
1921 · DK

National Film
Film distribution
1930 · DE

Stal
Radios
1934 · PL

Artcraft Pictures
Film production
1918 · US

Spalding & Bros
Sporting goods
1905 · US

Arri
Film cameras
1930 · DE

Ace Heating Technology
1923 · US

Canadian Northern
Railways
1909 · CA

Royal Films
Film production
1938 · CH

Algo
Magazine
1929 · ES

International Business Machines
Office machines
1924 · US

Auping
Mattresses
1929 · NL

Sosna
Cosmetics
1922 · US

Ate a Ways
Foods
1938 · US

Wörter

LACTOPEPTINE.

Lactopeptine
Pharmaceuticals
1882 · UK

MAGGI

Maggi
Foods
1899 · DE

OTOE

Otoe Food Products
1888 · US

THE CONTINENTAL

The Continental
Weapons
1887 · US

WORTH

The Canfield Rubber Company
Brushes
1886 · US

Firestone
Firestone
Tires
1900 · US

COLGATE'S

Der Tag
Der Tag
Newspaper
1905 · DE

Colgate
Toothpaste
1905 · US

TIFFANY & CO.
Tiffany & Co.
Jewellery
1905 · US

VARIETY

CHOCOLATES G.B.
G. B. Chocolates
1906 · CA

Variety
Film magazine
1905 · US

WINCHESTER

Winchester
Weapons
1907 · US

Tétraline

Tetraline
Chemicals
1909 · CH

Giotil

Giotil
Washing powder
1910 · Leroi · DE

WILKINSON

Wilkinson
Razors
1907 · UK

J◇B

Job
Leather products
1909 · FR

VASGUIT

Vasguit
Chemicals
1911 · DK

BIANCHI

Bianchi
Bicycles
1908 · IT

VITAL

Vital
Cosmetics
1909 · NO

MAZETTI

Mazetti
Chocolates
1911 · SE

GÖTA

Göta
Foods
1908 · SE

PALL MALL

Pall Mall
Cigarettes
1910 · UK

NESNAH

Neshnah
Foods
1912 · US

Stollwerck

Stollwerck
Chocolates
1910 · DE

Hercules

Hercules
Milling
1914 · US

ITALa

Itala
Automobiles
1919 · IT

REGO

Hardwick & Magee Company
Carpets
1912 · US

FIXFIT

Fixfit
Saddles
1915 · US

Nobel

Alfred Nobel & Co.
Explosives
1920 · DE

BENZ

Benz & Cie.
Automobiles
1910 · F. H. Ehmcke · DE

RIGHTO

Granite City Soap Company
1915 · US

WAVO

Wavo
Hair curlers
1914 · US

RADIX

Radix
Bicycles
1914 · SE

EXCELL

Theodore T. Wollens
Dental products
1915 · US

ESKIMO PIE

Eskimo Pie Corporation
Foods
1921 · US

VEVE

Vulkanverken
Machinery
1920 · SE

JELL-O

Jell-O
Marmelade
1922 · CA

LECTYN

Lectyn
Chemicals
1922 · US

LASHNEEN TRADE MARK REG.

Lashneen
Cosmetics
1920 · US

BOVRIL

Bovril
Foods
1922 · UK

woman

Woman
Magazine
1923 · UK

O·Cedar

O-Cedar
Furniture polish
1920 · US

E S S E X

Essex
Automobiles
1922 · UK

HAISS

George Haiss Manufacturing Company
Machinery
1922 · US

LETS GO!

Lets Go!
Foods
1921 · US

KODAK

Eastman Kodak Company
Photographic products
1922 · US

TIME

Time Magazine
1923 · US

Tissot & Fils
Watches
1924 · CH

Linovag
Floorings
1925 · CH

The Picturegoer
Movie magazine
1925 · UK

Carl Walther
Weapons
1924 · DE

Schweppes
Beverages
1925 · UK

Caterpillar
Construction machines
1925 · US

Osram
Light bulbs
1924 · UK

The S. Lemur Company
Soaps
1924 · US

Pirelli & Co.
Tires
1920 · IT

FYR-FOE

Jaeger Portable Power Corporation
Car parts
1925 · US

AKAI

Akai
Electronics
1929 · JP

KAUFHOF

Westdeutsche Kaufhof AG
Department stores
1933 · DE

Rewe

Rewe
Supermarkets
1927 · DE

Gevaert

Geveart
Film material
1934 · BE

BRAUN

Max Braun
Electronics
1934 · Will Münch · DE

KNORR

Knorr
Foods
1927 · IT

KOOL

Kool
Cigarettes
1933 · US

Canon

Canon
Photo cameras
1938 · JP

Kool-Aid

Kool-Aid
Beverages
1927 · US

ASPIRIN

Aspirin
Pharmaceuticals
1935 · DE

AZIZA

Aziza
Clothes
1938 · FR

metz en CO

Metz en Co.
Fabrics
1939 · NL

Nash

Nash-Kelvinator Corporation
Automobiles
1939 · US

noir

Noir
1930 · Marcel Arthaus · FR

GITANES

Gitanes
Cigarettes
1939 · FR

ROLEX

Rolex
Watches
1925 · UK

PHILIPS

Philips
Electronics
1935 · NL

Britt
Cosmetics
1939 · CH

Ludwig & Co.
Type foundry
1942 · DE

Wiener Werkstätte
Interior design
1903 · Koloman Moser · AT

Pesch
Yarns
1934 · FR

Hoya
Glass
1945 · JP

Ento London
Metal products
1932 · UK

Cellox
Soaps
1936 · DK

Emil Otto
Chemicals
1938 · DE

Bell
Foods
1943 · Gérard Miedinger · CH

Jubol
Pharmaceuticals
1909 · FR

Lemet
Bicycles
1923 · NL

Elite Film
Film distribution
1938 · CH

Cesar
Automobiles
1914 · IT

Amada
Foods
1924 · PL

Cibié
Film projectors
1938 · FR

Federal Rubber Company
1916 · US

Deutsche Blau-Gas-Gesellschaft
Gas
1926 · DE

Ansaldo
Engineering
1938 · IT

Koninklijke Hofjuweliers Berger
Jewellery
1919 · NL

Fim Fon Treibriemen
1926 · Fritz Rosen, Atelier Bernhard · DE

Taisho
Pharmaceuticals
1949 · JP

LOGO
MODERNISM

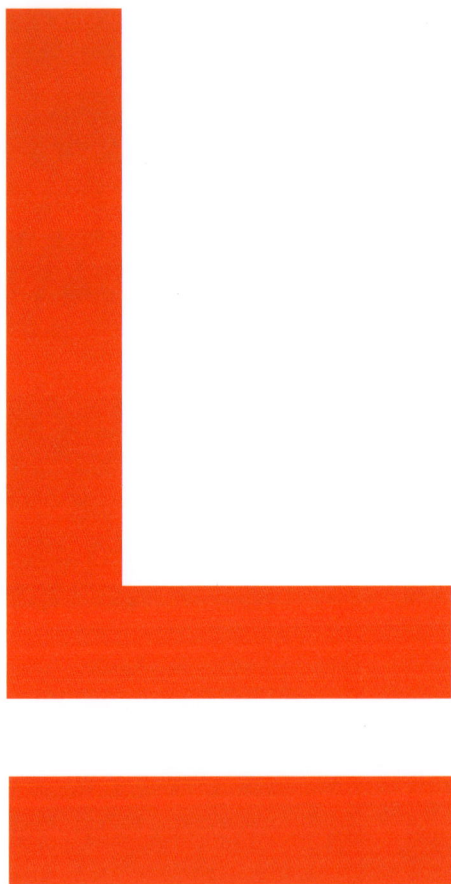

Logo
Jens Müller

Pick up any book about logos published 50 or 60 years ago and sooner or later you will come across references to how simplicity and directness serve as a counterbalance to our "complicated world." Since time immemorial the world has been perceived as complex, and the need for simple, clear signs is nothing new. We have to realize that these and similar statements made in the mid-20th century were part of the efforts of contemporary designers to free themselves from what they saw as the mystique surrounding commercial artists. The birth of modern graphics coincided with the moment when modern graphic designers were striving to create clear-cut systems and concepts rather than to display artistic genius. Of course, the late 19th century had produced a few design pioneers, which makes it almost impossible to determine exactly when the change in the perception of graphic design occurred. However, from the 1940s onwards, what might be termed Modernism in graphic design began to take hold. Over the next two decades, as international businesses and small enterprises alike set about revamping their corporate image, Modernist graphics started to appear across the globe in every area of graphic design. Perhaps the most obvious and most enduring changes are the result of the Modernist approach to logos. Representational images made way for simple shapes. Today, the zeitgeist, trends and technical advances are leading to different solutions, the roots of which are to be found in the design parameters set in the heyday of Modernism. It is worth revisiting that era.

Ethnologists, art historians and scholars have researched the origins of signs and symbols, producing a vast body of literature. While the subject of this book is the nature and design of the Modernist logo, it is also interesting to travel further back in history and focus on some of the logo's forerunners. The historiography of design takes us back to the dawn of human history, shedding light on the cave paintings of southern France and the rock art of North America and southern Africa. Rightly so, for it was from these, humanity's earliest forms of visual expression, that script and written language were developed. Here, too, we are sure to find the roots of the modern logo. However, if we are looking for indisputable precursors of the logo, it helps to establish what the precise purpose of the medium was and continues to be, namely a label and a distinguishing mark.

Researchers have regularly found notches or grooves on pottery dating from the dawning of the advanced civilizations of Asia, Africa and the Americas [→ 01]. These were both makers' marks and quality indicators. Chinese and Roman ceramics of somewhat later date bear even more distinctive markings that can easily be interpreted as direct forerunners of what would later become logos. So-called mason's marks have been found in tombs and other ancient structures dating back as far as 2000 BC. These abstract line graphics, each with its own specific characteristics, referred to a particular family or workshop [→ 02]. From this time, it was also the custom to brand farm animals. The current meaning of the word "brand," applied to an organization's trademark, goes back to a technique developed in much earlier times. The process of creating a logo out of signs and symbols was already practiced several thousand years ago. Keepers of livestock branded them with a single initial letter, or several interwoven letters, to identify the farmer or farming community to which they belonged. In the Middle Ages it was also customary for soldiers to be branded with the monogram or emblem of their warlord [→ 03].

A monogram, as its etymology suggests, was originally a single letter with embellishments of some kind. Today what we mean by a monogram is a design based on the initials of a person's given and family name. In the days of the Holy Roman Empire this type of monogram was most commonly used in European culture by monarchs and other rulers [→ 04]. It might consist of a handwritten signature or as a stamp or seal for use in official communications. These practical ways of identifying the sender of a document were later adopted by entrepreneurs and artists. One of the best-known and most striking examples of a monogram was the "AD" used for the first time in 1498 by the artist Albrecht Dürer.

Crusades, jousting tournaments and battles for land and other possessions all helped to shape medieval society and politics. In Europe, the High Middle Ages, between the 11th and 13th centuries, coincided with the introduction of heraldic devices—images of birds and animals, such as the eagle or the lion, symbolizing power, combined with colorful motifs and insignia of supremacy such as a crown, key or scepter [→ 05]. Such crests might represent estates, cities or noble families and their possessions, helping to distinguish one from another. Similarly, professional associations and other groups developed their own signs and symbols. Skilled artisans formed guilds, whose coats of arms bore emblems associated with their crafts. A trade guild's coat of arms was not only an early version of a seal of quality. At a time of widespread illiteracy, it was also a much-needed badge of recognition for business people operating in only recently established towns and cities.

In Japan in the same historical period, mon ("signs" or "emblems") came into being. Based on stylized representations of plants or animals, usually monochrome and surrounded by a circle, these were first used to identify the imperial family and the families of the shoguns, or hereditary military commanders. From 1600 onwards they were adopted by people of all social classes [→ 06]. Like European coats of arms, they were handed down from generation to generation in accordance with a specific set of rules. For many years, mon played only a minor role in everyday Japanese life but with the passage of time they came to be used as identifying marks for a family business. The famous logo of the automobile manufacturer Mitsubishi is an abstract combination of the mon of the two founding families.

With industrialization in the second half of the 18th century, nearly every area of commerce underwent gradual change. Companies extended their geographic areas of operation and an entirely new class of customer emerged, as factory workers earned considerably more than their forebears. Urban development led to different consumer behavior and an increase in the supply of goods, which in turn sparked off the product market. Under these new selling conditions it was more vital than ever before to distinguish one supplier from another, whether selling food, furniture or fashion. In many cases, elements from a family coat of arms became a company's first logo. For example, in 1878, one of the founders of the German stationery manufacturer Pelikan registered his family crest, the pelican, as the company trademark and brand name. Pelikan owes its continuing international fame to that decision [→ 07].

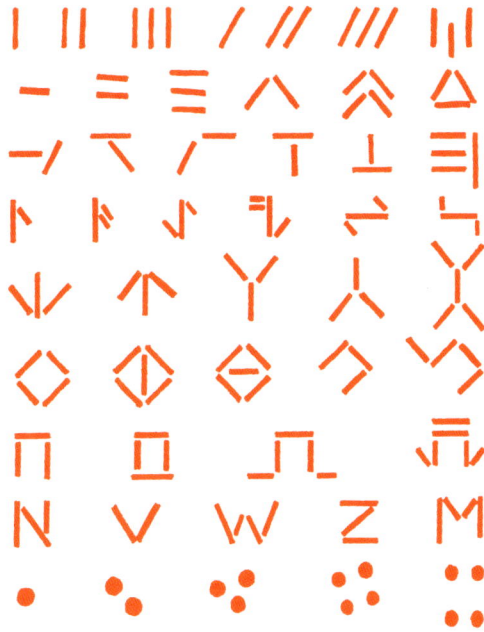

03
Medieval soldiers being
branded, copper engraving,
1616 (detail)

Mittelalterliche Brandmarkung
von Soldaten; Kupferstich
aus dem Jahr 1616 (Detail)

Marquage de soldats au
fer rouge. Gravure sur
cuivre de 1616 (détail)

In the 19th century, easily recognizable figure depictions like the pelican were a common form of visual imagery. Following in the tradition of trade guilds' coats of arms, a logo was always intended to create a clear, eye-catching link with the advertiser and/or its products. At this period, there were very few examples of abstract, non-representational signs. One of the earliest was the logo of the English William Bass brewery, whose products have displayed a red triangle since around 1875. Revolutionary for its time, the logo was streets ahead of all the competition and even now stands out from other brewers' more traditional visual identities. An interesting historical detail: the Bass triangle was the first-ever trademark to be registered in the United Kingdom and is hence the most strongly protected.

With a few exceptions, Modernist logos only began to appear in any number in the 1920s. Influenced by the De Stijl and Bauhaus art and design movements, the still-new discipline of commercial art changed significantly at this time. Turning to abstract shapes and skilfully intermingling them with geometric forms, commercial artists created designs quite unlike the figurative images that had so far dominated their work. Oskar Schlemmer's 1922 Bauhaus logo is a perfect example of the move towards abstract graphics [→ 08]. Writing in April 1926 in *Die Form*, the magazine of the Deutsche Werkbund (German Association of Craftsmen), the designer Johannes Molzahn, a close associate of the Bauhaus group although never a member, traced the thought process of an avant-garde artist bringing a logo design to fruition. "The meaning of the brand is paramount and the form is determined only by visual and mechanical laws that are intrinsic to design. Here, as in engineering, function dictates form. In reality, the creation of a brand is not so much an artistic problem as a technical and scientific one, involving both wit and imagination. Just like a machine, an aesthetically pleasing form is no more than the result of perfect construction combined with the objective of achieving the best performance." This philosophy is immediately apparent in groundbreaking logo designs like those of Wilhelm Deffke or Karl Schulpig [→ 09]. Many of the succeeding generation of international designers, such as Paul Rand and Yusaku Kamekura, acknowledge the Bauhaus and its achievements as a major influence on their creations.

Even so, it was not until the 1940s that the Modernist logo truly began to play a major role in new designs or in the reworking of existing ones. Ultimately, it was the Swiss Style typography, initially developed by 1920s avant-garde designers and later known as International Typographic Style, that helped Modernist design to achieve its final global breakthrough in the 1950s [→ 10]. Switzerland escaped much of the upheaval caused by World War II, which meant that its designers could continue to develop ideas and applications of abstract graphics, which in turn went on to inspire the new, post-war generation of designers in neighboring countries. One major contribution to the spread of the Swiss Style came from the magazine Graphis, founded in Zurich in 1944, and its yearbook Graphis Annual. The annual in particular, with its selection of Modernist graphic art from all over the world, was considered the definitive trade publication and influenced designers on every continent. In retrospect, the Swiss Style appears to have represented a finite period in the history of design which set the artistic tone, especially for such media as book jackets and posters, but which underwent partial change as new influences, such as Pop Art, began to emerge. However, its impact on the field of logo design was so radical that graphic art of the period can be seen as a genuine turning point in the history of the medium. Fundamental design parameters and methods changed, as did people's perception of the logo. Now, for the first time, as logos came into use across the board, designers were free to experiment with them.

Throughout the 1960s, as integrated corporate design systems became the norm, the logo's field of application broadened even further. The unified company image with its specific colors, typography and imagery was gradually catching on. The designer's individual method of dealing with signs and symbols was superseded by a rational, systematic approach [→ 11]. Until the introduction of the design manual, many companies routinely used different and often playful variations on their logos for different media of communication, such as posters, annual reports and such like. Even so, apart from barely noticeable alterations in a very few logos, these variations had little effect. Only the digital revolution in media production in the 1990s brought about real change in logo design. To begin with, few designers exploited the extra possibilities offered by digital image processing and most updates to logos were purely cosmetic. Adding a drop shadow or introducing other three-dimensional effects were among the most common. In recent years, purely 3-D logos have become increasingly popular [→ 12]. Because of their complexities of color and design, 3-D logos cannot be produced in single-color versions without losing important details of the design. The old ground rules, which made it impossible to include color or too many details because of reproduction problems, no longer apply thanks to advances in printing technology.

Today it seems that the logo gives designers greater freedom than ever before, but it also makes it more vital than ever to stick to a manageable number of basic design parameters. The three main chapters, entitled "Geometric", "Effect" and "Typographic", which in turn are divided into numerous sub-categories, take this representative selection of logos and pinpoint the most important basic forms, as well as the design possibilities they offer. Leafing through the collection, it might seem at first glance that there is nothing more to add. On closer inspection, it becomes clear that by combining the design parameters introduced in the book there is still much to discover about the process of design.

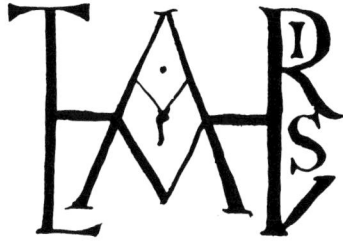
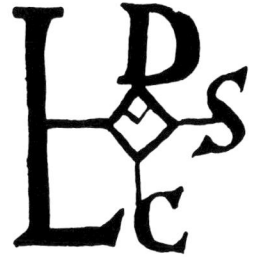
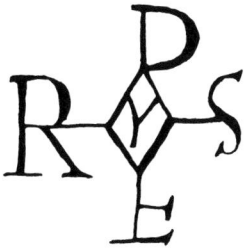

04

Monograms of Frankish and
Holy Roman/German emperors,
between 768 and 921

Monogramme fränkischer und
römisch-deutscher Herrscher
zwischen 768 und 921

Monogrammes de souverains
francs et romains germaniques
entre 768 et 921

05
Typical examples of family and
trade guild coats of arms

Typische Darstellungen verschiedener Familien- und Zunftwappen

Représentations caractéristiques
de différents blasons familiaux
et corporatifs

Logo
Jens Müller

Nimmt man Publikationen über Logos zur Hand, die vor 50 oder 60 Jahren veröffentlicht worden sind, wird dort früher oder später stets auf die „komplizierte Welt" verwiesen, in der das Elementare oder Vereinfachte zum Ausgleich und zur Bewältigung dient. Die Welt wird also schon eine ganze Weile als komplex wahrgenommen und der Bedarf an einfachen und eindeutigen Zeichen ist nicht ganz neu. Man muss diese und ähnliche Ausführungen aus der Mitte des 20. Jahrhunderts heute neben anderen Aspekten als versachlichende Legitimation von Gestaltern verstehen, die sich von der mystischen Aura des Werbekünstlers befreien wollten. Denn die Geburtsstunde der modernen Grafik geht einher mit jener des modernen Grafikdesigners, der sich statt von künstlerischem Genie eher von Nüchternheit, Konzept und Systematik lenken ließ. Selbstverständlich gab es einzelne Vordenker auch vor dieser Zeit, gegen Ende des 19. Jahrhunderts, und eine Bestimmung des exakten Zeitpunktes der Veränderung des Berufsverständnisses ist kaum möglich. Dennoch ist zu erkennen, dass sich ab den 1940er-Jahren so etwas wie die Moderne im Grafikdesign durchzusetzen begann. Spätestens in den beiden folgenden Jahrzehnten sind Arbeiten neuen Stils in nahezu allen Teilen der Erde und in sämtlichen Bereichen des Grafikdesigns zu finden. Internationale Konzerne wie auch lokale Kleinunternehmen verändern ihren visuellen Auftritt. Der modernistische Ansatz hat beim Medium Logo vielleicht die deutlichsten und nachhaltigsten Veränderungen mit sich gebracht. Gegenständliche Zeichen wurden endgültig von einfachen, grafischen Formen abgelöst. Trend, Zeitgeist und technische Weiterentwicklung führen heute zwar zu veränderten Lösungen, ihre Wurzeln liegen dennoch in den Gestaltungsparametern jener Hochphase des Modernismus. Ein Blick zurück lohnt also.

Ethnologen, Kunsthistoriker und Designwissenschaftler haben die Ursprünge von Zeichen und Symbolen ausführlich erforscht und umfangreiche Literatur dazu verfasst. Auch wenn in diesem Buch das modernistische Logo und seine Gestaltungsformen im Vordergrund stehen, ist es interessant noch etwas weiter in die Geschichte zurückzugehen und den Fokus auf verschiedene Vorfahren des Mediums Logo zu lenken. Die designbezogene Geschichtsschreibung wirft ihr Licht vielfach bis in die Frühzeit der Menschheit und führt die Höhlenbilder Südfrankreichs oder Felszeichnungen in Nordamerika und Südafrika an. Zu Recht, denn aus diesen ersten visuellen Äußerungen der Menschheit entwickelten sich letztlich Schrift sowie geschriebene Sprache. Und mit Sicherheit finden sich hier auch die fundamentalen Wurzeln des heutigen Logos. Sucht man aber nach ganz eindeutigen Vorfahren, ist es zunächst hilfreich sich der bis heute unverändert zweckgebundenen Aufgabe des Mediums Logo bewusst zu werden: Kennzeichnung und Unterscheidung.

Aus der Entstehungszeit früher Hochkulturen in Asien, Afrika und Amerika datieren keramische Arbeiten, auf denen Forscher systematische Einkerbungen fanden [→ 01]. Diese dienten der Markierung unterschiedlicher Hersteller und als Hinweise auf abweichende Qualitäten. Auf chinesischer und römischer Keramik etwas späteren Datums waren konkretere Kennzeichnungen von noch größerer Eindeutigkeit zu finden, die endgültig als direkte Vorläufer der späteren Markenzeichen zu interpretieren sind. Auf Grabmälern und anderen historischen Bauwerken, die bis auf 2000 v. Chr. zurückdatiert werden können, fanden sich sogenannte Steinmetzzeichen. Diese abstrakten Strichgrafiken verwiesen auf unterschiedliche Familien oder Werkstätten und hatten ihre eigene Systematik [→ 02]. Zur gleichen Zeit war es bereits auch üblich Nutztiere mittels Brandzeichen zu markieren. Das heutige Verständnis des Begriffs „Branding" für die Kennzeichnung einer Marke geht auf diese in der Frühzeit entwickelte Technik zurück. Für das bis heute praktizierte Verfahren der Brandzeichnung wurden schon vor mehreren tausend Jahren eigene Zeichen und Symbole entwickelt. In der Nutztierhaltung wurden dazu einzelne oder verbundene Buchstaben verwendet, die für den Besitzer oder eine Farmgemeinschaft standen. In der Zeit mittelalterlicher Schlachten war es auch üblich, Soldaten per Brandmarkung mit dem Signum oder Monogramm ihrer Kriegsherren zu kennzeichnen [→ 03].

Ein solches Monogramm war, wie sich etymologisch ableiten lässt, ursprünglich ein ausgestalteter Einzelbuchstabe. Heute verstehen wir darunter vor allem die kombinierte Gestaltung von Anfangsbuchstaben eines Vor- und Nachnamens. Schon in die Zeit des Heiligen Römischen Reichs Deutscher Nation zurückdatierend, ist diese Buchstabenmarke vor allem in der europäischen Kultur ein von Herrschern und Monarchen verwendetes Zeichen [→ 04]. Es wurde sowohl als handschriftliche Signatur als auch in Form von Stempel oder Siegel für die administrative Kommunikation eingesetzt. Diese praktischen Absenderkennungen machten sich später auch Unternehmer und Künstler zunutze. Eines der bis heute bekanntesten und markantesten Monogramme ist beispielsweise das von Albrecht Dürer 1498 erstmals verwendete „AD".

Kreuzzüge, das ritterliche Turnierwesen sowie Kämpfe um Land und andere Besitztümer bestimmten Gesellschaft und Politik des Mittelalters. Zur Zeit seiner europäischen Hochblüte zwischen dem 11. und 13. Jahrhundert entstanden die Wappen: gegenständliche Darstellungen von Kraft ausstrahlenden Tieren wie dem Adler oder dem Löwen, verbunden mit farbigen Mustern und Darstellungen von Machtinsignien wie Krone, Schlüssel oder Zepter [→ 05]. Sie kennzeichneten Ländereien, Adelsfamilien oder Städte sowie deren Besitztümer und halfen, sich voneinander abzugrenzen. Parallel entwickelten auch nicht adelige Berufsgruppen und andere Gemeinschaften eigene Zeichen und Symbole. Handwerker schlossen sich zu Zünften zusammen und entwickelten Wappen, die gegenständlich eine visuelle Kurzform der jeweiligen Tätigkeit abbildeten. Diese Zunftwappen waren nicht nur eine Art frühes Qualitätssiegel, sondern aufgrund des noch weit verbreiteten Analphabetismus eine notwendige Kennzeichnung für die Unternehmer in den noch jungen Städten.

In Japan entstanden zeitgleich die sogenannten Mon (dt. „Zeichnung, Muster"). Basierend auf stilisierten Darstellungen von Pflanzen oder Tieren, meist einfarbig in einem umrandeten Kreis platziert, kennzeichneten sie zunächst die Kaiserfamilie und den japanischen Kriegsadel, ab 1600 schließlich auch Familien aller Stände [→ 06]. Ähnlich wie die europäischen Wappen wurden sie nach bestimmten Regeln von Generation zu Generation vererbt. Im täglichen Leben spielten die Mon lange Zeit eine untergeordnete Rolle, erst im Lauf der Geschichte wurde es üblich die Symbole auch als öffentliche Kennzeichnung eines Familienunternehmens zu verwenden. So ist das bekannte Logo des Automobilherstellers Mitsubishi eine abstrahierte Kombination der Mon beider Gründerfamilien.

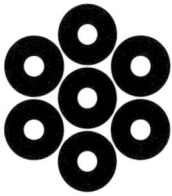

06
Examples of Japanese *mon*, whose forerunners were family crests dating back as far as the 12th century

Beispiele japanischer Mon, deren Vorläufer seit dem 12. Jahrhundert als Familien- zeichen in Gebrauch waren

Exemples de *mon* japonais ; leurs précurseurs étaient utilisés comme signes familiaux depuis le XIIᵉ siècle

07
Development of the logo of
the stationery manufacturer
Pelikan between 1873 and
2003, which originated from
a family crest

Entwicklung des Logos des
Schreibwarenherstellers Pelikan
zwischen 1873 und 2003; seine
Ursprünge liegen in einem
Familienwappen

Évolution du logo du fabricant
d'articles d'écriture Pelikan
entre 1873 et 2003 ; les
origines du logo remontent
à un blason familial

Mit der Industrialisierung zur zweiten Hälfte des 18. Jahrhunderts veränderten sich nach und nach fast alle Branchen. Unternehmen erweiterten ihre geografische Reichweite. Mit den im Vergleich zu ihren vorherigen Lebensumständen nun besser-gestellten Fabriksarbeitern entstand eine ganz neue Käuferschicht. Die Urbanisierung führte zu einem veränderten Konsumverhalten und einem Anstieg des Angebots; eine Art Initialzündung des Produktmarkts ereignete sich. Ob Lebensmittel, Möbel oder Kleidung – Differenzierung war in der veränderten Marktsituation notwendiger als je zuvor. In vielen Fällen wurden Elemente aus Familienwappen zu ersten Markenzei-chen. Der Pelikan als Wappentier der Familie des deutschen Schreibwarenherstellers wurde 1878 beispielsweise zum Logo und Markennamen des Unternehmens. Ihre inter-nationale Bekanntheit verdankt die Marke bis heute auch dieser Entscheidung [→ 07]. Figürliche Darstellungen, wie der genannte Pelikan, waren im 19. Jahrhundert eine übliche Form der Visualisierung. Aus der Tradition der Zünftewappen heraus wurde angestrebt, dass ein Logo eine deutliche und plakative Verbindung zum Unternehmer oder zum Angebot des Unternehmens herstellte. Nur vereinzelt entstanden bereits zu dieser Zeit abstrakte und nicht-gegenständliche Zeichen. Eines der ganz frühen Beispiele ist die englische Brauerei William Bass, die spätestens seit 1875 ein rotes Dreieck als Logo auf ihre Erzeugnisse druckte. Die damals revolutionäre Kenn-zeichnung hob sich mehr als deutlich von der gesamten Konkurrenz ab und unterschei-det die Marke bis heute von der eher traditionell geprägten visuellen Erscheinung anderer Bierbrauer. Als interessantes Detail der Geschichte war das Bass-Dreieck das aller-erste überhaupt in Großbritannien angemeldete und damit geschützte Markenzeichen.

Von einigen Ausnahmen abgesehen begann die erste Phase modernistischer Logos jedoch erst in den 1920er-Jahren. Von den künstlerischen und grafischen Be-wegungen um De Stijl und Bauhaus geprägt, veränderte sich die noch junge Disziplin der Gebrauchsgrafik in dieser Zeit maßgeblich. Der Griff zu abstrakten Formen und die gekonnte Kombination geometrischer Elemente führten zu neuen Lösungen, die einen extremen Gegensatz zu den bis dahin vorherrschenden gegenständlichen Aus-drucksformen darstellten. Das 1922 von Oskar Schlemmer entworfene Logo für das Bauhaus selbst ist ein ideales Exempel für den Übergang zur abstrakten Grafik [→ 08]. Im April 1926 erschien in der Werkbund-Zeitschrift *Die Form* ein Artikel des dem Bauhaus nahestehenden Gestalters Johannes Molzahn, worin die Gedankengänge der Avantgardisten zum modernen Logo auf den Punkt gebracht werden: „Der Marken-sinn ist absolut und die Form wird allein bestimmt von optisch-mechanischen Gesetzen, die die Gestalt nach sich ziehen; hier fordert Funktion eine Form in derselben Weise wie im Maschinenbau. Die Markenfrage ist in Wirklichkeit kein künstlerisches Problem zuerst, vielmehr ein technisch-wissenschaftliches und lebendig-psychisches; die ästhetische Form ist hier genau wie bei der Maschine nur das Resultat vollkommener Konstruktion, mit dem Sinn höchster Leistungsfähigkeit." Diese Philosophie wird in Pionierarbeiten der modernen Logogestaltung wie etwa von Wilhelm Deffke oder Karl Schulpig unmittelbar spürbar [→ 09]. Auch zahlreiche internationale Gestalter der nächsten Generation wie Paul Rand oder Yusaku Kamekura nannten das Bauhaus und seine Errungenschaften wichtige Einflussfaktoren ihrer Arbeit.

Dennoch begann sich das modernistische Logo bei Neuentwürfen oder Über-arbeitungen alter Zeichen erst im Laufe der 1940er-Jahre flächendeckend durch-zusetzen. Die wiederum durch die Avantgardisten der 1920er-Jahre begründete Bewegung der Schweizer Typografie, später auch als „International Typographic Style" bezeichnet, verhalf der modernen Grafik schließlich ab den 1950er-Jahren endgültig zum Durchbruch – auch international [→ 10]. In der durch den Zweiten Weltkrieg weniger belasteten Schweiz konnten sich Ideen und Ansätze der abstrakten Grafik weiterent-wickeln, und sie wurden nach Ende des Krieges von einer neuen Gestaltergeneration dankbar aufgenommen. Einen nicht unwesentlichen Beitrag zur Verbreitung des Schweizer Stils dürften dabei die 1944 in Zürich gegründete Zeitschrift Graphis und ihr Jahrbuch Graphis Annual geleistet haben. Vor allem das Jahrbuch mit einer Aus-wahl moderner Arbeiten aus aller Welt war so etwas wie das Leitmedium jener Zeit. Es erreichte und beeinflusste Gestalter auf allen Kontinenten. Bezogen auf Medien wie Buchumschläge oder Plakate stellt der Schweizer Stil rückblickend eine abge-schlossene Ära der Designgeschichte dar, die gestalterisch den Ton angab, später aber zumindest in Teilen durch neue Einflüsse – unter anderem aus der Pop Art – verändert wurde. Der Einfluss im Bereich des Logos war jedoch so einschneidend, dass man das damalige Schaffen als wirkliche Zäsur in der Entwicklung des Mediums werten kann. Grundlegende Gestaltungsparameter, die sowohl die Entwurfstechnik als auch die Wahrnehmung von Markenzeichen verändert haben, wurden damals erstmals in voller Bandbreite angewendet und ausgelotet.

Im Laufe der 1960er-Jahre wurde das Anwendungsfeld des Logos durch inte-gral konzipierte Corporate-Design-Systeme noch einmal erweitert. Einheitliche Unterneh-mensauftritte mit Normen zu Farbigkeit, Typografie, Bildsprache und anderen Elementen setzten sich zunehmend durch. Reglementierte Systematik und Ordnung lösten den bis-lang individuellen Umgang mit Zeichen ab [→ 11]. Bis zur Einführung von Design-Manuals war es in vielen Unternehmen üblich, das Logo in verschiedenen Kommunikationsmedien (Plakat, Geschäftsbericht etc.) ganz unterschiedlich und oft auch spielerisch variierend einzusetzen. In ihrem grundsätzlichen Aussehen wurden die Logos durch diese Verän-derungen jedoch nur unwesentlich und in Einzelfällen beeinflusst. Erst die digitale Revolution im Bereich der Medienproduktion in den 1990er-Jahren verursachte Verän-derungen in der Logoausgestaltung selbst. Erweiterte Möglichkeiten der Bildbearbeitung am Computer führten zunächst zu eher rein kosmetischen Aktualisierungen zahlreicher Zeichen. Das Hinzufügen eines Schlagschattens oder das Einfügen anderer dreidimen-sionaler Effekte waren die gängigen Eingriffe. In den letzten Jahren entstanden verstärkt auch rein dreidimensionale Logos [→ 12]. Aufgrund ihrer Komplexität können 3D-Logos nicht einfarbig wiedergegeben werden, ohne dabei wesentliche Gestaltungselemente zu verlieren. Alte Grundregeln, nach denen Farbigkeit oder zu viele Details infolge von Problemen in der Reproduzierbarkeit ausgeschlossen waren, gelten dank fortgeschrittener Drucktechnik nicht mehr.

Das Logo bietet heute also scheinbar mehr Gestaltungsfreiraum denn je. Umso notwendiger ist der Blick auf die überschaubare Anzahl grundlegender Design-parameter. Die drei Hauptkapitel „Geometrisch", „Effekt" und „Typografisch", die wiederum aus zahlreichen Subkategorien bestehen, zeigen dabei die wichtigsten Grundformen und Entwurfsmöglichkeiten auf, die in dieser repräsentativen Menge von Logos zu finden sind. Beim Durchblättern dieser Sammlung scheint es zunächst so, als wäre alles schon einmal da gewesen. Bei genauerem Hinsehen wird jedoch deutlich, dass in der Kombination der vorgestellten Gestaltungsparameter noch unlimitierte Möglichkeiten liegen, die es im Entwurfsprozess zu entdecken gilt.

08

Logo of the Bauhaus in Weimar, designed by Oskar Schlemmer in 1922

Logo des Staatlichen Bauhauses in Weimar, entworfen 1922 von Oskar Schlemmer

Logo du Bauhaus de Weimar, dessiné en 1922 par Oskar Schlemmer

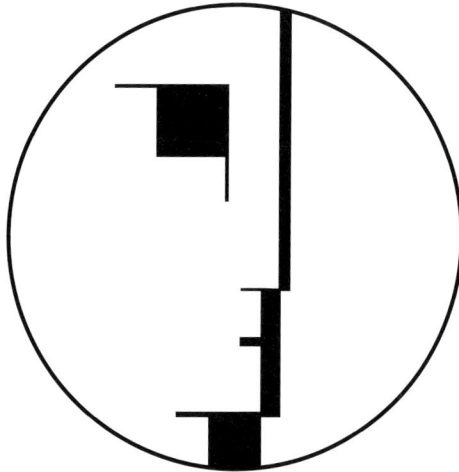

09

Designs from the 1920s by German logo pioneers Karl Schulpig (left), Johannes Molzahn (center) and Wilhelm Deffke (right)

Entwürfe der deutschen Logopioniere Karl Schulpig (links), Johannes Molzahn (Mitte) und Wilhelm Deffke (rechts) aus den 1920er-Jahren

Réalisations des pionniers allemands du logo Karl Schulpig (colonne de gauche), Johannes Molzahn (colonne centrale) et Wilhelm Deffke (colonne de droite) datant des années 1920

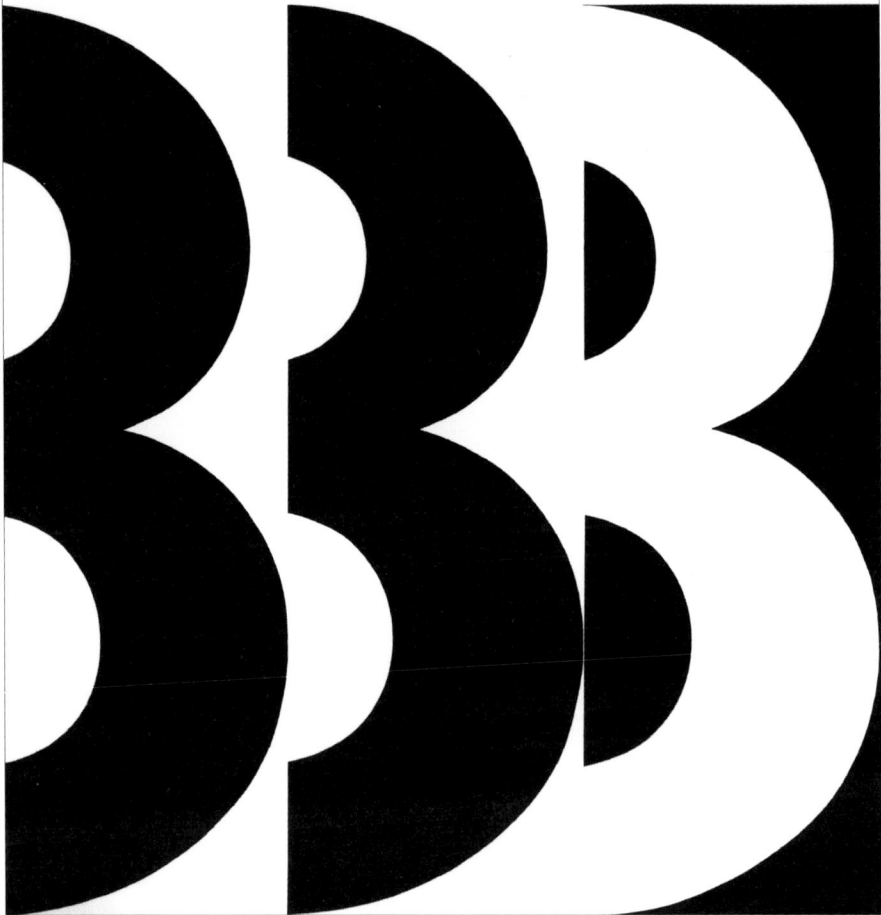

33ª Biennale
Internazionale
d'Arte

Venezia
18 Giugno
16 Ottobre
1966

Riduzioni ferroviarie

N. 1064/66 Esente da bollo Min. Fin. N. 37465 dell'11/5/66.
Stampa: Poligrafico G. Colombi S.p.A. - Milano-Pero - design / Bob Noorda - Unimark

10
Poster for the 33rd Venice Biennale, created
by the Dutch designer Bob Noorda in 1966 for
the Milan office of Unimark International

Plakat zur 33. Biennale in Venedig,
entworfen 1966 vom niederländischen
Gestalter Bob Noorda für das Mailänder
Büro von Unimark International

Affiche de la 33ᵉ Biennale de Venise
dessinée en 1966 par le designer
néerlandais Bob Noorda pour le bureau
milanais d'Unimark International

Logo
Jens Müller

Lorsqu'on passe en revue les publications parues voici cinquante ou soixante ans autour du logo, on tombe tôt ou tard sur un passage évoquant ce « monde compliqué » auquel l'élémentaire et la simplification doivent servir de contrepoids et d'outils de contrôle. Le fait que le monde soit perçu comme complexe ne date donc pas d'hier, et le besoin de signes simples et intelligibles n'est pas vraiment nouveau. Tout comme d'autres aspects, cette explication et d'autres de la même veine avancées au milieu du XXᵉ siècle doivent être comprises comme une recherche de légitimité objective de la part des designers, qui voulaient se débarrasser de l'aura mystique entourant l'artiste affichiste. De fait, la naissance du graphisme moderne est indissolublement liée à celle d'un graphiste moderne moins inspiré par le génie artistique que guidé par la sobriété, la conceptualisation et la systématique. Des précurseurs isolés ont bien sûr existé dès avant cette époque, vers la fin du XIXᵉ siècle, ce qui rend difficile de désigner le moment précis où la conscience du métier a changé chez les professionnels. Reste qu'à partir des années 1940 on observe que quelque chose que l'on pourrait appeler la modernité commence à s'imposer dans le domaine du design graphique. Au plus tard pendant les deux décennies suivantes, des travaux représentant ce nouveau style apparaissent un peu partout dans le monde et dans tous les secteurs du graphisme. Des groupes internationaux aussi bien que de petites entreprises régionales rénovent alors leur présentation visuelle. C'est peut-être dans le domaine du logo que l'esprit moderniste a produit les changements les plus manifestes et les plus durables. Si les tendances, l'esprit du temps et les évolutions techniques conduisent aujourd'hui à des solutions divergentes, celles-ci n'en plongent pas moins leurs racines dans les paramètres créatifs de cette apogée de la modernité. Un regard rétrospectif ne peut donc être qu'enrichissant.

Les ethnologues, les historiens de l'art et les spécialistes du design ont analysé en détails les origines des signes et des symboles de l'humanité et produit une immense littérature sur ce sujet. Même si le logo moderne et ses manifestations formelles constituent l'objet principal du présent ouvrage, il n'est pas inutile de remonter un peu plus haut dans l'histoire et de mettre un coup de projecteur sur quelques ancêtres de ce média. L'historiographie du design fait souvent remonter jusqu'à l'aube de l'humanité en citant les peintures préhistoriques du sud de la France et les dessins pariétaux d'Amérique du Nord ou d'Afrique du Sud. À juste titre, car c'est à partir de ces premières manifestations visuelles de l'humanité que se sont finalement développés l'écriture et le langage écrit, et c'est aussi là qu'on trouvera les racines primordiales du logo actuel. Lorsqu'on cherche toutefois les ancêtres qui coulent de source, il s'avère utile de saisir la fonction du logo qui, aujourd'hui comme hier, ressort d'un usage utilitaire : caractérisation et démarcation.

De l'apparition des premières civilisations en Asie, en Afrique et en Amérique datent des pièces de céramique sur lesquelles les chercheurs ont trouvé les premières entailles systématiques ⁽→⁰¹⁾. Celles-ci servaient à identifier différents fabricants et à signaler des qualités divergentes. Sur les céramiques chinoises et romaines d'époques un peu plus tardives, on a trouvé des caractérisations encore plus claires qui ne laissent subsister aucun doute sur le fait qu'elles sont les précurseurs directs des futures marques commerciales. Sur des tombeaux et des édifices historiques qui peuvent être datés jusqu'à 2000 avant notre ère, on a trouvé des «marques de tâcherons». Ces gravures linéaires abstraites renvoyaient à différents ateliers ou familles et avaient leur propre systématique [→ 02]. À la même époque, le marquage des bêtes au fer rouge est déjà une pratique courante. La compréhension de l'anglais «branding» pour désigner la caractérisation d'une marque commerciale remonte à cette technique apparue à la fin de la préhistoire. Dans le cadre de la pratique du marquage des bêtes, qui s'est conservée jusqu'à nos jours, des signes et des symboles ont été développés voici plusieurs milliers d'années. Dans le domaine de l'élevage, on utilisait des lettres isolées ou combinées représentant le propriétaire ou une communauté fermière. À l'époque des batailles médiévales, il était aussi courant de marquer les soldats du signet ou du monogramme de leur commandant [→ 03].

Comme l'indique l'étymologie du terme, le monogramme a d'abord été une lettre isolée intégralement dessinée. Aujourd'hui, le terme désigne surtout une graphie visuelle combinant les initiales d'un prénom et d'un nom de famille. Dès l'époque du Saint Empire romain germanique, ce type de sigle fut utilisé par les princes et les souverains – avant tout dans la culture européenne [→ 04]. On le trouve alors aussi bien sous forme de signature manuscrite que de cachet ou de sceau dans le cadre de communications administratives. Plus tard, les entrepreneurs et les artistes tirent à leur tour parti de ces caractérisations d'expéditeur de nature pratique. Un des monogrammes les plus célèbres reste à ce jour le sigle «AD» utilisé pour la première fois en 1498 par Albrecht Dürer.

Le monde des croisades, de la chevalerie et des tournois, mais aussi les conflits autour de la conquête de territoires ou d'autres biens ont déterminé la société et la politique du Moyen Âge. À l'apogée de cette période historique, entre les XIe et XIIIe siècles, apparaissent les blasons, représentations figurées d'animaux rayonnant de force comme l'aigle ou le lion, représentations associées à des motifs colorés et des insignes de pouvoir comme la couronne, les clés ou le sceptre [→ 05]. Les blasons servent à marquer des terres, à caractériser des familles nobles ou des villes ainsi que leurs propriétés, et à se démarquer les uns des autres. En même temps, des groupements professionnels appartenant au tiers état et d'autres communautés développent à leur tour leurs propres signes et symboles. Les artisans se regroupent en corporations et développent des blasons qui représentent leur activité par un raccourci figuré. Ces blasons corporatifs n'étaient pas seulement une sorte de label de qualité, mais aussi, dans le contexte d'un analphabétisme encore largement répandu, une caractérisation incontournable pour les entrepreneurs des jeunes métropoles.

Design system developed by
FHK Henrion in the 1960s for
management consultancy Metra
and its international subsidiaries

In den 1960er-Jahren von FHK
Henrion entwickeltes Zeichensystem
für die Unternehmensberatung
Metra und deren internationale
Tochterunternehmen

Système de signes développé dans
les années 1960 par FHK Henrion
pour la société de conseil Metra et
ses filiales internationales

À la même époque, on voit apparaître au Japon les insignes héraldiques appelés mon (fr. dessin, motif). Créés sur la base de représentations stylisées de végétaux ou d'animaux généralement monochromes placées dans un cercle clairement cerné, les mon caractérisent d'abord la famille impériale et la noblesse guerrière du Japon et, pour finir, à partir de 1600, également les familles de toutes les classes de la société [→ 06]. Un peu comme les blasons en Europe, ils se transmettent de génération en génération selon des règles bien précises. Dans la vie quotidienne, il devint ensuite courant d'utiliser ce type de symboles pour la caractérisation publique d'une entreprise familiale. C'est ainsi que le célèbre logo du constructeur automobile Mitsubishi est une combinaison abstraite des mon des deux familles fondatrices.

Avec la révolution industrielle de la seconde moitié du XVIIIe siècle, presque toutes les branches de l'industrie évoluent peu à peu. Les entreprises étendent leur rayon d'action géographique. Avec les ouvriers d'usines, dont le statut était alors comparativement meilleur, une toute nouvelle couche d'acheteurs voit le jour. L'urbanisation croissante modifie les habitudes de consommation et entraîne une augmentation de l'offre. Il se produit ainsi une sorte de mise à feu initiale du marché des produits. Alimentaire, mobilier ou habillement – dans le cadre des nouvelles conditions du marché, il devient plus nécessaire que jamais de se démarquer. Bien souvent, les premières marques commerciales sont créées à partir d'éléments tirés de blasons familiaux. Pour citer un exemple, en 1878, le pélican, animal héraldique de la famille du fabricant d'articles d'écriture Pelikan, devint le logo et le nom de l'entreprise. C'est notamment à cette décision que cette marque doit jusqu'à aujourd'hui sa notoriété internationale [→ 07]. Au XIXe siècle, les représentations figurées comme le pélican deviennent une forme courante de représentation visuelle. Dans la tradition des blasons corporatifs, l'on cherche alors à ce qu'un logo exprime un lien clair et frappant avec l'entrepreneur ou l'offre de l'entreprise. Dès cette époque apparaissent aussi des signes abstraits et non figuratifs, mais ils sont encore l'exception. Un des tout premiers exemples en est le brasseur anglais William Bass qui, au plus tard en 1875, fit imprimer sur ses produits un triangle rouge utilisé comme logo. Cette caractérisation révolutionnaire se démarquait alors de manière pour le moins voyante de toute la concurrence et continue à distinguer aujourd'hui cette marque parmi les identités visuelles plutôt traditionnelles des autres brasseurs. Détail intéressant dans ce contexte, le triangle de Bass fut la toute première marque commerciale déposée – et donc protégée – enregistrée au Royaume-Uni.

À quelques exceptions près, il faut toutefois attendre les années 1920 pour voir s'ouvrir la première phase du logo moderne. À l'époque, le design graphique, discipline encore jeune, change de manière décisive sous l'influence des mouvements artistiques et graphiques de la mouvance De Stijl et du Bauhaus. L'utilisation de formes abstraites et la combinaison savante d'éléments géométriques conduisent alors à des solutions inédites qui sont en opposition maximale avec les formes d'expression figuratives jusqu'alors prédominantes. Le logo qu'Oskar Schlemmer conçoit précisément en 1922 pour le Bauhaus illustre parfaitement cette transition vers le graphisme abstrait [→ 08]. En avril 1926, la revue du Deutsche Werkbund *Die Form* publie un article de Johannes Molzahn, créateur proche du Bauhaus, qui dégage l'essentiel des réflexions de l'avant-garde du logo : « L'esprit de la marque est un absolu, la forme est exclusivement déterminée par des lois optico-mécaniques qui guident la création. Ici, la fonction crée la forme tout comme dans le domaine de l'ingénierie mécanique. En réalité, la question de la marque n'est pas un problème d'abord artistique, mais bien plutôt un problème technicoscientifique et concrètement psychique. Comme dans le cas de la machine, la forme esthétique n'est ici rien d'autre que le résultat d'une construction parfaite, l'objectif étant l'excellence des performances. » Cette philosophie est concrétisée le plus clairement dans les réalisations pionnières de Wilhelm Deffke et Karl Schulpig (→ 09). De nombreux designers internationaux de la génération suivante, comme Paul Rand ou Yusaku Kamekura, ont eux aussi cité le Bauhaus et ses acquis comme des influences importantes pour leur travail.

Mais c'est seulement au cours des années 1940 que le logo moderne commence à s'imposer largement dans le cadre de nouveaux projets ou lors du remaniement de signes déjà existants. Pour finir, à partir des années 1950, le mouvement de la typographie suisse – parfois appelé « International Typographic Style », fondé lui aussi par des avant-gardistes des années 1920, apportera une contribution décisive à la percée définitive de la création graphique moderne, notamment sur le plan international (→ 10). Dans une Suisse moins directement touchée par la Seconde Guerre mondiale, les idées et les orientations du graphisme international ont pu continuer de se développer et, à la fin de la guerre, elles vont être saluées par une nouvelle génération de graphistes – d'abord dans les pays voisins. Une contribution non négligeable à la diffusion du style suisse a été apportée par la revue Graphis, fondée en 1944 à Zurich, et par sa publication annuelle Graphis Annual. C'est surtout cette dernière, avec sa sélection de projets réalisés dans le monde entier, qui fut le média le plus influent de l'époque. Elle atteignit et influença des créateurs des cinq continents. Dans le domaine de la couverture de livre ou de l'affiche, le style suisse, considéré rétrospectivement, marque une phase révolue de l'histoire du design. S'il a donné le ton de la création à son époque, ce style sera ensuite modifié au moins en partie par de nouvelles influences – notamment celle du Pop Art. L'empreinte qu'il a laissée dans le domaine du logo a toutefois été telle qu'il faut considérer les créations de cette époque comme une véritable césure dans l'évolution du média. Certains paramètres fondamentaux qui ont révolutionné la technique de conception aussi bien que la perception des marques commerciales ont alors été appliqués et explorés pour la première fois dans toutes leurs implications.

unitymedia

DC
COMICS™

Sony Ericsson

Thomas Cook
Group

at&t

12
Three-dimensional logos,
used chiefly or almost exclusively
in color applications

Dreidimensionale Logos,
die hauptsächlich oder sogar
ausschließlich in farbiger
Anwendung funktionieren

Logos tridimensionnels
fonctionnant principalement,
voire exclusivement en couleurs

Au cours des années 1960, le logo élargit encore son champ d'application avec l'apparition de systèmes de corporate design conçus jusqu'aux moindres détails. Des images d'entreprise homogènes, entièrement normalisées en termes de couleurs, de typographie, de langage visuel ou d'autres aspects, s'imposent alors progressivement. Le systématisme et l'ordre réglés viennent désormais remplacer le traitement individuel du signe [→ 11]. Jusqu'à l'apparition du manuel de conception, les entreprises utilisaient leur logo de façon très différente selon les médias de communication (affiche, rapport de gestion etc.), souvent dans des versions ludiques. Sauf exception, ces changements n'altéraient guère l'aspect fondamental des logos. Avec la révolution numérique des années 1990 dans la production médiatique, on relève toutefois de vrais changements dans la conception de logos. Dans un premier temps, les nouvelles possibilités offertes par la conception graphique assistée par ordinateur conduisent à des actualisations plutôt cosmétiques de nombreux signes. L'ajout d'une ombre portée et l'insertion d'autres effets tridimensionnels sont alors les interventions les plus courantes. Au cours de ces dernières années se sont aussi imposés de plus en plus souvent des logos purement tridimensionnels [→ 12]. Leur complexité en termes de couleurs et de design fait que les logos en 3D ne peuvent être produits en version monochrome sans perte d'aspects importants du design. Les anciennes règles de base qui excluaient la couleur ou l'excès de détails pour des raisons liées à des problèmes de reproductibilité n'ont plus cours aujourd'hui grâce aux progrès des techniques d'impression.

Le logo offre donc aujourd'hui apparemment plus d'espace de liberté créatrice que jamais. Cela rend d'autant plus nécessaire d'avoir une vue d'ensemble des paramètres fondamentaux du design, somme toute limités en nombre. Les trois chapitres principaux « Géométrique », « Effet » et « Typographique », eux-mêmes subdivisés en nombreuses sous-catégories, présentent les principales formes fondamentales et possibilités créatives que l'on peut recenser dans cette somme représentative de logos. En feuilletant cette compilation, la première impression sera peut-être que tout a déjà existé. Mais à y regarder de plus près, on réalisera clairement que la combinaison des paramètres de création présentés recèle encore des possibilités illimitées qu'il s'agit de découvrir lors du travail de conception.

Viva Modernism!

R. Roger Remington

Modernism, in its broadest definition, is contemporary thought, character or practice. More specifically, Modernism describes for the arts a set of cultural tendencies and associated cultural movements, affirming the power of human beings to make, improve and reshape their environment. Modernism is the projection of an ideology encompassing awareness of the production process and the final destination of its products.

The quintessential Modernist designer Massimo Vignelli sets the birth of Modernism as coinciding with the publication of the Diderot and d'Alembert *Encyclopédie* in the middle of the 18th century. This work was the great contribution of the Enlightenment, a unique moment of transition in the history of mankind from an agrarian society to an industrial one, from a religion-dominated culture to a liberal and progressive vision of the world. In the encyclopedia was to be found the last expression of crafts and an early view of the new Machine Era. Also evident was the recognition of the need for a different way of designing artifacts. No longer was the artisan the master of the end product, but a new figure was emerging, someone devising products manufactured by machines, from glass to china, from steel to fabrics, from paper to type and more. The Enlightenment generated a new way of thinking as people looked forward to a new social order. The French Revolution accelerated man's evolution and gave new strength to ideas. The modern man was born, liberated from the bind of oppressing and confining boundaries from the past. New horizons stimulated minds in every area from the sciences to the arts, from politics to commerce. The advent of the steam engine at the beginning of the 19th century brought power to industry. Products of all kinds had to be designed for the new production processes. Mechanization took command, from railways to textiles. Even agriculture was mechanized. Steel bridges spanned the new era. Everything was now designed, at the beginning in a rather naive way and later in a more conscious way, thus expressing the new technologies and the new sensibilities. Industrial and technological change always gives rise to social change which, in turn, affects artistic expression. Creative expressions become a mirror, always reflecting society.

Marx and Engels provided a voice for the needs of a different social justice. A new way of seeing the human condition gave rise to new ideologies covering every aspect of the nascent society emerging from the Industrial Revolution. In the middle of the 19th century, William Morris reacted against the stylistic commonality caused by the improper use of the new industrial processes, advocating a new attention to the design of products, from furniture to textiles.

The design and building of London's Crystal Palace heralded the emergence of Modernism through architecture. This unique building of cast-iron and glass was constructed in 1851 for the Great Exhibition at Hyde Park which showcased the newest products of many nations. Its design forecast by years the glass curtain walls of Gropius's architecture of the 1920s.

The profile of the modern designer was therefore starting to take shape. At the beginning of the 20th century in Germany, Peter Behrens was already the model for the modern industrial designer, covering with his work the whole field of design, applying new mental processes and new expressions. He was the first designer to face the industrial needs of communication and the real inventor of corporate identity, the expression of a company vision and commitment to integrity and quality. Behrens was also a founding member of the Deutsche Werkbund, which played a major role in integrating design and industry. A noteworthy publication of the Werkbund from 1921 entitled *XX Eigen-Marken* (Twenty Personal Brands) presented for the first time a collection of identity marks and logotypes from its members, many of which break with traditional forms of identity of the period.

Other European avant-garde movements each did their best to radically sever connections with the traditional past and contribute to shaping modern design thought and practice. This new wave of creative thought and activity cut across many boundaries beyond design to painting, sculpture, architecture, dance, music, poetry and more. Contributors came from many parts of Europe. The Constructivists in Russia were the major players of the European avant-garde and El Lissitzky was the seminal father of this movement. For this break-away Modernist, "Not even the new was new enough for him."[1] The Cubist painters in Paris suggested new ways of seeing the world and shaping visual form. The De Stijl group in the Netherlands brought their utterly unique inventions to this initiative to break away dramatically from traditional forms. One of their members, painter Piet Mondrian, wrote: "At every moment of the past all variations of the past were 'new.' But it was not THE new. We should not forget that we stand at the end of a culture, at the end of everything old."[2] The Futurists in Italy and the Dada group in Switzerland and Berlin were instrumental in liberating typography.

The geographic center of much of this dynamic change was Germany. In 1927, led by Kurt Schwitters, designers from many parts of Germany came together to form a group known as the "Ring Neue Werbegestalter" (Circle of Modern Advertising Designers). Among its members were Jan Tschichold, Max Burchartz, Willi Baumeister, along with many others. This group of graphic designers held exhibitions and meetings throughout Germany showing off their progressive graphics and advocating avant-garde approaches in their work. Much of the Modernist European expression in design became unified at the Bauhaus in Germany. This experimental school, especially in its Dessau phase, was the first to determine the ideological and formal boundaries of the design profession, its enriched sensitivities and sense of purpose.

The thrust of European Modernism was brought to America prior to World War II and, following the conflict on the crest of America's post-war economic boom, corporate identity became the goal of most businesses and industries. Every firm needed a new corporate logo or symbol, and a modern look became the norm for every business. Progressive American designers such as Lester Beall, Paul Rand and William Golden met the challenge and thus began the golden age of corporate identity in the United States. This worldwide impetus was to last well into the 1970s.

In the late 1980s, the ideals of Modernism were being critically reviewed and tested. Deconstructivism was a trend born from the postmodernist wish to replace

Modernism. Skeptics were asking, is Modernism just a style? Designers were also asking if a new design approach had temporary or permanent values. In response to their critics, objective minds felt that it was necessary to understand the difference between developing and replacing. As Vignelli has strongly stated, "Replacing Modernism implied a misunderstanding of the basic notion of Modernism. It is not a style but a dynamic attitude in continuous flux, with solid foundations based on rational processes. Styles are just the opposite, ephemeral manifestations of the speculative desires of producers." [3] While there remain doubters, for many of its supporters today Modernism is alive and well, because its *raison d'être* is permanent and its imperatives are historically valid. Its critics and its advocates continue to argue the case. In spite of this philosophical dichotomy of view, the Modernists still hold to their utopian goal of making the world better by design.

References Cited
[1] El Lissitzky: unpublished work
[2] Hollis, Richard: Swiss Graphic Design; Yale University Press, New Haven 2006; p.15
[3] Vignelli, Massimo: About Modernism; personal letter, 2012

13
AEG booklet from 1909 using the company's visual identity created by Peter Behrens

AEG-Werbebroschüre von 1909 im von Peter Behrens entwickelten Erscheinungsbild

Brochure AEG de 1909 utilisant l'identité visuelle de la firme créée par Peter Behrens

Es lebe die Moderne!
R. Roger Remington

Ganz allgemein gesprochen versteht man unter „Moderne" zeitgenössisches Denken, Sein und Handeln. Im engeren Kontext der Kunst ist die Moderne eine Reihe kultureller und verwandter Strömungen, die uns die Fähigkeit des Menschen bestätigen, seine Umgebung zu formen, zu verbessern und umzugestalten. Sie ist die Vorausschau einer Ideologie, zu der ein Verständnis für den Herstellungsprozess und die endgültige Bestimmung ihrer Produkte gehören.

Massimo Vignelli, der archetypische Designer der Moderne, nennt als Geburtsstunde seiner Epoche die Veröffentlichung von Diderots und d'Alemberts *Encyclopédie* in der Mitte des 18. Jahrhunderts. Dieses Werk gilt als großartigste Leistung der Aufklärung, einer in der Geschichte der Menschheit einzigartigen Übergangzeit von der Agrar- zur Industriegesellschaft, von einer durch die Religion bestimmten Kultur zu einer toleranten, fortschrittlichen Weltsicht. In der Enzyklopädie traten ein letztes Mal die Handwerke in den Vordergrund, gleichzeitig bot sie einen ersten Blick auf das neue Maschinenzeitalter. Zudem wurde dort bereits von der Notwendigkeit gesprochen, neue Methoden zur Gestaltung von Gegenständen zu entwickeln. Nicht mehr der Handwerker war Meister des Endprodukts, ein neuer Berufsstand bildete sich heraus: einer, der die von Maschinen hergestellten Produkte ersann, ob nun aus Glas oder Porzellan, Eisen oder Stoff, Papier oder Schrifttypen. Im Zuge der Aufklärung entwickelte sich eine neue Art des Denkens, die Menschen lebten in Aussicht auf eine neue soziale Ordnung. Die Französische Revolution trieb die Evolution des Menschen noch weiter voran, neue Gedanken verschafften sich Raum. Der moderne Mensch wurde geboren, ein Mensch, den keine erdrückenden, beengenden Schranken mehr behinderten. Neue Horizonte regten in allen Bereichen das Denken an, ob in der Wissenschaft oder der Kunst, in der Politik oder im Handel. Das Aufkommen der Dampfkraft Anfang des 19. Jahrhunderts versorgte die Industrie mit Energie. Hilfsmittel aller Art für die neuen Produktionsabläufe mussten entworfen werden, die Mechanisierung hielt überall Einzug, ob bei der Eisenbahn oder in der Textilindustrie. Selbst die Landwirtschaft wurde mechanisiert. Stahlbrücken überspannten die neue Ära. Alles war nun gestaltet – anfangs noch eher naiv, später sehr bewusst. In der Gestaltung fanden die neuen Technologien und das neue Empfinden ihren Ausdruck. Industrielle und technische Neuerungen haben immer auch soziale Veränderungen zur Folge, die wiederum die künstlerische Ausdruckskraft beeinflussen. Der kreative Ausdruck ist ein Spiegel, der unweigerlich die Gesellschaft reflektiert.

Marx und Engels verliehen der Notwendigkeit einer sozialen Gerechtigkeit ihre Stimme. Eine neue Sicht auf die *conditio humana* ließ neue Ideologien erstehen, in denen jeder Aspekt der Gesellschaft, die sich gerade aus der industriellen Revolution löste, abgedeckt wurde. Mitte des 19. Jahrhunderts plädierte William Morris als Reaktion auf die einfallslose Gestaltung von Objekten, zurückzuführen auf den falschen Einsatz der neuen industriellen Herstellungsweisen, für eine größere Aufmerksamkeit gegenüber der Gestaltung von Gegenständen, vom Möbelstück bis zur Textilie.

Mit Entwurf und Errichtung des Londoner Crystal Palace war die Moderne schließlich auch in der Architektur angekommen. Dieses unvergleichliche Bauwerk

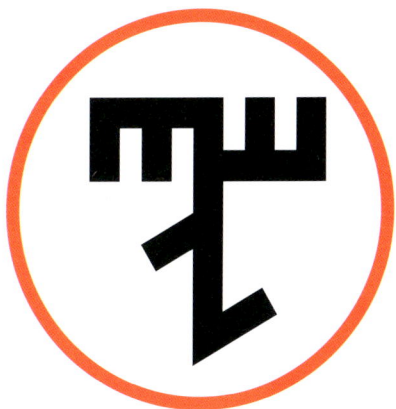

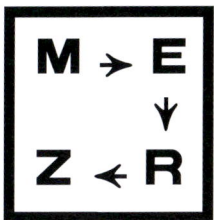

14
Logotypes by Karl Bültmann,
Kurt Schwitters, Hans Karl
Michel and Otto Firle (from left
to right) from the early 1920s

Logoentwürfe von Karl Bültmann,
Kurt Schwitters, Hans Karl Michel
und Otto Firle (von links nach rechts)
aus den frühen 1920er-Jahren

Logos conçus au début des
années 1920 par (de g. à dr.)
Karl Bültmann, Kurt Schwitters,
Hans Karl Michel et Otto Firle

aus Gusseisen und Glas wurde 1851 für die Great Exhibition im Londoner Hyde Park errichtet, bei der die neuesten Produkte aus aller Herren Länder vorgestellt wurden. Seine Gestaltung nahm die gläsernen Vorhangfassaden von Walter Gropius aus den 1920er-Jahren um Jahrzehnte vorweg.

Allmählich bildete sich ein Profil des modernen Designers heraus. In Deutschland galt Peter Behrens zu Anfang des 20. Jahrhunderts als Vorbild des modernen Industriedesigners. Seine Arbeit deckte alle Bereiche der Gestaltung ab und ließ neue Denkprozesse und neue Ausdrucksformen einfließen. Als erster Designer beschäftigte er sich auch mit den Ansprüchen der Industrie hinsichtlich ihrer Kommunikation. Er ist der eigentliche Erfinder der Corporate Identity, dem Ausdruck einer Firmenvision und der Verpflichtung zu Integrität und Qualität. Behrens war außerdem Gründungsmitglied des Deutschen Werkbunds, der eine wesentliche Rolle beim Zusammenspiel von Gestaltung und Industrie einnahm. Eine einflussreiche Veröffentlichung des Werkbunds aus dem Jahr 1921 mit dem Titel *XX Eigen-Marken* stellte erstmalig eine Reihe von Markenzeichen und Logotypen seiner Mitglieder vor, die vielfach mit den traditionellen Signets der damaligen Zeit brachen.

Auch andere europäische Bewegungen der Avantgarde lösten nach Kräften alle Verbindungen zur Vergangenheit und warteten mit eigenen Vorstellungen auf, um das moderne Design in Theorie und Praxis weiterzuentwickeln. Diese neue Welle kreativen Denkens und Handelns erstreckte sich über die bloße Gestaltung hinaus bis hin zu Malerei, Bildhauerei, Architektur, Tanz, Musik, Lyrik und weiter. Die Beiträge stammten aus vielen Teilen Europas. Die russischen Konstruktivisten führten die Liga der europäischen Avantgarde an, mit El Lissitzky als bahnbrechendem Gründungsvater der Bewegung. Für den revolutionären Vertreter der Moderne war „nicht einmal das Neue neu genug".[1] Die Pariser Maler des Kubismus legten neue Möglichkeiten nahe, die Welt zu sehen und visuelle Formen zu gestalten. Die niederländische Gruppe De Stijl sagte sich mit ihren eigenwilligen Erfindungen radikal von den traditionellen Formen los. Wie eines ihrer Mitglieder, der Maler Piet Mondrian, schrieb: „In jedem Moment der Vergangenheit waren alle Variationen der Vergangenheit ‚neu'. Aber es war nicht DAS Neue. Wir dürfen nicht vergessen, dass wir am Ende einer Kultur stehen, am Ende alles Alten."[2] Die Futuristen in Italien und die Dadaisten in der Schweiz und Berlin waren maßgeblich daran beteiligt, die Typografie zu befreien.

Geografischer Mittelpunkt vieler dieser dynamischen Veränderungen war Deutschland. Unter dem Vorsitz von Kurt Schwitters trafen sich 1927 Designer aus allen Teilen des Landes zur Gründung der als Ring Neuer Werbegestalter bekannten Gruppe. Dieser Kreis von Grafikern, dem neben Jan Tschichold, Max Burchartz und Willi Baumeister viele andere angehörten, organisierte in ganz Deutschland Ausstellungen und Versammlungen, in denen sie ihre fortschrittliche Grafik präsentierten und avantgardistische Ansätze ihres Gewerbes propagierten. Ein Großteil der europäischen Strömungen der Moderne fand sich im deutschen Bauhaus wieder. Diese experimentelle Schule legte, vor allem in ihrer Zeit in Dessau, als Erste die ideologischen und formalen Grenzen des gestaltenden Berufs fest und sprach von dem dafür erforderlichen Einfühlungsvermögen und dem Vorrang der Zweckdienlichkeit.

Der Grundgedanke der europäischen Moderne war schon vor dem Zweiten Welt-krieg nach Amerika gelangt. Im gewaltigen wirtschaftlichen Aufschwung der Nach-kriegszeit verlangten die meisten Unternehmen und Industrien der USA nach einer Corporate Identity. Jede Firma benötigte ein neues Logo oder Symbol, ein moderner Look wurde Norm für jedes Unternehmen. Fortschrittliche amerikanische Designer wie Lester Beall, Paul Rand und William Golden nahmen die Herausforderung an, und damit begann in den Vereinigten Staaten das goldene Zeitalter der Corporate Identity – ein weltweiter Siegeszug, der sich bis in die 1970er-Jahre hinein fortsetzen sollte.

Ende der 1980er-Jahre wurden die Ideale der Moderne einer kritischen Neu-bewertung unterzogen. Der Dekonstruktivismus als Trend entstand aus dem post-modernen Wunsch heraus, die Moderne abzulösen. Skeptiker erhoben die Frage, ob die Moderne nicht ein bloßer Stil sei. Auch Designer dachten darüber nach, ob ein neuer Gestaltungsansatz kurzzeitige oder dauerhafte Werte darstelle. Als Reaktion auf diese Kritik vertraten objektive Beteiligte die Ansicht, dass es notwendig sei, den Unterschied zwischen Entwickeln und Ersetzen zu verstehen. Wie Vignelli so nachdrücklich fest-stellte: „Die Moderne zu ersetzen – dem Gedanken liegt ein Missverständnis vom Grundkonzept der Moderne zugrunde. Sie ist kein Stil, sondern eine dynamische Ein-stellung, die ständig im Fluss ist, aber ein solides, auf rationalen Abläufen beruhendes Fundament hat. Ein Stil ist genau das Gegenteil davon, eine flüchtige Manifestation der spekulativen Wünsche der Hersteller."[3] Zweifler gibt es nach wie vor, aber für viele Fürsprecher der Moderne ist sie heute so jung wie eh und je, weil ihr Daseinsgrund nie veraltet und ihre Ansprüche historisch gerechtfertigt sind. Kritiker und Verteidiger stehen sich nach wie vor gegenüber. Und trotz dieser philosophischen Gegensätze halten die Vertreter der Moderne an ihrem utopischen Ziel fest, die Welt durch Design besser zu machen.

Literaturzitate
[1] Lissitzky, El: Unveröffentlichte Arbeit
[2] Hollis, Richard: Swiss Graphic Design; Yale University Press, New Haven 2006; S. 15
[3] Vignelli, Massimo: Über Modernismus; Persönlicher Brief, 2012

 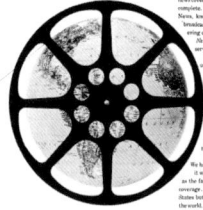

15

Examples of print advertising
for CBS Television, designed
by William Golden in 1951
and using his "eye" symbol
as main characteristic

Beispiele für Werbung des
Fernsehsenders CBS, 1951
von William Golden entworfen,
bei der sein markantes „Eye"-
Symbol im Mittelpunkt steht

Publicités de la chaîne de
télévision CBS, conçues en
1951 par William Golden autour
du célèbre symbole de l'œil

Vive la modernité !

R. Roger Remington

Dans son acception la plus large, la modernité est une pensée, un caractère ou une pratique attachés à la contemporanéité. Dans l'art, la modernité décrit un ensemble de tendances culturelles et de mouvements qui affirment le pouvoir de l'être humain de créer, améliorer et remanier son environnement. La modernité est la projection d'une idéologie consciente du processus de production et de la destination finale de ses produits.

Massimo Vignelli, designer moderne par excellence, fait remonter la naissance de la modernité à la publication de l'*Encyclopédie* de Diderot et d'Alembert au milieu du XVIIIe siècle. Ce travail a été la grande manifestation des Lumières, ce moment unique dans l'histoire de l'humanité qui marque le passage d'une société agraire à une société industrielle, d'une culture dominée par la religion à une vision du monde progressive et libérale. Dans l'*Encyclopédie* se trouvent à la fois la dernière expression de l'artisanat et une première approche de la nouvelle ère des machines. S'y manifeste aussi comme une évidence la nécessité de concevoir les objets manufacturés selon d'autres critères. L'artisan n'est plus le maître du produit final : un nouvel acteur apparaît, qui dessine les produits fabriqués par des machines – du verre à la porcelaine, de l'acier aux étoffes, du papier aux caractères d'imprimerie. Les Lumières ont donné naissance à une nouvelle manière de penser au moment où les gens vivaient dans l'attente d'un nouvel ordre social. Plus tard, la Révolution française donne un coup d'accélérateur à l'évolution humaine et insuffle une nouvelle vigueur à ces idées. L'homme moderne est né, l'homme libéré des chaînes de l'oppression et des limitations contraignantes du passé. De nouveaux horizons stimulent les esprits dans tous les domaines, des sciences aux arts, de la politique au commerce. Au début du XIXe siècle, l'avènement de la machine à vapeur stimule puissamment l'industrie. Les produits de tout type doivent être dessinés en fonction des nouveaux processus de fabrication. La mécanisation prend les rênes – du chemin de fer au textile. L'agriculture elle-même se mécanise. Les ponts en acier se tendent au-dessus de l'ère nouvelle. Tous les objets sont désormais « designés », d'abord un peu naïvement, plus tard d'une manière consciente qui permet aux nouvelles technologies et sensibilités de s'exprimer. Les évolutions industrielles et technologiques entraînent toujours dans leur sillage des changements sociaux qui affectent à leur tour l'expression artistique. Les expressions créatives deviennent toujours un miroir qui reflète la société.

Marx et Engels se sont fait les porte-parole du besoin d'une justice sociale différente. Une nouvelle manière d'aborder la condition humaine donne naissance à de nouvelles idéologies qui couvrent tous les aspects de la société née de la révolution industrielle. Au milieu du XIXe siècle, William Morris réagit contre la morosité stylistique due à l'utilisation impropre des nouveaux processus industriels et prône une attention nouvelle au design des produits – des meubles aux tissus.

La conception et la construction du Crystal Palace à Londres annoncent l'émergence de la modernité en architecture. Ce bâtiment tout à fait unique en fonte et en verre fut construit à Hyde Park à l'occasion de l'Exposition universelle de 1851, qui présentait les produits les plus récents de nombreuses nations. Son design anticipait de bien des années les murs-rideaux en verre que l'architecte Gropius allait concevoir dans les années 1920.

Le profil du designer moderne commence à prendre forme. Dès le début du XXᵉ siècle, en Allemagne, Peter Behrens est le modèle du designer industriel moderne. Son travail couvre tout le champ d'application du design en s'appuyant sur des processus mentaux et des modes d'expression inédits. Behrens fut le premier designer à répondre au besoin de communication de l'industrie et le véritable inventeur de l'identité graphique, qui donne une expression visuelle à l'engagement d'intégrité et de qualité de l'entreprise. Behrens fut aussi membre fondateur du Deutscher Werkbund, qui jouera un rôle de premier plan en conciliant design et industrie. En 1921, une mémorable publication du Werkbund intitulée *XX Eigen-Marken* (Vingt marques maison) présente pour la première fois un recueil de marques et de logotypes créés par ses membres, dont beaucoup rompent avec les formes d'identité graphique traditionnelles qui prévalent à l'époque.

D'autres mouvements d'avant-garde européens ont contribué de leur mieux à rompre les ponts avec le passé traditionnel et à élaborer la pensée et les pratiques du design moderne. Cette nouvelle vague d'activité intellectuelle et créative déborde vers bien des domaines situés au-delà du design : peinture, sculpture, architecture, danse, musique, poésie, etc. Ses contributeurs sont originaires de nombreuses régions d'Europe. Les constructivistes russes sont les principaux acteurs de l'avant-garde européenne. El Lissitzky est le père absolu du mouvement. Pour ce champion de la modernité, « même la nouveauté n'était pas assez nouvelle. »[1] À Paris, les peintres cubistes inaugurent de nouvelles manières de voir le monde et de concevoir la forme visuelle. En Hollande, les membres du groupe De Stijl enrichissent de leurs inventions tout à fait uniques cet effort pour se libérer radicalement des formes traditionnelles. L'un d'entre eux, le peintre Piet Mondrian, écrit alors : « De tout temps, toutes les variations passées ont été "nouvelles". Mais ce n'était pas LA nouveauté. N'oublions pas que nous nous trouvons à la fin d'une culture, à la fin de tout ce qui est ancien. »[2] Les futuristes en Italie et les dadaïstes en Suisse et à Berlin ont joué un rôle majeur dans la libération de la typographie.

Le centre de toute cette dynamique du changement est l'Allemagne. En 1927, des designers de nombreuses régions d'Allemagne forment autour de Kurt Schwitters un groupe connu sous le nom de « Ring Neuer Werbegestalter » (Cercle des nouveaux graphistes publicitaires), dont les membres comptent notamment Jan Tschichold, Max Burchartz, Willi Baumeister, pour n'en citer que quelques-uns. Ce groupe de graphistes organise des expositions et des rencontres dans toute l'Allemagne, présentant leur graphismes progressifs et défendant l'approche avant-gardiste de leur travail. Une bonne part de l'expression moderne européenne a été unifiée au Bauhaus en Allemagne. Cette école expérimentale, particulièrement pendant la phase de Dessau, fut la première à définir les lignes idéologiques et formelles du métier de designer, de ses sensibilités enrichies et de son sens utilitaire.

La vague de la modernité arrive aux États-Unis avant la Seconde Guerre mondiale. À l'apogée du boom économique d'après-guerre, la définition de l'identité visuelle devient l'objectif de la plupart des entreprises et industries américaines.

Toutes ont alors besoin d'un nouveau logo ou symbole. Une image moderne est la norme pour toute entreprise. Les designers américains progressistes comme Lester Beall, Paul Rand et William Golden relèvent le défi, marquant le début de l'âge d'or de la *corporate identity* aux États-Unis. Les effets de cette dynamique mondiale seront encore perceptibles pendant une bonne partie des années 1970.

À la fin des années 1980, une révision critique soumet les idéaux de la modernité à rude épreuve. Le déconstructivisme est une mode née du désir de remplacer la modernité. Les sceptiques se demandent si la modernité n'est qu'un style et les designers s'interrogent à leur tour pour savoir si une nouvelle approche du design est porteuse de valeurs temporaires ou permanentes. En réponse à leurs critiques, les esprits objectifs ressentent la nécessité de faire comprendre la différence entre remplacement et évolution. Comme Vignelli l'a déclaré avec une grande pertinence : « Remplacer la modernité relevait d'un malentendu touchant la notion fondamentale de modernité. La modernité n'est pas seulement un style, mais une attitude dynamique en perpétuel mouvement, avec des bases solides reposant sur des processus rationnels. Les styles en sont l'exact contraire : des manifestations éphémères des désirs spéculatifs des fabricants. »[3] Si les incrédules persistent, pour beaucoup de ses défenseurs la modernité est aujourd'hui vivante et se porte bien parce que sa raison d'être est d'ordre permanent et que ses impératifs ont une validité historique. Entrée détracteurs et défenseurs de la modernité, le débat se poursuit. Malgré la divergence des points de vue, les modernes restent fidèles à leur objectif utopique d'améliorer le monde par le design.

Références des citations
[1] Lissitzky, El : Travail non publié
[2] Hollis, Richard : Swiss Graphic Design, Yale University Press, New Haven 2006, p. 15
[3] Massimo Vignelli à propos de la modernité : lettre personnelle, 2012

R. Roger Remington is Vignelli Distinguished Professor Emeritus of Design at the Vignelli Center for Design Studies at Rochester Institute of Technology, Rochester, New York, USA

R. Roger Remington ist emeritierter Vignelli Distinguished Professor of Design des Vignelli Center for Design Studies am Rochester Institute of Technology, Rochester, New York, USA

R. Roger Remington est professeur émérite de design du Vignelli Center for Design Studies à l'Institut de technologie de Rochester, New York, États-Unis

G

Different periods in the relatively short history of design are marked either by a trend towards greater simplicity or a counter-trend away from it. Such changes of approach were probably at the root of the conflict many graphic artists experienced between free artistic expression and commercial design. Modernist designers gladly seized on the rules and visual vocabulary of geometry. Circles, triangles, rectangles and squares were able to transmit clear and emphatic signs. Many successful logos also incorporated visual references to the advertiser's name and/or line of business. This sometimes means that a second or even a third look at the logo is required to interpret the full meaning.

Die unterschiedlichen Epochen der noch relativ jungen Designgeschichte sind bestimmt durch den Trend hin zu bzw. den Gegentrend weg von einer verstärkten Sachlichkeit in der Gestaltung. Hier spiegelt sich vermutlich der in vielen Gestalter-persönlichkeiten steckende Zwiespalt zwischen freiem künstlerischem Ausdruck und einem – weniger anfechtbaren – verwissenschaftlichten Entwurf wider. Moder-nistische Gestalter griffen die Geometrie mit ihrer Formensprache und ihrem Regel-werk jedenfalls dankbar auf. Aus Kreisen, Dreiecken, Rechtecken oder Quadraten konstruierten sie eindeutige und kraftvolle Zeichen. Das Einfügen von visuellen Hinweisen auf den Namen oder die Tätigkeit des jeweiligen Unternehmens gelang dennoch in vielen Fällen. Hierzu ist beim Betrachter jedoch mitunter ein zweiter oder dritter Blick auf das Zeichen notwendig.

Les différentes époques de l'histoire encore relativement jeune du graphisme sont marquées par la tendance à une sobriété créative accrue, ou bien par le courant opposé qui s'en éloigne. Ceci traduit sans doute le dilemme de bien des graphistes entre création artistique libre et travail le plus scientifique possible, c'est-à-dire inattaquable. Le fait est que les graphistes modernes ont été heureux d'accueillir dans leur travail la géométrie, avec son langage formel et son cortège de règles. À partir de cercles, de triangles, de rectangles ou de carrés, ils ont conçu des signes aussi clairs que puissants. L'intégration de références visuelles aux noms ou à l'activité des entre-prises concernées n'en a pas moins été réussie dans bien des cas. Il est vrai que ces réalisations nécessitent parfois un second ou un troisième regard.

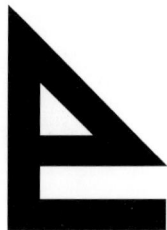

Light Publicity
Design
1962 · Makoto Wada · JP

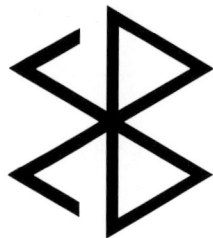

Ernst Beutler
Interior design
1940s · Hans Hartmann · CH

**2nd Congresso Panamericano
de Arquitetos, São Paulo**
Architectural congress
1962 · João Carlos Cauduro · BR

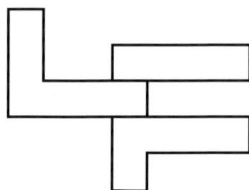

Lamm-Frates Company
Real estate
1971 · Crawford Dunn · US

Securit SA
Office furniture
1961 · Alexandre Wollner · BR

Sola y Tortas
Lighting systems
1972 · Lydia Casellas · ES

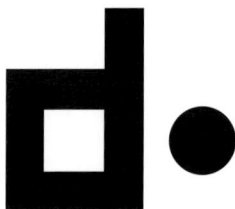

Dewag-Dia-Dresden
Photographic services
1965 · Johannes Brase · DE-GDR

M. Medicke
Industrial trade
1965 · Peter Mantwill · DE-GDR

Enciclopedia Fatos e Fotos
Publishing
1966 · Pinto Ziraldo · BR

Companhia General de Minas
Mining
1962 · Alexandre Wollner · BR

Klingenthal
Textiles
1960s · Anonymous · DE

Takahashi Shoji
Industrial recycling
1960s · Nakajo Masayoshi · JP

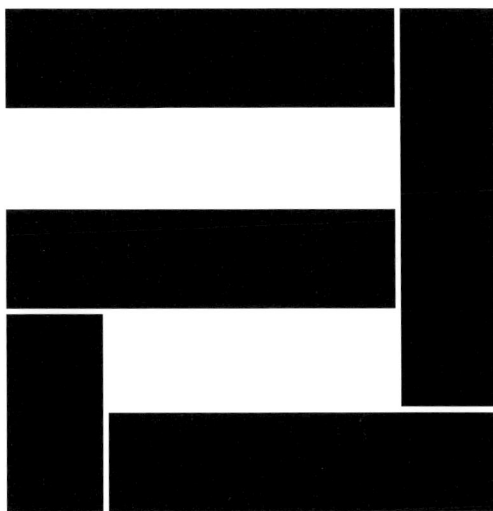

Artwood Büromöbel
Office furniture
1960s · Ernst Roch · CA

Sanyo Electric
1970 · Tomoichi Nishiwaki,
Inada Akira · JP

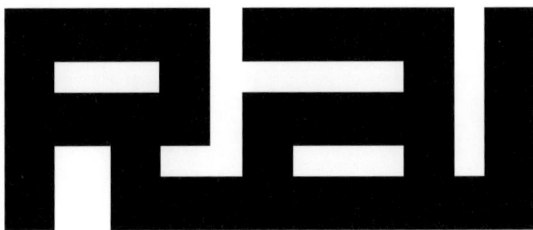

RAI Radiotelevisione Italiana
Broadcasting
1954 · Erberto Carboni · IT

Ingenieurbüro für Planung und
Steuerungssysteme
Planning and control systems
1973 · Heinz Schwabe · DE

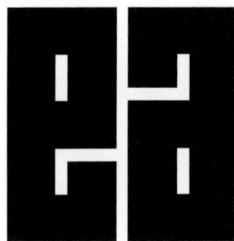

Europäisch-Arabische Bank,
Frankfurt am Main
1973 · Heinz Schwabe · DE

Indústrias Paramount
Clothing
1963 · Alexandre Wollner · BR

Witthöft Werk für Spulenkörper &
Isoliererzeugnisse
Heating technology
1965 · Johannes Brase · DE-GDR

Marketing Italia S.p.A.
Research institute
1960s · Cecco Re · IT

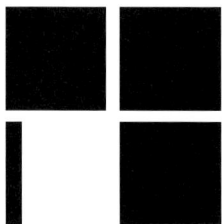

Philosophische Bibliothek, Hamburg
Publishing
1989 · Jens Peter Mardersteig · DE

Weimar-Werk
Machinery
1965 · Fritz Deutschendorf · DE-GDR

Ediciones Mundonuevo
Publishing
1950s · Rómulo Macció · AR

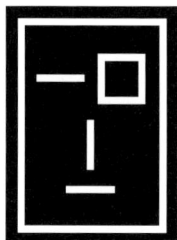

Jana
1970s · Hannes Schober,
Wolfram Reinhardt · DE

P.I.E. Facilities
Life insurance
1971 · Arthur Eckstein · US

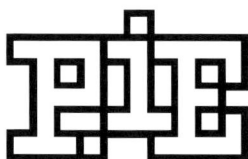

Bonifica
Landscape planning
1968 · Enzo Mari · IT

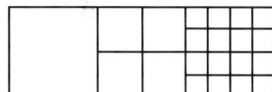

Muster-Schmidt Verlagsgesellschaft
Publishing
1905 · Christian Hansen-Schmidt · DE

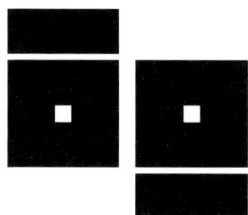

Action Graphique Paris
Design
1959 · Gérard Ifert · FR

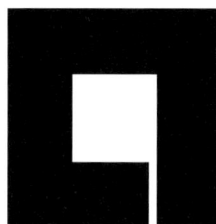

I.J.J. Koroknay & Associates
Urban planning
1967 · Imre Koroknay · CA

Treffpunkt
Television show
1979 · Odermatt+Tissi · CH

Welthandelsfirma
Import-export
1980 · Odermatt+Tissi · CH

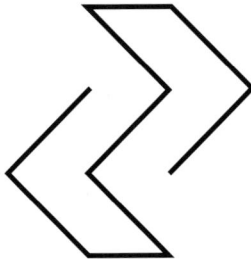

Ministerium für Verkehr
Department of transport
(proposed design)
1970s · Helmut Schmid · DE

SIMAT Italestero
Postal services
1971 · Ornella Noorda · IT

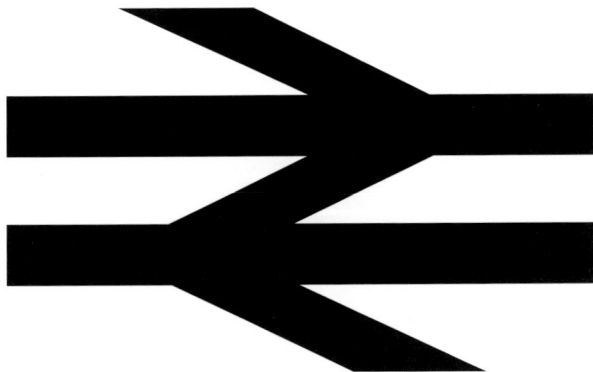

British Railways Board
Public transport
1964 · Gerald Barney, Milner Gray, Rupert Armstrong,
Collis Clements/Design Research Unit · UK

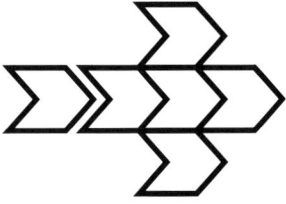

Ullian
Publishing
1962 · Etienne Bucher · FR

Import-Export
1960s · Andrzej Zbrozek · PL

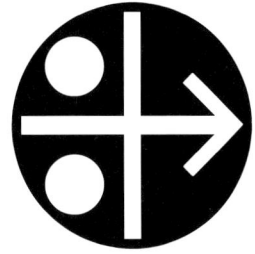

Schweizerische Reisekasse
Travel fund
1960s · Rudolf Bircher · CH

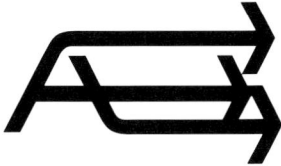

Committee of Aluminum Producers
1960s · Saul Bass · US

Ferrovie Nord Milano
Public transport
1981 · R. Nava, D. Soffientini,
A. Ubertazzi · IT

SGS
Microcircuit sales conference
1965 · Bob Noorda/
Unimark International · IT

Chemdorff
Chemicals
1970 · Francisco Marco Vilar/
Grupo de Diseño · ES

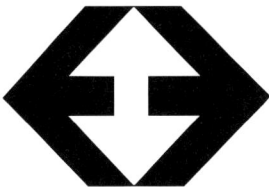

Austral Líneas Aéreas
Airline
1966 · Guillermo Gonzáles Ruiz · AR

Nederlandse Spoorwegen
Public transport
1967 · Tel Design Associated · NL

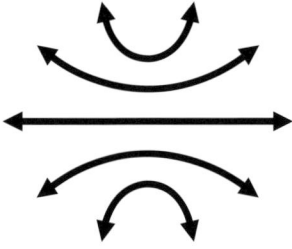

Corning Class
Works foundation
1974 · Robert Hagenhofer · US

Coco Ernesto Transportes
Transport
1976 · Jorge Sposari · AR

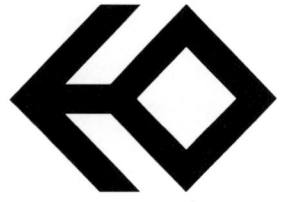

Ediciones de Occidente
Publishing
1964 · Amand Domènech · ES

**Centre d'Etudes et de Développement
des Relations Internationales**
Student exchange program
1968 · Jacques Douin · FR

Flugsýningin 1969
Aviation history exhibition
1969 · Thröstur Magnusson, Hilmar
Sigurdsson/Argus Advertising · IS

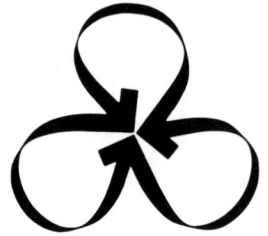

Carrefour de la Belle Epine
Shopping center
1969 · Théodore Stamatakis/
Créations Stama · FR

Fotograbado Vene
Prepress services
1967 · Gerd Leufert · VE

Montello Tour
Tourism
1977 · Peter Vetter · IT

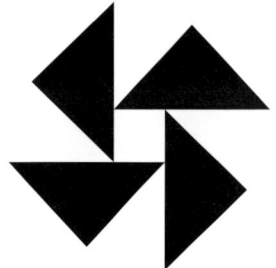

Sarag
Advertising
1965 · Anonymous · DE

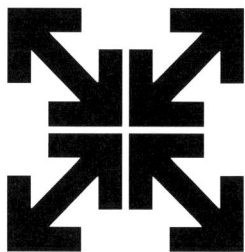

Park City Hospital
1978 · Joe Dieter · US

City of Emeryville
City identity
1973 · William Carson,
Douglas Williams · US

Ximenes Hnos
Import-export
1960s · Gerd Leufert · VE

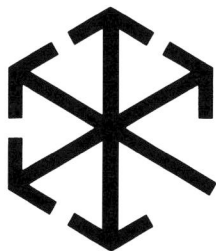

Ingeniörforlaget
Publishing
1967 · Bruno Oldani · NO

Museum Voor Schone Kunsten, Ghent
Art museum
1967 · Antoon de Vijlder · BE

Instituto Mexicano de Opinión Pública
Market research
1975 · Ernesto Lehfeld · MX

293

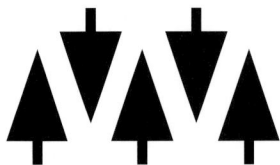

West Coast Landscape Construction
Landscape design
1960s · Conrad E. Angone · US

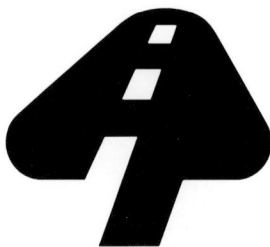

Road Construction Enterprise
Highway construction
1980 · Ivan Dvoršak,
Matjaz Bertonceli · YU

Moldoplast
Plastics
1965 · Amand Domènech · ES

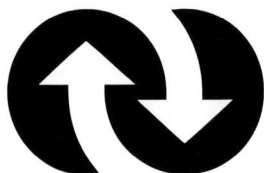

New Life Movement Association
Civic education
1975 · Kiyoshi Kyoi · JP

Brødr. Søyland
Construction machines
1965 · Erik Fjellberg · NO

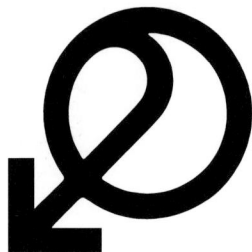

La Nouvelle Encyclopédie
Publishing
1960s · Christin Delorme · FR

**Werbeagentur Gerber, Geiß,
Kunert & Co.**
Advertising
1972 · Rainer E. Kunert · DE

Bunka
Publishing
1970 · Shigeo Fukuda · JP

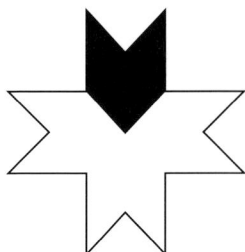

John Sandwick Studios
Design
1969 · Bill Hyde · US

Asphalt Roofing
Building materials
1983 · Terry Lesniewicz/Al Navarre · US

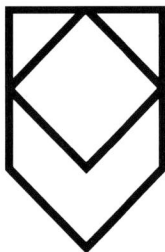

Indústrias Villares
Construction company
1967 · João Carlos Cauduro,
Ludovico Antonio Martino · BR

Swissair
Airline
1952 · Rudolf Bircher · CH

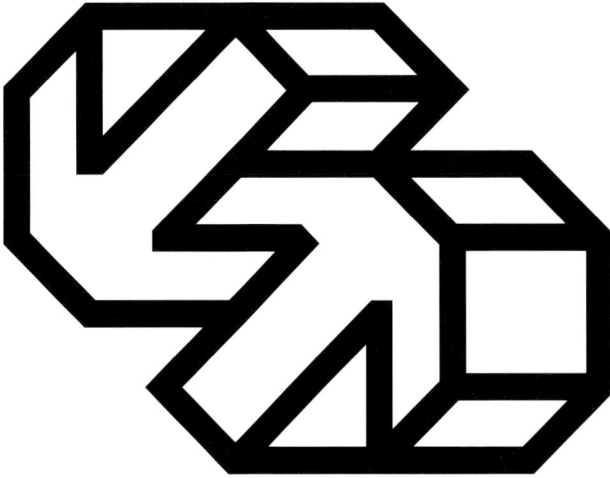

Camera di Commercio I.A.A. di Milano
Chamber of commerce
(part of integrated logo system)
1972 · Mimmo Castellano · IT

Design-Zentrum Baden-Württemberg
Design association
1956 · Herbert W. Kapitzki · DE

Japan Socialist Party
1961 · Makoto Wada · JP

Neuenschwander, Bern
Thermal engineering
1950s · Robert Sessler · CH

Hecker Elektronik
Electronics
1976 · Manfred Wutke · DE

De Wolf
Advertising
1960s · De Wolf · BE

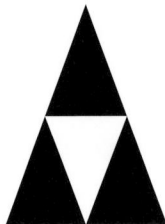

Bede Aircraft
Kit-plane manufacturer
1961 · Read Viemeister/
Vie Design Studios · US

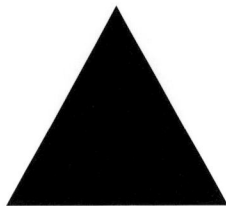

Japan General Arts Corporation
1970 · Gan Hosoya · JP

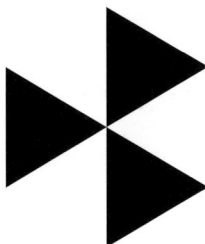

Diethelm Werbeagentur
Advertising
1964 · Walter J. Diethelm · CH

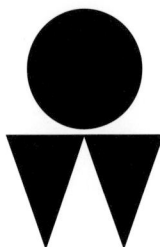

M. H. D. Odziez Włókno
Textiles
1964 · Andrzej Zbrozek · PL

P. A. Fitzgerald & Co.
Engineering
1960s · Raymond Kyne · IE

Aero-Cargo
Air freight
1965 · Félix Beltrán · CU

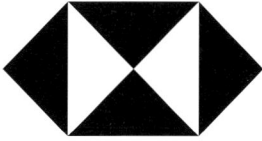

**Hongkong and Shanghai
Banking Corporation**
1983 · Henry Steiner · HK

SJV Warmtecentrum
Thermal engineering
1966 · Benno Wissing/Total Design · NL

Moffitt & McDaniel
Architecture
1971 · Ray Engle · US

W. S. Inwalidów
1972 · Kazimierz Mann,
Jarosław Jasiński · PL

Jewish Foundation
Cultural organization
1960s · Ivan Chermayeff, Heiner
Hegemann/Chermayeff & Geismar · US

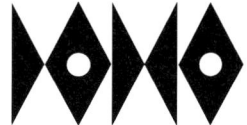

Norconsult
Management consultancy
1968 · Bruno Oldani · NO

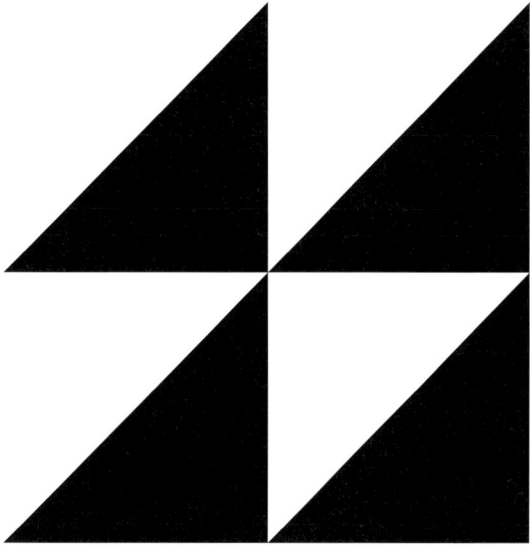

Nizzoli Associati
Urban planning
1965 · A. G. Fronzoni · IT

Domo
Grocery
1956 · Hanns Lohrer · DE

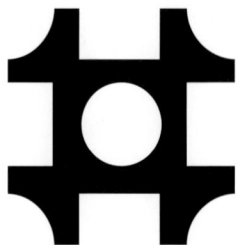

Holland, Hannen & Cubitts
Construction company
1958 · Romek Marber · UK

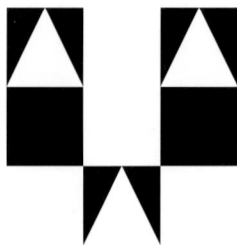

S. C. Fromagerie
Foods
1965 · Luc Van Malderen · BE

Stabilimenti Chimici Italiani
Chemicals
1968 · A. G. Fronzoni · IT

American Motors Corporation
Automobile company
1969 · Walter P. Margulies/
Lippincott & Margulies · US

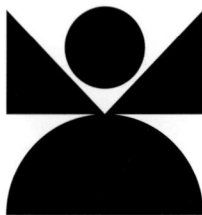

Mlad
Wooden toys
1974 · František Bobáň · CZ

FRESPO Fresas de Exportación
Import-export
1977 · Jaime Gutierrez Lega · CO

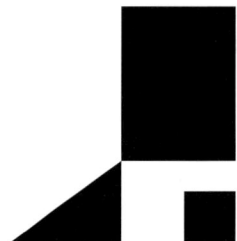

Schuhhersteller
Footwear
1972 · Jerzy Leontiew · PL

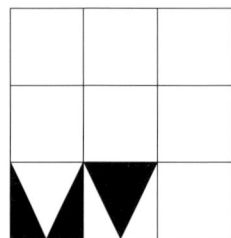

Münchner Volkshochschule
Education
1973 · Rolf Müller · DE

Novum
Design group
1958 · Helmut Lortz · DE

Gense
Stainless steel
1960s · Rolf Lagerson, Stig Bark · SE

Brazilian Institute of Geography and Statistics
1960s · Magalhães, Noronha & Pontual · BR

Institut d'Esthétique Industrielle, Brussels
Industrial design institute
1960 · Michel Olyff · BE

Sten Jacobsson Konsult
Management consultancy
1950s · Lars Bramberg · SE

Schweizerische Bundesbahn, Bern
Federal railway
1970 · Kurt Wirth · CH

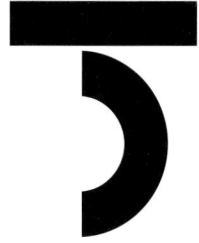

Deciep
1972 · Félix Beltrán · CU

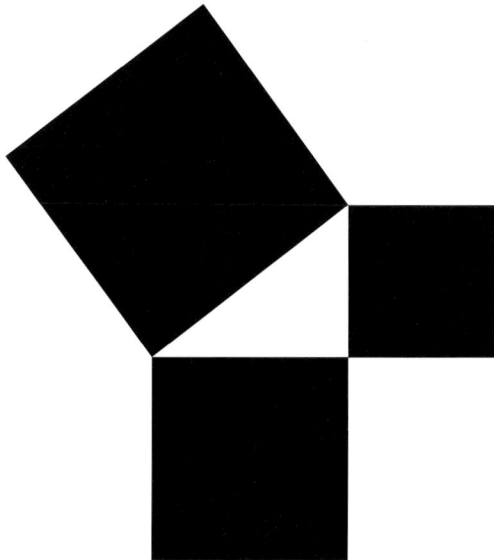

Club You May
Nightclub
1969 · Tomoichi Nishiwaki, Akisato Ueda · JP

Industrial Trainers
1965 · John Gibbs, T.J. Attwood/ Unit Five Design · UK

Financial Parameters, Willowdale
Investment
1970 · Manfred Gotthans, Chris Yaneff/Chris Yaneff · CA

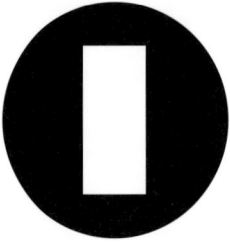

Order-Mation
Electronic automation
1963 · David J. Goodman/
Porter & Goodman Design · US

Oral Editora
Publishing
1968 · Pinto Ziraldo · BR

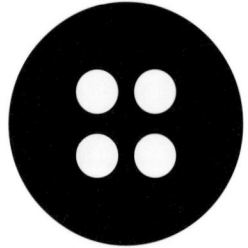

Muestra
Market research
1961 · Rómulo Macció · AR

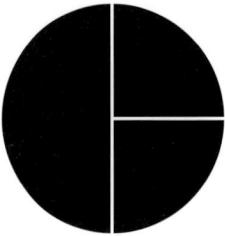

Chicago Graphics
Printing
1970s · James Lienhart · US

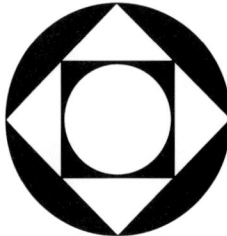

Summa Corporation
Business investment management
1971 · Mario Zamparelli,
Jean-Claude Müller · US

Crystalex Nový Bor
Glass
1983 · Vincenc Kutáč,
Stanislav Kovár · CZ

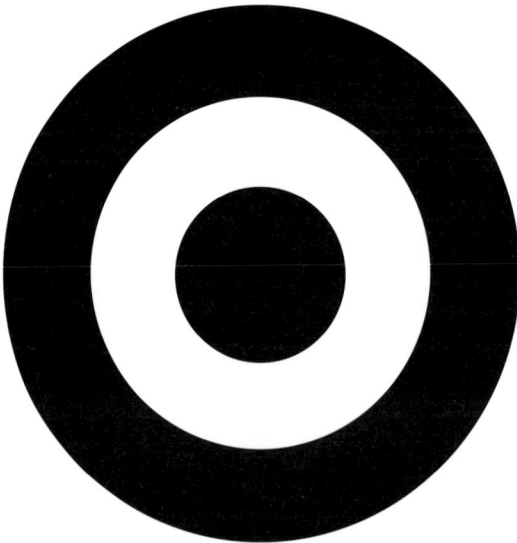

Pam
Fuel oil
1966 · Benno Wissing,
George Koizumi/Total Design · NL

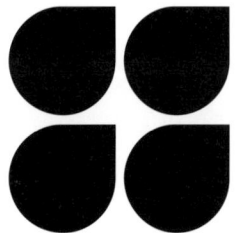

Target
Supermarket chain
1970 · Unimark International · US

Pam
Fuel oil
1966 · Benno Wissing,
George Koizumi/Total Design · NL

Eiran Lämpö
Plumbing
1969 · Jukka Veistola/Sok · FI

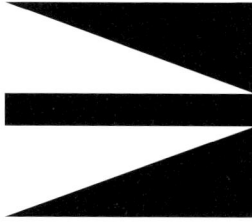

The British National Export Council
1962 · Negus & Negus · UK

British Ministry of Transport Test Station
Vehicle certification
1959 · Kinneir, Calvert & Associates · UK

Gruppo Bodino
Architecture
1979 · Giovanni Brunazzi · IT

Terra-Bio-Chemie
Chemicals
1967 · Paul Klahn · DE

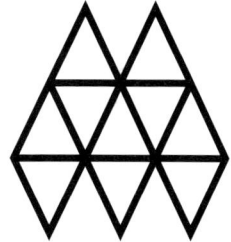

Associated Colleges of the Midwest
1968 · Charles MacMurray/
Latham Tyler Jensen · US

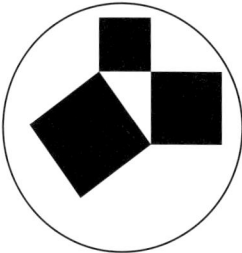

Deutsche Feinmechanik und Optik
Trade organization for optical products
1982 · Rolf Müller · DE

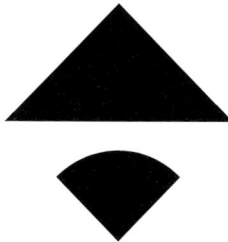

Viscosuisse
Textiles
1965 · Hans Hurter · CH

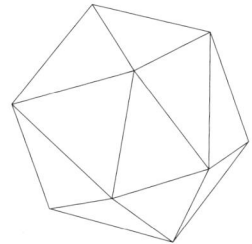

Robert Zeidman Associates
Industrial design
1960s · George Tscherny · US

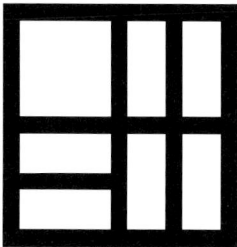

Light Metal Founders Association
1968 · Roger O. Denning · UK

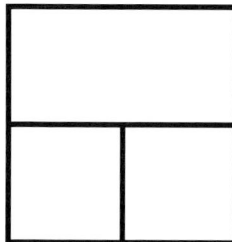

Taniguchi, Takamiya & Associates
Architecture
1980 · Takenobu Igarashi,
Akinori Nagao · JP

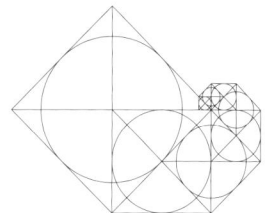

Hans Winterhager
Engineering
1960s · Klaus Winterhager · DE

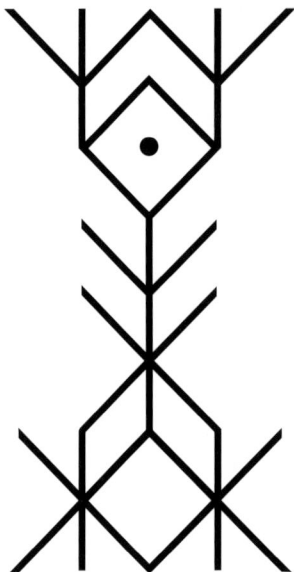

Shinichi Kusamori
Publishing
1969 · Makoto Wada · JP

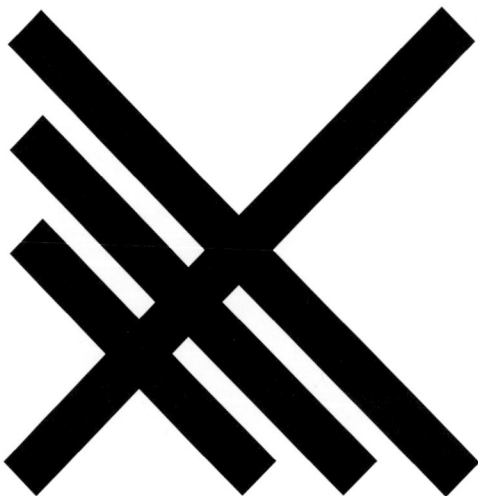

Photolithographic School
1960s · Gerd Leufert · VE

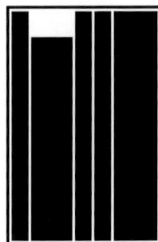

Fehr'scher Taschenbuchladen, St. Gallen
Bookstore
1960s · Jost Hochuli · CH

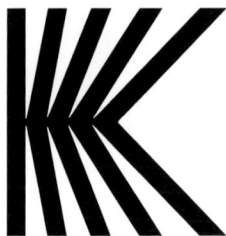

Kanbe
Textiles
1973 · Akisato Ueda · JP

Arteper
Art center
1972 · A. G. Fronzoni · IT

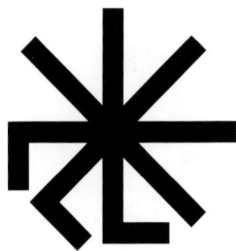

Annual of Architects
1971 · Dicken Castro · CO

Pacific Data Images
Computer animation
1983 · Kip Reynolds · US

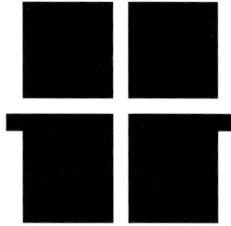

Kobe Shinbun Shuppan
Publishing
1975 · Yoshitake Komoriya · JP

Chrysler
Automobiles
1962 · Lippincott & Margulies · US

Tequila Mexicano
Alcoholic drinks
1982 · Félix Beltrán,
Teresa Echartea · CU/MX

Congreso Interamericano de Vivienda
Housing congress
1968 · Gerd Leufert · VE

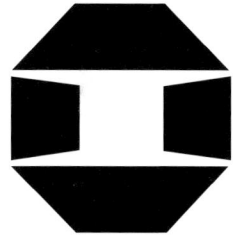

Icomi Minérios
Mining
1962 · PVDI · BR

Macmillan of Canada
Publishing
1967 · Leslie Smart · CA

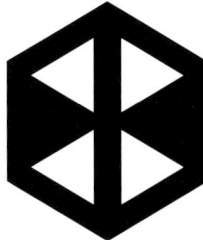

Schmolz & Bickenbach
Steel
1957 · Wolf D. Zimmermann · DE

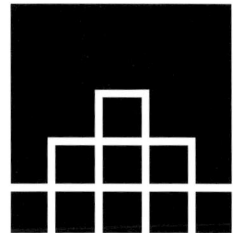

Kulturhistorisches Museum
1965 · Hans Schlapmann · DE-GDR

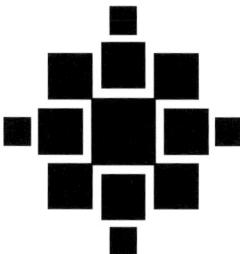

Diatech
1989 · Gil L. Strunck · BR

Akustik-Ground Tongeräte
Sound equipment
1980 · Klaus Richter · DE

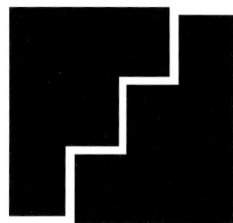

Financiera Faciema
Bank
1975 · Guillermo Gonzáles Ruiz · AR

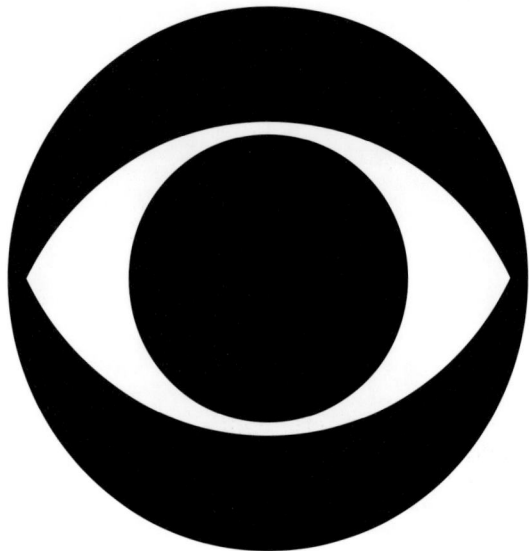

CBS Television
Broadcasting
1954 · William Golden · US

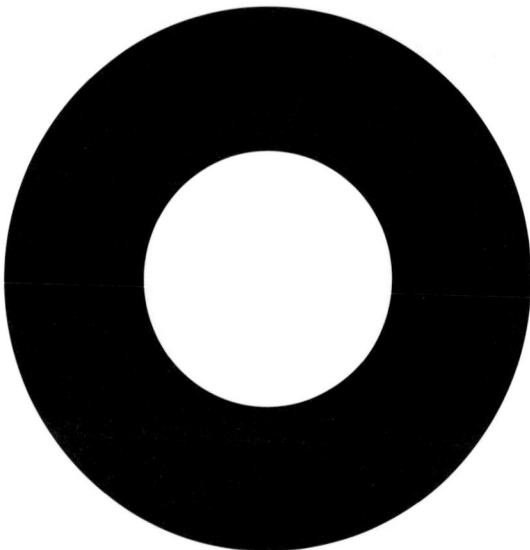

Blue Circle Group
Cement and paints
1966 · Henrion Design Associates · UK

Girsberger
Furniture
1955 · Carl B. Graf · CH

Nissan Koku Service
Travel agency
1981 · Tadasu Fukano · JP

The Nihon Keizai Shimbun
Economics journal
1966 · Hiromu Hara/Nippon Design Center · JP

Disco-Partes
Automobile parts
1968 · John Lange · VE

Dayton Hudson Corporation
Retail
1970s · Vance Jonson · US

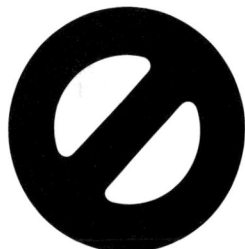

The Nihon Keizai Shimbun
Economics journal
1966 · Hiromu Hara/
Nippon Design Center · JP

Buchreihe über Sozialarbeit
Publishing
1980 · Anonymous · DE

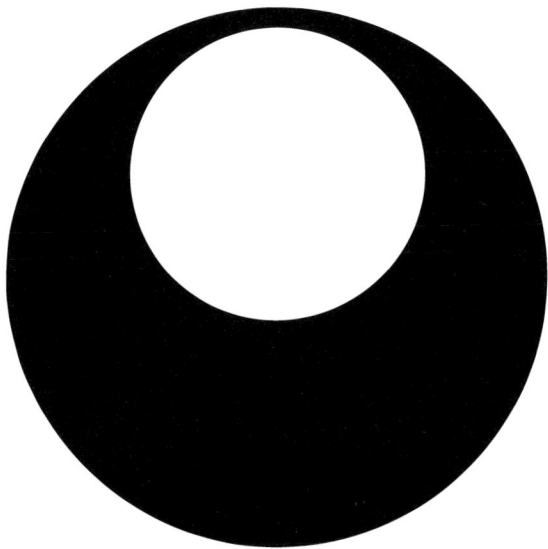

Willi Pfanner
Printing
1968 · Christian Lippauer · CH

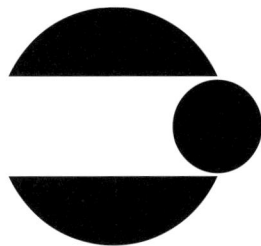

TransCanada Pipelines
Energy supplier
1969 · E. J. Morrison/
Stewart & Morrison · CA

Enertec
Solar energy
1979 · Jorge Sposari · AR

Schule für Kinder Stiftung
Charity
1985 · Niklaus Troxler · CH

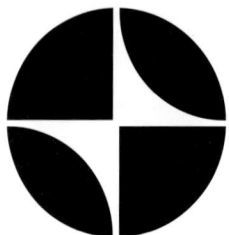

Meer-Terrasse
Real estate
1976 · Bruno K. Wiese · DE

**International Union of
Geodesy and Geophysics**
1968 · Hansruedi Widmer/Devico AG · CH

Jung-Kang Spice
Spices
1960s · T. S. Jisang · CN

Le Point
Publishing
1966 · Michel Waxman · BE

Milgrom
Textiles
1970 · Rolf Strub/Mafia · FR

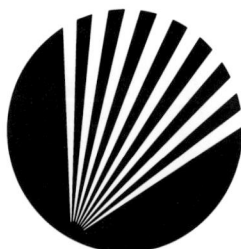

Japan Amateur Sports Association
1974 · Kazumasa Nagai · JP

Seiko Shoji
1983 · Yasuhisa Iguchi · JP

Boston Belting Company
1895 · US

ABC7 Los Angeles
Broadcasting
1970s · G. Dean Smith · US

Der Kinderbuchverlag
Publishing
1971 · Sonja Wunderlich · DE-GDR

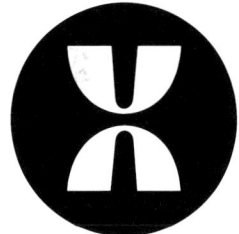

The Citizens Bank of Kuwait
1980 · Young Jae Cho · KR

Nippon Cultural Broadcasting Systems
1958 · Kenji Ito · JP

Howard Miller Clock Co.
Watches
1960s · Irving Harper/
George Nelson & Co. · US

Royal Micrographics
Microphotography systems
1969 · Primo Angeli · US

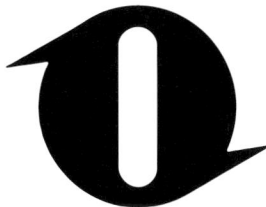

OriolAvia Soviet Avstriskoe
Aviation
1967 · Vladimir Chaika · RU

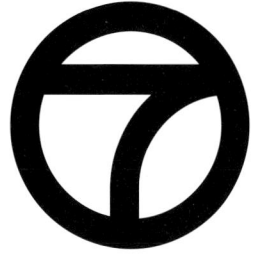

Schweizerischer Werkbund, Bern
Craft association
1962 · Marcel Wyss · CH

Boehringer Kinderpräparate
Pharmaceuticals
1965 · Wolf D. Zimmermann · DE

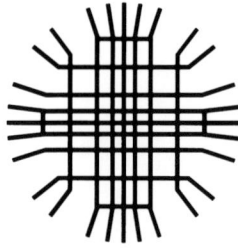

Carlos Celis Arquitectos, Caracas
Architect
1969 · Gerd Leufert · VE

Slieve Bawn Co-operative
Crafts
1974 · Peter Dabinett · IE

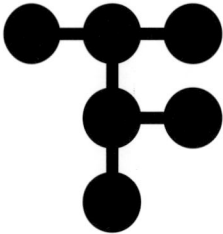

Telefusion
Broadcasting
1962 · Atelier Stadelmann Bisig · CH

**Conseil du Centenaire
de la Confédération**
Commemorative foundation
1966 · George Huel · CA

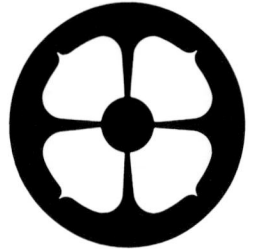

Schwaderlapp Keramik
Ceramics
1962 · Jupp Ernst · DE

Ceag Grubenlampen
Mining lamps
1963 · Walter Breker · DE

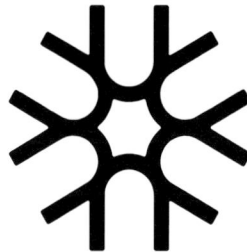

Union
1970s · Robert Hagenhofer · US

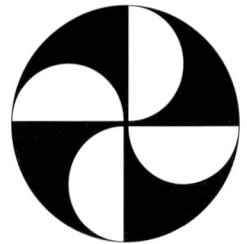

People Plus
Employment agency
1970 · Leslie Smart · CA

Postisäästöpankki
Bank
1960 · Pauli Numminen · FI

Copp Clark
Financial markets advisor
1973 · Gottschalk+Ash · CA

Companhia Sol de Seguros
Insurance
1960s · Aloísio Magalhães/PVDI · BR

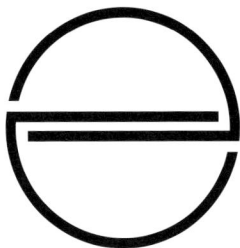

Krankenpflegeschule Zürich
Medical school
1960s · Students of Kunstgewerbeschule
Zürich · CH

Izrom
Light bulbs
1972 · Asher Kalderon · IL

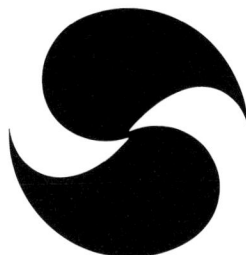

P. Wellhauser Super-Jet
Lawn sprinklers
1959 · Michel Martina · CH/FR

F.lli Oggioni
Furniture
1958 · Giulio Confalonieri, Ilio Negri · IT

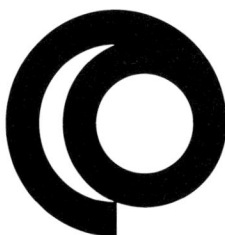

Feldmühle
Paper
1963 · Wolfgang Heuwinkel · DE

Hydroscience
Water pollution control
1970s · Robert Hagenhofer · US

San Lorenzo
Silverware
1970 · G. & R. Associati · IT

Staten Island Mental Health Society
1970s · Robert Hagenhofer · US

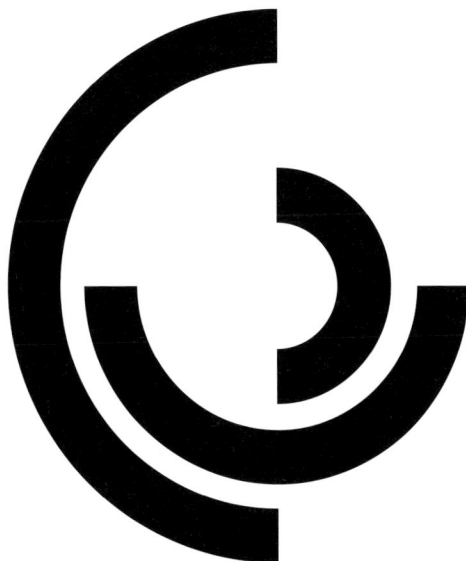

12th Triennale di Milano
Architecture and industrial art exhibition
1959 · Roberto Sambonet · IT

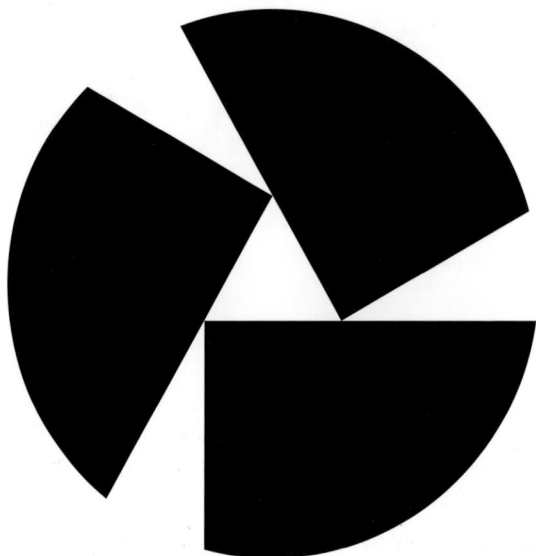

Banco Nacional
Bank
1974 · PVDI · BR

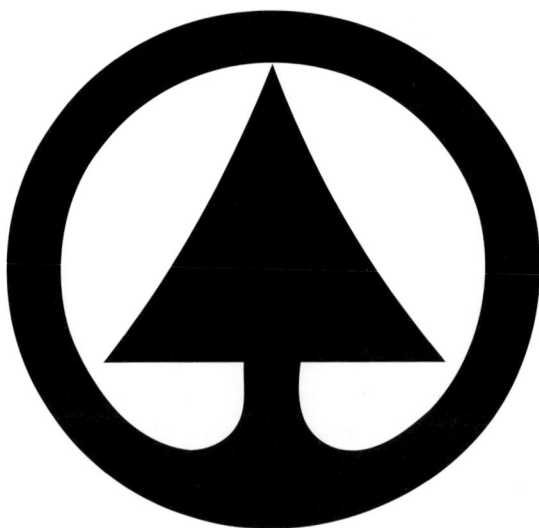

Exportbank
Bank
1960s · Gérard Miedinger · CH

Konsum
Wines
1965 · Erhard Müller · DE-GDR

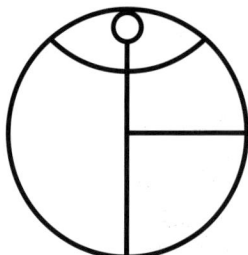

Gymnaestrada Basel
Gymnastics world cup
1968 · Herbert Leupin · CH

Spar
Supermarket chain
1968 · Raymond Loewy/CEI · UK

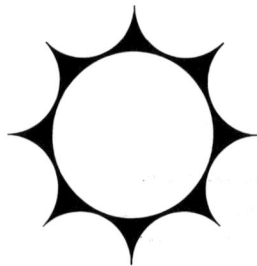

VEG Saatzucht Zierpflanzen
Flowers
1965 · Herbert Vogel · DE-GDR

Brockmann
Timber merchant
1974 · Walter Breker · DE

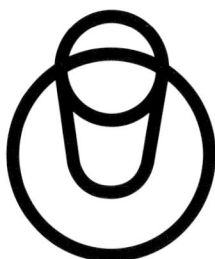

California Dairy Association
1966 · Thomas Laufer · US

Jelen Forest
1963 · Miloš Ćirić · YU

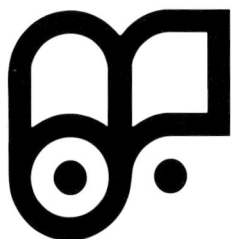

Manifestica Graficke
Design association
1979 · Miloš Ćirić · YU

Journal of the History of Biology
Academic journal
1968 · David Ford · US

RSSA Komi
Civil airline
1960s · Igor Borisović,
Leonid Nikolaevič Rabičev · RU

Niagara University Art Festival
1966 · Richard De Natale · US

Karten-Druckerei Karl Werner
Printing
1957 · Hermann Eidenbenz · CH

W. Euler
Paper
1961 · Willy Faltin · DE

Boise Cascade Corporation
Land development
1963 · G. Dean Smith · US

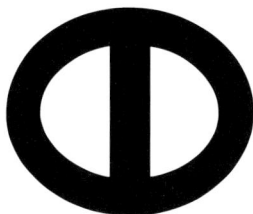

Signa Design Consultants
1953 · Louis le Brocquy · IE

Automobil Club der Schweiz
Automobile drivers association
1950s · Josef Müller-Brockmann · CH

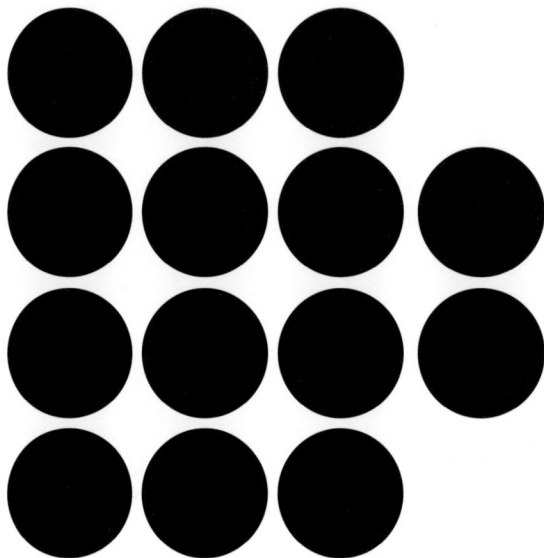

Cristallerie Daum
Glass
1970 · Leen Averink · FR

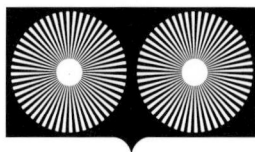

Òliba
Record label
1970 · Francesc Guitart · ES

Hemus
Pencils
1960s · Anton Metchknev · BG

Verband der Volkstheater
Theater association
1970s · Peter Steiner · DE

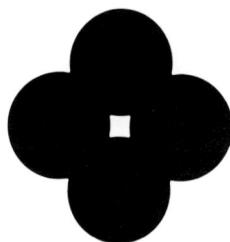

Vereinigung Zentrum, Witikon
Shopping center
1969 · Ernst & Ursula Hiestand · CH

Raymond Lee & Associates
Advertising
1969 · Raymond Lee · CA

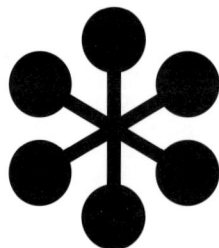

Hyvon-Kudeneule
Clothing
1950 · Matti Viherjuuri · FI

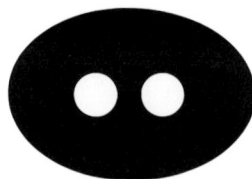

Fiorucci
Cold meats
1975 · Rinaldo Cutini · IT

Die Brücke
Cultural association
1960s · Peter Riefenstahl · DE

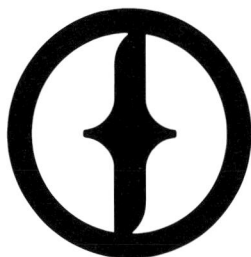

Fabryka Samochodów Warszawie
Automobiles
1980 · Tytus Walczak · PL

Patterson Plaza
Shopping center
1979 · Henry Steiner, Paul Cheung ·
US/HK

Dr. Kurt Ruelke
1914 · Julius Gipkens · DE

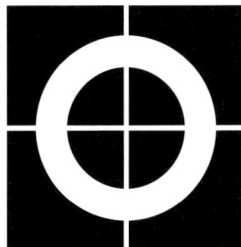

Maruishi
Millinery
1980 · Yonefusa Yamada,
Shin Szaki · JP

Handelsschule
Business school
1960s · Jupp Ernst · DE

Onimus-Outils
Transportation
1950s · Robert Sessler · CH

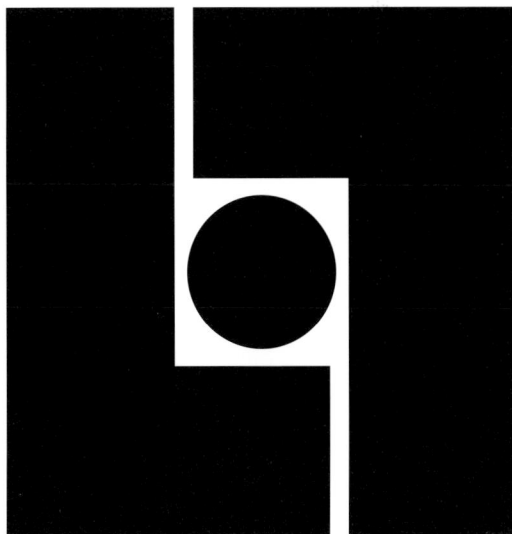

ICSID Annual Congress
Design congress
1967 · Laurent Marquart/
Jacques Guillon Designers · CA

Gesellschaft für Gerichtliche Medien
Legal publishing
1965 · Gerhard Voigt · DE-GDR

Lincocin Upjohn Company
Pharmaceuticals
1960s · Will Burtin · US

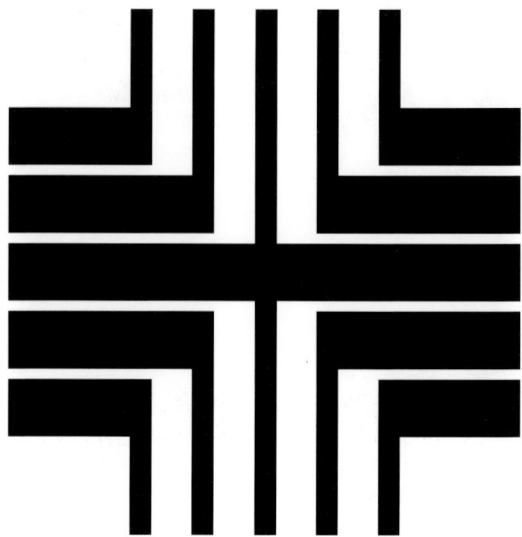

Pitney Bowes
Business equipment
1971 · Robert A. Gale · US

Helvetas Fonds für Entwicklungshilfe
Development aid
1965 · Christian Lang · CH

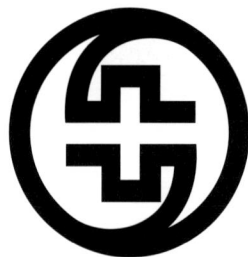

Stiftung Schweizer Spitzensport
Sports foundation
1972 · Hansruedi Scheller · CH

Schweizer Radio
Broadcasting
1978 · Roland Hirter · CH

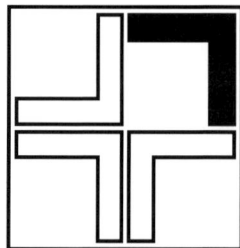

System Three
Market research
1966 · Ian Bradbery · UK

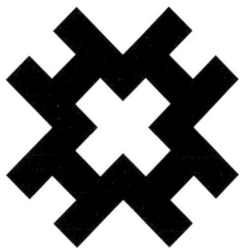

Hollister
Medical supplies
1979 · Jack Weiss, Randi Robin · US

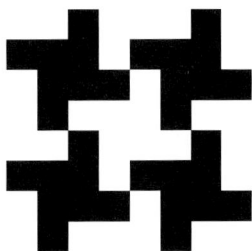

Maestrelli
Textiles
1960s · Franco Grignani · IT

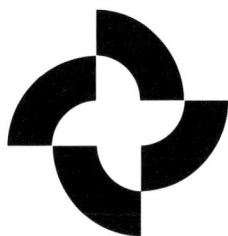

Museo de Arte, Caracas
Museum
1983 · Gerd Leufert · VE

Canadian Guild of Crafts
National crafts trust
1964 · Heiner Hegemann/
Chermayeff & Geismar · CA

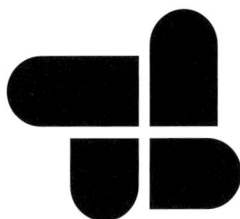

Blutzentrale, Stuttgart
Blood donation
1970s · Hannes Schober,
Wolfram Reinhardt · DE

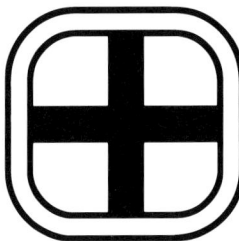

Ekco Containers
1960s · Don Marvine/
Latham Tyler Jensen · US

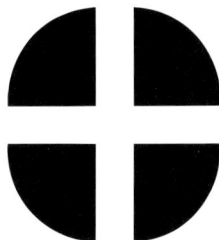

Da Costa & Asociados CA
Market research
1969 · Reynaldo Da Costa · VE

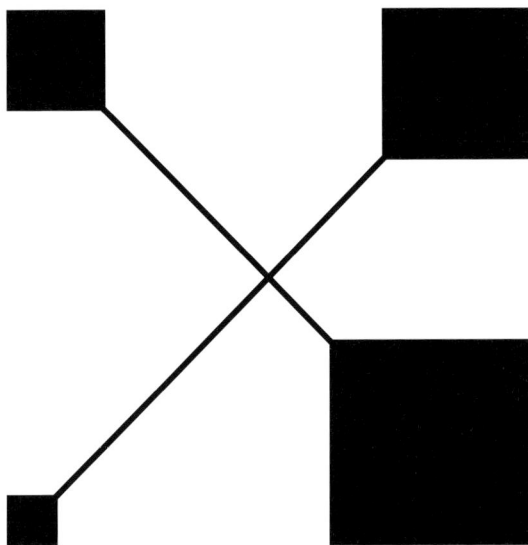

Asia
Ski manufacturing
1960s · Gan Hosoya · JP

Pavia Municipality Town Hall
1981 · R. Nava, D. Soffientini,
A. Ubertazzi · IT

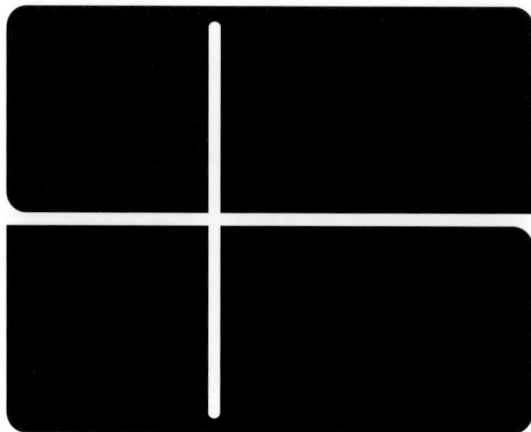

ScandinavSian Windows
1969 · David J. Plumb · UK

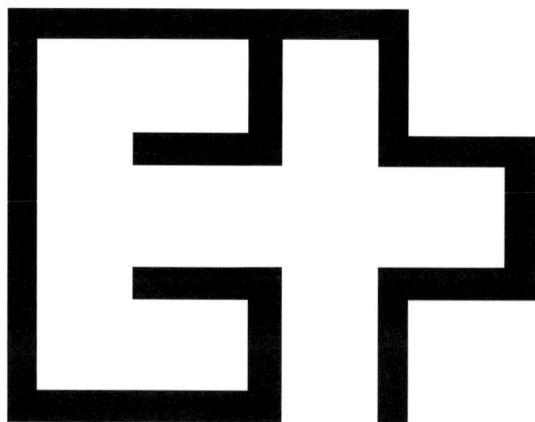

Schweizerische Landesausstellung, Lausanne
Exhibition
1964 · Armin Hofmann · CH

Beekman Downtown Hospital
1969 · Philip Gips · US

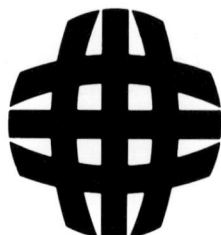

I Propilei
Publishing
1965 · Daniele Baroni · IT

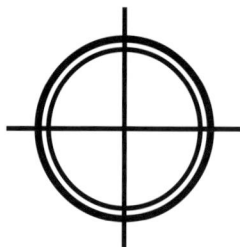

Junger Instruments AB
Precision technology
1968 · Geoffrey Woollard/
Allied International Designers · UK

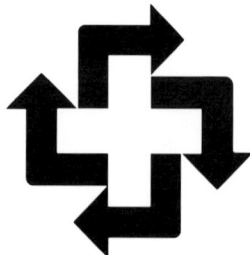

Hospital Management Systems Society
Healthcare organization
1967 · Beau Gardner · US

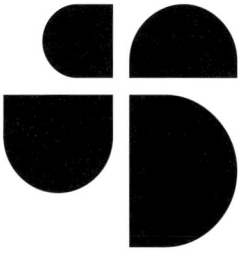

F. Hoekendijk Kerk
Church
1971 · Jan Jaring · NL

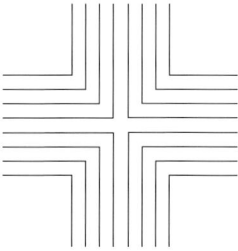

Red Cross International, Havana
Aid agency
1958 · Félix Beltrán · CU

B+S Sägewerk
Sawmill
1960s · Hans-Joachim Brauer · DE

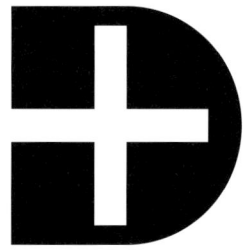

Salisbury Theological College
1967 · Keith Murgatroyd · UK

Hospitales Unidos de Barcelona
Hospital association
1959 · Ribas & Creus · ES

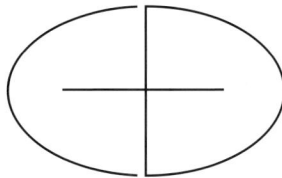

Dillman+Danaher
Investment
1970 · Allan W. Miller · US

Bouwmij Janssen
Construction company
1964 · Marcel Pijpers · NL

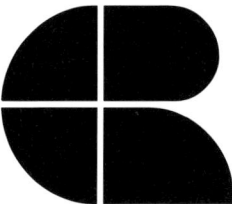

Communication+Design
1972 · Gerold Schmidt · DE

Kirchengemeinde Buchthalten
Church
1960s · Peter G. Ulmer · CH

Capital Planning Resources
Real estate
1974 · Mike Quon · US

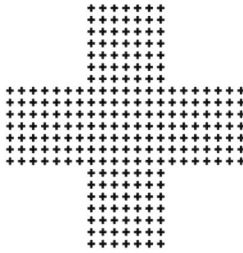

University of Utah Medical Center
Health center
1980 · Michael Richards,
Bill Swensen · US

M+N+P
Design
1960 · Aloísio Magalhães, Luiz Fernando
Noronha, Artur Lício Pontual · BR

Punkte

Grand Dinner Theater
1982 · Joseph Boggs · US

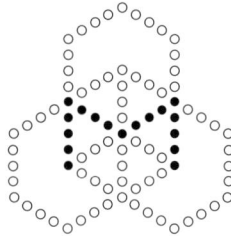

Rautatiekirjakauppa
Public transport
1964 · Bror B. Zetterborg · FI

Metra International
Management consultancy
1958 · Henrion Design Associates · UK

Matvörur Hf.
Foods
1969 · Thröstur Magnusson, Hilmar
Sigurdsson/Argus Advertising · IS

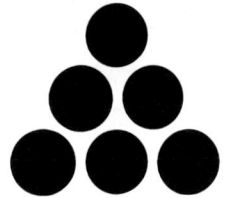

Sigen
Nuclear research
1975 · Giovanni Brunazzi · IT

Escuela de Administración Pública
School
1971 · Dicken Castro · CO

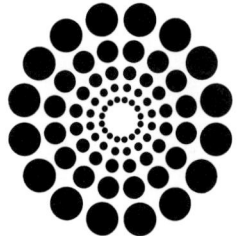

Reuters
News agency
1966 · Crosby, Fletcher, Forbes · UK

Exhibition Services
1960s · Erberto Carboni · IT

Roosevelt University
1971 · Edward Hughes · US

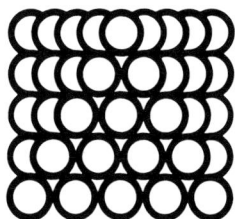

Centro Médico Docente La Trinidad
Hospital
1972 · Gerd Leufert · VE

Labora Mannheim
Laboratory equipment
1974 · Erwin Poell · DE

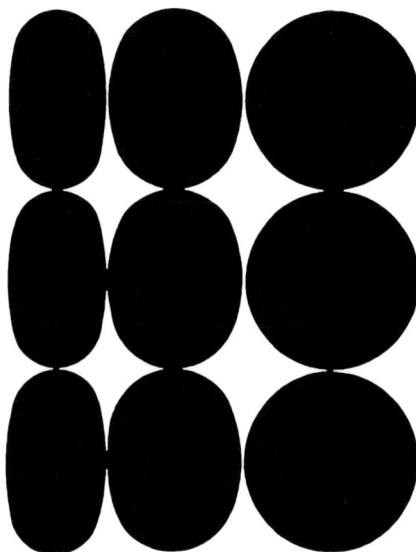

Taichi Shoji
Public relations
1981 · Ishine Nituma,
Taijiro Nakayama · JP

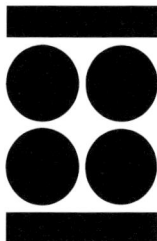

Banco del Estado
Bank
1977 · Dicken Castro · CO

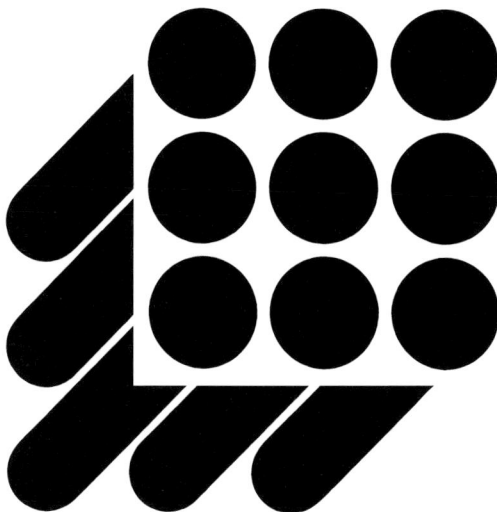

Conicit
Research institute
1970 · Gerd Leufert · VE

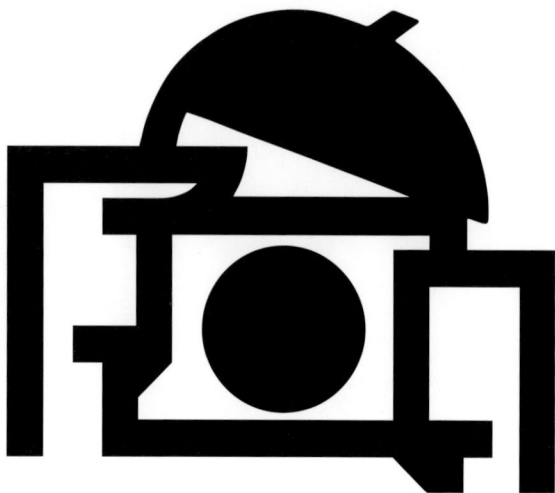

Das Aktuelle Bild der DEWAG
Advertising services
1965 · Herbert Prüget · DE-GDR

AGM
Miniature models
1967 · Bob Gill · US/UK

International Paper Company
Paper and packaging
1959 · Lester Beall · US

Sungarden
Real estate
1973 · John Spatchurst · AU

Paclett
Paper
1960s · Ingo & Christine Friel · DE

Editorial Fabril
Publishing
1962 · Rómulo Macció · AR

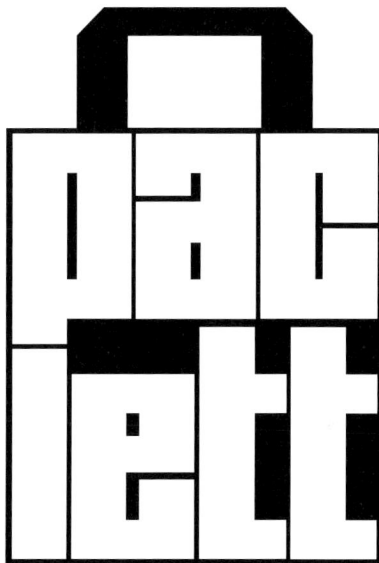

Curling Club Basel
Sports organization
1967 · Jürg Spahr · CH

VEB Fernmeldewerk
Telecommunications
1965 · Alfons Hopf · DE-GDR

Jöns
Transportation
1970s · Heinz Schwabe · DE

Alessio Bassi
Metal goods
1960s · Giancarlo Guerrini · IT

Steelcase
Furniture
1970 · Vance Jonson · US

Danish Agricultural Marketing Board
Foods
1963 · Adam Moltke · DK

Mál & Menning
Publishing
1968 · Thröstur Magnusson, Hilmar
Sigurdsson/Argus Advertising · IS

Venezuelan Supply
Industrial gloves
1952 · Gerd Leufert · VE

Cercle du Livre Economique
Publishing
1968 · Lonsdale Design · FR

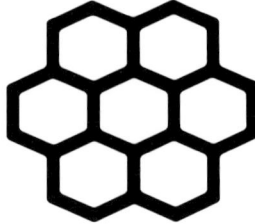

Sveriges Biodlares Riksförbund
Federation of beekeepers
1969 · Ove Engström · SE

Oppi
School furniture
1968 · Osmo Omenamäki · FI

Shiroya
Laundry
1965 · Mitsuhiko Sasao/
McCann Erickson-Hakuhodo · JP

Nihon-Reiyon
Textiles
1965 · Shigeo Fukuda · JP

**Comédiens Associés
du Québec**
Federation of actors
1971 · Raymond Bellemare · CA

Oy Airam
Light bulbs
1961 · Kyösti Varis · FI

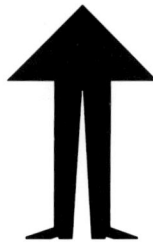

Post Magazine
1969 · Shigeo Fukuda · JP

Berg- & Hüttenindustrie
Metallurgy
1965 · Werner Duda · DE-GDR

**Canadian Arthritis &
Rheumatism Society**
Healthcare
1965 · Eiko Pech/Stewart & Morrison · CA

L'Elefante
Furniture
1967 · Bob Noorda/
Unimark International · IT

Krefina Bank
1960s · Robert Geisser · CH

Walther Raebel & Sohn
Clothing
1965 · Karl-Jürgen Härtel · DE-GDR

Uusikivalehti
Magazine
1950s · Martti A. Mykkänen · FI

Playboy Magazine
1953 · Arthur Paul · US

Boles-Aero
Travel agency
1962 · Jerry Braude · US

Fritz Feinhals Werbeberater
Advertising
1953 · Heinz Schwabe · DE

Exlibris
1950s · René Althaus · CH

Association of the Swedish Book Trade
1969 · Erik Ellegaard Frederiksen · DK

Kyodo Nyugyo
Dairy products
1965 · Ikko Tanaka · JP

Clay-Adams
Medical instruments
1967 · Bruce Blackburn/
Chermayeff & Geismar · US

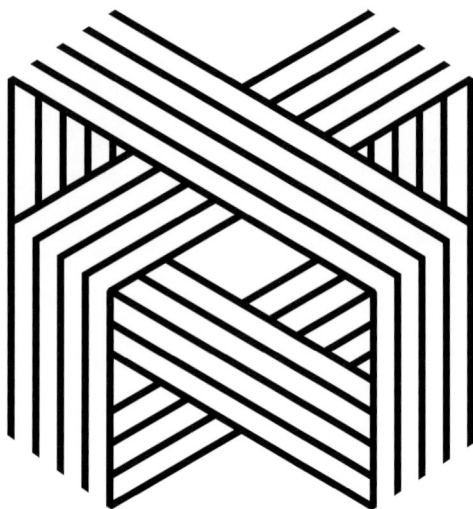

Grand Prix du Ruban d'Or de l'Emballage
Packaging award
1969 · Daniel Maurel/Chourgnoz Publicité · FR

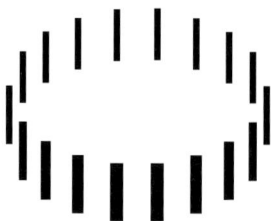

Deutsches Filmmuseum
Film museum
1984 · Philipp Teufel, Günter Illner · DE

Nylon de México
Clothing
1970s · Lance Wyman · US

Erik Ellegaard Frederiksen
Industrial design
1960 · Erik Ellegaard Frederiksen · DK

Arflex
Furniture
1971 · Giancarlo Iliprandi · IT

Eina
Design school
1967 · Pérez Sánchez · ES

Meacham Companies
1969 · Robert P. Gersin · US

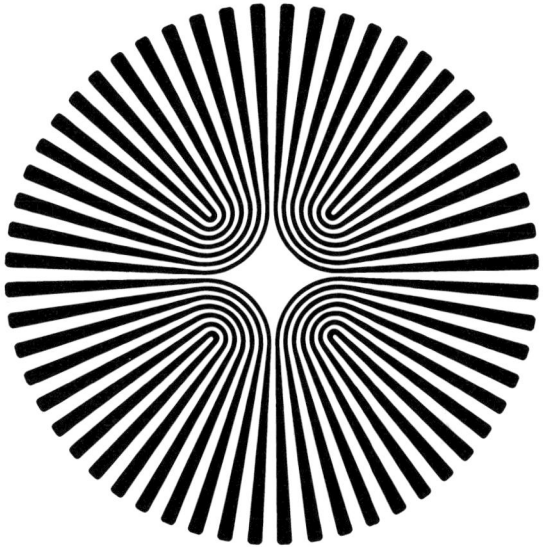

Ingrid
Cosmetics
1970 · Franco Grignani · IT

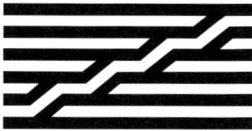

Centre Georges Pompidou
Cultural center
1975 · Jean Widmer · FR

Hotel & Public Building Equipment Group
Interior design
1967 · Negus & Negus · UK

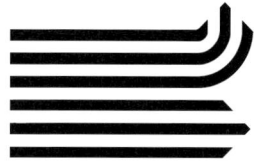

Palacio de Pioneros, Havana
Youth center
1975 · Félix Beltrán · CU

IASA Indústrias de Azulejos
Tiles
1971 · Roberto Amaro Lanari · BR

Sterling Life
Insurance
1981 · Kenneth Hollick · UK

Asociación Argentina de Psicoterapia
Psychotherapy
1971 · Norberto H. Coppola · AR

Aboa Development
1974 · Akisato Ueda · JP

Van Gelder
Paper
1968 · Karen Munck/
Allied International Designers · UK

Continental Airlines
1968 · Saul Bass & Associates · US

Bagnasco
Restaurant chain
1968 · Piero Ottinetti · IT

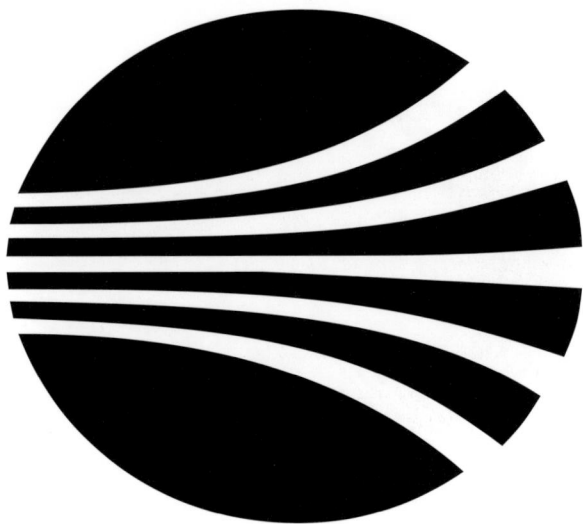

Transamerica Pyramid
Skyscraper
1969 · Jerry Berman · US

Olympic Games, Moscow 1980
1980 · Vladimir Arsentyev · RU

Republic Corporation
Holding company
1968 · Robert Miles Runyan · US

**American Association
of Department Stores**
Retail federation
1970s · Vincent Ceci · US

Electrorama
Lighting
1970 · Jean Delaunay/Look · FR

326

Rockwell International
Manufacturing conglomerate
1968 · Saul Bass & Associates · US

ON Associates
Music publishing
1970 · Shin Nagamatsu,
Kyoji Nakatani · JP

The I Club
Private club
1982 · Henry Steiner,
Jennings Ku · HK

Nijverdal ten Cate
Textiles
1960 · Gerard Wernars · NL

Cefina JMW
Jewish social-work foundation
1969 · Otto Treumann · NL

Ministerstwo Przemysłu Lekkiego
Ministry of light industry
1960s · Witold Surowiecki · PL

Stalling Filmsatz
Typesetting
1975 · Bruno K. Wiese · DE

Raffold
Conveyor systems
1970 · David J. Plumb · UK

Grupo Cinco
Architecture
1978 · Allan W. Miller/Animex · MX

Nawinta Mineralbrunnen
Mineral water
1979 · Manfred Wutke · DE

Stiftung Volkswagenwerk
Humanities and science research funding
1965 · Klaus Grözinger,
Peter Riefenstahl · DE

Woolmark
International wool secretariat
1964 · Franco Grignani · IT

Laboratoires Sarbach
Pharmaceutical laboratory
1966 · Erich Brenzinger/
Chourgnoz Publicité · FR

Stamps Sales
1973 · Ernesto Lehfeld · MX

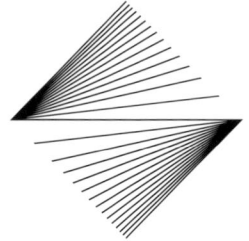

Chemiefaserkongress
Congress on synthetic fibers
1975 · Rolf Müller · DE

Suruga Bank
1965 · Kazumasa Nagai · JP

Industrial Design USA
Exhibition
1966 · George Nelson · US

Tack Leisure Building
1977 · Shintaro Ajioka · JP

Equipamento de Hoy
Furniture
1971 · Ricardo Blanco · AR

Saumweber & Stecher
Construction company
1974 · Oanh Pham Phu · DE

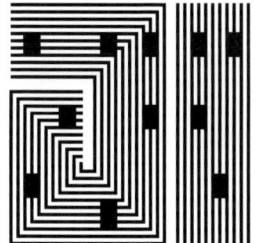

Asturiana de Informática
Computer systems
1967 · José Santamarina/
Elías & Santamarina · ES

Colt Heating & Ventilation
1965 · Henrion Design Associates · UK

Teppichfabrik Niedek-Velour
Carpets
1983 · Paul Effert · DE

The Fiber Union
1982 · Joe Dieter · US

Moatti
Antiques
1972 · Jean Delaunay/Look · FR

Taubman Shopping Center
1971 · Robert P. Gersin · US

Toyo Jitsugyo
Marble surface care
1982 · Masahiro Shimizu · JP

Ilford
Photographic materials
1966 · Ronald Armstrong/
Design Research Unit · UK

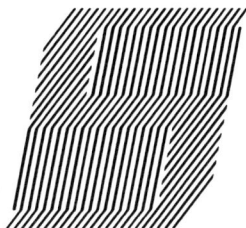

Fukusuke
Commemorative event
1981 · Helmut Schmid · DE/JP

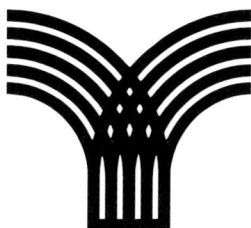

Industrias de Alta Tecnología
Technological development
1978 · Alfonso Capetillo Ponce,
Jack Vermonden · MX

Estudio Uno
Design
1979 · Gerd Leufert · VE

Yoshino
Interior design
1976 · Koichi Watanabe · JP

**Japanese Association for
Expo '70, Osaka**
World's fair organization
1969 · Nakajo Masayoshi · JP

Imasco
Consumer goods
1970 · Rolf Harder, Ernst Roch/
Design Collaborative · CA

Pacific Fuel Trading
1983 · Tatsuhito Yamamoto · JP

Uitgeverij Spaarnestad
Publishing
1968 · Tel Design Associated · NL

Station Hotel, Kyoto
1960s · Yorikazu Hirata · JP

Community Krsko Region
Flag
1982 · Judita Skalar · YU

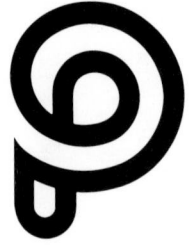

Universidad Simón Bolívar
University
1969 · Gerd Leufert · VE

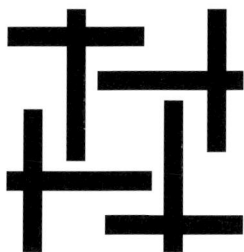

**Canadian Conference on
Church and Society**
1968 · Julien Hébert · CA

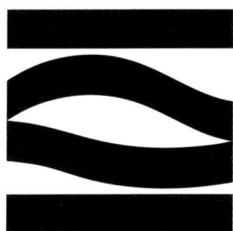

AZ Grupo Gráfico
Design
1970 · Pedro Ariño · ES

**Companhia Nacional
de Tecidos Nova América**
Textiles
1968 · Joaquim Redig · BR

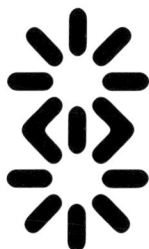

Performance Maximus
Sports center
1968 · J. R. Weiss/
The Design Partnership · US

C.O.N.I.
Commemorative event
1972 · Mimmo Castellano,
Michele Spera · IT

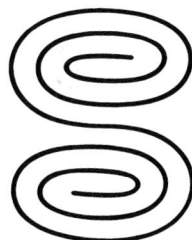

Steiger & Deschler Webereien
Weaving
1950s · Otl Aicher · DE

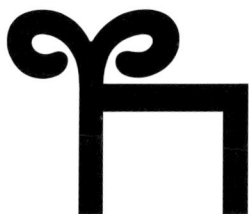

Lodex
Textiles
1967 · Andrzej Bertrandt · PL

Tennis Unlimited
Sports club
1968 · Appelbaum & Curtis · US

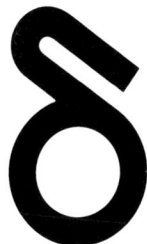

Dechy Publicité
Advertising
1962 · Dechy Publicité · BE

Gütesiegel Echt Silber
Silver quality mark
1975 · Hans Karl Rodenkirchen · DE

Industrie und Handelskammer
Trade organization
1979 · Rolf Müller · DE

Keio
Department store
1962 · Yoshio Hayashi · JP

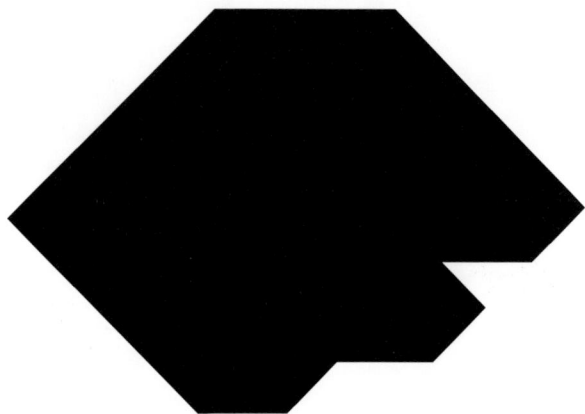

Base Finanza
Investment
1987 · A. G. Fronzoni · IT

Indian Airlines
1973 · Benoy Sarkar · IN

**Fukuoka City
Public Transport**
1979 · Fumio Koyoda · JP

Homare Bowling Center
Sports facility
1972 · Shuji Torigoe · JP

Belair
Airline
1979 · Armin Vogt · CH

Merinoteks
Yarns
1970s · Andrzej Stypułkowski · PL

Tower Industries
Stone surfaces
1981 · Thomas Ohmer, Koji Takei · US/JP

Estudio Actual
Art gallery
1968 · Nedo Mion Ferrario · IT/VE

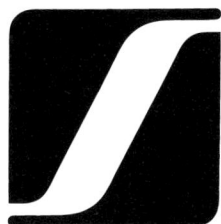

Seiyu Stores
Supermarket chain
1974 · Jitsuo Hoashi · JP

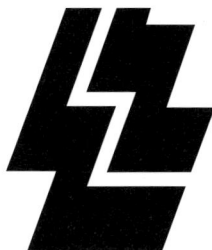

ERCOA
Machinery
1975 · Elías García Benavides · ES

Melbourne Whiting
Construction company
1968 · Hans R. Woodtli · CH

Mizuno Print
Printing
1976 · Kazuharu Fuji · JP

Leykam
Paper
1981 · Madeleine Bujatti · AT

Messaggeria Emiliana
Parcel service
1963 · Valeriano Piozzi/Piozzi & Cima · IT

Elektrowatt Zürich
Energy and industry holding company
1973 · Odermatt+Tissi · CH

Legler Industria Tessile
Textiles
1968 · Jörg Hamburger · CH

vh Verlag
Publishing
1970s · Helmut Schmid · DE

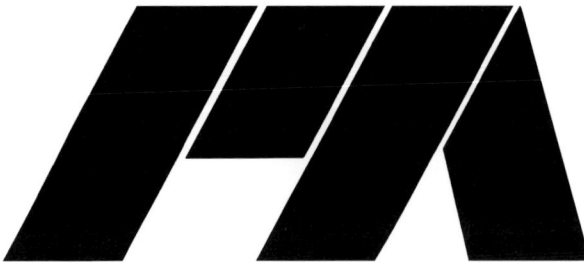

Kingsway Public Relations
Communications company
1973 · Kate Osbar · UK

Panart
Artist management
1969 · Rod Dyer · US

Via Rail Canada
Public transport
1978 · Anonymous · CA

VAW
1970s · Heinz Schwabe · DE

Flughafen Immobilien Gesellschaft
Real estate
1970s · Peter G. Ulmer · CH

Overseas Marketing Corporation
Technological development
1967 · Chandrashekhar Kamat/
Design Research Unit · UK

International Scientific Systems
Data processing
1963 · Fletcher, Forbes, Gill · UK

Matthews Real Estate
1979 · Duane Wiens, Arvid Wallen · US

Fiat Costruzioni & Impianti
Automobile engineering
1972 · Giovanni Brunazzi · IT

Academic Aye Computer
Computing
1980 · Minoru Takahashi · JP

Morse Shoe
Footwear
1968 · Herman & Lees Associates · US

Yeye
Cosmetics
1967 · Armando Milani · IT

Aldo Maspero
Furniture
1971 · Studio GSZ · IT

Ideal Science Industry
Printing
1979 · Shigeo Fukuda · JP

Kunimatsuya
Retail
1979 · Koichi Watanabe · JP

Docenave Navegação
Shipping operator
1967 · PVDI · BR

Handi Polstermöbel
Furniture
1970s · Werner Hartz · DE

SG6
Technology sales conference
1967 · Salvatore Gregorietti/
Unimark International · IT

**Institut für Latein-Amerikanische
Studien der Universität St. Gallen**
Education
1981 · Jost Hochuli · CH

Groupe Kastuan
Urban planning
1970 · Pham Ngoc Tuan · FR

Argos Industrial
Textiles
1958 · Alexandre Wollner · BR

Sapio
Olive oil
1971 · Mimmo Castellano · IT

N. Busquets
Plumbing
1971 · Enric Huguet · ES

Etcetera
1966 · Nakajo Masayoshi · JP

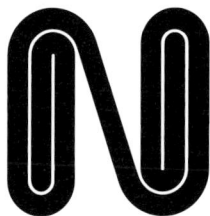

Leela
Clothing
1960s · Henry Steiner · HK

Vieta
Audio equipment
1968 · Pérez Sánchez · ES

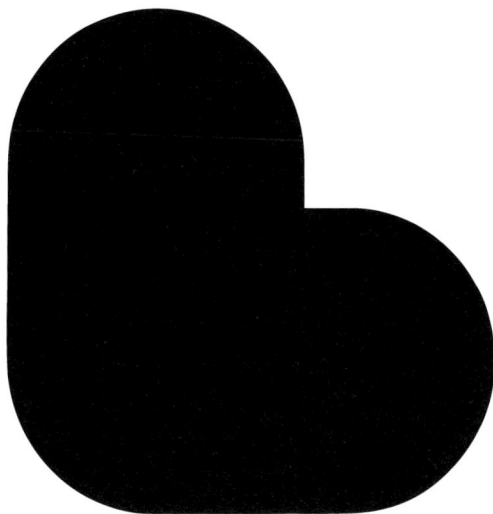

Nortextil
Clothing
1966 · Paul Brand · NO

Schappe International
1965 · Hanns Lohrer · DE

Labor Abbigliamento
Clothing
1972 · Giovanni Brunazzi · IT

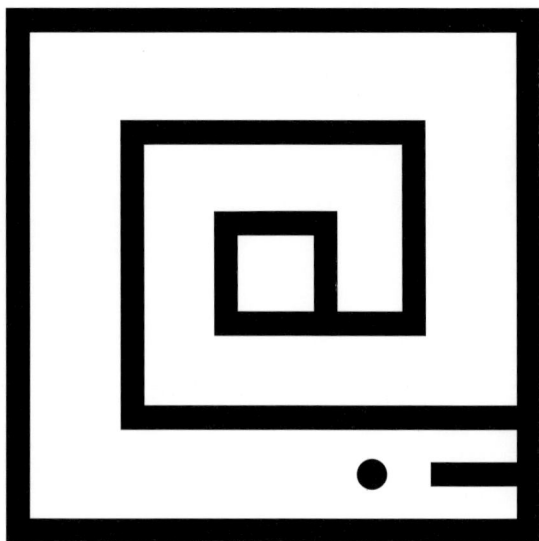

Marktgass-Passage Apotheke
Pharmacy
1964 · Paul Sollberger · CH

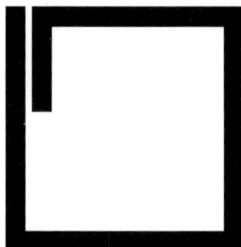

E. H. Schelling Rümlang
Container trade
1960 · Odermatt+Tissi · CH

El Al
Airline
1963 · Otto Treumann · NL

Iveco
Vehicle manufacturer
1978 · Carlo Malerba · IT

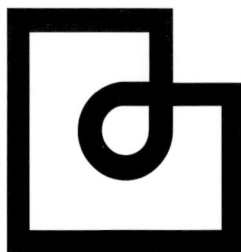

Complejo Plástico, Isla Margarita
Art center
1970 · Nedo Mion Ferrario · VE

Hans-Kjell Larsen
Architecture
1970 · Paul Brand · NO

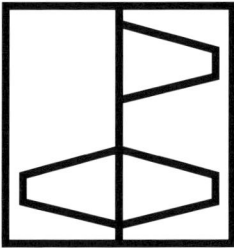

Plieger
Sanitation
1958 · Wim Crouwel/Total Design · NL

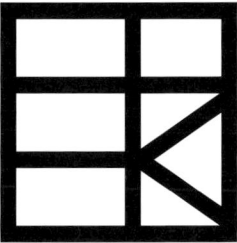

Carl Steinherr
Design
1964 · Carl Steinherr · NL

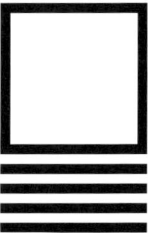

Universität der Künste, Berlin
University of the arts
1960s · Helmut Lortz · DE

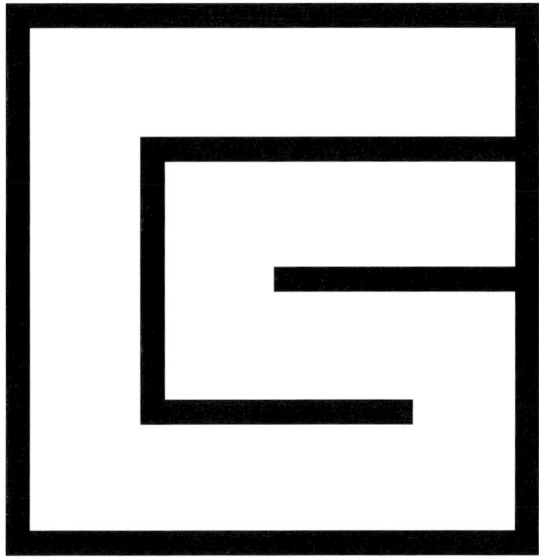

LaSalle Steel
Steelworks
1962 · Morton Goldsholl · US

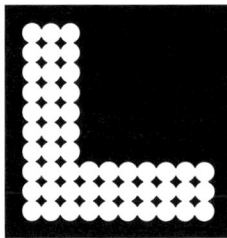

Constructora Los Alamos
Construction company
1969 · José Santamarina/
Elias & Santamarina · ES

La Cie J. B. Rolland & Fils
Paper
1960 · George Huel · CA

Nordisk Film
Film production
1968 · Paul Brand · NO

Apotheke Ehrensberger
Pharmacy
1950s · Helmuth Kurtz · CH

Comitato per la Seta Italiana
Committee for Italian silk
1960s · Franco Grignani · IT

K. Täumer & Söhne Ziegeldächer
Roofer
1961 · Otto Kuchenbauer · DE

Veeder-Root
Counting control devices
1960s · Chermayeff & Geismar · US

Textilhaus Kemmerling
Clothing
1950s · Robert Sessler · CH

Kohlenversorgungs AG
Coal
1963 · Igildo Biesele · CH

Torii & Co.
Pharmaceuticals
1977 · Kazuo Tanaka · JP

Ospinas y Cia.
Construction company
1974 · Dicken Castro · CO

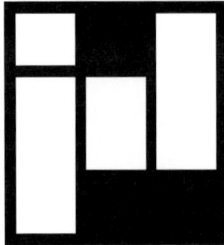

International Research & Development
Research and development
1964 · David Caplan · UK

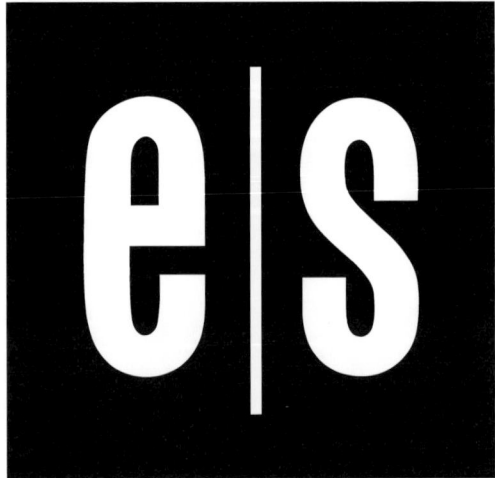

Eugen Schmidt
Furniture
1955 · Helmut Lortz · DE

Scott Paper
Toilet paper
1960s · Hiram Ash/
George Nelson & Co. · US

Mani Tese
Sustainability
1970 · Pino Tovaglia · IT

Viktoria Verlag
Publishing
1950s · Kurt Toggweiler · CH

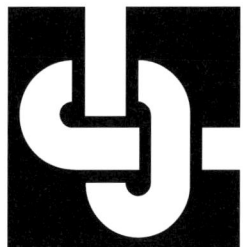

Home Store
1973 · João Carlos Cauduro,
Ludovico Antonio Martino · BR

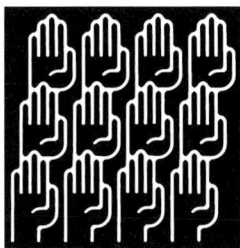

Litton Industries
Electrical systems
1958 · Robert Miles Runyan · US

Novotar
Concrete construction
1973 · František Bobáň · CZ

Tuna Çelik
Metalworks
1982 · Burhan Tastan · TR

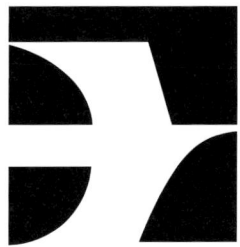

Zins
Clothing
1967 · Daniel Maurel/
Chourgnoz Publicité · FR

Polaha & Somers
1970 · Ronald Cutro · US

Van Besouw
Looms
1968 · Gerard Wernars · NL

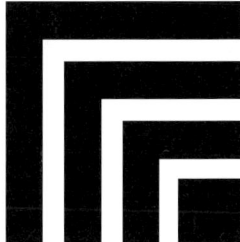

Československé Státní Aerolinie
Airline (proposed design)
1960s · Jiří Rathouský · CZ

**Raymond Chabot
Martin Paré & Associates**
Accounting
1982 · Vasco Ceccon · CA

Nippon Unit Load
Container companies
1977 · Koichi Watanabe · JP

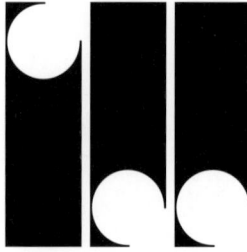

Instituto de Diseño
Design institute
1964 · Gerd Leufert · VE

Werb'-Günther
Advertising and publishing
1965 · Hace Frey · DE

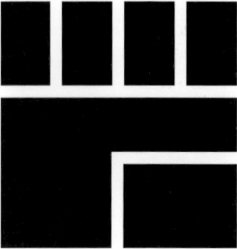

Editorial Estela
Publishing
1971 · Enric Satué · ES

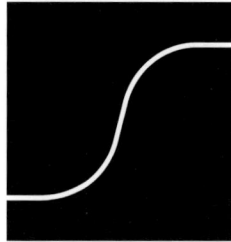

Symphonic Electronic Corporation
Consumer electronics
1969 · Jean Morin, John Murray · CA

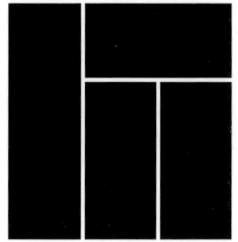

De Vlissingsche Courant
Newspaper
1927 · NL

**Registro Tumori del Piemonte
e la Valle D'Aosta**
Cancer research institute
1971 · Giovanni Brunazzi · IT

Alfred Scherz Verlag
Publishing
1953 · Paul Sollberger · CH

Mursten og Fliser Producenter
Bricks
1969 · Ove von Späth · DK

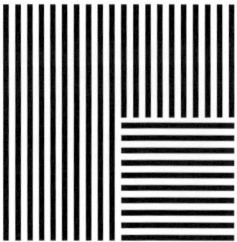

Centro di Cultura G. Puecher
Cultural center
1969 · Franco Grignani · IT

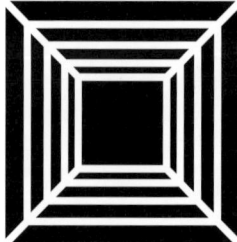

Glendale Center Theater
1979 · Scott Engen · US

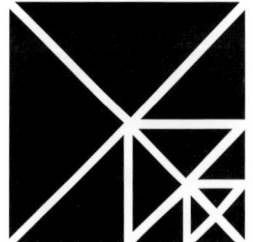

Ministerio de Desarrollo Económico
Ministry of economic development
1968 · Dicken Castro · CO

Municipality of the City of Buenos Aires
1979 · Eduardo A. Cánovas · AR

Versandhaus Neckermann
Mail order (proposed design)
1960s · Wolfgang Freitag · DE

Larsen Design Office
1976 · Tim Larsen · US

Ansbacher Siegel
Printing
1970s · Robert Hagenhofer · US

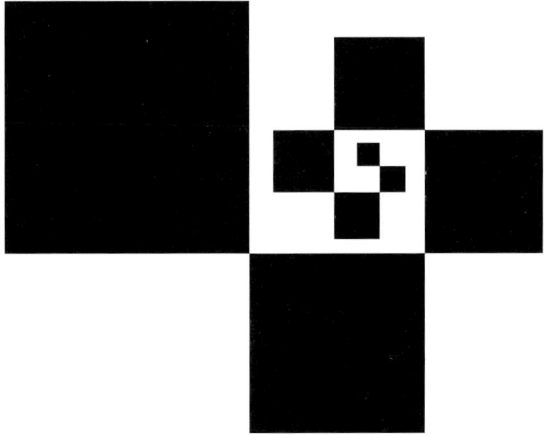

Terimobel
Real estate
1967 · Julian Key · BE

Olivetti Systed
Educational institution
1971 · Walter Ballmer · IT

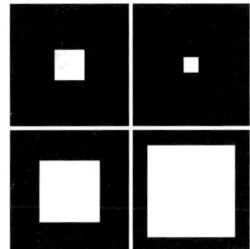

Eurodomus
Interior design book series
1956 · Giulio Confalonieri · IT

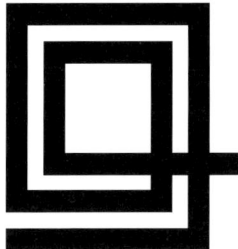

Olivetti
Business machines
1956 · Marcello Nizzoli · IT

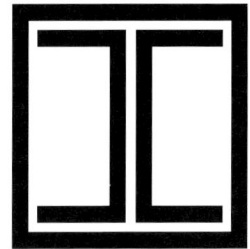

Jacob Bek
Metalworks
1961 · Winfried J. Jokisch · DE

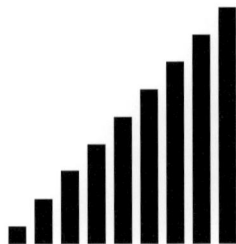

Tequila Mexicano
Liquor
1982 · Félix Beltrán · CU/MX

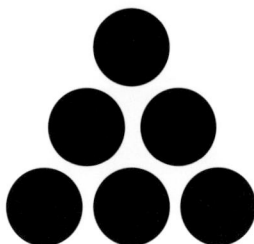

Augusto Avanzini
Adhesive products
1964 · Dante Bighi · IT

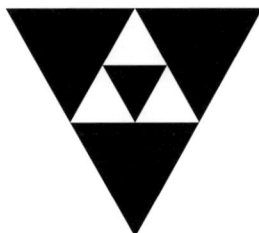

Delfim Araújo SA
Investment
1966 · João Carlos Cauduro, Ludovico
Antonio Martino · BR

Delta Werbegesellschaft
Advertising
1972 · Gerold Schmidt · DE

Gralglas
Glass
1950 · Otl Aicher · DE

Asakura Architects & Associates
1971 · Hiroshi Manzen · JP

Gomes de Almeida Fernandes
Construction company
1964 · Paulo de Tarso Mello,
Cleuton Sampaio · BR

Christian Broadcasting Network
1982 · George McGinnis · US

Roussel Uclaf
Pharmaceuticals
1963 · Raymond Loewy/CEI · FR

Alpeadria Dos Ljubljana
Tourism
1981 · Ivan Dvoršak · YU

Reggio Leasing
1989 · Silvio Coppola · IT

Kashiyama
Clothing
1977 · Kazumasa Nagai · JP

Alpine
Sporting goods
1980 · John M. Alexander · US

Seterie Argenti
Textiles
1986 · Max Huber · IT

A. Diethelm
Painting tools and supplies
1957 · Carlo L. Vivarelli · CH

Intercontinentale Assicurazioni
Insurance
1970 · Vittorio Antinori · IT

Editora Delta
Publishing
1960s · Aloísio Magalhães/PVDI · BR

Packer Enterprises
Investment
1983 · Yarom Vardimon · IR

Art Grafische Werkstätten
Design
1960s · Ryszard Dudzicki · PL

Kreis Deckt Dächer, Dübendorf
Roofers
1961 · Hansruedi Scheller · CH

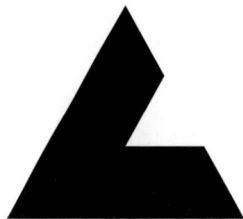

Anton Lihl
Advertising
1970 · Oanh Pham Phu · DE

Gérard Miedinger
Design
1960s · Gérard Miedinger · CH

Tidningen Arbetet
Paper
1968 · Bertil Andersson-Bertilson · SE

Asbestzementwerk Magdeburg
Asbestos
1965 · Horst Jacob · DE-GDR

Interwerba
Advertising
1965 · Interwerba · CH

Spółdzielnia Rybołówstwa
Fishing cooperative
1960s · Ryszard Dudzicki · PL

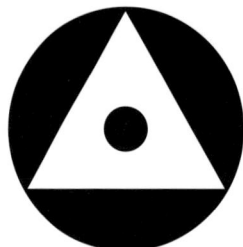

Amann Möbel
Furniture
1972 · Werner Hartz · DE

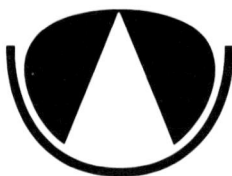

Carl A. Donald Excavation
1957 · Ernst Roch/
Design Collaborative · CA

Max R. Diethelm
Architecture
1964 · Walter J. Diethelm · CH

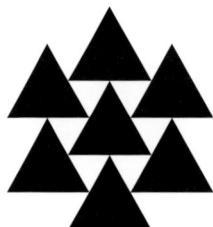

Forest History Society
Educational institution
1960s · Russell A. Sandgren · US

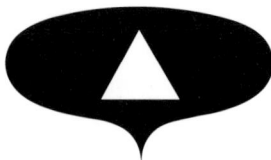

Hotel Kirishima
1960s · Kenji Ito · JP

Associated Spring
Industrial trade
1958 · Armin Müller · US

**Staatliche Schule für
Kunst und Handwerk**
Art school
1946 · Robert Sessler · CH/DE

Vision Photography
1969 · Rod Dyer · US

**Escuela Superior de
Administración Pública**
Higher education
1970 · Claude Dietrich · PE

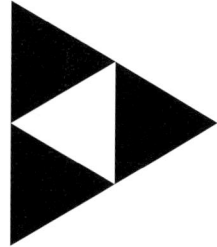

Monte Ávila Editores
Publishing
1968 · Gerd Leufert · VE

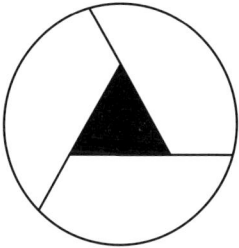

P. Barberini
Optical products
1964 · Till Neuburg · CH

Peter Kwasny
Spray paints
1964 · Werner Keidel · DE

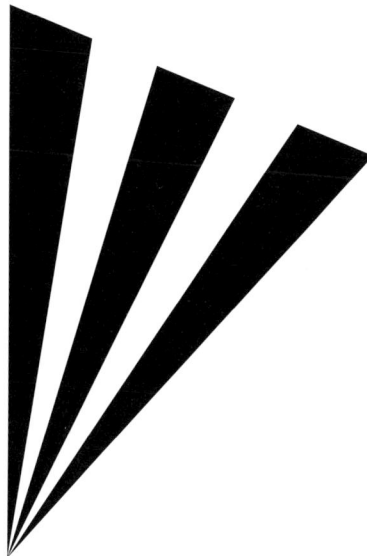

Triad Institute for Urban Research
1969 · Charles Fuhrman · US

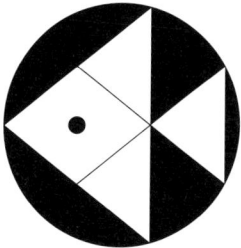

Textil Fischer
Textiles
1950s · Kurt Toggweiler · CH

WDR Westdeutscher Rundfunk
Broadcasting
1968 · Graphicteam Köln · DE

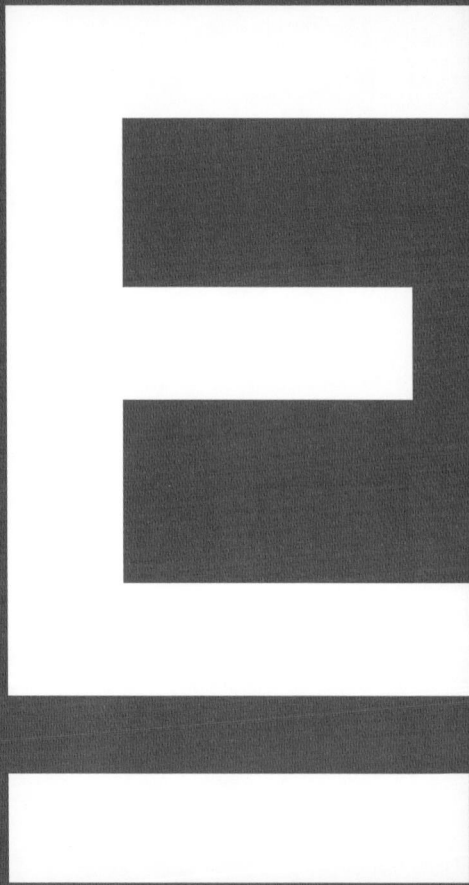

Effekt

Effect

Simply playing with basic geometric shapes can provide a variety of graphic solutions. Even so, it is only by adding extra effects that designers can exploit the full range of possibilities. Among typical techniques currently used in logo design are mirror imaging, duplication and cropping. In the main, a finished logo design will not be the result of a single set of specifications. The most exciting and idiosyncratic logos rely simultaneously on several effects. A look at more recent work reveals that, whatever the new and constantly changing trends may be, designers are still happy to fall back on the methods described on the following pages.

Das Spiel mit den einfachen geometrischen Grundformen erlaubt bereits eine Vielzahl unterschiedlicher grafischer Lösungen. Erst durch die Anwendung weiterer Effekte lässt sich jedoch die ganze Bandbreite an Möglichkeiten ausschöpfen. Ein Fokus auf Methoden wie Spiegelung, Verdopplung oder Zerschneiden verdeutlicht gängige Schemata in der Gestaltung von Logos. Oft fand in den realisierten Zeichen nicht nur ein einzelner Gestaltungsparameter Anwendung, vielmehr führte die Kombination mehrerer Effekte zu spannungsreichen und individuellen Logoentwürfen. Untersucht man Arbeiten neueren Datums, erweisen sich die im folgenden beschriebenen Methoden – unabhängig von sich verändernden Gestaltungstrends – als noch immer in Anwendung.

Le jeu sur les formes géométriques fondamentales offre déjà un grand nombre de possibilités graphiques. C'est seulement par l'application d'effets supplémentaires que toute la palette des possibilités peut être épuisée. Une concentration sur des méthodes comme la réflexion, le redoublement ou le découpage fait apparaître des schémas courants dans la création de logos. Souvent, le signe final ne procède pas seulement d'un seul paramètre de création. Au contraire, c'est la combinaison de plusieurs effets qui produit des résultats captivants et individuels. Lorsqu'on analyse des réalisations récentes, on s'aperçoit que les méthodes décrites ci-après ont conservé toute leur validité – indépendamment des tendances changeantes de la création.

G.E.A.P.
Typesetting
1978 · Alfredo de Santis · IT

Maurice Barthalon
Electricity
1968 · Gérard Guerre/Technés · FR

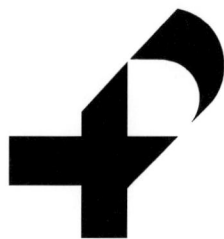

Rotbuch Verlag
Publishing
1975 · W. Tatlin · DE

Fairchild
Publishing
1966 · Philip Franznick/
Franznick & Charney · US

Gerber
Advertising
1960s · Gerber Werbeagentur · CH

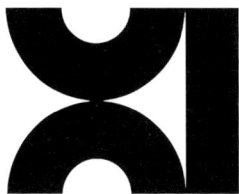

Universidad de Ingenieria
Engineering university
1965 · Claude Dietrich · PE

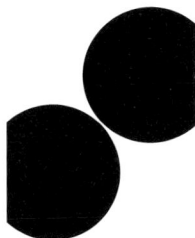

Club Selector
Nightclub
1964 · Takeshi Otaka · JP

Hotel Takase
1967 · Takeshi Otaka · JP

Meridional Companhia de Seguros
Insurance
1960s · Joaquim Redig · BR

Buenos Aires City Hall
1971 · Studio González Ruiz &
Shakespear · AR

Miyata
Beauty salon
1978 · Toshinori Nozaki · JP

National Homes Construction
Construction company
1976 · Barrett & Gaby · US

Cordex
TV sets
1962 · Lala Méndez Mosquera · AR

Optima Corporation
1978 · Lewis van der Beken,
Norm Holtzman · US

Grandi Motori Trieste
Engineering
1970 · Giovanni Brunazzi · IT

Gazette Printing
1969 · William J. Campbell · CA

Comforto
Furniture
1974 · Ettore Vitale · IT

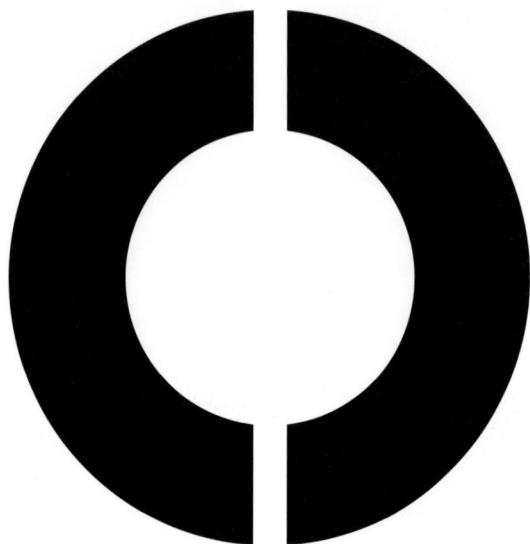

Clenet Coachworks
Automobiles
1977 · Marty Neumeier · US

Sanyo
Electronics
1963 · Shigeo Fukuda · JP

Tokyo Financing Bank
1969 · Yoshio Hayashi · JP

Pepsi-Cola
Beverage
1960s · Ivan Chermayeff,
Gene Secander · US

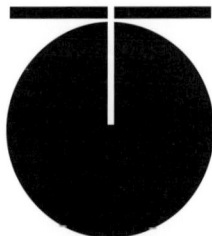

Österreichischer Bundesverlag
Publishing
1980 · Anonymous · AT

International Ocean Exposition
1973 · Kazumasa Nagai · JP

Toyo Jozo
Wines
1968 · Kazumasa Nagai · JP

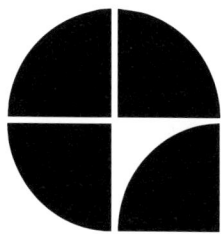

CO.FE.MO. di P. Moreschi & Figli
Metal processing
1967 · Pietro Amadei · IT

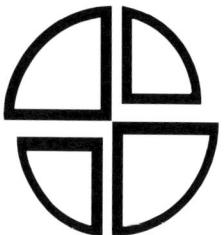

Companhia Coronado de Hoteis
Hotel chain
1968 · João Carlos Cauduro,
Ludovico Antonio Martino · BR

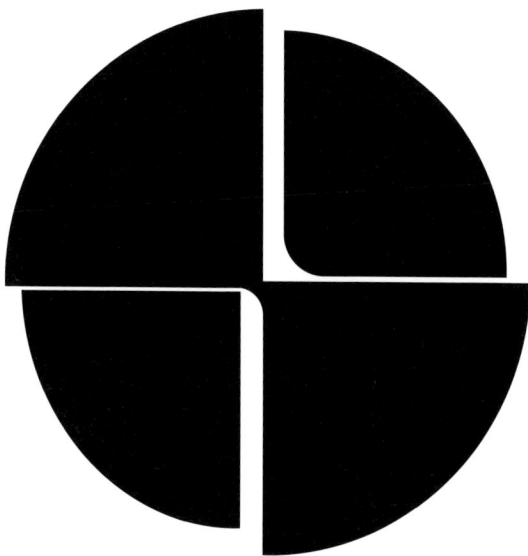

Usines du Pied-Selle
Kitchens
1964 · Raymond Loewy/CEI · FR

Teleflex
Cable systems
1968 · David L. Burke · US

Atelier Chourgnoz
Design studio
1960s · Jean-Marie Chourgnoz · FR

Turun Kala
Foods
1962 · Bror B. Zetterborg · FI

Delco
Packaging
1963 · Lance Wyman · US

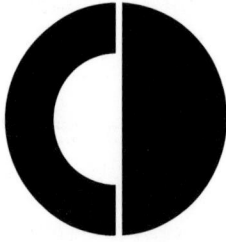

Cramer Druck
Printing
1972 · Gerold Schmidt · DE

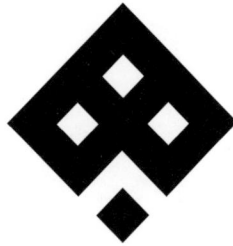

Passagen Verlag
Publishing
1985 · Anonymous · AT

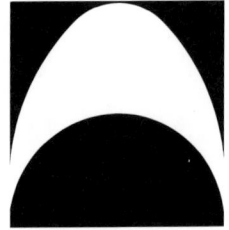

Komeito
Political party
1970 · Hiroshi Ohchi · JP

**5th International Labour
Film Festival, Montreal**
1967 · Georges Beaupré · CA

Instituto de Ciencia Animal
Livestock management and research
1969 · Félix Beltrán · CU

Centro de Turismo Nova Lindóia
Tourism
1962 · Alexandre Wollner · BR

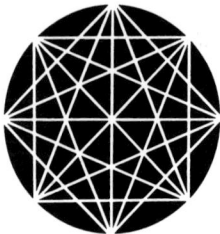

Gouda Garden
Yarns
1969 · Ralph Prins · NL

Scic
Kitchens
1965 · Franco M. Ricci · IT

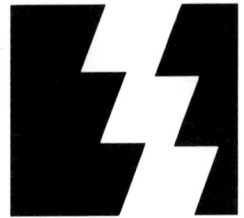

Urban Research Corporation
Development
1968 · David L. Burke · US

Ediciones Unidas
Publishing
1971 · Francesc Guitart · ES

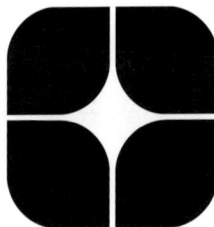

Statens Informasjonstjeneste
National parks
1966 · Paul Brand · NO

Centro Arredamento Moderno
Interior design
1973 · Amedeo Bergamasco · IT

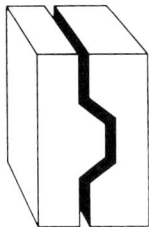

Harvey Cowan
Architecture
1969 · James Donahue/
Cooper & Beatty · CA

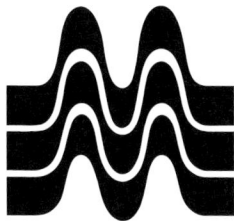

Marcona Mining Corporation
1969 · Robert Pease · US

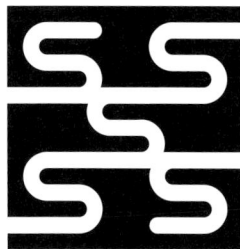

Sturm Söhne Solingen
Climate technology
1970 · Hans Karl Rodenkirchen · DE

Women's Fashion Factory
1965 · Jan Hollender · PL

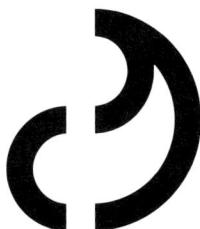

Centro Profesional de Dibujantes
Graphic designers association
1959 · Nedo Mion Ferrario · VE

Eastman Kodak
Photographic equipment
1983 · Joe Selame · US

Urological Surgery Center
Hospital
1979 · Eduardo A. Cánovas · AR

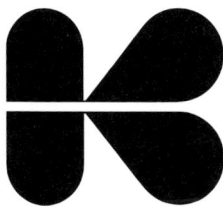

Kobashi Photo Studio
1974 · Ken'ichi Hirose · JP

Sakata International
Trading
1983 · Ikuya Kimura · JP

S.E.I.
Encyclopedia
1968 · Giorgio Maltisotto/Sitcap · IT

Washington Mutual
Savings bank
1968 · Ken Parkhurst · US

Celstar
Polystyrene products
1970 · Bruno Oldani · NO

Maestro
Foods
1970 · Morten Peetz-Schou · DK

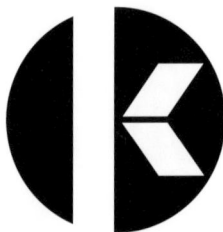

Osakeyhtiö Konttoritarpeita
Engineering
1959 · Jukka Pellinen · FI

Michel Olyff
Design
1960s · Michel Olyff · BE

Quorum Corporation
Acquisitions and development
1983 · Denise Spaulding · US

Continental Petroleum
1979 · J. Barton · US

Pussy - Agencia de Modelos
Modeling agency
1969 · Pedro Ariño · ES

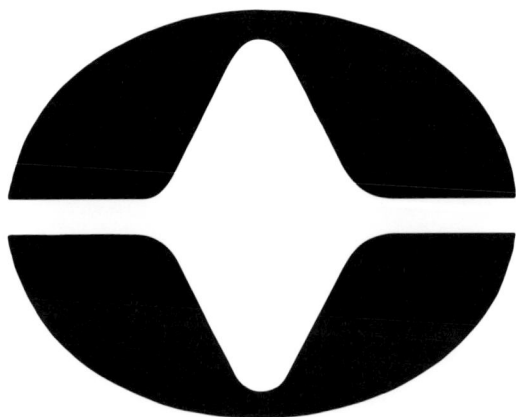

Ifanger
Turning tools
1960s · Milo Schraner · CH

Olin Mathieson
Chemicals
1970s · Lippincott & Margulies · US

Wiener + Deville
Advertising
1965 · Anonymous · CH

**American Computer and
Communications Company**
Computer services
1971 · Conrad E. Angone · US

Tessitura di Giussano
Textiles
1970 · Silvio Coppola · IT

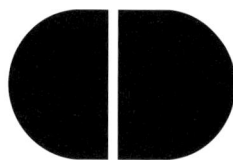

Centro Di
Publishing
1968 · A. G. Fronzoni · IT

Aksel Kjersgaard
Furniture
1960s · Anonymous · DK

System- und Flugelektronik
Flight systems development
1972 · Rainer E. Kunert · DE

F.lli de Dominicis
Patent office
1968 · Patrizia Pataccini/
Studio Cortesi · IT

Tipofilm Cortometraggi Pubblicitari
Advertising
1965 · Enzo Careccia/Opit Pubblicità · IT

IBM Western Region
Computer systems
1968 · Gerry Rosentswieg · US

Servizi Finanziari Internazionali
Financial services
1968 · Ilio Negri · IT

Imprimerie Jouve
Printing
1950s · Aldo Calabresi · IT/FR

National Theatre, London
1971 · Henrion Design Associates · UK

Röntgen Technische Dienst
X-rays
1964 · Charles Jongejans · NL

Ramón Sopena
Publishing
1964 · Ribas & Creus · ES

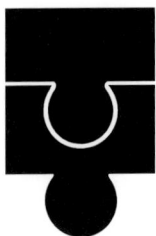

EDP Technology
Computer software
1968 · Arnold Saks · US

San Francisco
Rehabilitation workshop
1964 · Michel Dattel · US

Teach Yourself Books
Publishing
1969 · Peter Cope · UK

Tate & Lyle
Sugar
1967 · Henrion Design Associates · UK

House of Packaging
1967 · Rod Dyer · US

Groep De Bondt
Construction company
1968 · Rob Buytaert · BE

Comité de Solidaridad con Vietnam
Political committee
1967 · Félix Beltrán · CU

L'Artiere
Gift shop
1972 · Franco M. Ricci · IT

Nomina
Research institute
1982 · Rolf Müller · DE

**Young Homebuilders
of Northern California**
1969 · Robert Pease · US

Light House
Lamps
1963 · Bruno Oldani · NO

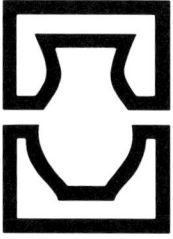

Keramische Werke
Ceramics
1965 · Martin Rosette · DE-GDR

Noritsu
Boilers
1967 · Takeshi Otaka · JP

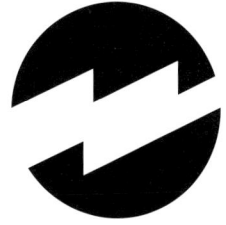

Optik Meier
Optician
1967 · Anonymous · DE

The Science Council of Canada
Scientific advisory group
1970 · Peter Steiner/
Gottschalk+Ash · CA

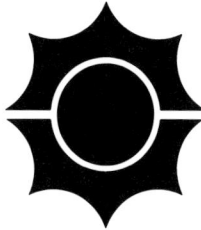

Joyo Bank
1965 · Yoshio Hayashi · JP

Cronmatch
Matches
1965 · W. M. de Majo · UK

Rabitz Druck
Printing
1961 · Hans Karl Rodenkirchen · DE

Drumlin Farms
Agriculture
1968 · Manfred Gotthans/
Chris Yaneff · CA

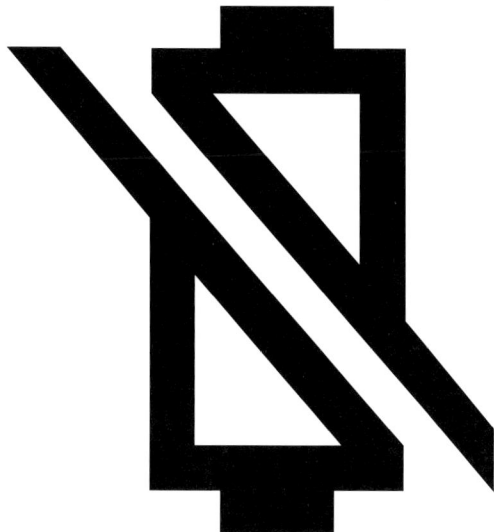

Cantoni
Textiles
1960s · Studio Boggeri · IT

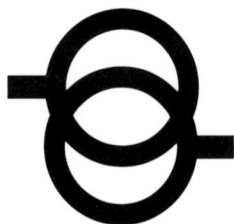

Wunderwald-Krawatten
Ties
1950 · Walther Bergmann · DE

Bofinger+Reinhardt
Design
1970s · Bofinger+Reinhardt · DE

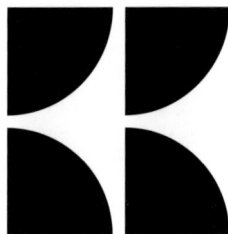

Karl Kessel
1965 · Félix Beltrán · CU

Gugelmann & Cie
Textiles
1960s · Hansruedi Widmer/
Devico AG · CH

Livraria 2 Cidades
Bookstore
1962 · Ludovico Antonio Martino · BR

Weston Woods
Film production
1960 · Jon Aron · US

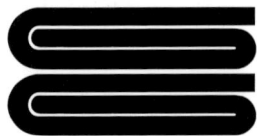

Illy Caffé
Coffee
1959 · Dante Bighi · IT

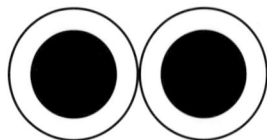

Grupo Cobalto
Cinemas
1969 · Álvaro Sotillo · VE

All-Terrain Vehicle
Off-road vehicles
1969 · Leslie & Philip Smart · CA

Olle Eksell Design
Design
1969 · Olle Eksell · SE

Marine Sciences Corporation
Underwater research
1961 · Frank R. Cheatham/
Porter & Goodman Design · US

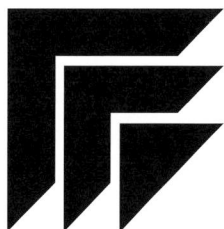

Takarabune
Clothing
1982 · Shuzo Murase,
Jun Yoshida, Toshinori Nozaki · JP

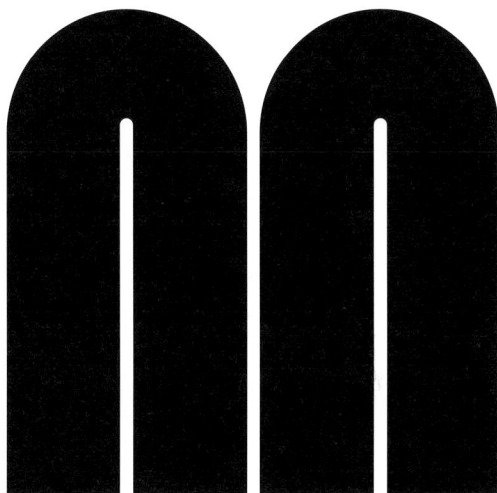

Paul Maurel
Bookstore and art gallery
1968 · Daniel Maurel/Chourgnoz Publicité · FR

Smith Stevens Architects
1971 · Paul M. Levy · US

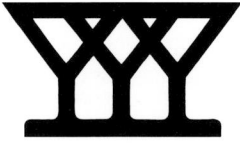

Vereinigte Böhmische Glasindustrie
Glass
1950 · Walter Sauer · DE

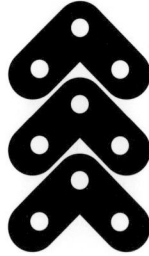

H. H. Ehrlich, Erfurt
Metal constructions
1965 · Karl-Jürgen Härtel · DE-GDR

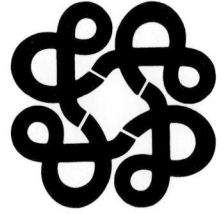

Howarth & Smith Monotype
Typesetting
1963 · Carl Brett/
Hiller Rinaldo Associates · CA

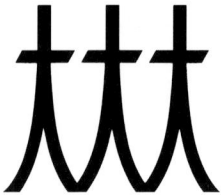

Towers Merchants
Grocery
1966 · Chris Yaneff · CA

Totalgas
Fuel oil
1965 · Ilio Negri, Michele Provinciali,
Pino Tovaglia · IT

St. Cloud Library
Public library
1975 · Peter Seitz · US

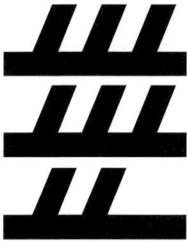

Württembergischer Kunstverein
Art association
1979 · Kurt Weidemann · DE

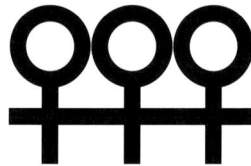

**Junior Women's
Association of Wheaton**
1968 · James Lienhart/RVI Corp. · US

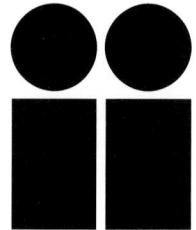

Studio Idea II
Advertising
1970 · Renato Romiti/Studio Idea II · IT

Helsingin Kaupungin Sähkölaitos
Electronics
1960 · Martti A. Mykkänen · FI

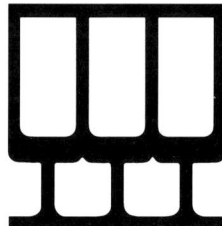

Glaswerke Ilmenau
Glass
1965 · Karlheinz Herke · DE-GDR

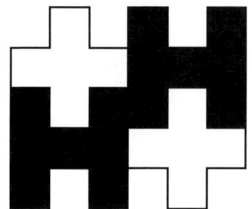

Asociación para el Desarrollo Hospitalario
Hospital association
1969 · Ribas & Creus · ES

Metropolitan Life Insurance
1967 · Sandgren & Murtha · US

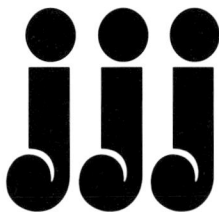

Junket Dessert
Foods
1960 · Appelbaum & Curtis · US

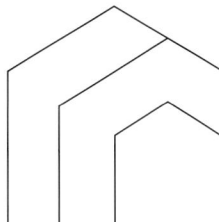

Whitehall Development
Construction company
1968 · Michael Van Elsen/
Hiller Rinaldo Associates · CA

Heller
Radio advertising
1967 · Robert Pease · US

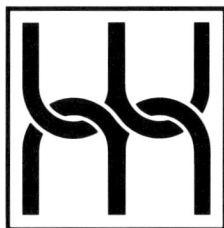

Mab & Mya
Textiles
1962 · Bertil Andersson-Bertilson · SE

Grace
Jewellery
1982 · Koichi Nakai, Ichiro Nakai,
Tetsuo Hiro, Tetsuo Togasawa · JP

Sbrissa
Foods
1964 · Enzo Scarton/Alfa Studio · IT

Bolsa de Valores do Rio de Janeiro
Stock exchange
1966 · Nelson Motta, Renato Landim · BR

Momicor
Chemical research laboratories
1977 · Armando Milani,
Maurizio Milani · IT

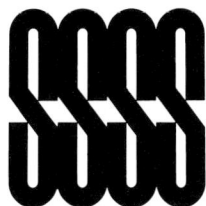

Comitato per la Seta Italiana
Silk marketing
1962 · Franco Grignani · IT

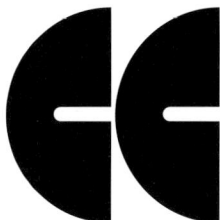

Carlo Ciarli
Advertising
1968 · Carlo Ciarli · IT

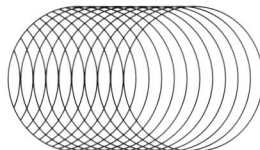

Helipot
Potentiometers
1947 · Lou Frimkess · US

Raster

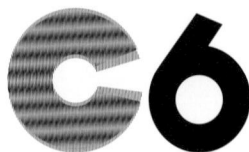

Cinema Six
Movie rentals
1968 · Bob Gill · US/UK

**Gütezeichen für Erzeugnisse
der Deutschen Emailindustrie**
Enamel quality mark
1986 · Bruno K. Wiese · DE

Dai-ichi-shoji
Chemical products
1968 · Hiroshi Ohchi · JP

Ciba Photochemie
Photochemicals
1970s · Annemarie Staehlin,
Erwin Giger · CH

Lemon Tree Productions
Music productions
1968 · Clarence Lee · US

Agroquímica Rafard
Chemicals
1977 · PVDI · BR

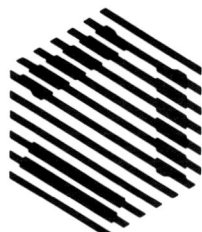

Xellos Havana
Stamps
1970 · Félix Beltrán · CU

Sato Design Room
1978 · Shigeru Sato · JP

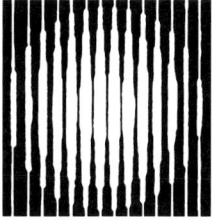

Skan Camera G-M Laboratories
1968 · Henry Robertz/
The Design Partnership · US

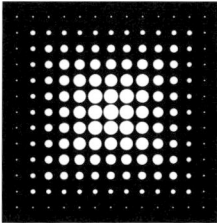

Reclamo-Standard
Printing
1967 · Bruno Oldani · NO

Ratiobau
Property development
1965 · Hanns Lohrer · DE

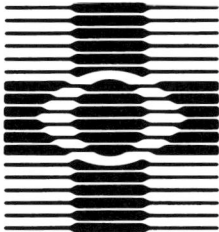

Ljós & Orka
Light installations
1968 · Throstur Magnusson, Hilmar
Sigurdsson/Argus Advertising · IS

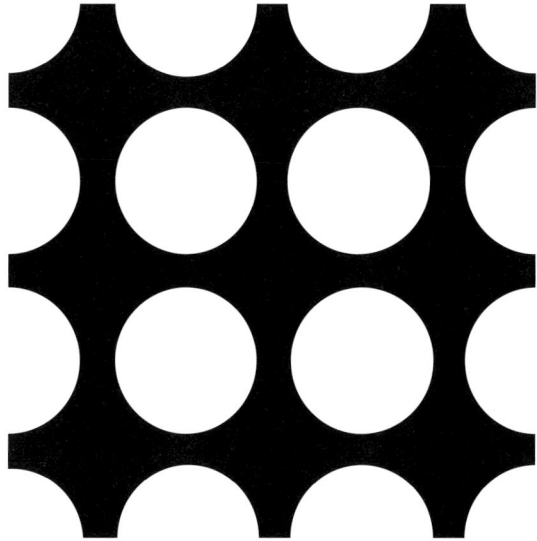

**Research Center for
Personality Development**
Research institute
1970s · Dick Krueger · US

Speakeasy Club
Nightclub
1967 · Crosby, Fletcher, Forbes · UK

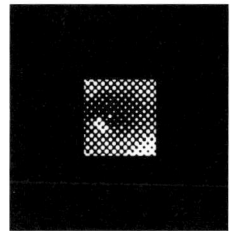

Highland Baptist Hospital
1981 · Tony Bead · US

Terituono
Raincoats
1965 · Theodoor Manson · IT

Continental Bank Money Card
Bank card
1970s · James Lienhart · US

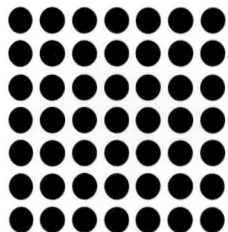

Secretaria de Educação e Cultura do Estado da Guanabara
Ministry of education and culture
1969 · Aristo Rabin · BR

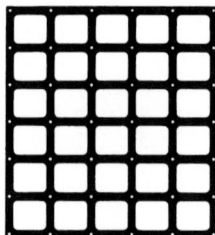

El Farol
Oil company magazine
1969 · Gerd Leufert · VE

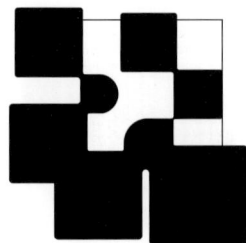

Schwitter Klischees
Prepress services
1959 · Karl Gerstner · CH

Imbalplast
Wrapping paper
1967 · Ilio Negri · IT

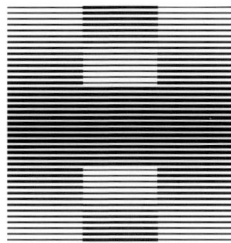

Hauserman
Movable walls
1970 · Paul M. Levy · US

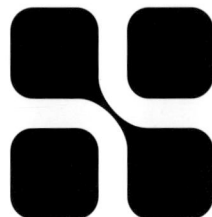

Nikkei Printing
1973 · Koichi Takahashi · JP

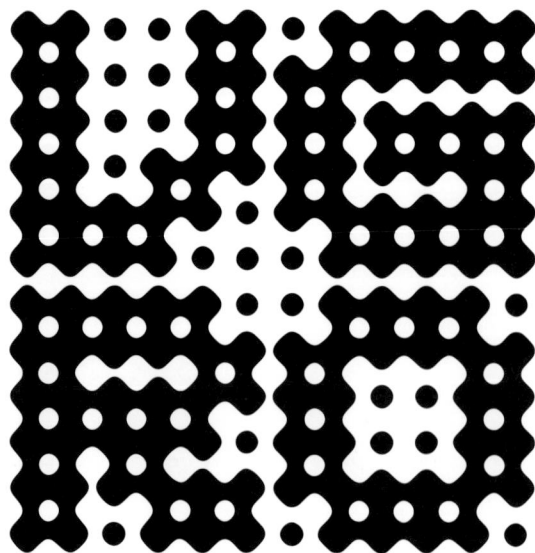

The Krystal Company
Fast-food chain
1975 · Chermayeff & Geismar · US

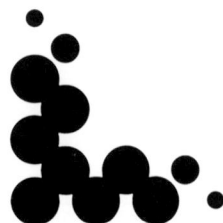

Vereniging van Grafische Reproductie Ondernemingen
Association for graphic reproduction
1958 · Gerard Wernars · NL

Lucentum Baloncesto
Sports association
1979 · Fernando Medina · ES

Media Services, University of Utah
1983 · Scott Engen · US

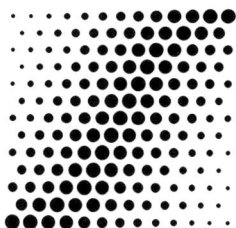

Passpoint Auto Wash
Car wash
1969 · Heinz Waibl/
Unimark International · IT

Bund Freischaffender Foto-Designer
Association of freelance photo designers
1986 · Rolf Müller · DE

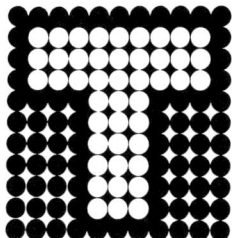

Peter Seitz & Associates
Design
1988 · Peter Seitz · US

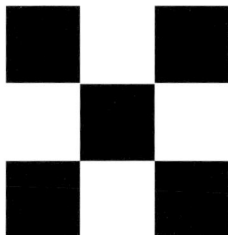

ENEL
Energy supplier
1967 · Ilio Negri · IT

Camera di Commercio I.A.A. di Milano
Chamber of commerce
1972 · Mimmo Castellano · IT

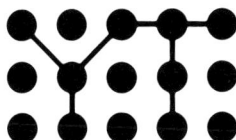

Struthers Electronics Corporation
1976 · Arthur Eckstein · US

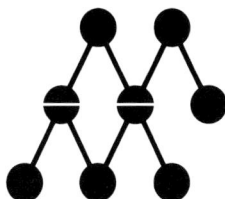

Yoshihiro Tatsuki
Photography
1965 · Makoto Wada · JP

Medium
Furniture
1972 · Pérez Sánchez · ES

Enrico Tronconi
Lighting
1971 · Ilio Negri · IT

Suzuki
Clothing
1969 · Shigeo Fukuda · JP

Television Opinion Panel
Television voting
1969 · John Gibbs/Unit Five Design · UK

Vermont Import & Export
Sporting goods
1962 · Stephen Dunne/Unimark International · US

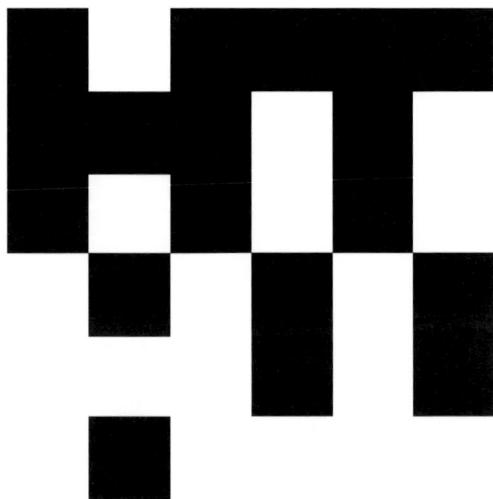

Heinz Terhardt
Photography
1965 · Anonymous · DE

Banco Andrade Arnaud
Bank
1960 · DPZ · BR

Bank of Dallas
1982 · Jack Evans · US

Pavarini
Furniture
1946 · Walter Ballmer · IT

GB
Publishing
1950 · Raoul A. Brink · DE

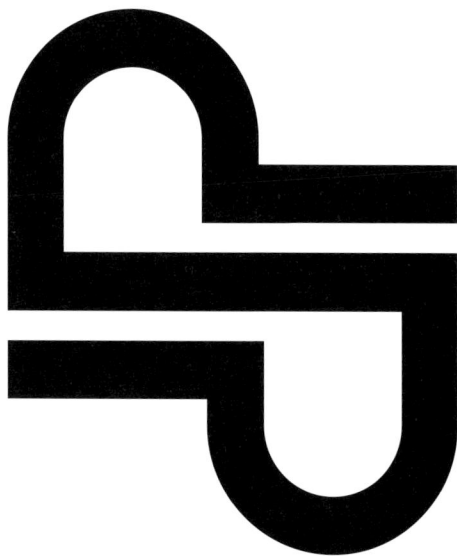

McHenry Medical Group
1965 · Bruce Beck · US

Fog & Mørup
Furniture
1960s · Anonymous · DK

Nils Nessim
Carpets
1958 · Olle Eksell · SE

VEB Funkwerk
Audio technology
1965 · Fritz Deutschendorf · DE-GDR

Granula
Plastics
1962 · Paul Bühlmann · CH

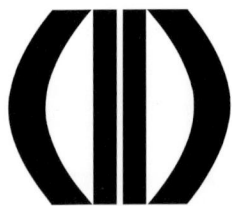

Major Holdings & Development
Property management
1969 · John S. Brown · CA

**Union of Municipal and
Government Employees**
1968 · Thröstur Magnusson, Hilmar
Sigurdsson/Argus Advertising · IS

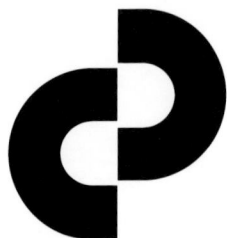

Cultural Presentations
1968 · Arnold Saks · US

Rose-Marie Joray
Design
1960s · Rose-Marie
Joray-Muchenberger · CH

British Celanese
Acetates and chemicals
1969 · Raymond E. Meylan/Artes
Graphicae · UK

Lease Plan Nederland
Automobile hire
1967 · Ralph Prins · NL

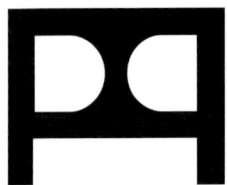

Publi-pistas
Advertising
1969 · Enric Huguet · ES

Metropolitana Milanese
Public transport
1963 · Bob Noorda/
Unimark International · IT

Librairie des Sciences
Bookstore
1968 · Michel Waxman · BE

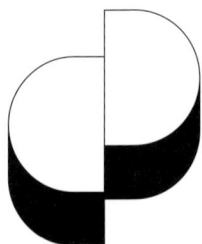

Benoît de Pierpont
Design
1969 · Benoît de Pierpont · BE

Kasparian
Furniture
1955 · Allen Porter/
Porter & Goodman Design · US

Road Safety
Department of transport
1969 · Clarence Lee · US

New Man
Clothing
1968 · Raymond Loewy/CEI · FR

Mobil Wall
Furniture
1964 · Heinz Waibl · IT

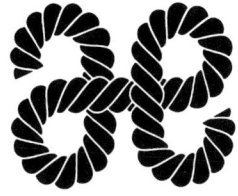

Seilerei Haas
Ropes
1960s · Ernst Roch · CA

db Drogerie Bazaar
Pharmacy
1970s · Anonymous · NL

Decoradora Marina Blanco
Interior design
1969 · José Santamarina/
Elias & Santamarina · ES

European Community, Brussels
1973 · Dieter Urban · DE

Manuel Albo
City tours
1979 · Yutaka Sato · JP

Diversified Products
Wholesale
1964 · Frank R. Cheatham · US

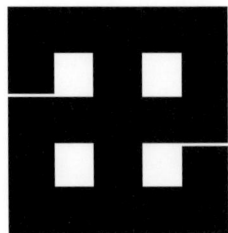

Alfons Eder
Design
1958 · Alfons Eder · FI

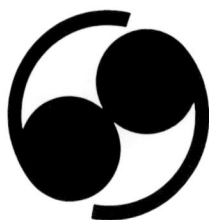

**6th International Congress of the
Society of Industrial Designers**
1968 · Roger O. Denning · UK

Metal 2 Indústria Metalurgica
Metal foundry
1963 · João Carlos Cauduro · BR

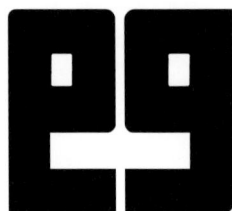

Editions Edigraf
Publishing
1966 · Maurice Leclercq · BE

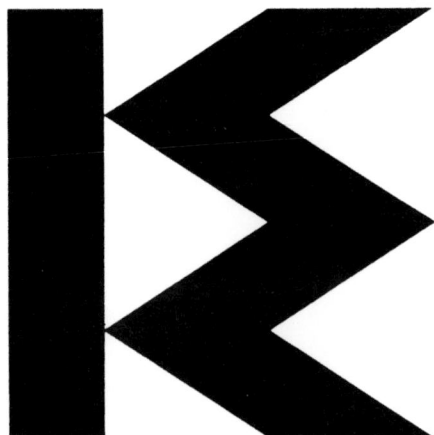

Laroche Pelletier Graphistes, Montreal
Design
1968 · Yvon Laroche,
Pierre-Yves Pelletier · CA

Kilkenny Design Workshops
Design center
1963 · Louis le Brocquy · UK

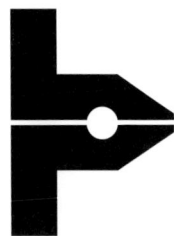

Centro Cultural Tercer Mundo
Cultural center
1969 · Emiro Lobo · VE

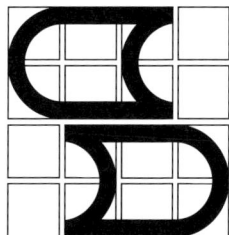

Enciclopedia della Stampa
Encyclopedia of printing
1968 · Giovanni Brunazzi · IT

Savage Sloan
Design
1961 · Savage Sloan · CA

D. C. Heath
Publishing
1970 · Herman & Lees Associates · US

Dansilar
Stockings
1955 · Hanns Lohrer · DE

Hotel Zürich
1960s · Eugen & Max Lenz · CH

Serem
Care for the disabled
1970s · Julián Santamaría · ES

Norpapp Industri
Packaging
1970 · Paul Brand · NO

Short Line
Transportation
1960s · Malcolm Grear · US

Stierli & Kobelt
Metal goods
1960s · Peter Schaufelberger · CH

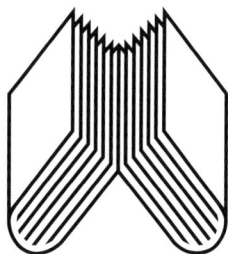

Biblioteca Nacional
National library
1971 · Gerd Leufert · VE

Sutro and Co.
Stockbrokers
1970 · G. Dean Smith · US

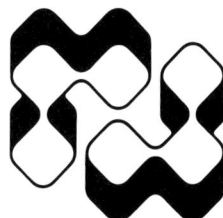

Berenschot, Bosboom
Management consultancy
1969 · Jaap Frank · NL

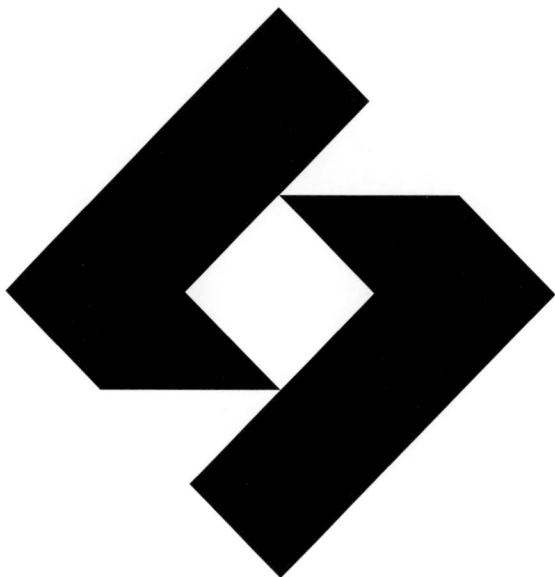

J. Mosterd
Air cleaning machines
1971 · Jan Jaring · NL

Turner Color Works
Paint
1960s · Tetsuo Katayama · JP

Association of Food Retailers
1960s · Hans Hartmann · CH

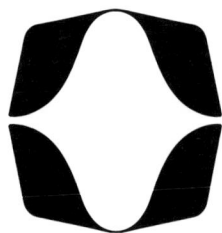

Schwind Radiohandel
Radios
1940s · Walter Herdeg · CH

Werbegesellschaft
Advertising
1961 · Helmut Keppler · DE

Coronado Shopping Center
1970s · Gollin, Bright & Zolotow · US

Institutet för Färgfoto
Photography
1969 · Bertil Andersson-Bertilson · SE

El Nuevo Grupo
Theater
1967 · John Lange · VE

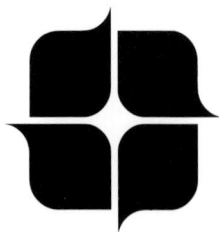

International Janitor
Heating systems
1968 · Ulrich Haupt/
Allied International Designers · UK

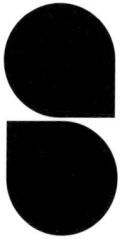

Sanibel Monoprix
Sanitary products
1966 · Jean Delaunay/Havas Conseil · FR

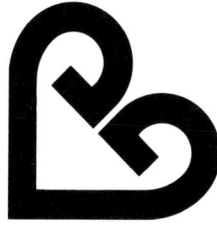

Ber Gold Inc.
1976 · Stuart Ash/Gottschalk+Ash · CA

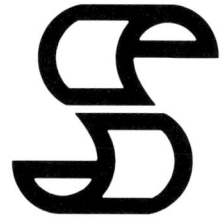

Rank Xerox
Photocopiers
1950s · Marcello Minale · UK

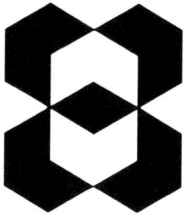

Noble Lowndes International
Insurance
1968 · David Caplan · UK

Royal Garden Hotel
1960s · Ronald Armstrong · UK

Offset-Haus
Printing
1960s · Walter Bangerter · CH

Ecos
Security services
1969 · Ricardo Blanco · AR

Royal Garden Hotel
1960s · Ronald Armstrong · UK

The Conservation Trust of Puerto Rico
Ecological and heritage conservation
1968 · Chermayeff & Geismar · US

Universidad Tecnológica Nacional
University
1966 · Ricardo Blanco · AR

Petite Maison Shimazaki
Clothing
1977 · Akira Hirata, Hiroshi Tada · JP

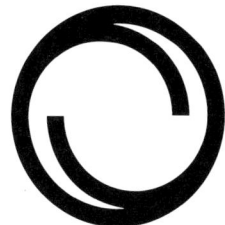

Roto Smeets
Printing
1968 · Marcel Pijpers · NL

375

Multiprocessors
Furniture
1981 · Gustavo Gómez-Casallas,
Rodrigo Fernández · CO

Tanner
Model aircraft
1950s · Marcel Wyss · CH

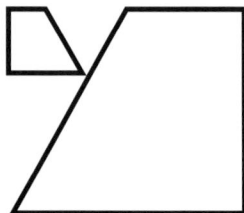

Dutch Pavilion, Expo '70, Osaka
World's fair stand
1969 · Total Design · NL

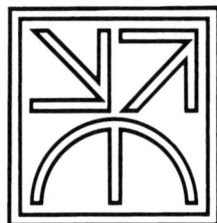

Metall
Machinery
1966 · Jan Jaring · NL

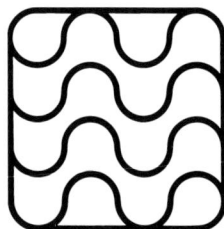

Visual Design Program
Design education
1970 · Manuel Espinoza · VE

Honbo Office
Real estate
1979 · Takenobu Igarashi · JP

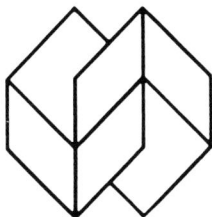

Banco Mercantil do Brasil
Bank
1969 · Aloísio Magalhães/PVDI · BR

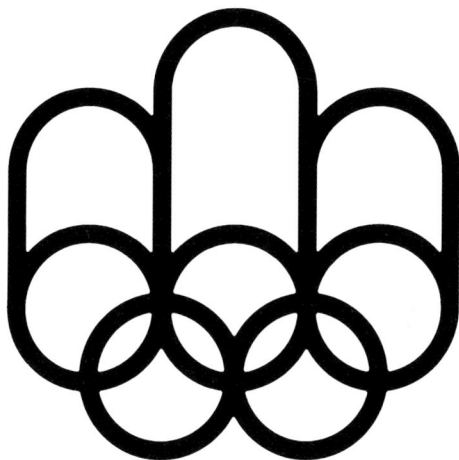

Olympic Games, Montreal 1976
1976 · George Huel · CA

Broome County
Transportation
1960s · Fritz Gottschalk/
Gottschalk+Ash · CA

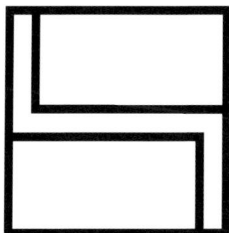

Wilkhahn Sitzmöbel
Furniture
1964 · Rolf Müller · DE

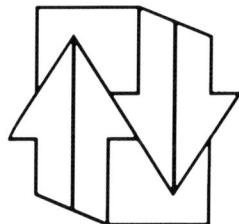

Del Libro sin Arco, Caracas
Publishing
1971 · Gerd Leufert · VE

Ets Roland
Paper bags
1962 · Raymond Loewy/CEI · FR

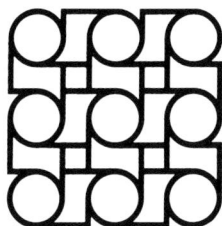

Revista del Colegio de Arquitectos
Architectural magazine
1970 · Álvaro Sotillo · VE

Beckers
Inks
1968 · Stig Arbman · SE

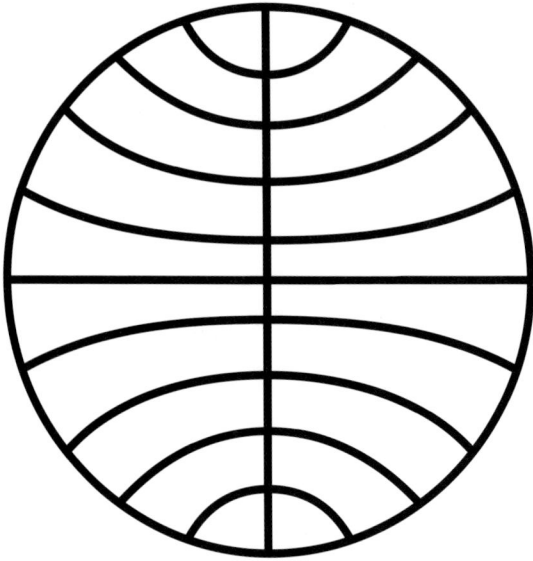

Pan American Airlines
1950 · Edward Larrabee Barnes,
Charles Forberg, Ivan Chermayeff · US

L'Opéra de Québec
Opera
1971 · Yvon Laroche,
Pierre-Yves Pelletier · CA

Laboratoire de Cosmétologie Biologique
Cosmetics
1968 · Gilles Fiszman · FR

Sosiaalihuollon Keskusliitto
Social services
1958 · Olof Eriksson · FI

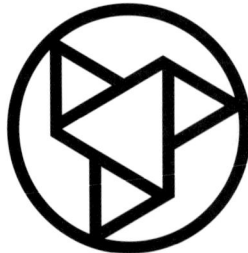

Pieter Schoen
Paint
1963 · Karel Suyling · NL

Manifattura Valle dell'Orco
Plastics
1952 · Egidio Bonfante · IT

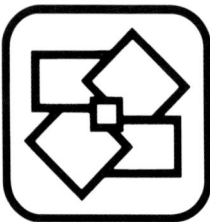

Saldos de Papel
Paper
1983 · Olga Dorantes/
Saxdid Diseño · MX

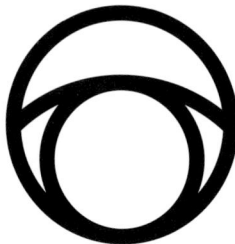

Spectrum Möbel
Furniture
1960 · Teun Teunissen van Manen · NL

Internationale Verkehrsausstellung München
Transport exhibition
1963 · Ernst Ruchay · DE

Pepsi-Cola International
Beverage
1975 · Richard Hess · US

Pelican Films
Film production
1960s · S. Neil Fujita · US

Ota Dental Clinic
1974 · Koichi Watanabe · JP

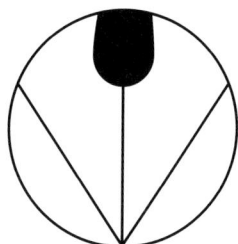

Flora Olomouc
Flower festival
1970s · Jan Rajlich · CZ

Canadian Film Institute
1962 · Georges Beaupré · CA

Tourism Association
1970 · Tomás Vellvé · ES

Fundación Mito Juan Pro-Música
Record label
1969 · Nedo Mion Ferrario · VE

Boda Glasbruk Glassworks
1960s · Bertil Andersson-Bertilson · SE

Institute for Expoart Control
1960s · Ludvík Feller · CZ

Deutsche Medizin-Messe
Medical exhibition
1978 · Michael Herold · DE

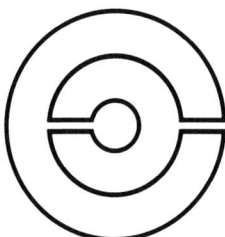

Concordia S.P.R.L.
Insurance
1965 · Antoon de Vijlder · BE

CHIARIFORTI

Chiari & Forti
Foods
1969 · Bob Noorda/
Unimark International · IT

Worldport Corporation
Furniture
1958 · Read Viemeister · US

Mar Beach
Watersports club
1960s · Nedo Mion Ferrario · VE

Sigtay
Light bulbs
1968 · Michel Olyff · BE

Ohio Center
Banquet hall
1975 · Chermayeff & Geismar · US

Watney Combe Reid & Co.
Brewing
1960s · Milner Gray/
Design Research Unit · UK

Saffa Cartiera
Paper
1966 · Walter Del Frate · IT

Sardinhas Coqueiro
Tinned sardines
1958 · Alexandre Wollner · BR

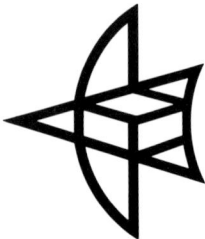

Internationale Luftfrachtgesellschaft
Air freight
1963 · Erich Unger · DE

AT & T
Telecommunications
1969 · Saul Bass · US

L. S. Croth & Co.
Insurance law office
1969 · John S. Brown · CA

International Public
Relations Association
1966 · Hans Kleefeld/
Stewart & Morrison · DE/US

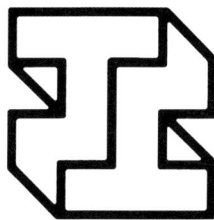

Ikola Design
1979 · Gale William Ikola · US

Hamburger Großdruckerei
Printing
1940s · Gust Hahn · DE

Das Band
Clothing
1960s · M. Rudin · CH

Metrocraft
Publishing
1977 · Don Connelly · US

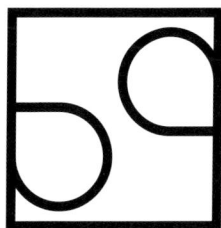

Qualitätssiegel Echt Silber
Silver quality mark
1974 · Hans Karl Rodenkirchen · DE

The Bellwood Company
Doors
1961 · Joseph Weston · US

A. S. Nicholson & Son
Timber
1965 · Jack Reid/
Hiller Rinaldo Associates · CA

Olle & Wolter Verlag
Publishing
1978 · Anonymous · DE

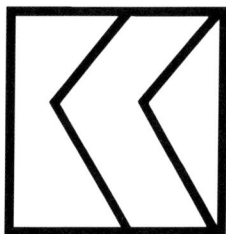

Kuwahara
Automobiles
1981 · Sogen Onishi · JP

Nacional de Resinas
Plastics
1978 · Fernando Rión · MX

Société Prénatal
Baby products
1966 · Rudi Meyer · FR

Collège de Maisonneuve
School
1969 · George Huel,
Pierre-Yves Pelletier · CA

Erik Jørgensen Møbelfabrik
Furniture
1960s · Anonymous · DK

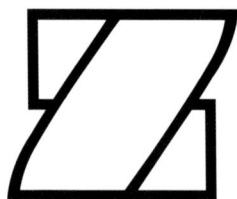

Zinnober Verlag
Publishing
1984 · Jan Buchholz, Peter Albers · DE

Kato Insatu
Printing
1973 · Sumio Hasegawa · JP

Administración Pública
Magazine
1970 · Claude Dietrich · PE

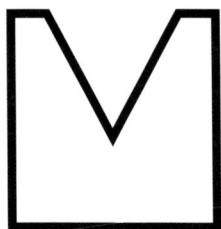

Meplex
Metal goods
1969 · Klaus Hofmann · CH

Planning One
Interior design
1979 · Kazuo Kanai · JP

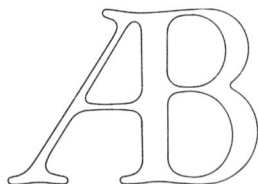

Anthony Blond
Publishing
1962 · Fletcher, Forbes, Gill · UK

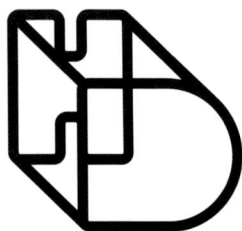

Horacio Durán
Furniture
1971 · Ernesto Lehfeld · MX

Fundação Bienal de São Paulo
Art foundation
1965 · PVDI · BR

Kuraray
Safety glass
1964 · Tadasu Fukano · JP

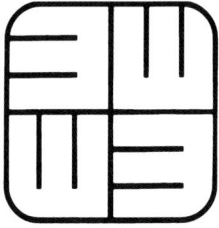

Emme Edizioni
Publishing
1967 · Salvatore Gregorietti/
Unimark International · IT

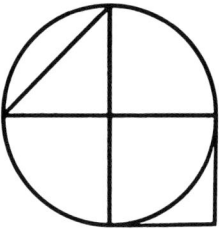

Anivo
Furniture
1967 · Rudolf Verelst · BE

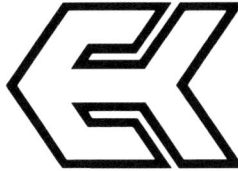

H. Schneider
Ceramics
1969 · Kurt Wirth · CH

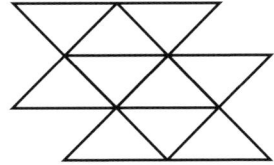

**Technical School of
Advertising and Design**
1965 · Günter Junge · DE-GDR

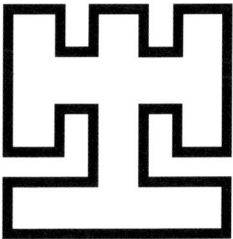

Eduard Keller
Import-export
1972 · Hansruedi Scheller · CH

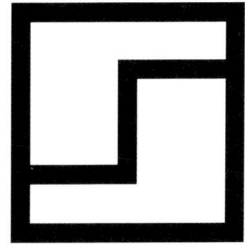

Hong Kong Hilton
Hotel
1960s · Henry Steiner · HK

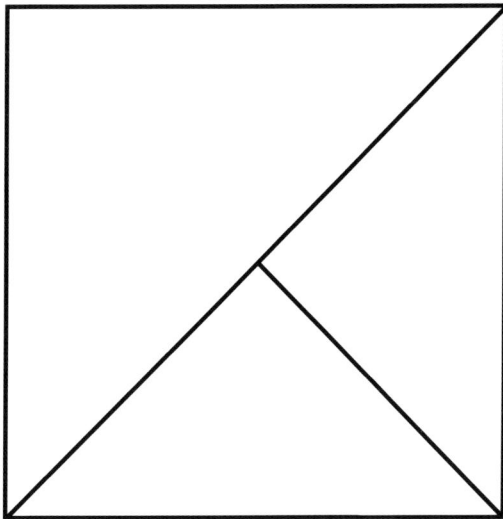

Tamminen & Havaste
Architecture
1969 · Seppo Polameri · FI

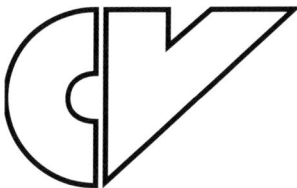

Claudius Verlag
Publishing
1986 · Werner Richter · DE

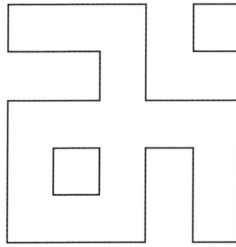

Städtische Kunsthalle Düsseldorf
Art gallery
1967 · Walter Breker · DE

Union
Political party
1950s · Heinz Schwabe · DE

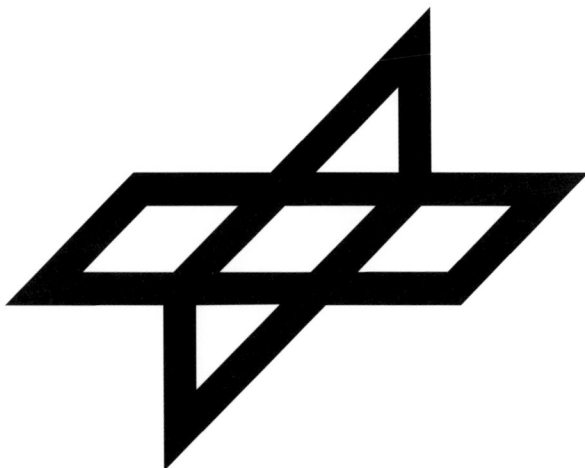

Deutsche Luft und Raumfahrtgesellschaft
German aerospace
1970s · Bruno K. Wiese · DE

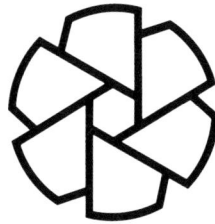

Plüss-Staufer
Chalk
1968 · Hans R. Woodtli · CH

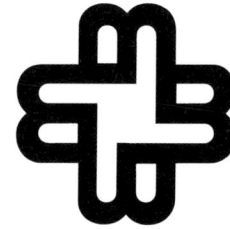

Broadbents of Southport
Clothing
1967 · Tony Forster · UK

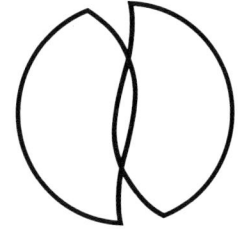

Birrificio Angelo Poretti
Brewing
1960s · Michele Provinciali · IT

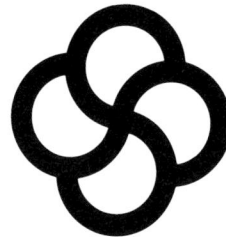

Swedish Union
1960s · Bertil Andersson-Bertilson · SE

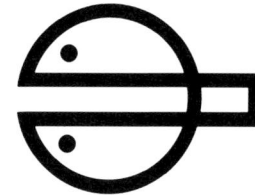

Fischerei Cürten
Fishing
1960s · Klaus Winterhager · DE

Panam Propaganda
Advertising
1959 · Alexandre Wollner · BR

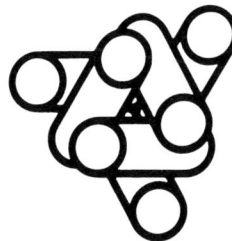

IPI
Prefabricated building parts
1973 · Mimmo Castellano · IT

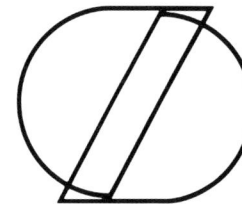

**Instituto de
Orientación en Arte, Caracas**
Art academy
1969 · Nedo Mion Ferrario · VE

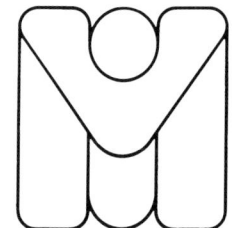

Verzekerings Maatschappij
Insurance
1968 · Hartmut Kowalke,
Christine Witt/Total Design · NL

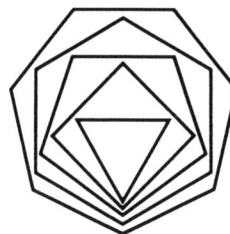

**IUPAC Conference on
Physical Organic Chemistry**
1971 · Gisela Buomberger · CH

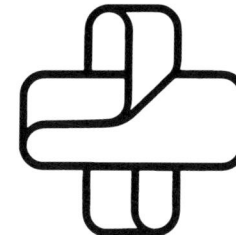

Tosama Domžale
Hygiene products
1977 · Ivan Dvoršak · YU

Brot & Backwarenfabrik Bergen
Bakers
1965 · Klaus Grosche · DE-GDR

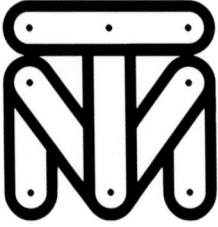

Mobiltecnica
Metal furniture
1967 · Piero Sansoni · IT

Bunte Stube Ahrenshoop
Ceramics
1965 · Georg Hülsse · DE-GDR

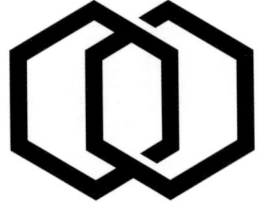

Polska Firma Handlowa
Import-export
1960s · Stephan Śledziński · PL

Westinghouse Learning Corporation
Education
1967 · Tom Woodward · US

Packaging Design Magazine
1966 · Andrew Kner · US

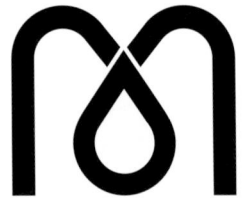

Metro Sprinkler
Fire extinguishers
1968 · Appelbaum & Curtis · US

Otto Harberer
Ventilation systems
1940s · Paul Sollberger · CH

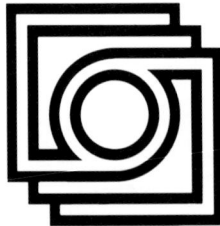

Infor-Información Organizada
Advertising
1970 · Nedo Mion Ferrario · VE

Laboratório Maurício Villela
Pharmaceuticals
1960s · Aloísio Magalhães/PVDI · BR

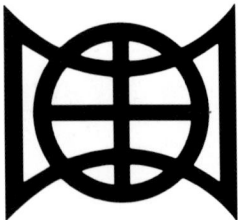

Panorama
Exhibition
1965 · Rudolf Graßmann · DE-GDR

Sitos-Werke
Baking powder
1960s · Walter M. Kersting · DE

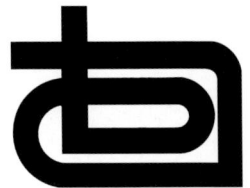

Sociedad Bolivariana de Arquitectos
Society of architects
1968 · Gerd Leufert · VE

Petroleum Refinery
1960s · Tadeusz Pietrzyk · PL

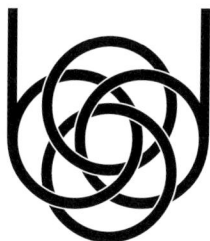

Blaine Karsten & Deirdre Michael
Wedding commemoration
1976 · Rockford Mjos · US

Sociedad Bolivariana de Arquitectos Society of architects
1968 · Gerd Leufert · VE

Suomen Akateeminen Urheiluliitto
Sports association
1969 · Jukka Veistola, Tapio
Korpisaari, Antti Laiho/Sok · FI

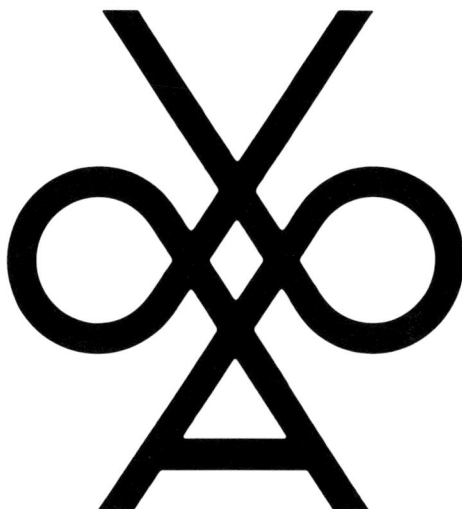

Kansai Electric
Energy supplier
1960s · Shichiro Imatake · JP

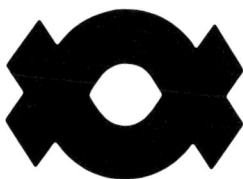

**Instituto Nacional de
Cultura y Bellas Artes**
Cultural institute
1965 · Gerd Leufert · VE

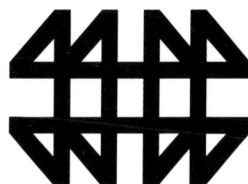

Vaccari Zincografica
Printing
1970 · Ivan Vaccari · IT

Stephens Biondi Decicco
Design
1960s · Stephens, Biondi, Decicco · US

Suomen Säästöpankkiliitto
Bank
1968 · Matti Viherjuuri/
Markkinointi Viherjuuri · FI

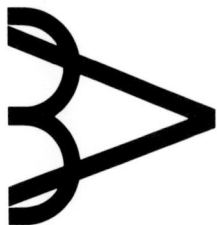

Ateneo de Boconó
Cultural association
1963 · Nedo Mion Ferrario · VE

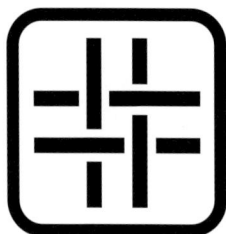

Pramassolwerk
Chemicals
1965 · Walter Seifert · DE-GDR

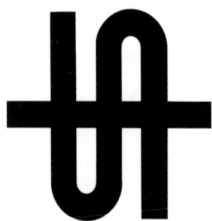

Werres & Geuertz
Rental cars
1954 · Hans Karl Rodenkirchen · DE

Ateneo de Boconó
Cultural association
1963 · Nedo Mion Ferrario · VE

The Empire Life Assurance Company
Insurance
1968 · James D. Taylor/
Rous & Mann Press · CA

Cinema of the University of California
1971 · Harry Murphy, Bud Thon/
Harry Murphy & Friends · US

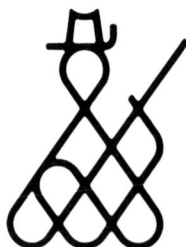

Tikkaustuote
Textiles
1966 · Rolf Christianson · FI

The Empire Life Assurance Company
Insurance
1968 · James D. Taylor/
Rous & Mann Press · CA

Cooperative Kopernik
Metalworks
1965 · Wladyslaw Brykczynski · PL

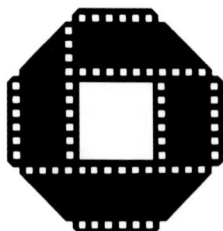

Telespazio
Space technology
1967 · Sergio Ruffolo · IT

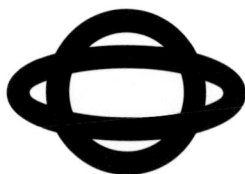

**Ministerium für Handel
und Versorgung Arkalaine**
Trade association
1965 · Ingo Arnold · DE-GDR

Cooperative Kopernik
Metalworks
1965 · Wladyslaw Brykczynski · PL

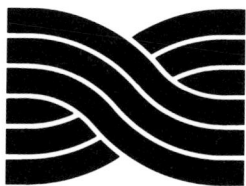

Casa de la Amistad
Social organization
1978 · Félix Beltrán · CU

Sørliemøbler
Furniture
1960s · Anonymous · NO

Diseñadores Comerciales
Design
1963 · Amand Domènech · ES

PGH Harzer
Clothing
1965 · Horst Jacob · DE-GDR

Hanf- und Leinenverkaufsgesellschaft
Hemp and linen
1940s · Hermann Eidenbenz · CH

GB
Vinyl production
1960s · Jiří Rathouský · CZ

Stella-Meta Filters
Water filtration
1972 · Tor A. Pettersen/
Lock Pettersen · UK

Colecciones Venezolanas
Art exhibition
1969 · Manuel Espinoza · VE

Toninelli
Art gallery
1960s · Erberto Carboni · IT

National Economics Editions
Publishing
1966 · Franciszek Winiarski · PL

Cooperative Walter
Textiles
1968 · Wladyslaw Brykczynski · PL

Editions René Julliard
Publishing
1957 · Marcel Jacno · FR

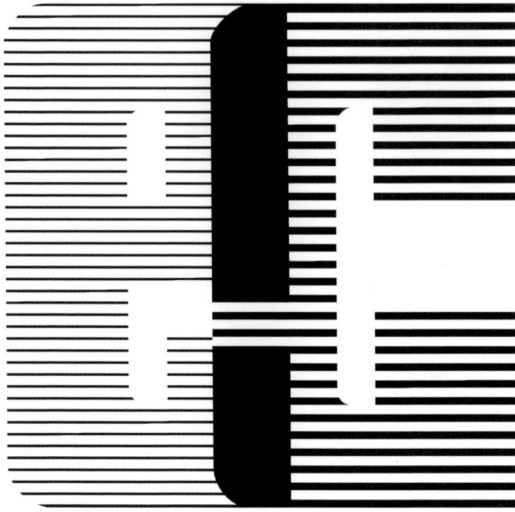

Eurocheque
Banking
1968 · Heinz Schwabe · DE

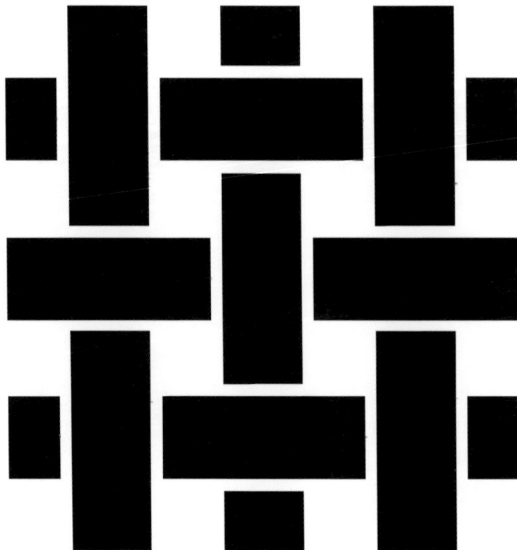

Kristjan Kristjansson
Design
1960 · Kristjan Kristjansson · IS

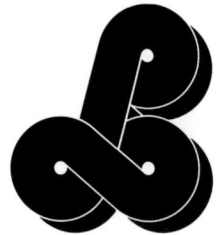

Lucassen
Furniture
1967 · Tel Design Associated · NL

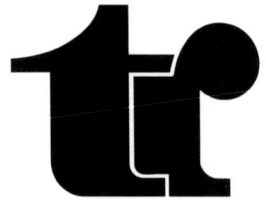

Jack Lenor Larsen
Textiles
1962 · James S. Ward, Arnold Saks · US

Tapeten-Ring
Wallpaper manufacturers
trade association
1972 · Siegfried W. Küchler · DE

Pattloch Verlag
Publishing
1976 · Klaus Imhoff · DE

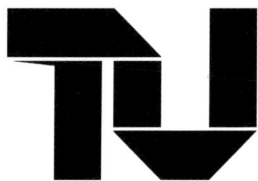

Urbanistico Territoriale
Urban development
1970 · Michele Spera · IT

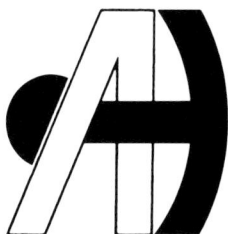

Aldus Books
Publishing
1966 · Romek Marber · UK

Crédit Agricole
Bank
1969 · Raymond Gid · FR

British Aluminium
1959 · Abram Games · UK

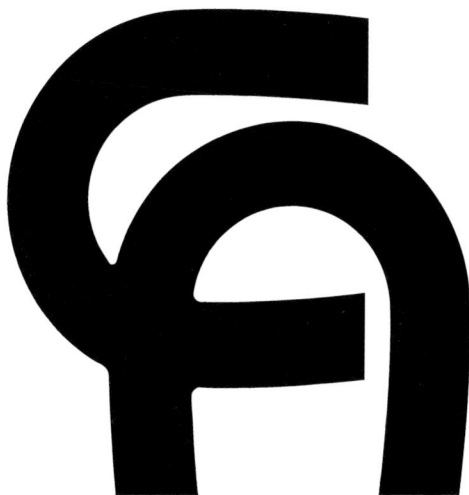

Pentamarmi
Marble quarries
1972 · Mimmo Castellano · IT

Boffi
Interior fittings
1971 · Mimmo Castellano · IT

Canada Wire and Cable Company
1969 · René Demers/
Hiller Rinaldo Associates · CA

C.O.N.I.
National Olympic committee
1970 · Mimmo Castellano · IT

Shearson Hammill
Investment
1963 · Philip Gips/Gips & Danne · US

Positif/
Négatif

Positiv/
Negativ

Positive/
Negative

Bayerischer Rundfunk
Broadcasting
1962 · Richard Roth · DE

Polar International Brokerage
Investment
1962 · Eckstein-Stone · US

Promociones Pando
Construction company
1981 · Elías García Benavides · ES

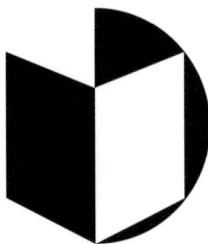

Openbare Bibliotheek
Public library
1958 · Ralph Prins · NL

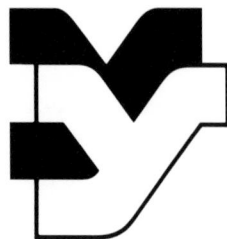

Yamamura Senkaku
Leather dyeing
1980 · Kuniharu Masubuchi,
Ikuo Masubuchi · JP

Untergrundbahn
Public transport (proposed design)
1960s · Hans Weckerle · DE

Bero-Kaffee & Extrakt
Coffee
1965 · Otto Kietzmann · DE-GDR

Pflanzenfettkombinat Velten
Foods
1965 · Conrad Priem · DE-GDR

Fritz Steck
1950s · Eugen & Max Lenz · CH

Xerca
Publishing
1969 · Rémy Peignot · FR

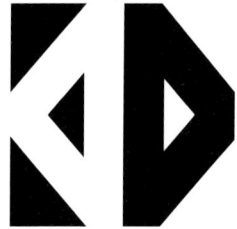

Davis Delany
Printing
1960s · A. Ross, B. Thompson · US

DIMAC
Mexican designers association
1972 · Ernesto Lehfeld · MX

F.lli Dioguardi
Construction company
1963 · Mimmo Castellano · IT

CKG
Real estate
1975 · Masatoshi Shimokawa · JP

Centrade Bank
1970 · Eugen & Max Lenz · CH

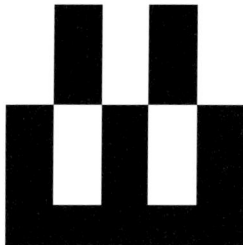

Wallace & Hess Studio
Design
1962 · Hess & Antupit · US

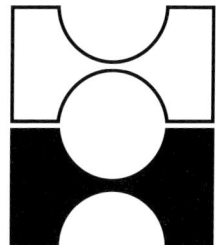

Hans Hesse
Architecture
1968 · M. van Winsen · NL

Novamedical
Pharmacy
1964 · Piero Sansoni · IT

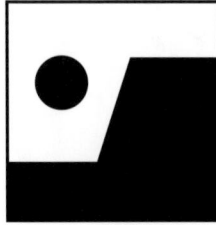

Tekstil-Opplysning
Textiles
1967 · Per Einar Eggen/
Alfsen, Becker & Bates · NO

Petrochemia
Chemicals
1960s · Wladyslaw Brykczynski · PL

Fiol-Biblioteket
Book series
1966 · Morten Peetz-Schou,
Bent Danielsen · DK

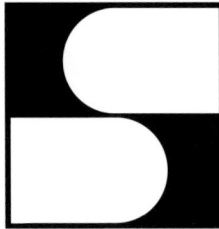

Staff & Schwarz Leuchtenwerk
Lighting
1965 · Anonymous · DE

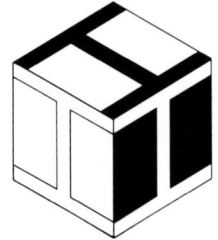

Harrison Wholesale Company
1967 · H. B. Smith, Franz Altschuler · US

Foire Internationale de Bruxelles
Trade fair
1965 · Luc Van Malderen · BE

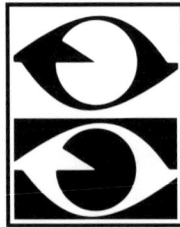

**Vereinigung Selbstständiger
Augenoptikermeister**
Opticians association
1970s · Anonymous · DE

Hasegawa Interior
Interior design
1974 · Akisato Ueda · JP

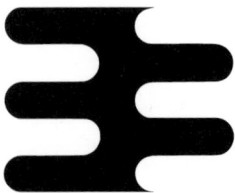

Stahl für die Welt von Morgen
Steel congress
1965 · Anonymous · DE

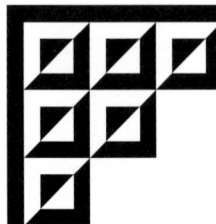

Ferrero Süsswaren
Confectionery (proposed design)
1960s · Eugen & Max Lenz · CH

Hala Mirowska
Department store
1964 · Roman Duszek · PL

Notec
Linen
1966 · Emilia Nozka-Paprocka · PL

Interplan
Interior design
1964 · James Lienhart/RVI Corp. · US

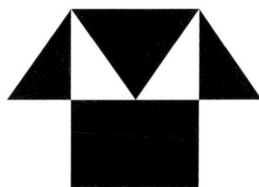

Maebara Coating
1983 · Yasaburo Kuwayama · JP

Dřevokombinát
Timber
1969 · František Bobáň · CZ

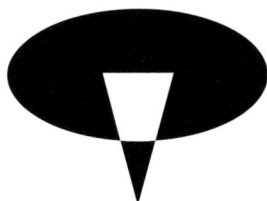

Lindell
Art supplies
1959 · Inkeri Vallioja · FI

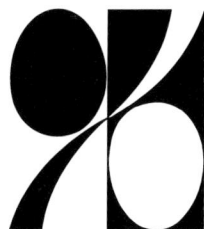

Union des Moulins à Huile de Provence
Vegetable oil manufacturers union
1964 · Design Groupe Viaud · FR

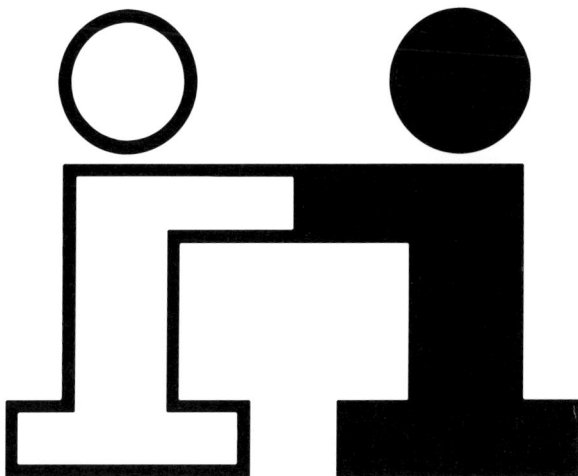

Kurt Versen
Lighting
1963 · Rudolph de Harak · US

Ideal Lebensversicherung
Insurance
1963 · Erich Unger · DE

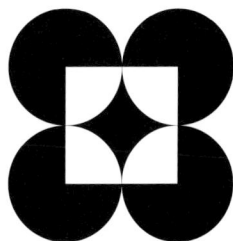

Aerlod Teoranta
Airline
1960s · Richard Geiger/Signa · IE

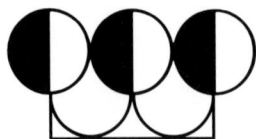

Antonio Corona
Photocopiers
1964 · Carmelo Cremonesi/
Stile-Advertising · IT

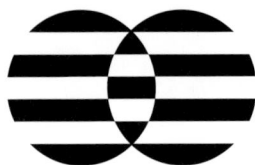

Sandra Berler
Photography gallery
1970s · Lance Wyman · US

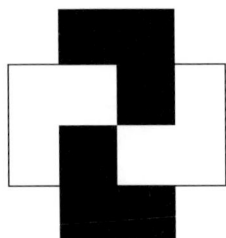

K. Thienemanns
Publishing
1973 · Ernst Strom · DE

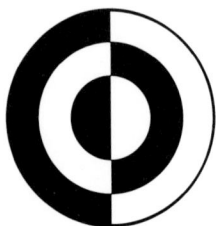

Petrochemia
Petroleum refinery
1960s · Jerzy Cherka · PL

Circolo Nautico Imperia
Yacht club
1972 · Giovanni Brunazzi · IT

Leipziger Wollkämmerei
Weaving
1965 · Ruth Weber · DE-GDR

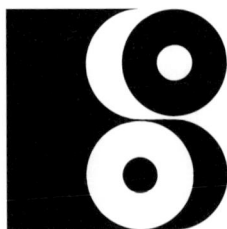

Tage Poulsens Møbelsnedkeri
Furniture
1960s · Anonymous · DK

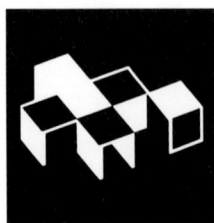

Bay State Abrasives
Bonded abrasive products
1960s · Malcolm Grear · US

Zenhanren
Agriculture
1967 · Yoshio Hayashi · JP

Mitsui Knowledge Industry
Communications
1971 · Gan Hosoya · JP

Khourie & Lawrence Associates
Interior design
1968 · Bill Hyde · US

Richard Hühnerkopf
Liquors
1973 · Heinz Schwabe · DE

396

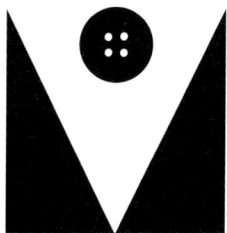

Melka
Clothing
1958 · Olle Eksell · SE

Russell & Hinrichs
Design
1966 · Tony Russell, Kit Hinrichs · US

Nahrungs- und
Genußmittelbetrieb, Halberstadt
Foods
1965 · Peter Hamann · DE-GDR

Nurmen Konepaja
Metal goods
1968 · Kyösti Varis · FI

Lebensversicherungen
Insurance
1950s · Heinz Schwabe · DE

Katsuyama Bowling Center
1971 · Gan Hosoya · JP

Galanteria Drewna
Toys
1967 · Emilia Nozka-Paprocka · PL

Forschervereinigung
Researchers association
1950 · Walther Bergmann · DE

Sukuwall Kojimachi
Hotel
1988 · Shigeo Fukuda · JP

Nederlandse Stichting voor Statistiek
Statistics office
1969 · Tel Design Associated · NL

Thomas & Kurzberg
Printing
1950s · Jupp Ernst · DE

Ind Coope
Brewing
1950s · Abram Games · UK

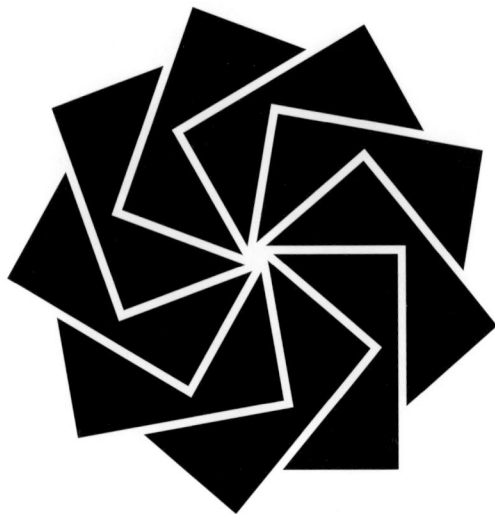

Gooische Glas- en Verfhandel
Craft supplies
1967 · Ben Bos/Total Design · NL

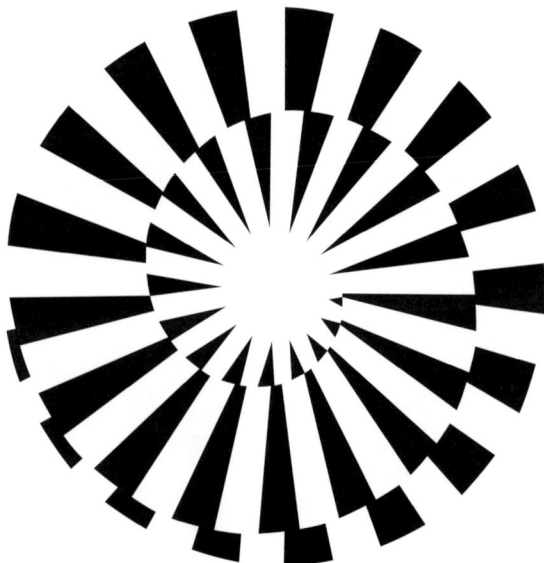

Olympic Games, Munich 1972
1972 · Coordt von Mannstein/
Graphicteam Köln · DE

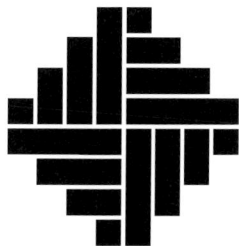

Royfund
Investment
1969 · Rolf Harder/
Design Collaborative · CA

Marché International de Rungis
Market halls
1967 · André Chante/
Hollenstein Création · FR

Gardena
Gardening tools
1970 · Hannes Schober,
Wolfram Reinhardt · DE

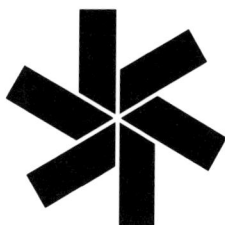

Stokke & Blindheim Möbelfabrikk
Furniture
1965 · Paul Brand · NO

Le Nordet
Theater
1971 · Raymond Bellemare · CA

Accurate Diamond Tools
Cutting tools
1976 · Ronald Cutro · US

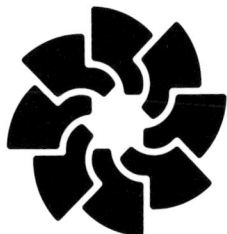

ISLO
Aluminum foundry
1978 · Ernesto Lehfeld · MX

Concretex Engenharia de Concreto
Concrete
1973 · João Carlos Cauduro,
Ludovico Antonio Martino · BR

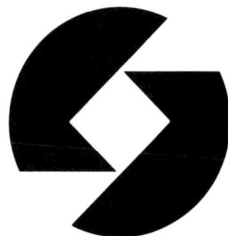

Precisa
Technical instruments
1976 · Manuel Sanchez · MX

Saitama Bank
1973 · Kazumasa Nagai · JP

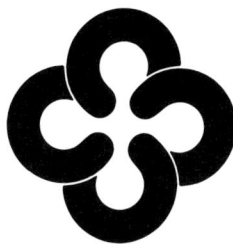

Mochiya
Bakery
1960s · Susumu Kimura · JP

Stichting Rijnmond-Nordzeekanal
Transportation
1960s · H. P. Doebele · NL

Controls Company
1960s · John Massey · US

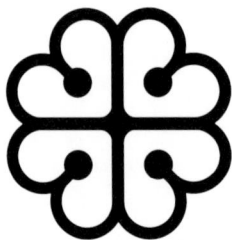

City of Montreal
City identity
1981 · George Huel · CA

Ontario Ministry of Labour
Government office
1978 · Roslyn Eskind, David Gibson · CA

Toyo Rayon
Synthetic fibers
1964 · Takeshi Otaka · JP

Turbocompresores
Air-conditioning
1981 · Monica Morales · MX

Duzan
Ceiling and roof-building
1960s · Lars Bramberg · SE

Saim Solar
Heating systems
1972 · Silvio Coppola · IT

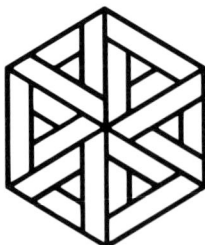

Historisches Museum Frankfurt am Main
Historical museum
1970 · Herbert W. Kapitzki · DE

Finnkino Oy
Movie rentals
1965 · Kyösti Varis · FI

Diateknikk
Audio-visual systems
1967 · Paul Brand · NO

Aco
Machinery
1970 · Gerd Leufert · VE

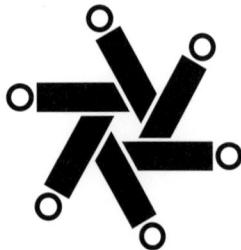

Idea Books
Publishing
1969 · Roberto Innocenti · IT

Sundt & Company
1969 · Bruno Oldani · NO

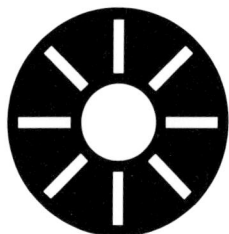

**National Institute
of Industrial Research**
1964 · Eduardo A. Cánovas · AR

Prose Recycling
1983 · Peter G. Ulmer · CH

Norm Scudellari
Photography
1970 · Leslie Smart · CA

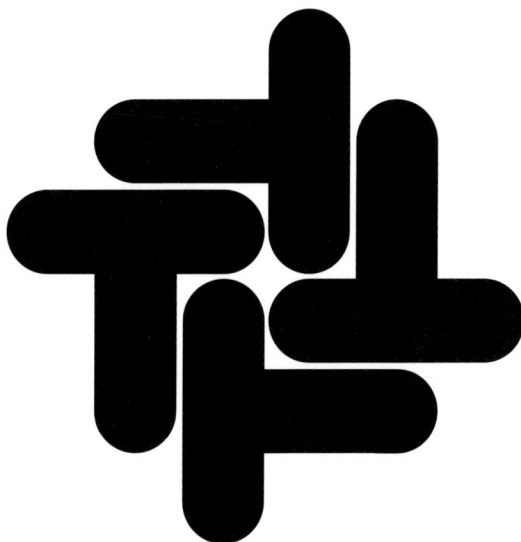

Titan Fasteners
Fittings and washers
1968 · Appelbaum & Curtis · US

Falcinelli Ceramiche
Wall and floor tiles
1973 · Franco Grignani · IT

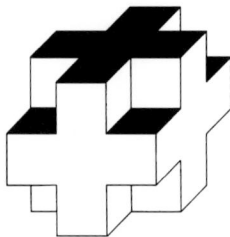

University of Chicago
Hospitals and clinics
1971 · Edward Hughes · US

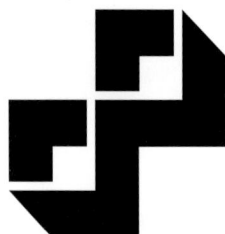

Hino Architect & Engineering
1975 · Tadamasa Katsube · JP

Dresdner Packungsbetrieb
Packaging
1965 · Fritz Panndorf · DE-GDR

Daiichi Zoen Doboku
Landscape architecture
1981 · Akira Hirata, Hiroshi Mori · JP

Museo Nacional
Museum
1970 · Félix Beltrán · CU/MX

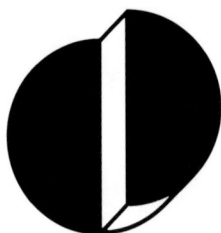

Facility Technology & Management
Computer systems
1969 · Eskil Ohlsson · US

Institute of Urban Planning
1960s · Shigeo Fukuda · JP

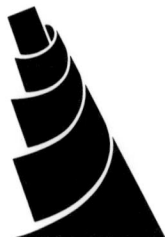

New Left Books
Publishing
1970 · Ken Garland · UK

402

Francisco Soler
Construction company
1972 · Francesc Guitart · ES

**British Organisation for the
Development of Exports**
1968 · John Gibbs/Unit Five Design · UK

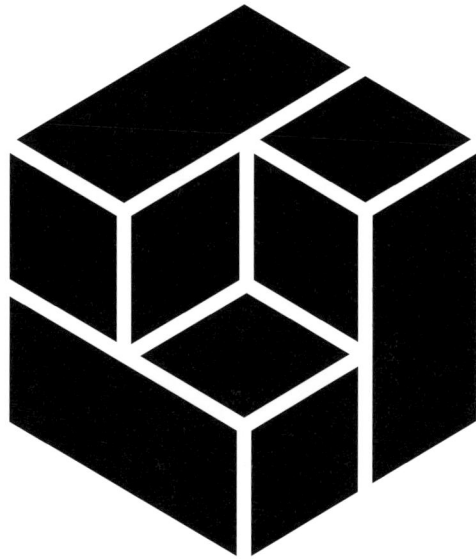

Haraldssøn
Office furniture
1968 · Paul Brand · NO

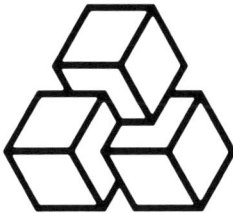

Banco do Estado do Rio Grande
Bank
1965 · Aloísio Magalhães/PVDI · BR

Pictogramma
Art gallery
1971 · Michele Spera · IT

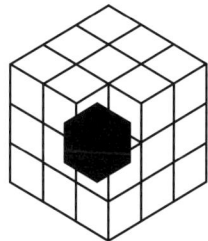

Marion Shop
Toys
1971 · Luciano Francesconi · IT

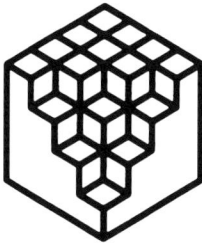

L'Escalier
Clothing
1970 · Michele Spera · IT

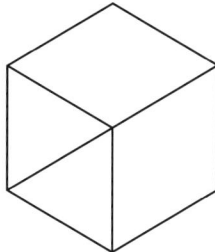

Otto Zapf Möbel
Furniture
1965 · Wolfgang Schmidt · DE

Colegio de Arquitectos
School of architecture
1977 · Álvaro Sotillo · VE

American Can Company
Can manufacturer
1967 · George Tscherny · US

Univerza v Mariboru P. A.
University
1980 · Ivan Dvoršak · YU

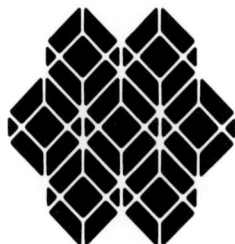

The Icehouse, San Francisco
1975 · Michael Vanderbyl · US

Se.Co.A.
Management consultancy
1973 · Da Centro Disegno · IT

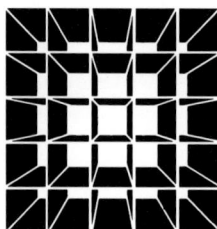

Hewitt Associates
Management consultancy
1982 · Jack Weiss, Randi Robin · US

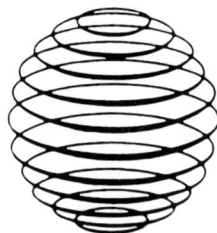

Hemisphere Club
Lunch club
1970 · George Nelson · US

G. Jantsch Druckerei
Printing
1980 · Hermann Zapf · DE

Vita Farmac
Pharmaceuticals
1955 · Ryszard Sidorowski · PL

The California State Exposition
Exhibitions
1966 · Saul Bass & Associates · US

Equity Funding Corporation of America
Insurance
1969 · Gary Hinsche/
Robert Miles Runyan · US

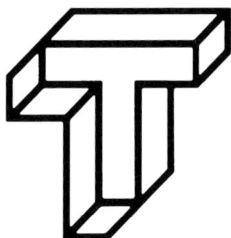

Quinpool Centre Developments
1977 · Rick Cartledge · CA

Matui Architectural Office
Planning office
1977 · Akisato Ueda · JP

Tornaghi Mobiliere
Furniture
1979 · R. Nava, D. Soffientini,
G. Romani, A. Ubertazzi · IT

Standard Show Services
Exhibitions
1968 · Ernst Roch/
Design Collaborative · CA

Empaques de Cartón Titán
Packaging
1970s · Lance Wyman · US/MX

Kuresa
Adhesive films and papers
1980 · Claude Dietrich · PE

Meyster
Publishing
1977 · Anonymous · DE

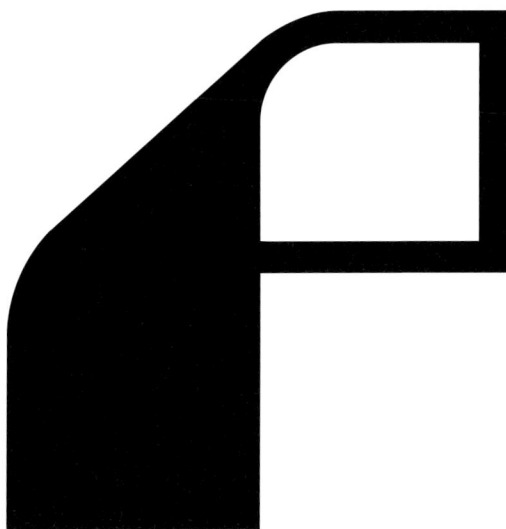

Fotoklub Maribor
Photographers club
1975 · Ivan Dvoršak · YU

Harmonic Groupement
Industrial investment
1973 · Jean Delaunay/Look · FR

Peter Paulsen
Real estate
1978 · Harry Murphy, Stanton Klose · US

Michael Novak
Architecture
1975 · Lanny Sommese · US

Sabco
Trucks
1967 · Jay Hanson · US

Telimena
Textiles
1965 · Witold Surowiecki · PL

H. Wesselo en J.J. van Voorst
Architecture
1970 · Jan Jaring · NL

Policomer
Import-export
1971 · Enric Huguet · ES

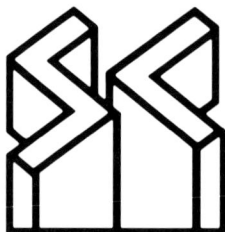

System Creates
Planning office
1978 · Takao Yoguchi · JP

Fapasa
Road construction
1958 · Enric Huguet · ES

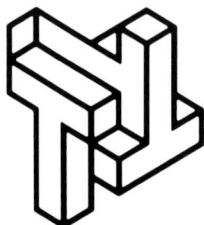

Investors Diversified Services
Financial management
1977 · Gale William Ikola · US

Tetsuya Ohta
Design
1980 · Tetsuya Ohta · JP

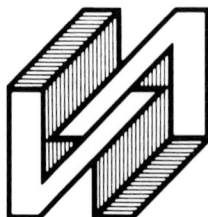

Vetreria Angelana
Glass
1981 · Francesco Burcini · IT

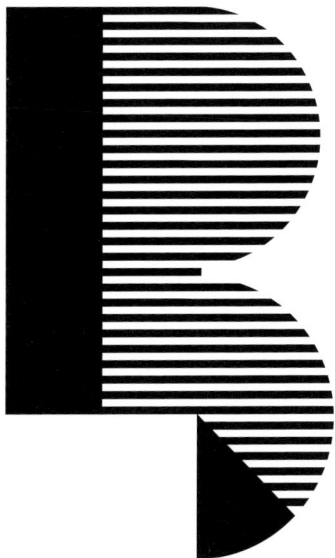

Leonblu
Furniture
1971 · Silvio Coppola · IT

Estructuras Activas
Industrial design
1970 · Nedo Mion Ferrario · VE

Webeg Baugesellschaft
Construction company
1972 · Siegfried W. Küchler · DE

Banque Nationale de Paris
Bank
1967 · A. Baier/Delpire-Advico · FR

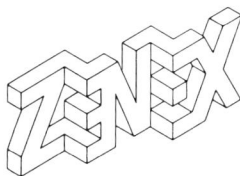

Fairlawn Industries
1970 · David Leigh · US

Redi-Mix Associates
Construction company
1980 · Richard Wittosch · US

Container Corporation of America
Packaging
1958 · Ralph E. Eckerstrom · US

Zenex
Construction company
1981 · Tony Forster · UK

Dimension
Broadcasting
1960s · Franz Wagner · US

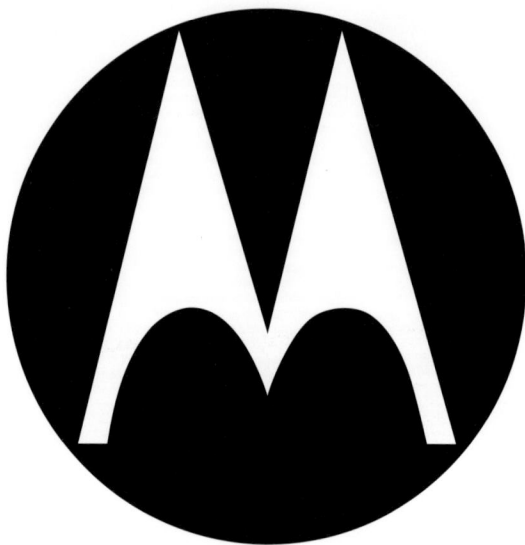

Motorola
Telecommunications
1952 · Morton Goldsholl · US

Marufuku
Ceramics
1979 · Kazuharu Fuji · JP

Facit
Furniture
1960s · Anonymous · SE

Kona Inn
Hotel
1970 · Clarence Lee · US

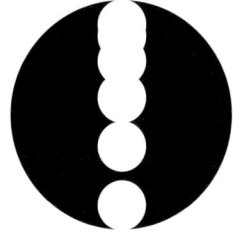

Bank of Iwate
1971 · Shigeo Fukuda · JP

Ontario Trucking Association
Transportation
1974 · Peter Adam/
Gottschalk+Ash · CA

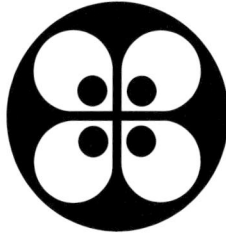

R. Murray & Son
Construction company
1970 · Raymond Lee · CA

Kokusai International
Travel agency
1969 · Jim Miho · JP

Ono City Ironware Cooperative
Workers association
1982 · Ikuya Kimura · JP

Tele-Tape Productions
Television studios
1968 · Seldon G. Dix Jr. · US

Meiji
Chocolates
1967 · Tadashi Ohashi · JP

René Gigandet
Design
1960s · René Gigandet · CH

Suginoko Academy
School
1983 · Yasuhisa Iguchi · JP

Kowa Art Printing
1979 · Kimito Ohashira · JP

United Semiconductor
Electronics
1967 · Carl Seltzer · US

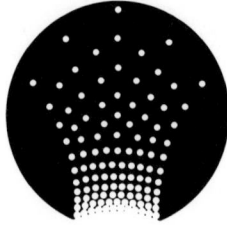

Miss Universe Contest
Beauty pageant
1978 · Joe Vera, Francisco Tellez · MX

Cinémathèque Suisse
Movie theater
1960s · Roger-Virgile Geiser · CH

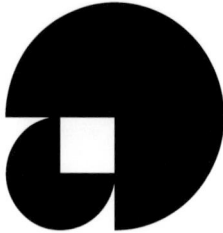

Prestigio Linoleum
Flooring
1958 · Roberto Sambonet · IT

H. Te Laake
Watches
1967 · Bruno K. Wiese · DE

Schweizer Druckerei
Printing
1960s · Roger-Virgile Geiser · CH

Miyanami Engineering
1980 · Shunji Ninomi · JP

Paracom
Sporting goods
1977 · Mike Quon, Chris Zoulamis · US

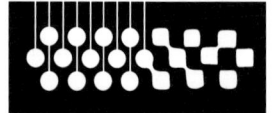

Kimberly-Clark Corporation
Munising Paper Division
1957 · Morton Goldsholl · US

Kyoho
Textiles
1969 · Tomoichi Nishiwaki,
Akisato Ueda · JP

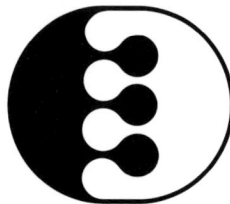

Dr. Wander
Pharmaceuticals
1967 · Peter Megert · CH

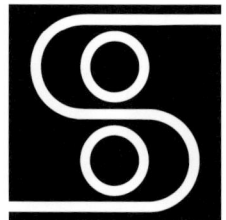

Sonika
Tape recorders
1960s · Bob Noorda · NL

Trade Fair for Silk Products
1960s · Jun Tabohashi · JP

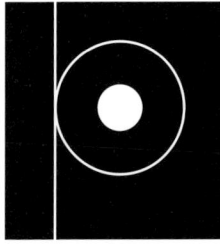

Photo Set
1971 · Hans Hurter · CH

BDK Kulturorganisation
Cultural organization
1950s · Eugen Hotz · CH

ZDF/Zweites Deutsches Fernsehen
Broadcasting
1961 · G. W. Hörnig · DE

Atelier Moderner Beleuchtungskörper
Lighting
1940s · Karl J. Weiss · CH

Arndt-Verlag
Publishing
1963 · Anonymous · DE

Rochester Institute of Technology
University
1966 · R. Roger Remington · US

Bunnosuke Syokuhin
Foods
1978 · Hiroyuki Okuda · JP

Les Assurances Nationales
Insurance
1968 · Pascal Besson · CH

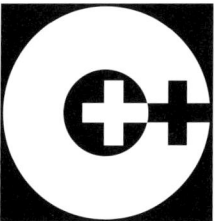

Red Cross Blood Donation
1960s · Hans Hartmann · CH

Capper-Neill
Construction company
1967 · Rupert Armstrong, Milner
Gray/Design Research Unit · UK

Elektrochemie und Plaste Halle
Chemicals and plastics
1965 · Gerhard Voigt · DE-GDR

Galleria Peccolo
Art gallery
1971 · Franco Grignani · IT

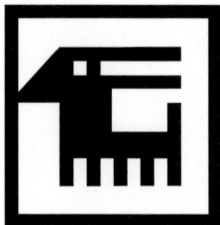

Népművészeti és Háziipari V.
Folk art trading
1964 · István Szekeres · HU

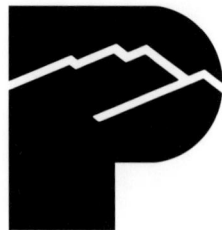

Pila
Tourism
1979 · Giovanni Brunazzi · IT

International Airport Consultants of Montreal
Airport management
1970 · Julien Hébert · CA

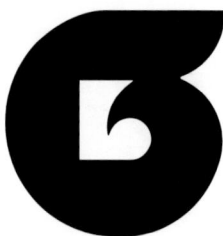

Gulf Life Holding Company
Insurance
1975 · Jack Evans · US

Redaelli-Como
1978 · Pietro Galli · IT

Exposition Belge des Transports
Exhibition committee
1964 · Julian Key · BE

Cellulose and Paper Factory
1960s · Ernst Roch · CA

La Comète
Film advertising
1960s · Bob Noorda · IT

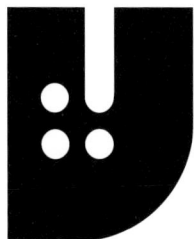

Vega
Clothing
1977 · Raúl Shakespear,
Ronald Shakespear · AR

VEB Hydrocarbon
Fuel company
1965 · Horst Müller · DE-GDR

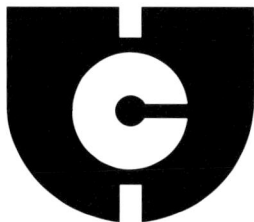

Weather Routing
Weather forecasting
1978 · Bill Bundzak · US

Sun Art Printing
1983 · Hiroshi Manzen · JP

Aspa-Plast-System
Frames
1977 · Walter Hergenröther · IT

Bertelsmann Buchclub
Book club
1957 · Sepp Huber · DE

Kuachukov Závod
Footwear
1964 · Sotir Sotirov · BG

Doubinski Frères
Furniture
1965 · Raymond Loewy/CEI · FR

Marcello Masi
Office machines
1973 · Rinaldo Cutini · IT

T

Typographique

Typografisch

Typografie

Typographie

Alongside abstract or semi-representational images, lettering and word-marks play a key role in modernist logos. While the meaning of a symbol-based logo can only be deciphered when words of explanation are added, typographic signs are instantly "legible". In addition to popular word-marks, usually showing the full name of the company, single letters or combinations of letters represent a special kind of typographic logo. Following in the age-old tradition of the monogram, one or more single letters stand for a company's complete graphic identity.

Neben den abstrakten oder teilgegenständlichen Zeichen gehört auch die Kategorie der Buchstaben- oder Wortmarke zu den modernistischen Logos. Während symbolbasierte Zeichen oft nur im Zusammenspiel mit erklärender Schrift ihre Bedeutung erhalten, sind typografische Zeichen direkt „lesbar". Ergänzend zur weitverbreiteten Wortmarke, die meist den vollständigen Unternehmensnamen abbildet, stellen Einzelbuchstaben bzw. Buchstabenkombinationen eine besondere Gruppe im Bereich der typografischen Logos dar. Nach der Tradition historischer Monogramme verweisen hier nur einzelne Buchstaben auf den kompletten Wortlaut eines Unternehmens.

À côté des signes abstraits ou partiellement figuratifs, certains logos modernes relèvent encore d'une autre catégorie, celle des sigles et des logotypes. Alors que les signes symboliques prennent tout leur sens dans l'interaction avec l'écrit qui les éclaire, le signe typographique est directement « lisible ». Complétant le logotype largement répandu, qui reproduit généralement le nom complet de l'entreprise, les lettres isolées ou les combinaisons de lettres constituent un groupe particulier dans le domaine du logo typographique. Dans le sillage du monogramme traditionnel, seules des lettres isolées renvoient ici au nom complet de l'entreprise.

Avery
Label maker
1970s · Saul Bass & Associates · US

Azuma Drive-In
1975 · Akisato Ueda · JP

Mechanikai Művek
Heating technology
1970 · István Szekeres · HU

Aluminum Company of America
1970s · Saul Bass & Associates · US

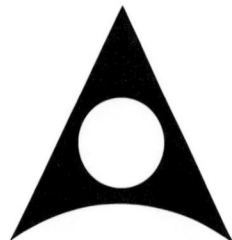

San Francisco International Airport
1969 · Thomas Laufer & Associates · US

Studio di Architettura
Design and architectural school
1981 · A. G. Fronzoni · IT

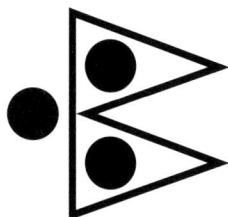

**Staatliche Akademie
für Grafik, Druck und Werbung**
Design school
1950s · Franz Hermann Wills · DE

E. Breuninger
Textiles
1948 · Hanns Lohrer · DE

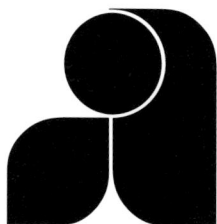

**Arbeitsgemeinschaft
kultureller Institutionen**
Cultural association
1960 · Walter Breker · DE

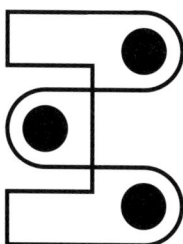

Bagel Druck
Printing
1971 · Walter Breker · DE

Verkehrsverein Basel
Tourism
1968 · Armin Hofmann · CH

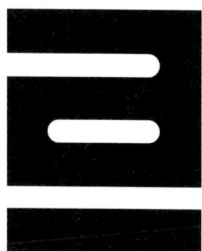

Allied Casting
Construction company
1960s · Kramer, Miller, Lomden,
Glassman Inc. · US

Houtoku
Furniture
1980 · Shunji Ninomi · JP

Boles Aero
Caravans
1960s · Jerry Braude · US

Abbott
Pharmaceuticals
1960s · Don Ervin/
George Nelson & Co. · US

Bunka Hyoronsha
Publishing
1982 · Makoto Yoshida · JP

Félix Beltrán
Design
1960 · Félix Beltrán · CU

Chemische Werke Buna, Schkopau
Chemicals
1965 · Gerhard Voigt · DE-GDR

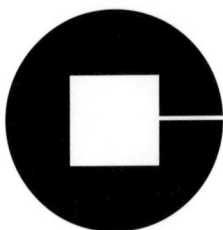

Carl Christiansen
Construction company
1961 · Werner Hartz · DE

Continentale Versicherungen
Insurance
1970 · Ulrich Schürmann · DE

Clark Technologies
Mechanical engineering
1975 · R. Roger Remington · US

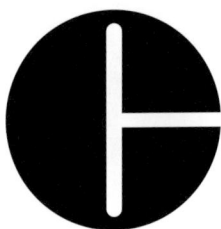

Colmers
Grocery
1966 · Kenneth Hollick · UK

Centrum-Warenhaus
Department store
1965 · Herbert Prüget · DE-GDR

Continental Can
Canning and packaging
1972 · Anspach Grossman Portugal · US

Commodore
Computer systems
1965 · Chris Yaneff · CA

Diblo Holding
Import-export
1979 · Joe Vera, Francisco Tellez · MX

Cayena
1978 · Hugo Arapé · FR

Caterpillar Tractor
Construction equipment
1967 · Lester Beall · US

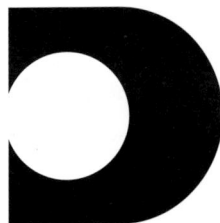

Delta Tooling
Machinery
1960s · Mort Walsh · CA

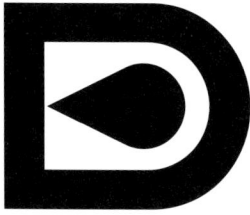

Clichy Distugil
Plastics
1967 · Jacques Nathan-Garamond · FR

Edwin Vogt & Partner
Printing
1982 · Armin Vogt · CH

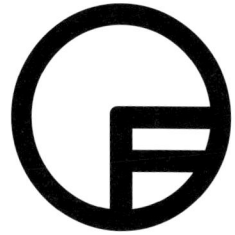

Famos
Textiles
1976 · R. Nava, D. Soffientini, G. Romani,
A. Ubertazzi · IT

Défilé Foires
Exhibition
1970s · Jan Rajlich · CZ

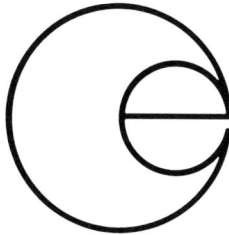

Edition Leipzig
Publishing
1975 · Sonja Wunderlich · DE-GDR

Fuji Kyuso
Haulier
1978 · Shinichi Takahara · JP

E-Marke
Crayons
1960s · Walter Breker · DE

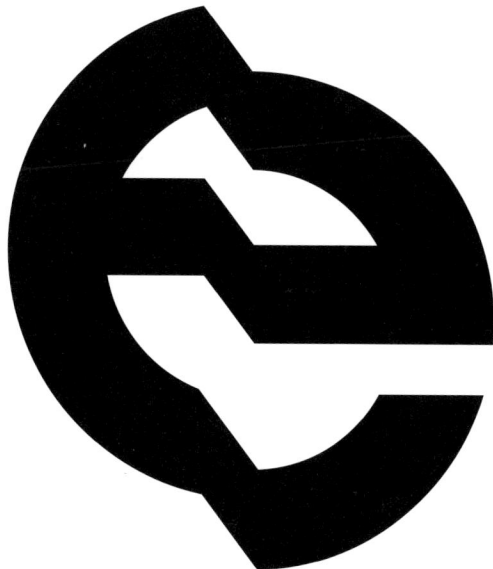

Electrolux
Domestic appliances
1962 · Marcel Wyss · CH

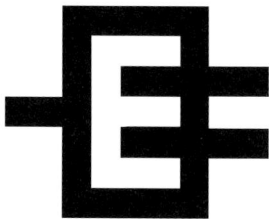

Ediltur
Travel agency
1975 · Alfredo de Santis · IT

Formation Furniture
1965 · Fletcher, Forbes, Gill · UK

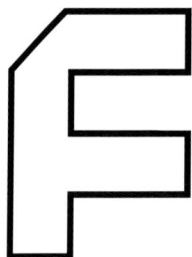

Stadt Gelsenkirchen
City identity
1970s · Eberhard Hippler · DE

Georg Jensen Sølvsmedie
Product design
1969 · Morten Peetz-Schou,
Ulla Heegaard · DK

Friesland Bank
1973 · Wim Crouwel · NL

Nederlandse Gasunie
Energy supplier
1965 · Otto Treumann · NL

22nd International Geographical
Congress, Ottawa
1969 · Fritz Gottschalk, Ian Valentine/
Gottschalk+Ash · CA

Oy Aero Finnair
Airline
1966 · Kyösti Varis · FI

George Gärtner
Advertising
1971 · G. W. Hörnig · DE

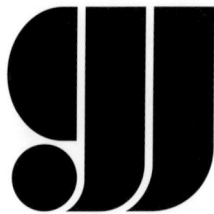

Verkehrsverein Grindelwald
Tourism
1969 · Hans Hartmann · CH

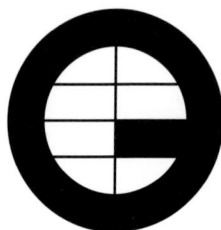

Schweizer Filmarchiv
Film archive
1950 · Hermann Eidenbenz · CH

Girad
Bank
1960s · Emil O. Biemann · US

Graphic Designers Association
1979 · Kazuo Kishimoto · JP

Hotel
1956 · Félix Beltrán · CU/MX

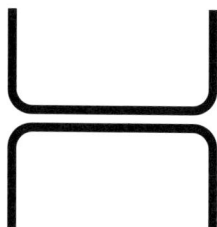

L. Holzer & Co.
Tables
1968 · Ken Garland · UK

Kempinform
Campsite
1983 · István Szekeres · HU

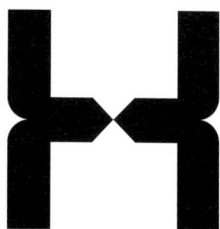

Halifax Shopping Center
1961 · Ernst Roch/
Design Collaborative · CA

Hilton
Hotel chain
1964 · Anonymous · US

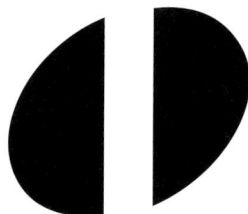

Ishigami Nikko
Gems
1982 · Harukata Yano, Hiro Terao · JP

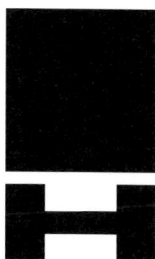

Hunziker Transporte Rüschlikon
Haulier
1960s · Hansruedi Scheller · CH

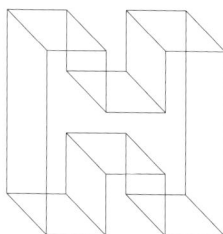

Hammerplast Manchester
Glass
1975 · Keith Murgatroyd,
Tony Forster · UK

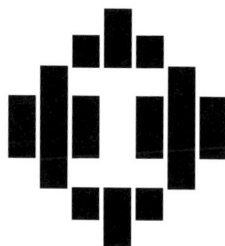

Intersport
Sporting goods
1962 · David J. Goodman/
Porter & Goodman Design · US

Haslett Warehouse & Transportation
1964 · Robert Pease · US

Hormicuba
Concrete
1972 · Félix Beltrán · CU

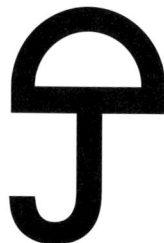

Jochan Regenschirme
Umbrellas
1982 · Hans-Peter Frantz · DE

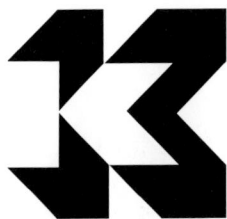

Krestmark Aluminum
1975 · Jack Evans · US

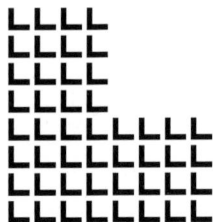

Letra y Linea
Printing
1982 · Félix Beltrán · CU/MX

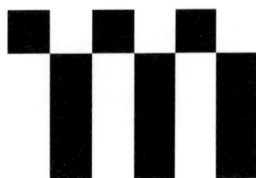

Telco Marketing Services
Investment information
1970 · David L. Burke · US

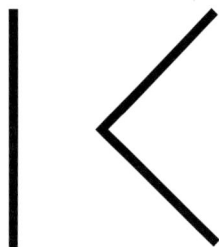

Rolf Koller
Advertising
1967 · Michael Freisager · CH

Leona Textiles
1970s · Lance Wyman · US

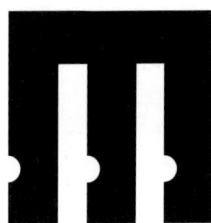

Meisterschule für Buchdrucker
Printing school
1960s · Hermann Virl · DE

Kartografický
Cartography
1968 · Zdeněk Ziegler · CZ

R. Müller & Cie.
Textiles
1963 · Paul Bühlmann · CH

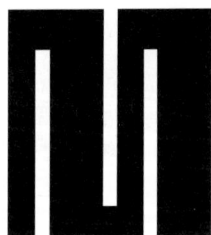

M Products
Construction materials
1969 · Arthur Cole · UK

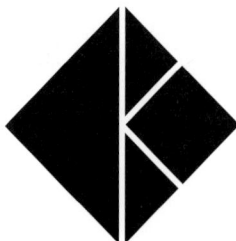

Keller & Co.
Printing
1967 · Anonymous · CH

Merck
Pharmaceuticals
1950s · Enzo Rösli · CH

Mitchell Travel Service
Travel agency
1960s · Robert R. Overby · US

National Bank of Canada
1979 · Vasco Ceccon · CA

NAF
Real estate
1980 · Shigeo Katsuoka · JP

Quintus International
1973 · Dwight Frazier, Paul Hauge/
Newmarket Design Associates · US

International Coffee Organization
1969 · PVDI · BR

Platicone
Engineering
1975 · Pietro Galli · IT

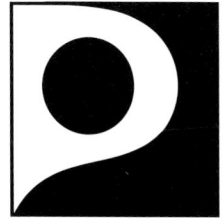

Progil
Chemicals
1968 · Raymond Loewy/CEI · FR

County Transport Company
1982 · Öve Engström,
Ingvar Johansson · SE

Pfauen Mode
Textiles
1964 · Armin Hofmann · CH

Polygraph-Export
Printing machines
1965 · Dieter Lehmann · DE-GDR

Racine Press
Printing
1964 · Rudolph de Harak · US

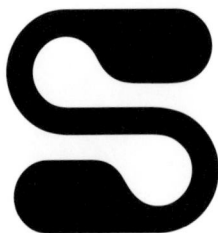

Systems Professional
Civil engineering
1968 · Usher & Follis Design · US

Schweppes
Beverages
1963 · Leen Averink · FR/UK

Refratechnik
Steelworks
1950 · Walter Breker · DE

New Style Industry
1979 · Kao Yu-Lin · TW

Tel Design Associated
Design
1967 · Tel Design Associated · NL

Sparkasse Berlin
Bank
1960 · Hans Adolf Albitz · DE

P. L. Spagnolo
Furniture
1980 · Marcello d'Andrea · IT

Bestime
Watches
1983 · Ove Engström, Kurt Karlsson · SE

Sitcap
Advertising
1956 · Emanuele Centazzo, Sitcap · IT

G. F. Smith & Son
Security technology
1965 · Eurographics · UK

Tigamma
Lighting technology
1969 · Silvio Coppola · IT

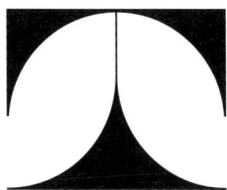

Tecno
Furniture
1954 · Roberto Mango,
Osvaldo Borsani · IT

G. Wegele
Elevator technology
1963 · Peter Steiner · DE

Yuasa Beauty Parlor
Cosmetics
1977 · Masaaki Ishii · JP

Thomson International
Harvesting equipment
1969 · James Cross · US

The Wickes Company
Kitchens
1970 · John Greiner/Unimark International · US

Yonex
Sports equipment
1975 · Takahisa Kamijyo · JP

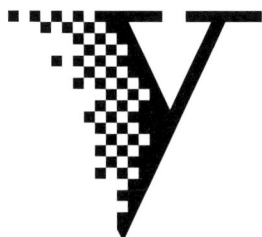

Verlaine
Furniture
1983 · George Delany · US

Warner Communications
Entertainment group
1972 · Saul Bass & Associates · US

Zingg
Furniture
1962 · Werner Mühlemann · CH

Veto
Electronics
1968 · Veniero Bertolotti/Studio 4 · IT

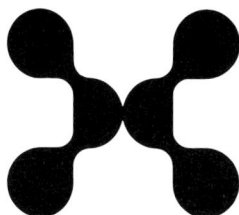

Ken'ichi Hirose's Design Office
1974 · Ken'ichi Hirose · JP

Ring Railway
Transportation
1980 · S. M. Shah · IN

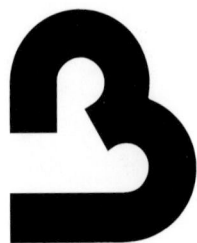

Barazzoni F.lli
Kitchens
1968 · Ennio Lucini · IT

Dimati France
Office supplies
1960s · Ruut van den Hoed · US

Kulturmarkt Dillingen
Cultural association
1980 · Dieter Urban · DE

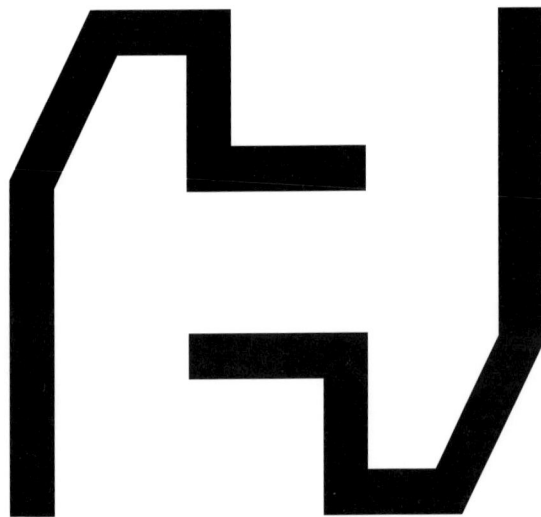

Element
Construction company
1960s · Marcel Wyss · CH

Construction Company
1976 · Bruno K. Wiese · DE

Marzari Artegrafica
Printing
1970 · Walter Ballmer · IT

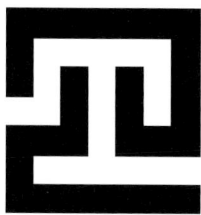

Thornton
Drawing instruments
1964 · Norman Stevenson,
Harry Ward · UK

Grupo Renovación
Institute of sociology
1970 · Álvaro Sotillo · VE

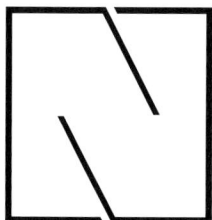

Newton Publishing
1968 · William Newton · CA

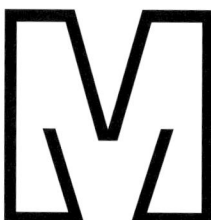

Mensch & Company
Paints
1960s · Armin Hofmann · CH

Eurocartera
Finance
1971 · Julián Santamaría · ES

Neográfica
Printing
1978 · Reynaldo Da Costa · VE

Le Panneau Magnétique
Magnetic advertising panels
1967 · Jacques Nathan-Garamond · FR

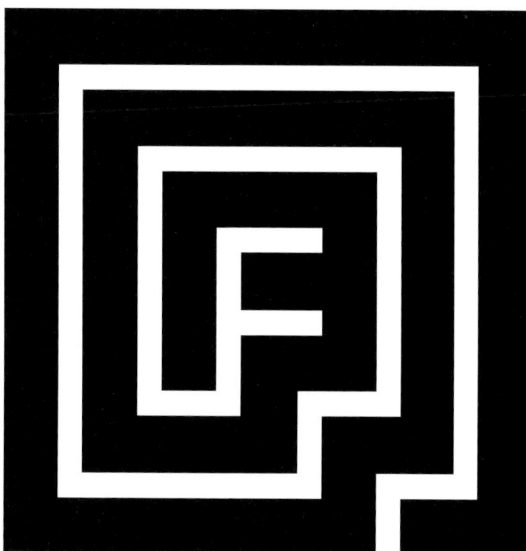

Findex
Computer systems
1978 · Jean-Claude Müller · US

Deux
Lettres

Zwei
Buchstaben

Two
letters

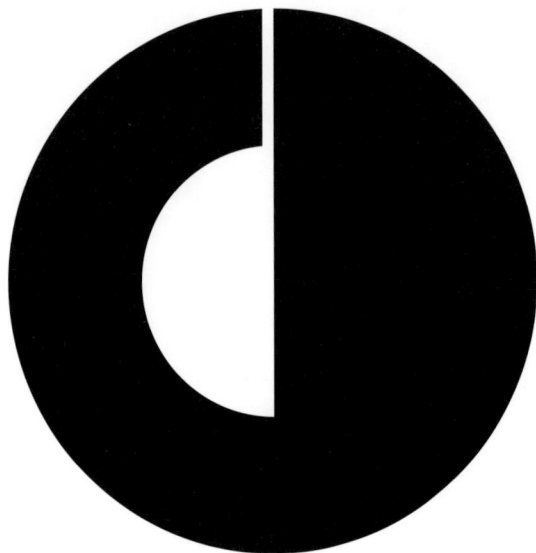

Consolidated Credits & Discounts Bank
1967 · Romek Marber · UK

Varian and Associates
Electronics
1966 · Giulio Citatto · US

Growth Fund of America
Investment
1969 · Carl Seltzer, James Marrin · US

Dalmine
Steel tubing
1947 · Remo Muratore/
Studio Boggeri · IT

JK Industriekontor
Industrial trading
1940s · Heinrich Steding · DE

Technical Center for Aluminum
1966 · Pál Szücs · HU

Alfieri & Lacroix
Printing
1952 · Franco Grignani · IT

Ready Steady Go!
Television program
1963 · Arnold Schwartzmann · UK

Leipziger Kommissions- und Buchhandel
Booksellers association
1971 · Sonja Wunderlich · DE-GDR

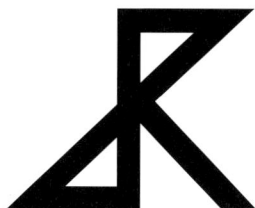

Alfred Ramel
Advertising
1960s · Alfred Ramel · CH

Manchester Polytechnic
Education
1978 · Hans & Pat Schleger · US

Hermann Rülke
Toys
1965 · Horst Süß · DE-GDR

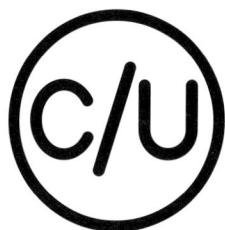

Cape Universal
Construction materials
1968 · Crosby, Fletcher, Forbes · UK

Canadian National Railway
Transportation
1959 · Allan Robb Fleming · CA

Gierre
Textiles
1968 · Armando Milani · IT

Ascoli Bottoni
Buttons
1968 · Silvio Coppola · IT

Field Work
Marketing consultancy
1969 · Piero Barca · IT

Nobel Bozel
Chemicals
1964 · Raymond Loewy/CEI · FR

Interior Forma
Furniture
1963 · Stephen Dunne/
Unimark International · US

Moelven Brug
Prefabricated houses
1968 · Paul Brand · NO

Integrated Plastics
1967 · Vello Hubel · CA

A. Tarlisio
Furniture
1968 · Silvio Coppola · IT

G. W. Furniture
1970 · Jean Morin, Denis L'Allier · CA

Fukuda Design
1981 · Masaki Fukuda · JP

Odermark
Clothing
1970s · Anonymous · DE

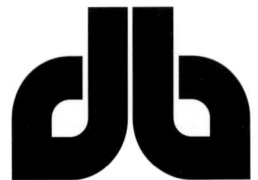

Didaktica
Language school
1977 · Carlo Marchionni · IT

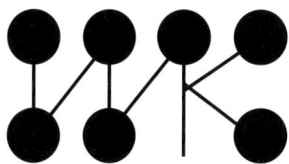

Werner Klapproth Werbung
Advertising
1960s · Werner Klapproth · CH

Slovakian Print Industry
1981 · Jiří Rathouský · CZ

Erhard & Asociados
Advertising
1972 · Carlos R. Erhard/
Erhard & Asociados · MX

Studio Del Frate
Design
1968 · Walter Del Frate · IT

Leisure Press
Publishing
1975 · Lanny Sommese · US

Euro Survey
1968 · Philippe Gentil · FR

Lead Development Association
Lead industry public relations
1968 · Crosby, Fletcher, Forbes · UK

Thorn Parsons
Electronics
1967 · Peter Rea · UK

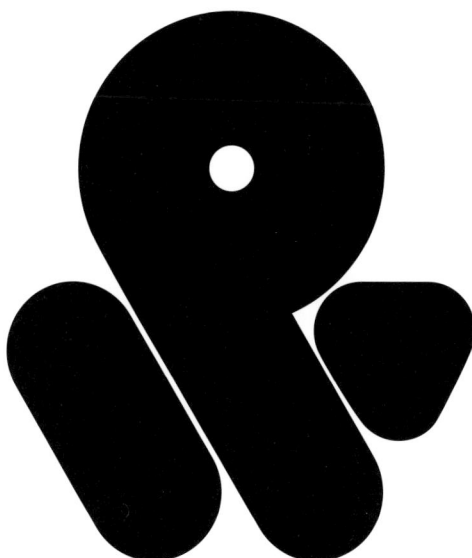

Palais Wittgenstein
Cultural space
1985 · Paul Effert · DE

Cinetechnica Madrid
Film production services
1981 · Fernando Medina · ES

Insel Taschenbuch
Publishing
1974 · Anonymous · DE

Euroceramica
Ceramics
1970 · Walter Ballmer · IT

Custom Builders
Construction company
1970s · Bob Swisher · US

Hans Schulz
1974 · Oanh Pham Phu · DE

BG
Brewing
1960s · Jacques Richez · BE

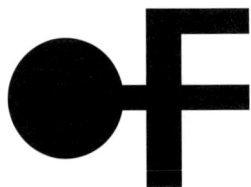

Centro Forme
Furniture
1975 · Heinz Waibl · IT

Richard Brack Stereo
Audio equipment store
1964 · Imre Koroknay · CA

United Dominion
Investment
1961 · Chris Yaneff,
Manfred Gotthans · CA

Transnoel
Haulier
1969 · Tomás Vellvé · ES

Ramon Reig Cabanas
Textiles
1966 · Ribas & Creus · ES

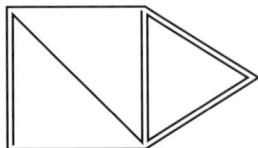

Nippon Design Center
1960 · Kazumasa Nagai · JP

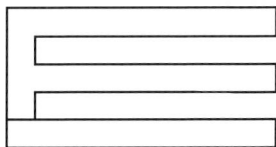

Fideg Elettronica
Electronics
1969 · A. G. Fronzoni · IT

La Carbonique Française
Production of carbon dioxide
1968 · Etienne Bucher · FR

Robert Campiche
Advertising
1960s · Robert Campiche · CH

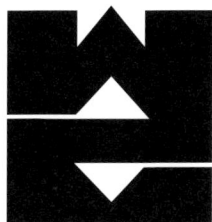

Eduard Franke, Erfurt
Machinery
1965 · Martin Rosette · DE-GDR

Julien et Mège
Industrial heat pumps
1969 · Technés · FR

Irrigation Company
1960s · Anthony Smith,
Roger Turpin · UK

Wohnbau Gröbenzell
Real estate
1970s · Hannes Schober,
Wolfram Reinhardt · DE

Time Life
Publishing (proposed design)
1969 · Arnold Saks · US

Cross and Trecker
Machinery
1981 · Mark Topczewski,
Frances Ullenberg, Ken Eichenbaum · US

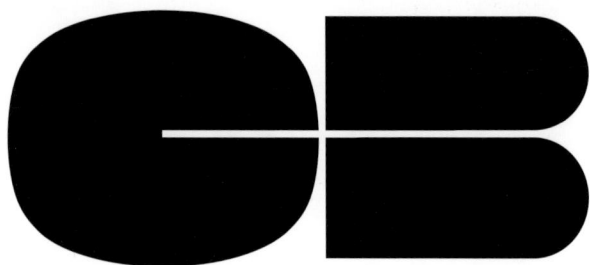

Carte Bleue
Bank
1967 · Daniel Maurel/Chourgnoz Publicité · FR

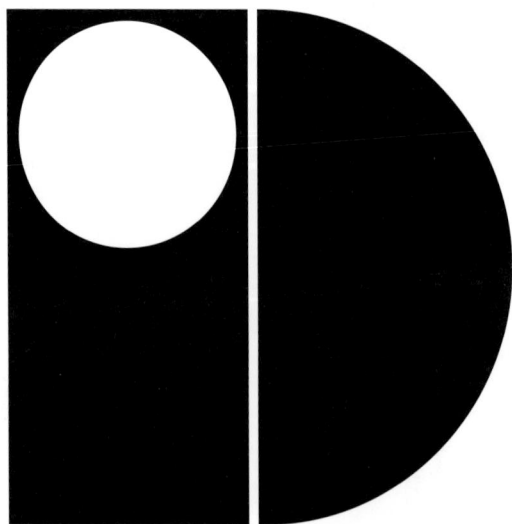

Owens-Illinois
Glass bottles
1970s · Chermayeff & Geismar · US

Kuwait National Petroleum Company
1968 · Crosby, Fletcher, Forbes · UK

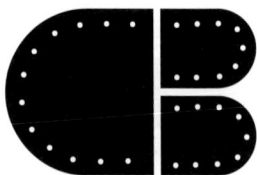

Cobbler's Bench
Footwear
1983 · Mo Lebowitz · US

Drevo Industries
Construction materials
1973 · František Bobáň · CZ

Lorilleux International
Inks
1971 · Alain Carrier · FR

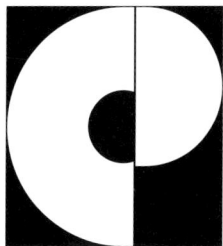

C. Paakkinen
Bakery
1963 · Rolf Christianson · FI

3M
Multi-technology products
1978 · Siegel & Gale · US

Society of Physical Therapists
1969 · Jay Hanson · US

Studio AX
Interior design
1979 · Othmar Motter · AT

Hans Neuburg
Advertising
1940s · Hans Neuburg · CH

Umemura Stainless
Steelworks
1964 · Yoshio Hayashi · JP

Morris Graphics
Printing
1966 · Leslie Smart · CA

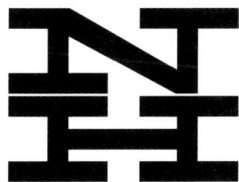

New Haven
Transportation
1954 · Herbert Matter · US

Greenwich Joinery
Carpentry
1973 · Kenneth Hollick · UK

Turri Casa
Furniture
1963 · Armando Milani · IT

Radiotelevisione Italiana
Broadcasting
1950 · Erberto Carboni · IT

E. M. Miller
Bank
1967 · Vance Jonson · US

Finland Designland
Quality mark
1968 · Eka Lainio/
Markkinointi Viherjuuri · FI

Smalteria Viterbese
Enamel
1961 · Italo Lupi · IT

Amnesty International
Human rights organization
1972 · Robert Sessler · CH

Besana Mobili
Furniture
1960 · Valeriano Piozzi/Piozzi & Cima · IT

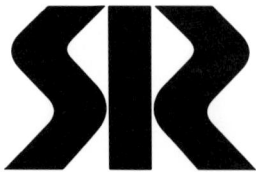

Salient Records
Record label
1969 · Rod Dyer · US

A. C. Distribuidora
1983 · Morfos Diseño · MX

Schweizerische Rückversicherung
Insurance
1960s · Walter Reichen, Max Lenz · CH

Orive Laboratorios Perfumes
1968 · Ribas & Creus · ES

Vesdre-Escaut
Textiles
1965 · Luc Van Malderen · BE

L'Acier Moulé, Paris
Steel
1970 · Albert Boton/Delpire-Advico · FR

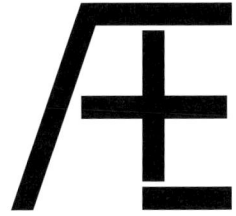

Albert Einstein Hospital
1961 · Alexandre Wollner · BR

Metallaufbereitung Erfurt
Metal processing
1965 · Lothar Freund · DE-GDR

Swiss TV
Broadcasting
1958 · Carlo L. Vivarelli · CH

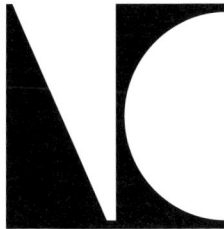

Norrland Center
Exhibition space
1967 · Lars Bramberg · SE

Paris Hilton
Hotel
1964 · Raymond Loewy/CEI · FR

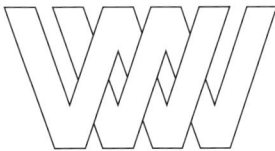

Wilson Walton International
Signs
1970 · Alan Fletcher/
Pentagram · UK

Cemer
Interior design
1970 · Marcello d'Andrea · IT

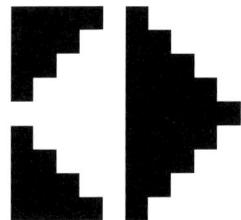

Kuwayama Design Room
1982 · Yasaburo Kuwayama · JP

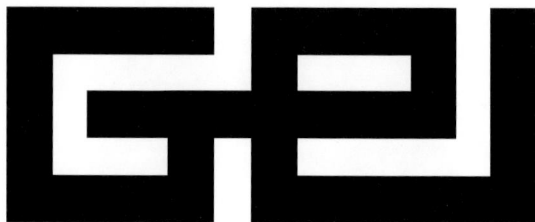

Robert Geisser
Design
1950s · Robert Geisser · CH

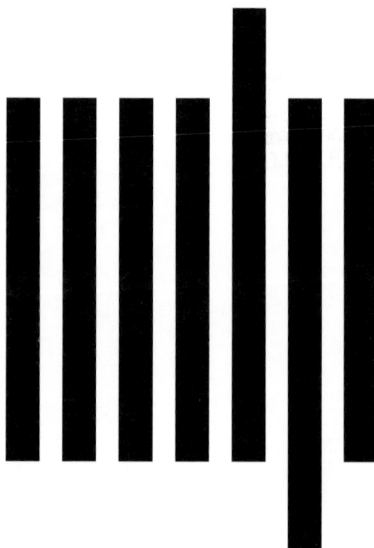

M.I.T. Press
Publishing
1962 · Muriel Cooper · US

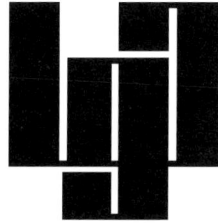

**Landesgewerbeamt
Baden-Württemberg**
Trade supervisory office
1956 · Herbert W. Kapitzki · DE

Cox of Watford
Furniture
1960 · Henrion Design Associates · UK

EFF Eidgenössische Versicherungs AG
Insurance
1950s · Helmuth Kurtz · CH

Actualité des Arts Plastiques
Magazine
1970 · René Ponot · FR

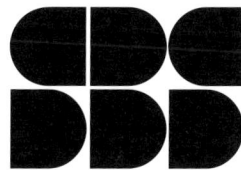

CBM Concrete Company
Construction materials
1970s · Bob Swisher · US

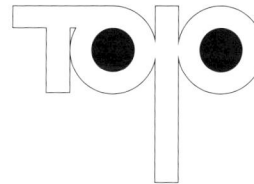

De Swaan Bonnist
Import-export
1960s · Gerard Wernars · NL

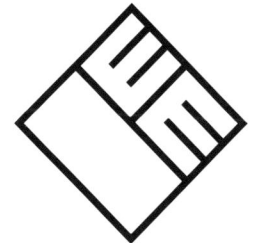

SBS Construction Management
1980 · James Lienhart, Al Navarre · US

Top Gallery
Art gallery
1970 · John Lange · VE

Istituto Euchimico Milanese
Chemical research
1967 · Armando Milani · IT

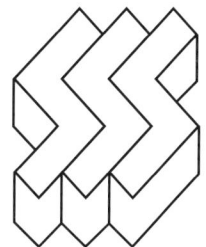

Verlag Michael Winkler
Publishing
1950s · Hermann Kosel · AT

IDI Cinematografica
Film production
1972 · Sergio Salaroli · IT

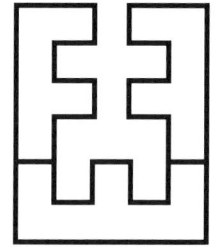

Sun Sano Sogei-Sha
Design
1982 · Yutaka Sato · JP

439

Shin Nihon Shokken
Foods
1981 · Tadashi Ishikawa,
Hideko Sakado · JP

Latham Tyler Jensen
Industrial design
1963 · Charles MacMurray,
Sherman Mutchnick · US

C. F. Christensen
Furniture
1950s · Anonymous · DK

International Gold Research
1983 · Hiroshi Fukushima · JP

ECTA-3
Design
1973 · Alberto Isern/ECTA-3 · ES

Pirelli
Tires
1960s · Albe Steiner · IT

The McBee Company
Office supplies
1964 · Rudy Eswarin/
Stewart & Morrison · CA

City Investment Trust
1971 · Ken Garland · UK

**International Telephone
& Telegraph Corporation**
1957 · Matthew Leibowitz · US

United States Steel Corporation
1960s · Emil O. Biemann/
Lippincott & Margulies · US

Cine Club de Valencia
Film club
1950s · Carlos Cruz-Diez · VE

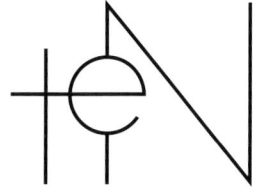

Dr. Te Neuss Großdruckerei
Printing
1950s · Heinz Schwabe · DE

Dai Nippon Printing
1954 · Kenji Ito · JP

Ente per lo Sviluppo dell'Artigianato
Craft workers agency
1964 · Martin Diethelm · CH

Plumbers & Mechanical Contractors
Association
1981 · Dennis Pehoski · US

American Gas & Chemicals
1960s · Stanley Eisenman,
David Enock · US

Canadian Industrial Advertisers
1968 · Anonymous · CA

Aok Kosmetik
Cosmetics
1967 · Anonymous · DE

Independent Photographers Service
1950s · Allan Robb Fleming · CA

Imprese Turistiche Barziesi
Travel agency
1960s · Cecco Re · IT

OHL Industrietechnik
Industrial services
1970 · Heinz Schwabe · DE

OSC Italia
1979 · Armando Milani,
Maurizio Milani · IT

Hatsune Industries Co.
Machinery
1979 · Kenji Kaneko · JP

General Química Layetana
Chemicals
1968 · José Baqués · ES

Design Projects Center
1960s · Leslie Smart,
Sid Bersudsky · CA

Illumination Industries
Lighting
1969 · Primo Angeli · US

CRL Products and Homewares
Mail order
1967 · Keith Murgatroyd · UK

Tobu
Department store
1971 · Kakutaro Iimori · JP

Instructional Systems Incorporated
Education training
1965 · Lance Wyman · US

Sie
Textiles
1967 · José Baqués · ES

Sun Spice
Spices
1960s · Koji Kato · JP

Compas
Travel agency
1970 · Manuel Espinoza · VE

Société Financière Européenne
Financial services
1960s · A. Baier/Delpire-Advico · FR

Società Nebiolo
Type foundry
1960 · Aldo Novarese · IT

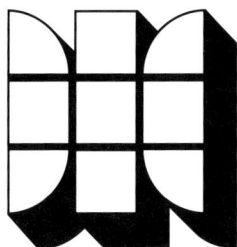

Diffusion Industrielle à Céramique
Ceramics
1968 · Serge Defradat/
Chourgnoz Publicité · FR

RTL Plus
Broadcasting
1989 · Anonymous · DE

New Product Management Group
Market research
1979 · Michael J. Russell,
Sylvia Sewell · UK

Ticino Vito
1980 · Max Huber · IT

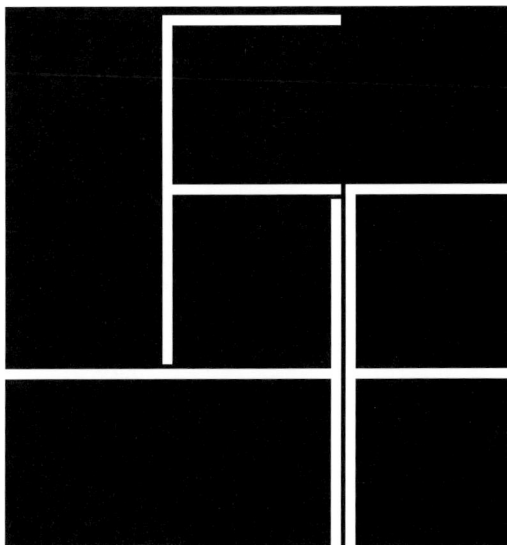

Fonderie Typographique Française
Type foundry
1962 · J. M. L. Richard · FR

La Gazzetta del Mezzogiorno
Newspaper
1965 · Mimmo Castellano · IT

33rd Biennale d'Arte, Venice
Art festival
1966 · Bob Noorda · IT

Integrated Design
Associates
1957 · Allen Porter · US

Foreningen af Danske Civiløkonomer
Association of business economists
1968 · Morten Peetz-Schou · DK

International Underwater Contractors
Underwater engineering
1970 · Jeanette Koumjian/
Russell & Hinrichs · US

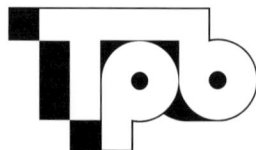

Tintoria Paolo Barzaghi
Industrial dyeing
1954 · Piero Ottinetti · IT

Illinois National Bank
1975 · Chermayeff & Geismar · US

General Felt Industries
Textiles
1978 · Philip Gips · US

100th Anniversary of the Printing
Industries of New York
1963 · Richard Danne/Gips & Danne · US

Institut Français du Pétrole
Petroleum research
1982 · George McGinnis · US

Compagnie Internationale
pour l'Informatique
Computer science
1968 · Alain Carrier · FR

CPT Corporation
Word processors
1973 · Peter Seitz · US

Dent Everyman
Publishing
1960s · John Alcorn · US

JWS
Machinery
1954 · Carlo L. Vivarelli · CH

Hammel, Green and Abrahamson
Architecture and engineering
1984 · Peter Seitz · US

Löw Schuhfabriken
Footwear
1955 · Leo Gantenbein · CH

Blatter Spieler Sachse Werbeagentur
Advertising
1966 · BSS Werbeagentur · DE

Impresa Finanza Investimento
Investment
1976 · Giovanni Brunazzi · IT

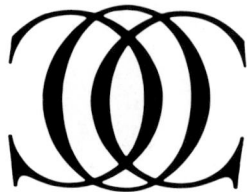

Aktieselskabet C. Olesen
Textiles
1956 · Acton Bjørn · DK

Linificio e Canapificio Nazionale
Textiles
1966 · Silvio Coppola · IT

RAI Radio Italiana
Broadcasting
1960s · Erberto Carboni · IT

800 År Jubilæum i Byen København
City anniversary
1967 · Børge Nebel · DK

Calefação Elétrica
Heating technology
1971 · Aristo Rabin · BR

Conditionarento Nord Italia
Climate technology
1973 · R. Nava, D. Soffientini,
G. Romani, A. Ubertazzi · IT

Dansk Fotografisk Forening
Photographers association
1970 · Morten Peetz-Schou · DK

**Stop and Save
Trading Stamp Corporation**
1962 · Henry Robertz/
The Design Partnership · US

Radio Corporation of America
Electronics and entertainment
1968 · Walter P. Margulies/
Lippincott & Margulies · US

DDI
Beverages
1969 · Morten Peetz-Schou,
Flemming Hedvard · DK

Art Directors Club (Germany)
Advertising
1964 · Vilim Vasata · DE

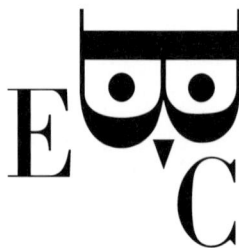

Educational Broadcasting Corporation
1960s · Walter Allner · US

Overseas Containers Ltd.
1975 · Implement · UK

Géo
Canned foods
1967 · Roman Duszek/
Lonsdale Design · FR

**Kupferschmiede und
Apparaturen C. Kunze**
Coppersmiths
1965 · Marlene Ramdohr-Bark · DE-GDR

ZIP Zündhölzer
Matches
1960s · Enzo Rösli · CH

Hygrade Fuels
1968 · Leslie Smart · CA

**International Minerals &
Chemicals Corporation**
1959 · Morton Goldsholl · US

**Canadian International
Paper Company**
1965 · Frank Lipari/
Gazette Printing Company · CA

Editions Desclée De Brouwer
Publishing
1953 · Michel Olyff · BE

Basler Kulturgemeinschaft
Cultural association
1940s · Hermann Eidenbenz · CH

447

Wörter

Words

seriaal
seriaal
seriaal
seriaal
seriaal

Seriaal Galerie
Art gallery
1968 · Pieter Brattinga · NL

ankit

Ankit Bombay
1973 · Yeshwant Chaudhary · IN

Speedaprint
Speedaprint
Speedaprint
Speedaprint
Speedaprint

Speedaprint
Printing
1968 · Robert Davies · UK

schwaben bräu
schwaben bräu
schwaben bräu
schwaben bräu

Schwaben Bräu
Brewing
1960s · Nelly Rudin · CH

KELVIN
KELVIN
KELVIN
KELVIN
KELVIN

Kelvin Research Corporation
1970s · Robert Hagenhofer · US

FILM FILM FILM

Jeremy Lepard Films
Film production
1967 · Rod Dyer · US

Kimo mag

Kimo
Furniture
1976 · Odermatt+Tissi · CH

Lumitype Deberny & Peignot
Type foundry
1963 · Rémy Peignot · FR

Comune di Parma
Twinning Parma-Ljubljana
1964 · Franco M. Ricci · IT

magnum

Magnum
Magazine
1954 · Kurt Schwarz · AT

m/ä/s/e/r

Mäser
Clothing
1969 · Ruedi Rüegg · CH

EEDV

Elektronische Datenverarbeitung
Data processing
1970 · Rainer Strempel · DE

22 22

Foto Studio 22
Photography
1961 · Albe Steiner · IT

julie T.

Julie T.
Clothing
1969 · Rudi Meyer/Publicis · CH

Ritz Italora
Watches
1972 · Da Centro Disegno · IT

Simon Suds
Car wash
1969 · John Kobold/
Hiller Rinaldo Associates · CA

Will Waller
Packaging
1968 · Edi Doswald · CH

Rasiom
Fuel oil
1968 · Giulio Confalonieri · IT

Swibar
Watches
1986 · Yeshwant Chaudhary,
Ashok Sood · IN

Koyo Office Planning
Computer systems
1983 · Hisahiro Umezawa · JP

Cinema
Television program
1966 · Yvon Laroche · CA

Biennale der Europäischen Grafik
Design festival
1982 · Erwin Poell · DE

Interdomo
Industrial design
1973 · Giulio Confalonieri · IT

Arnold
1950s · Otto Krämer · CH

Van der Vorm's
Construction company
1968 · Geoffrey Gibbons/
Allied International Designers · UK

Asics
Sporting goods
1977 · Herb Lubalin · US

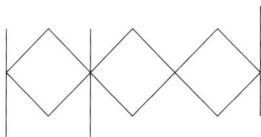

Pier Paolo Delitala
Furniture
1959 · Ilio Negri · IT

Groupe Design
Industrial design
1959 · Luc Van Malderen · BE

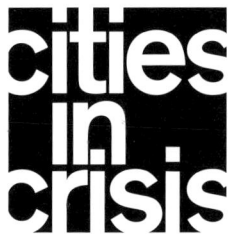

Cities in Crisis
Documentary movie
1967 · Dietmar R. Winkler · US

Logix Kepner-Tregoe
Education
1970 · Appelbaum & Curtis · US

Life
Magazine
1978 · Anonymous · US

Max Wiener
Textiles
1965 · Karlheinz Herke · DE-GDR

Arcus - Tonon Laburthe
Footwear
1973 · J.C. Jouis/Look · FR

Libreria Cortina
Bookstore
1965 · Italo Lupi · IT

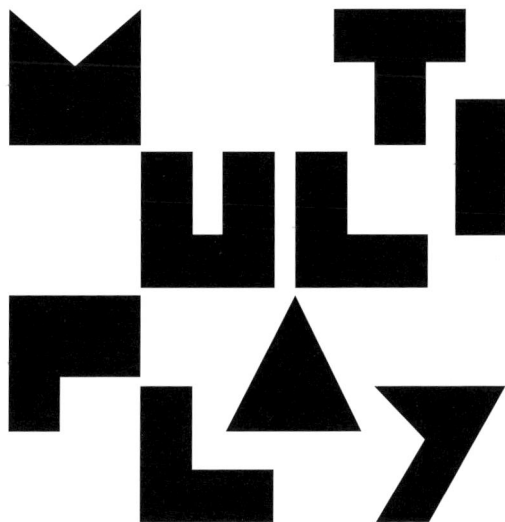

Multiplay
Toys
1970 · Ferruccio Soldati · CH

Pluvius
1955 · Uli Huber · DE

Ladybug
Magazine
1969 · Jay Dillon/Hess & Antupit · US

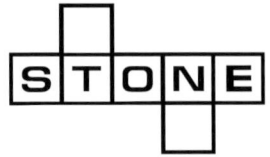

Stone Container Corporation
Packaging
1959 · Morton Goldsholl · US

Polyfor
Textiles
1970 · Rudi Meyer/Publicis · FR

L'eggs, Hanes Hosiery
Pantyhose
1970 · Roger J. Ferriter/
Lubalin, Smith, Carnase · US

United Supply Company
Plumbing suppliers
1966 · Appelbaum & Curtis · US

SISFI
Swiss-Italian trade union
1960s · Walter Ballmer · CH

Pacific
Theater group
1969 · Jerry Braude · US

Dunlop Footwear
1960s · Kenneth Lamble/Clements · UK

Ditto
Photocopiers
1960s · Morton Goldsholl
Design Associates · US

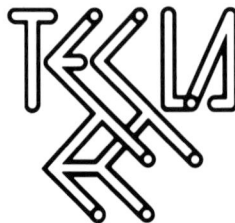

Tecla Tofano
Art exhibition
1969 · Manuel Espinoza · VE

KALA
Art gallery
1960s · Juan Carlos Destéfano · AR

boîte à musique

Boîte à Musique
Record store
1957 · Karl Gerstner/GGK · CH

KETCH

Ketch Giorgio Confezioni
Textiles
1972 · Giulio Confalonieri · IT

buri

Buri & Cie
Printing
1964 · Kurt Wirth · CH

otto

Otto
Textiles
1950s · Hanns Lohrer · DE

siex

Siex
Import-export
1967 · José Baqués · ES

sica

Sica
Textiles
1970 · Mimmo Castellano · IT

TESALA

Tecla Sala
Yarns
1963 · Joan Pedragosa · ES

Woolrich

Woolrich Manufacturing
Cotton
1966 · Kramer, Miller, Lomden,
Glassman Inc. · US

bopp

Arnold Bopp
Sound consultant
1960s · Walter Bangerter · CH

453

OTTO

Otto
Audio technology
1966 · Tomoichi Nishiwaki · JP

MONO

Legler Industria Tessile
Textiles
1948 · Eugen & Max Lenz · CH

Mono
Pencils
1960s · Takashi Kono · JP

RAIBOR

VISTA

AVANT GARDE

Raibor
Carpets
1964 · Theodoor Manson · IT

Vista
Magazine
1968 · Hess & Antupit · US

Avant Garde
Magazine
1960s · Herb Lubalin · US

CITIBANK

NASA

Grammo Studio

Citibank
1976 · Anspach Grossman Portugal · US

**National Aeronautics and
Space Administration**
1976 · Dane & Blackburn · US

Grammo Studio
Record store
1957 · Odermatt+Tissi · CH

National Zeitung
Newspaper
1960 · Karl Gerstner · CH

Mobil
Fuel oil
1964 · Ivan Chermayeff, Tom Geismar/Chermayeff & Geismar · US

Reinhard Holzwarenfabrik
Wooden goods
1961 · Odermatt+Tissi · CH

Socodac
Secretarial services
1966 · Gilles Fiszman · BE

Lowe
Film production
1967 · Studio González Ruiz &
Shakespear · AR

Baric Computing Services
1970 · Marcello Minale,
Brian Tattersfield · UK

Achille Serre
Cleaning services
1968 · Michael Tucker · UK

Riso Kagaku Corporation
Photocopiers
1980 · Anonymous · JP

Olivetti
Business machines
1971 · Walter Ballmer · IT

P

The Modernist logos featured in this book were in the main created over a period of about 40 years by graphic designers of varying ages and nationalities. Looking at the logos in this book, it could easily be assumed that none of the designers has an unmistakable style. However, when we explore the work of eight ground-breaking logo designers from different parts of the world and radically different backgrounds, the opposite seems to be true. Furthermore, this selection of works arranged in chronological order also shows how the art of the logo has continued to advance in this Modernist age.

Die meisten der in diesem Buch versammelten modernistischen Logos wurden in einen Zeitraum von etwa 40 Jahren von Gestaltern unterschiedlichen Alters und verschiedener Herkunft entworfen. Betrachtet man die Logos in der in diesem Buch vorliegenden Kategorisierung, entsteht leicht der Eindruck, so etwas wie die individuelle Handschrift eines Gestalters existiere bei diesem Medium gar nicht. Der Blick auf die Arbeiten von acht wegweisenden Logogestaltern, die aus verschiedenen Teilen der Erde stammen und grundverschiedene biografische Hintergründe haben, beweist das Gegenteil. Durch eine chronologische Sortierung der Arbeiten offenbaren sich außerdem visuelle Weiterentwicklungen innerhalb der Ära des modernistischen Logos.

La plupart des logos modernes réunis dans cet ouvrage ont été conçus sur une période d'une quarantaine d'années par des créateurs d'âges et d'origines diverses. En passant en revue les logos classés selon les catégories proposées dans ce livre, le lecteur aura facilement l'impression que quelque chose comme la griffe individuelle d'un designer n'existe pas dans ce médium. Un regard sur les réalisations de huit créateurs de logos issus de différentes régions du monde, avec des biographies très dissemblables, le convaincra du contraire. Le classement chronologique de leurs travaux permet en outre de reconnaître certaines évolutions visuelles pendant l'ère du logo moderne.

Adrian Frutiger was born in 1928 in Unterseen, Switzerland. From 1944 to 1948 he was an apprentice compositor in Interlaken before attending the Zurich School of Arts and Crafts, where Alfred Willimann and Walter Käch were among his teachers. He then started work as a graphic designer in Zurich. His first logotypes, typefaces and woodcuts date from this period. In 1952 Frutiger moved to Paris where he worked for the Deberny & Peignot type foundry. He completed his work on the Univers font in 1957 and in the years that followed it came into use worldwide and remains one of the most popular sans-serif typefaces. In 1962, Frutiger, Bruno Pfäffli and André Gürtler set up their own design studio at Arcueil near Paris. There they produced typefaces for a range of French companies and institutions, including Paris Charles de Gaulle airport, as well as several publishing houses and pharmaceutical firms. At the same time Frutiger taught in Paris at the École Estienne (1952–60) and the École des Arts Décoratifs (1954–68). In 1968 he developed the OCR-B font, which in 1973 was declared a worldwide standard machine-readable font that could also be used for passports and bank statements. Frutiger's 1978 book, *Der Mensch und seine Zeichen* (*Signs and symbols: their design and meaning*, 1989), has become a standard work on design literature and has been translated into seven languages. Published three years later, another book by Frutiger, *Type, Sign, Symbol*, is also hailed as a classic. In the 1970s and '80s, Frutiger produced the font that bears his name—Frutiger—as well as Glypha, Serifa and Avenir. He returned to his native Switzerland in 1992 and lived in Bremgarten near Berne. Until his death in the fall of 2015, he continued to work mainly for the typeface manufacturer Linotype on the digitalization and diversification of his successful fonts.

Adrian Frutiger

1928–2015 · CH

Adrian Frutiger wurde 1928 im schweizerischen Unterseen geboren. In Interlaken absolvierte er zwischen 1944 und 1948 eine Schriftsetzerlehre, an der Kunstgewerbeschule Zürich studierte er bei Alfred Willimann und Walter Käch, bevor er schließlich als Grafiker in Zürich zu arbeiten begann. Erste Zeichen, Schriftentwürfe und Holzschnitte entstanden in dieser Zeit. Frutiger zog 1952 nach Paris und wurde Mitarbeiter der Schriftgießerei Deberny & Peignot. Die Arbeiten an der Schriftfamilie Univers schloss er 1957 ab. In den folgenden Jahren verbreitete sich diese international und ist bis heute eine der am meisten genutzten serifenlosen Schriftarten. Gemeinsam mit Bruno Pfäffli und André Gürtler gründete Frutiger 1962 ein eigenes Grafikatelier in Arcueil bei Paris. Erscheinungsbilder für zahlreiche französische Unternehmen und Institutionen wurden realisiert, darunter der Pariser Flughafen, mehrere Verlage und Pharmaunternehmen. Nebenher lehrte Frutiger an der Ecole Estienne (1952–60) sowie an der Ecole des Arts Décoratifs (1954–68) in Paris. Im Jahr 1968 entwickelte er die Schrift OCR-B, die ab 1973 zum weltweiten Standard für maschinenlesbare Schriften erklärt wurde und auch in Ausweisen oder auf Kontoauszügen Anwendung fand. Sein 1978 veröffentlichtes Buch *Der Mensch und seine Zeichen* wurde zum Standardwerk der Designliteratur und erschien in sieben Sprachen. Drei Jahre später legte er mit *Type, Sign, Symbol* eine weitere Publikation zum Thema Zeichen und Logos vor, die heute als Klassiker gilt. In den 1970er- und 1980er-Jahren entstanden Schriften wie die nach ihm benannte Frutiger, zudem Glypha, Serifa oder Avenir. Im Jahr 1992 kehrte er in die Schweiz zurück und lebte in Bremgarten bei Bern. Hier arbeitete er bis zu seinem Tod im Herbst 2015 vor allem für den Schriftenhersteller Linotype an Digitalisierungen und Erweiterungen seiner erfolgreichen Fontentwürfe.

Europrint
Printing
1960 · Adrian Frutiger · CH/FR

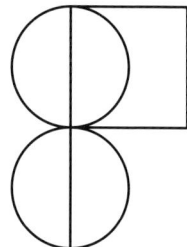

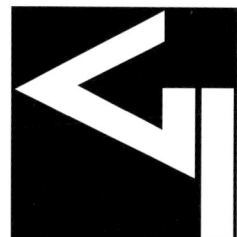

Imprimerie Hofer
Printing
1960 · Adrian Frutiger · CH/FR

Brancher Frères
Inks
1960 · Adrian Frutiger · CH/FR

Georges Johannet
Architecture
1960 · Adrian Frutiger · CH/FR

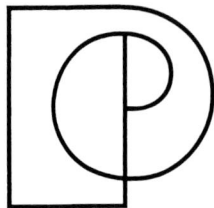

Prache de Franclieu
Commercial bookbinder
1962 · Adrian Frutiger · CH/FR

Demy Frères
Cement
1964 · Adrian Frutiger · CH/FR

Institut Atlantique, Paris
Research institute
1960s · Adrian Frutiger · CH/FR

Alpha & Omega
Religious magazine
1967 · Bruno Pfäffli,
Adrian Frutiger · CH/FR

Adrian Frutiger est né en 1928 à Unterseen, en Suisse. De 1944 à 1948, il suit une formation de typographe à Interlaken et étudie à l'École des arts et métiers de Zurich auprès d'Alfred Willimann et de Walter Käch, et il commence à travailler comme graphiste à Zurich. À cette époque voient le jour ses premiers projets de fontes, typos et bois gravés. En 1952, Frutiger s'installe à Paris et devient le collaborateur de la fonderie Deberny & Peignot. En 1957, il achève son travail sur la famille de polices de caractères Univers, qui se répand internationalement au cours des années suivantes et qui reste une des linéales les plus utilisées à ce jour. En 1962, Frutiger fonde son propre studio de graphisme avec Bruno Pfäffli et André Gürtler à Arcueil, près de Paris. Il crée les marques commerciales de nombreuses entreprises et institutions françaises, notamment Aéroports de Paris et diverses maisons d'édition et entreprises pharmaceutiques. Parallèlement, il enseigne à l'École Estienne (1952–60) et à l'École nationale des Arts Décoratifs (1954–68) à Paris. En 1968, il développe la police de caractères OCR-B ; à partir de 1973, elle devient le standard international des fontes lisibles par machine et est notamment utilisée pour les pièces d'identité ou les relevés de comptes. Son livre *Der Mensch und seine Zeichen*, paru en 1978 (*L'homme et ses signes*, 2000), est devenu une référence incontournable de la littérature graphique et a été publié en sept langues. Trois ans plus tard, Frutiger propose une autre publication autour des signes et des logos avec *Type, Sign, Symbol*, ouvrage aujourd'hui considéré comme un classique. Dans les années 1970 et 1980 voient le jour des polices comme la Frutiger qui porte son nom, mais aussi les Glypha, Serifa ou Avenir. En 1992, Frutiger rentre en Suisse, vivant désormais à Bremgarten, près de Berne. Jusqu'à sa mort à l'automne 2015, il y travaille à la numérisation et au développement de ses célèbres fontes, essentiellement pour le compte du créateur de polices de caractères Linotype.

Scoricentres
Steel industry
1970s · Adrian Frutiger · CH

Adrian Frutiger's design for steel producer Scoricentres' logo is a perfect example of his working method. Starting with a sketch, he moved step by step through a series of outlines until he achieved the perfect result. Scoricentres' corporate identity combines a sign designed by Frutiger and typography developed by Bruno Pfäffli.

Anhand seiner Entwürfe für das Zeichen des Stahlhersteller Scoricentres lässt sich Adrian Frutigers Vorgehen bei der Gestaltung beispielhaft nachvollziehen. Ausgehend von einer gezeichneten Form entwickelte er Schritt für Schritt weitere Formen bis zur perfekten Abstraktion. Das Zeichen wurde im Rahmen eines von Bruno Pfäffli entwickelten Grafiksystems in das Erscheinungsbild des Unternehmens eingebunden.

Les projets pour le logo de l'aciériste Scoricentres permet de suivre la démarche créative d'Adrian Frutiger. Partant d'une forme dessinée, il développe pas à pas d'autres formes jusqu'à parvenir à l'abstraction parfaite. Cet insigne fut intégré à l'identité visuelle de l'entreprise dans le cadre d'un système graphique développé par Bruno Pfäffli.

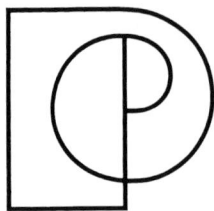

Prache de Franclieu
Commercial bookbinder
1962 · Adrian Frutiger · CH/FR

Demy Frères
Cement
1964 · Adrian Frutiger · CH/FR

Institut Atlantique, Paris
Research institute
1960s · Adrian Frutiger · CH/FR

Alpha & Omega
Religious magazine
1967 · Bruno Pfäffli,
Adrian Frutiger · CH/FR

Druckerei Winterthur
Printing
1967 · Bruno Pfäffli, Adrian Frutiger · CH/FR

L'Aéroport de Paris
Airport
1971 · Adrian Frutiger · CH/FR

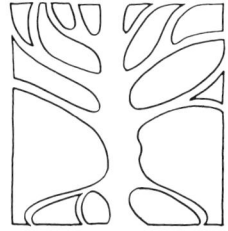

Schriftgießerei Haas
Type foundry
1970s · Adrian Frutiger · CH/FR

Brancher
Printing inks
1970 · Adrian Frutiger · CH/FR

Tissages Normands Réunis
Textiles
1970s · Adrian Frutiger · CH/FR

Musées Nationaux de France
Museums organization
1974 · Adrian Frutiger · CH/FR

Autoroute du Sud de la France
Highway
1975 · Adrian Frutiger · CH/FR

Paul Ibou

1939–2023 · BE

Paul Ibou was born in Antwerp in 1939. He studied in his native city from 1954 to 1962, attending first the Royal Academy of Fine Arts and then the Plantin Moretus Institute for Typography. On completing his studies he set up his own studio in the center of Antwerp. Working in every field of graphic design, he became one of Belgium's best-known designers. All his work, whether posters, postage stamps, books or corporate designs, is characterized by his Constructivist approach. He attracted special attention for his logo designs, which featured in many exhibitions and were frequently mentioned in a wide range of publications. Moreover, since the 1960s Ibou has published more than 50 books on art and design. He has acted as an advisor on design issues to the government of Flanders, worked for numerous corporate clients, and been a jury member at design competitions throughout the world. Ibou is renowned not only for his commercial work but also as a freelance artist, who continues to produce paintings and sculptures. These, too, bear his Bauhaus-influenced, experimental, geometric signature. In 1994, in Ostend, he organized the World Symbol Festival, an international exhibition and conference devoted entirely to the logo. Paul Ibou was appointed a Knight of the Order of King Leopold for his services to cultural life over many years. From 1985 to the end of his life he lived and worked in a historic castle in the small Belgian town of Zandhoven.

Paul Ibou wurde 1939 in Antwerpen geboren. In seiner Geburtsstadt studierte er zwischen 1954 und 1962 an der Koninklijke Academie voor Schone Kunsten und am Plantin Moretus Instituut. Anschließend machte er sich mit einem Büro im Stadtzentrum Antwerpens selbstständig. Hier war er in allen Bereichen des Grafikdesigns aktiv und wurde über die Jahre zu einem der bekanntesten belgischen Gestalter. Ein konstruktivistischer Ansatz ist das durchgängige Element aller seiner Arbeiten – ob Plakate, Briefmarken, Bücher oder Corporate Designs. Besonders seine Logoentwürfe brachten ihm auch internationale Anerkennung ein, die sich in zahlreichen Auszeichnungen sowie Erwähnungen in vielen Publikationen zeigte. Darüber hinaus veröffentlichte Ibou seit den 1960er-Jahren mehr als 50 eigene Bücher rund um Kunst und Design. Er war als Berater in Gestaltungsfragen für die flämische Regierung sowie für zahlreiche Unternehmen tätig und als Jurymitglied bei Designwettbewerben weltweit aktiv. Neben seiner auftragsbezogenen Arbeit wurde er als freischaffender Künstler bekannt und realisierte bis zu seinem Tod Skulpturen und Gemälde. Auch hier ist seine durch das Bauhaus geprägte experimentell-geometrische Handschrift zu finden. In Oostende organisierte er 1994 das „World Symbol Festival", eine internationale Ausstellung und Konferenz, die sich ausschließlich dem Medium Logo widmete. Für seine langjährigen kulturellen Verdienste wurde er mit dem königlichen Kronenorden zum Ritter erhoben. Ab 1985 lebte und arbeitete Paul Ibou in einem historischen Schloss im belgischen Zandhoven.

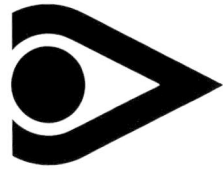

Grafo
Printing
1960 · Paul Ibou · BE

Scaldia
Paper
1963 · Paul Ibou · BE

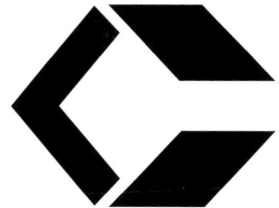

Charlier
Foods
1965 · Paul Ibou · BE

Antwerp-Tax
Taxi service
1967 · Paul Ibou · BE

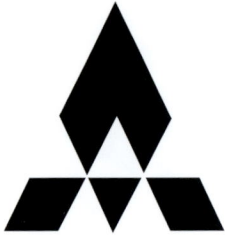

Artepik
Cultural center
1970 · Paul Ibou · BE

Soyuznefteexport
Fuel oil
1970 · Paul Ibou · BE

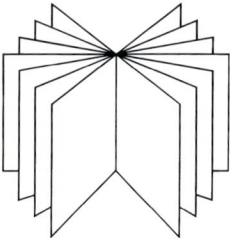

Antwerp Book Fair
1970 · Paul Ibou · BE

Suglo
Bakery
1973 · Paul Ibou · BE

Paul Ibou est né en 1939 à Anvers. De 1954 à 1962, il étudie dans sa ville natale à la Koninklijke Academie voor Schone unsten et au Plantin Moretus Instituut, puis il prend son indépendance en ouvrant une agence dans le centre d'Anvers. Il y déploie son activité dans tous les domaines graphiques et devient au fil des ans un des plus célèbres graphistes belges. Son approche constructiviste est l'élément constant de toutes ses réalisations – affiches, timbres, livres, corporate design. Ses créations de logos, tout particulièrement, lui valent la reconnaissance internationale, qui se manifeste par de nombreuses distinctions et citations dans des publications. À partir des années 1960, Ibou publie en outre plus de 50 livres sur l'art et le design. Il travaille comme conseiller en design pour le gouvernement flamand et de nombreuses entreprises et participe à des concours de design en qualité de membre du jury. À côté du travail de commande, il se fait aussi connaître comme artiste indépendant et réalise des sculptures et des peintures dans lesquelles on retrouve son écriture personnelle expérimentale et géométrique influencée par le Bauhaus. En 1994, il organise à Ostende le « World Symbol Festival », exposition et symposium exclusivement consacrés au logo. Il est fait chevalier de l'ordre de la Couronne pour son apport culturel au long cours. Paul Ibou vit à partir de 1985 dans un château historique à Zandhoven, en Belgique.

9 Biennale
Middelheim
Antwerpen

1967

8 BIENNALE MIDDELHEIM ANTWERPEN

11ᵉ Biënnale
Middelheim
Antwerpen
6 juni/3 okt. '71

8 biennale
middelheim
antwerpen

20 juni - 30 september '65

Middelheim
Sculpture Biennale Art festival
1965 · Paul Ibou · BE

In 1949 Antwerp held its first-ever exhibition of sculpture. Over the years, the
event in Middelheim Park has grown to
become an internationally respected
arts festival. In 1965, Paul Ibou, who
had only recently started out on his
career, was commissioned to create
designs for the eighth Biennale. In the
years that followed he based his graphics for posters and brochures on a
minimalist logo, with variations of shape
and detail for each show.

Im Jahr 1949 fand die erste Skulpturen-
ausstellung in Antwerpen statt. Über die
Jahre entwickelte sich die Veranstaltung
im Middelheim Park zum international
beachteten Kunstfestival. Der damals
gerade erst ins Berufsleben gestartete
Paul Ibou erhielt 1965 den Auftrag
für das Design zur achten Biennale.
Auf Basis seines reduzierten Logoent-
wurfs gestaltete er in den folgenden
Jahren Plakate und Broschüren für die
Veranstaltung, die jeweils mit Form und
Details des Markenzeichens spielen.

La première exposition de sculptures
fut présentée à Anvers en 1949. Au fil
des ans, l'événement du parc Middelheim
est devenu un festival d'art au retentis-
sement international. En 1965, Paul Ibou,
qui commençait tout juste sa carrière,
fut chargé de réaliser le design de la
huitième édition de la Biennale. Au cours
des années suivantes, sur la base de son
logo très sobre, il réalisera pour l'événement des affiches et des brochures qui
jouent chaque fois avec la forme et les
détails du sigle.

Mesy Shirts
Clothing
1974 · Paul Ibou · BE

Tolimpex
Customs office
1977 · Paul Ibou · BE

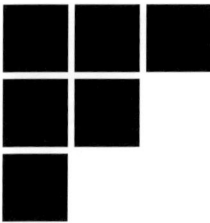

Frisol
Oil
1981 · Paul Ibou · BE

Medithek
Healthcare
1982 · Paul Ibou · BE

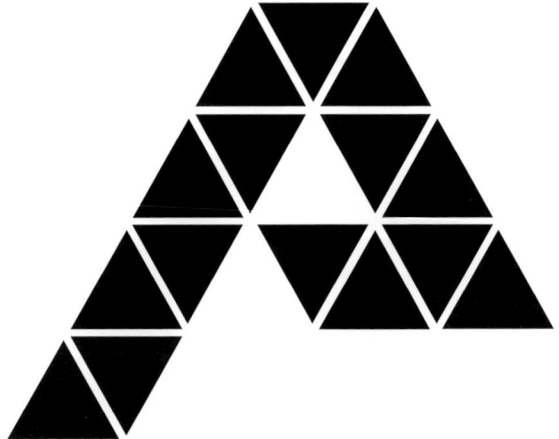

Government of Antwerp
Regional government office
1983 · Paul Ibou · BE

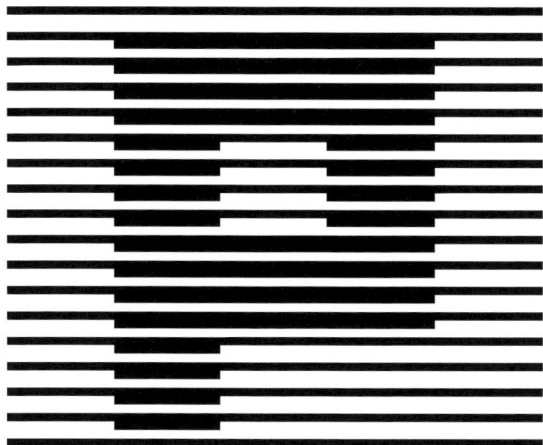

Pittors
Video services
1984 · Paul Ibou · BE

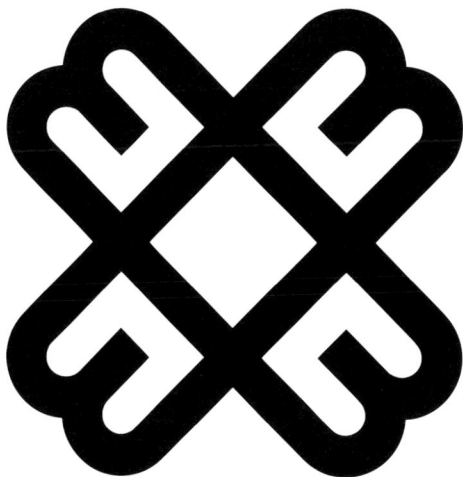

Belgian Bankers Association
1989 · Paul Ibou · BE

Linea
Art and design fair
1983 · Paul Ibou · BE

Mercator Press
Printing
1985 · Paul Ibou · BE

Cera
Financial services
1986 · Paul Ibou · BE

O.V.A.M.
Waste and soil management
1988 · Paul Ibou · BE

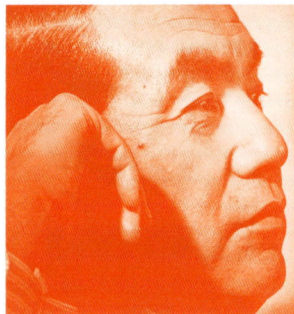

Yusaku Kamekura

1915–1997 · JP

Yusaku Kamekura was born in 1915 in Yoshida (now known as Tsubame). From 1935 to 1938 he studied for a degree in architecture at Tokyo's New Academy of Architecture and Industrial Arts, a private teaching institution modeled on the German Bauhaus. On graduation he worked for various advertising agencies and was also art director of several magazines. In 1951 he became a founder member of the Japan Advertising Arts Club, and in 1960 was one of the founder members of the Nippon Design Center. In 1962 Kamekura set up his own practice, where his work combining Constructivist elements with a traditional Japanese esthetic began to attract attention. In the following years he became one of Japan's best-known graphic designers. His work for the 1964 Tokyo Olympics and Expo '70 in Osaka brought him international recognition. Along with posters and packaging, trademarks were his preferred medium, which he explored in great detail. His book *Trademarks of the World*, published in 1956 and for which he spent five years collecting some 700 logos from across the world, was a standard work for the period. In 1978, he was appointed president of the newly founded Japan Graphic Designers Association and took on more administrative posts in international design organizations. Kamekura continued to work into old age and as late as 1985 created the logo for Nippon Telegraph and Telephone Corporation (NTT), one of the country's most recognizable corporate images. In the same year he launched and edited the magazine *Creation*, which in the space of five years ran to 20 issues charting developments in the world of graphic design. Kamekura died in Tokyo in 1997 aged 82 and is now regarded as one of Japan's most important designers of the 20th century.

Yusaku Kamekura wurde 1915 in Yoshida (heute: Tsubame) geboren. Von 1935 bis 1938 studierte er mit Schwerpunkt Architektur in Tokio an der Neuen Akademie für Architektur und Industriedesign, einem privaten Institut nach Vorbild des deutschen Bauhauses. Anschließend arbeitete er für Werbeagenturen und als Art Director mehrerer Zeitschriften. Im Jahr 1951 war er Gründungsmitglied des Japan Advertising Arts Clubs und 1960 des Nippon Design Centers. Ab 1962 war Kamekura selbstständig tätig und erregte mit seinen Arbeiten, die Elemente des Konstruktivismus mit traditioneller japanischer Ästhetik verbanden, zunehmend Aufmerksamkeit. In den folgenden Jahren stieg er zu einem der bestbekannten japanischen Grafikdesigner auf. Seine Arbeiten für die Olympischen Spiele in Tokio 1964 sowie für die Expo '70 in Osaka machten ihn auch international bekannt. Neben Plakaten und Verpackungen wurden Markenzeichen zu seinem bevorzugten Medium, mit dem er sich ausführlich beschäftigte. Sein 1956 veröffentlichtes Buch *Trademarks of the World*, für das er in fünf Jahren Arbeit rund 700 internationale Logos zusammentrug, war ein Standardwerk seiner Zeit. Er wurde 1978 Vorsitzender der neu gegründeten Japan Graphic Designers Association und übernahm weitere administrative Aufgaben in internationalen Designorganisationen. Bis ins hohe Alter arbeitete Kamekura an neuen Entwürfen und schuf noch 1985 mit dem Zeichen für das japanische Telekommunikationsunternehmen NTT eines der berühmtesten Markenzeichen des Landes. Im gleichen Jahr initiierte er das Konzept für *Creation*, ein Magazin, das über 20 Ausgaben innerhalb von fünf Jahren Entwicklungen im internationalen Grafikdesign dokumentierte. Kamekura verstarb 1997 im Alter von 82 Jahren in Tokio und gilt heute als einer der wichtigsten japanischen Designer des 20. Jahrhunderts.

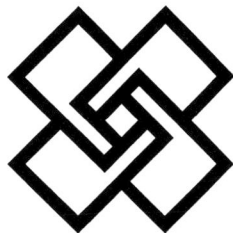

Daishowa
Paper
1954 · Yusaku Kamekura · JP

Nikon
Photography
1955 · Yusaku Kamekura · JP

Gendai Geijutsu Kenkyujo
Contemporary art institute
1957 · Yusaku Kamekura · JP

Good Design
Design institute and award
1957 · Yusaku Kamekura · JP

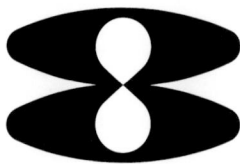

Television Network
1958 · Yusaku Kamekura · JP

Shell
Petroleum
1963 · Yusaku Kamekura · JP

Amagi Highland, Tokyo
Golf course
1965 · Yusaku Kamekura · JP

Child Ltd.
Children's clothing
1964 · Yusaku Kamekura · JP

Yusaku Kamekura naît en 1915 à Yoshida (aujourd'hui Tsubame). De 1935 à 1938, il suit des études principalement centrées sur l'architecture à la Nouvelle Académie d'Architecture et de Design industriel (Tokyo), une institution privée conçue sur le modèle du Bauhaus. Par la suite, il travaille pour des agences publicitaires et comme directeur artistique de plusieurs revues. En 1951, il devient cofondateur du Japan Advertising Arts Club, et en 1960 du Nippon Design Center. À partir de 1962, Kamekura prend son indépendance et commence à se faire remarquer par des travaux associant éléments constructivistes et esthétique japonaise traditionnelle. Au cours des années suivantes, il devient un des graphistes japonais les plus célèbres. Son travail pour les jeux Olympiques de Tokyo en 1964, puis pour l'Exposition universelle d'Osaka en 1970, lui assurent une renommée internationale. À côté d'affiches et d'emballages, les logos deviennent son médium privilégié et son centre d'intérêt principal. Son livre *Trademarks of the World* publié en 1956, pour lequel il réunira quelque 700 logos internationaux en cinq ans de travail, fut un ouvrage de référence de son époque. À partir de 1978, Kamekura est président de la toute nouvelle Japan Graphic Designers Association et accepte d'autres charges administratives dans des organismes de design internationaux. Kamekura travaillera à de nouveaux projets jusqu'à un âge avancé : en 1985, il crée une des marques commerciales les plus célèbres de son pays avec le logo de l'entreprise de télécommunications japonaise NTT. La même année, il lance le concept de *Creation*, un magazine qui, en cinq ans et 20 éditions, a documenté les évolutions du graphisme international. Kamekura s'éteint à Tokyo en 1997 à l'âge de 82 ans. Il est aujourd'hui considéré comme un des plus grands designers japonais du XXe siècle.

Nippon Hoso Kyokai
Broadcasting
1967 · Yusaku Kamekura · JP

Sangetsu
Wallpapers
1969 · Yusaku Kamekura · JP

**The Japan Society of Obstetrics
and Gynecology**
1970 · Yusaku Kamekura · JP

Meiji Seika Kaisha
Chocolate
1971 · Yusaku Kamekura · JP

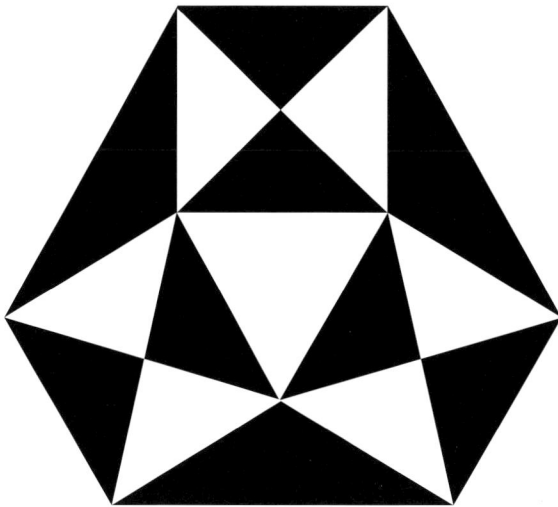

TDK – Tokyo Denki Kagaku Kogyo
Electronics
1966 · Yusaku Kamekura · JP

Association for the Promotion of
Traditional Craftsmanship
1975 · Yusaku Kamekura · JP

East-West Association for
Cultural Exchange
1978 · Yusaku Kamekura · JP

Fuji Bank
1979 · Yusaku Kamekura · JP

Nippon Telegraph
& Telephone Corp.
1985 · Yusaku Kamekura · JP

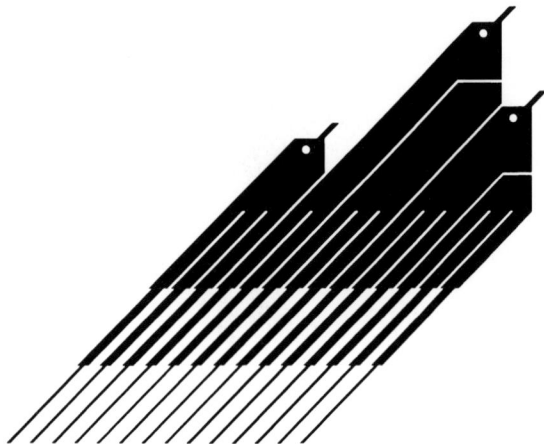

Cram School
1986 · Yusaku Kamekura · JP

TAK
Architecture
1992 · Yusaku Kamekura · JP

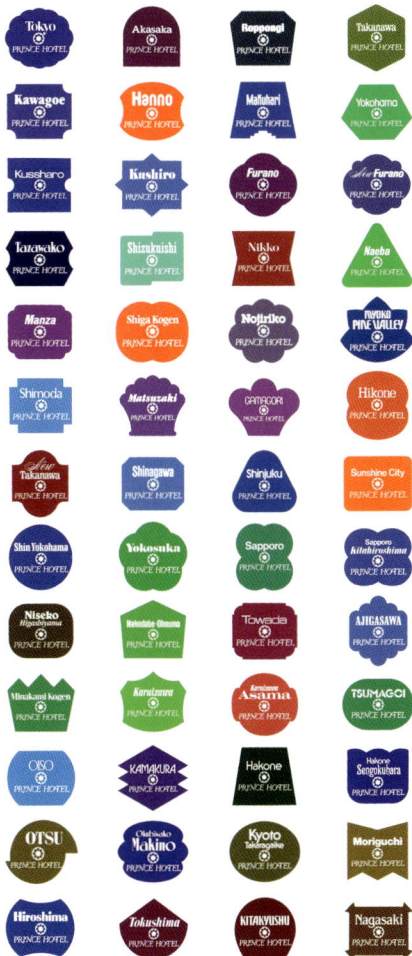

Up until 1968, the logo of the Prince Hotels chain was an old family coat of arms with a chrysanthemum in the center. Firstly, Yusaku Kamekura took the flower and transformed it into a symbol, on the white inner circle of which the locations of the hotels were shown. Secondly, he devised a system by which shapes, colors and typefaces could be interchanged to stand for individual hotels. Kamekura described his design as "a combination of Japanese elegance and Western beauty."

Die Hotelkette Prince Hotels verwendete bis 1968 ein altes Familienwappen mit einer Chrysantheme im Zentrum als Logo. Yusaku Kamekura abstrahierte die Blüte zu einem Symbol, bei dem die weißen Innenkreise auf die unterschiedlichen Standorte der Kette verweisen. Im zweiten Schritt wurde ein System konzipiert, das durch unterschiedliche Formen, Farben und Schriften die einzelnen Hotels individuell kennzeichnete. Kamekura beschrieb seine Lösung als „Kombination aus japanischer Eleganz und westlicher Schönheit."

Jusqu'en 1968, la chaîne hôtelière Prince Hotels avait eu pour logo un ancien blason familial conçu autour d'un chrysanthème central. Yusaku Kamekura simplifia cette fleur pour en faire un symbole dont les cercles intérieurs renvoient aux différentes implantations de la chaîne. Une seconde étape conduisit à concevoir un système dans lequel différentes formes, couleurs et écritures caractérisent individuellement les différents hôtels. Kamekura a décrit sa solution comme « combinaison d'élégance japonaise et de beauté occidentale. »

Stefan Kanchev

1915–2001 · BG

Stefan Kanchev was born in 1915 in Kalofer, Bulgaria. As a child he was taught to draw by his father, an icon painter. From 1933 he studied German philosophy in the capital Sofia. At the same time, he and an artist friend forged identity cards and other documents for anti-Fascists and Jews. In 1940 Kanchev entered the National Academy of Arts to study painting, but gave up his studies when he was hired as art director for a publishing house, so beginning his career as a graphic designer. In 1946, the People's Republic of Bulgaria came into being under Communist rule. In the same year Kanchev received his first commission to design a special stamp for the Bulgarian post office. Many more such assignments were to follow. Five years later he was appointed director of the state committee for graphic design. As such, Kanchev made crucial decisions on the use of graphics in numerous Bulgarian state corporations and institutions. Within a few years, trademark design became his main occupation. His work began to attract the attention of international design magazines and associations such as the International Center for the Typographic Arts and the American Institute of Graphic Arts, and a combination of exhibitions and publications made him one of the best-known and most respected figures on the international design scene. Between 1955 and 1985 Kanchev created around 2,000 trademarks, including logos for Bulgarian state television and the state-owned gas station chain. In the 1970s and '80s, Kanchev won many awards, but with the arrival of computers and the collapse of Communism he sank into oblivion. Only in recent years have several exhibitions and a book been devoted to the designer, who died in 2001, and whose work remains omnipresent in Bulgaria.

Stefan Kanchev wurde 1915 im bulgarischen Kalofer geboren. Von seinem Vater, einem Ikonenmaler, erhielt er bereits als Kind Zeichenunterricht. Ab 1933 studierte er zunächst Deutsche Philosophie in der Hauptstadt Sofia. In dieser Zeit fälschte er gemeinsam mit einem befreundeten Künstler auch Ausweise und andere Papiere für Antifaschisten und Juden. An der Nationalen Kunstakademie begann Kanchev 1940 ein Studium der Malerei. Mit Antritt der Position als künstlerischer Leiter eines Verlagshauses gab er sein Studium jedoch auf und begann eine Laufbahn als Grafikdesigner. 1946 wurde die Volksrepublik Bulgarien als kommunistischer Staat neu gegründet. Kanchev erhielt im gleichen Jahr einen ersten Auftrag für die Gestaltung einer Sonderbriefmarke der bulgarischen Post, dem noch viele weitere folgten. Fünf Jahre später berief man ihn zum Vorsitzenden der Staatskommission für Grafikdesign. In dieser Position entschied Kanchev maßgeblich über das Auftreten des bulgarischen Grafikdesigns in zahlreichen staatlichen Unternehmen und Institutionen mit. Der Entwurf von Markenzeichen wurde in den folgenden Jahren zu seiner bestimmenden Tätigkeit. Internationale Designmagazine und Verbände wie das International Center for the Typographic Arts oder das American Institute of Graphic Arts wurden auf seine Arbeiten aufmerksam und machen ihn durch Ausstellungen und Veröffentlichungen zu einer bekannten und respektierten Persönlichkeit der internationalen Designszene. Zwischen 1955 und 1985 entwarf Kanchev rund 2000 Markenzeichen, darunter das Logo des öffentlichrechtlichen Fernsehsenders oder der staatlichen Tankstellenkette des Landes. In den 1970er- und 1980er-Jahren erhielt Kanchev zahlreiche Auszeichnungen, geriet jedoch mit Aufkommen des Computers und dem Zerfall des kommunistischen Systems in Vergessenheit. Erst in den vergangenen Jahren wurde das Werk des 2001 verstorbenen Designers, das im heutigen Bulgarien noch immer omnipräsent ist, in mehreren Ausstellungen sowie einem Buchprojekt gewürdigt.

Applied Arts Center, Sofia
Cultural organization
1957 · Stefan Kanchev · BG

Kino Studio
Film studio
1957 · Stefan Kanchev · BG

Narodna Prosveta
Publishing
1957 · Stefan Kanchev · BG

Reklama
Advertising agency
1958 · Stefan Kanchev · BG

National Opera, Sofia
1960 · Stefan Kanchev · BG

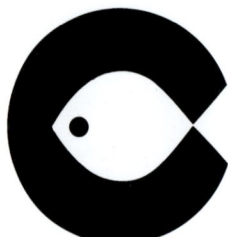

Sadala
Underwater fishing equipment
1960 · Stefan Kanchev · BG

Central Puppet Theater, Sofia
1963 · Stefan Kanchev · BG

Dunavia-Rousse
Canned foods
1963 · Stefan Kanchev · BG

Stefan Kanchev naît en 1915 à Kalofer, en Bulgarie. Dès son enfance, il apprend le dessin avec son père, un peintre d'icônes. À partir de 1933, il commence des études de philosophie allemande à Sofia, la capitale. À la même époque, il fabrique de fausses pièces d'identité avec un ami artiste pour des militants antifascistes et des juifs. En 1940, Kanchev suit des études de peinture à l'École nationale des Beaux-Arts, études qu'il abandonne toutefois lorsqu'il devient directeur artistique d'une maison d'édition et qu'il se lance ainsi dans une carrière de graphiste. En 1946, la Bulgarie est refondée comme État communiste sous le nom de République populaire de Bulgarie. La même année, Kanchev reçoit une commande pour la création d'un timbre spécial de la poste bulgare, première d'une longue série. Cinq ans plus tard, il est nommé président de la Commission nationale de graphisme. C'est à ce poste qu'il devient codécisionnaire de l'identité du graphisme bulgare de nombreuses entreprises et institutions d'État. Au cours des années suivantes, la création de logos devient son activité principale. Des magazines et des institutions de design internationales comme l'International Center for the Typographic Arts ou l'American Institute of Graphic Arts prennent connaissance de son travail – diverses expositions et publications vont faire de lui une des personnalités les plus connues et les plus respectées de la scène du design international. Entre 1955 et 1985, Kanchev a créé environ 2000 logos, notamment celui de la télévision publique ou celui de la chaîne de stations d'essence nationale de Bulgarie. Dans les années 1970 et 1980, Kanchev reçoit de nombreuses distinctions, mais sombre dans l'oubli avec l'arrivée de l'informatique et la chute du régime communiste. C'est seulement au cours de ces dernières années que l'œuvre du designer décédé en 2001, aujourd'hui encore omniprésent en Bulgarie, a été dignement célébrée à travers plusieurs expositions et d'un projet de livre.

Mineralni Vodi-Sofia
Mineral water
1963 · Stefan Kanchev · BG

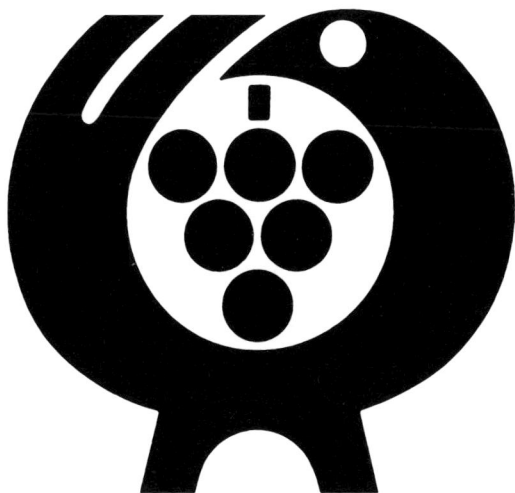

Vinsavod
Wine
1963 · Stefan Kanchev · BG

Zement Kombinat Wratza
Cement
1964 · Stefan Kanchev · BG

Bulgarian National Television
Broadcasting
1965 · Stefan Kanchev · BG

Balkancar
Forklift trucks
1966 · Stefan Kanchev · BG

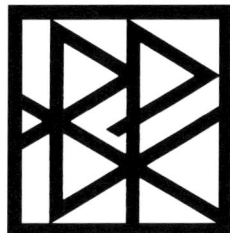

Building Materials
1966 · Stefan Kanchev · BG

Petrol
Gas stations
1964 · Stefan Kanchev · BG

For this oil company founded in 1932 Kanchev designed a trademark blend of lettering and imagery which could be used separately or together. His preparatory sketches reveal how he worked, always beginning with endless small drawings. The Petrol AD logos are still used to signpost nearly 500 gas stations across Bulgaria.

Für das 1932 gegründete Rohölunternehmen entwarf Kanchev eine Bild- und eine Wortmarke, die einzeln oder in Kombination verwendet werden konnten. Die dazugehörigen Skizzen aus dem Entwurfsprozess veranschaulichen seine Arbeitsweise, die immer mit unzähligen kleinen Zeichnungen begann. Bis heute sind die Petrol-Logos in Verwendung und kennzeichnen fast 500 Tankstellen in Bulgarien.

Pour cette entreprise pétrolière fondée en 1932, Kanchev créa un insigne et un logotype qui pouvaient être utilisés séparément ou combinés entre eux. Les croquis réalisés pendant le travail de conception illustrent la démarche du graphiste, qui commençait chaque projet par d'innombrables petits dessins. L'insigne et le logotype Petrol AD sont encore utilisés aujourd'hui et signalent presque 500 stations d'essence en Bulgarie.

State Music Hall, Sofia
Concert hall
1968 · Stefan Kanchev · BG

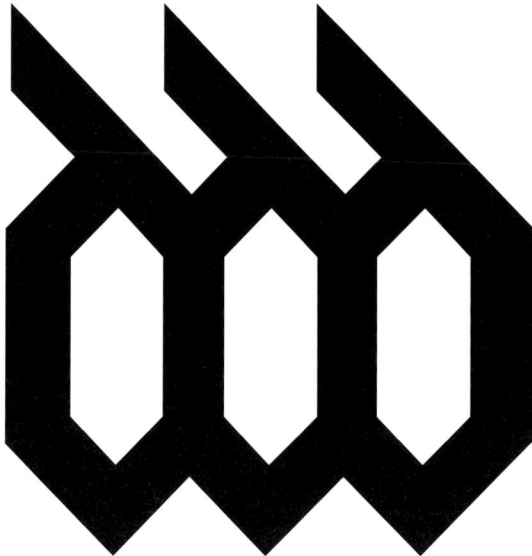

Nauka i Iskustvo
Publishing
1967 · Stefan Kanchev · BG

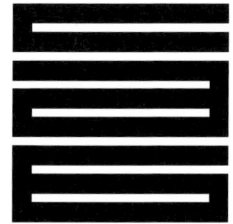

Union of Bulgarian Architects
1968 · Stefan Kanchev · BG

Bulgarian Center for Graphic Design
1970 · Stefan Kanchev · BG

DDD
Chemicals
1970 · Stefan Kanchev · BG

Feromagniti
Magnets
1970 · Stefan Kanchev · BG

Burton Kramer

*1932 · CA

Burton Kramer was born in 1932 in New York's Bronx neighborhood. From 1954 to 1957 he studied at the Institute of Design in Chicago and at Yale University School of Arts & Architecture, and also spent a year at the Royal College of Art in London. Kramer began his career as an assistant in Will Burtin's New York studio and as a designer for various corporate clients including the drug manufacturer Geigy. In 1961, he moved to Switzerland to work for the Erwin Halpern advertising agency, and it was there that he received the first awards for his work. After four years in Zurich he joined Paul Arthur Associates in Toronto, where he worked on graphics and signage for Expo '67. In 1967 he founded his own studio under the name of Burton Kramer & Associates—which later became Kramer Design Associates. Within a few years it was one of Canada's best-known design studios, with work mainly focused on creating complex corporate identities. In the 1970s Kramer developed logos for internationally respected institutions including the Royal Ontario Museum and the Canadian Broadcasting Corporation. In 1974 he took Canadian citizenship and in the same year became one of the first Canadian members of the design association Alliance Graphique Internationale. Between 1980 and 2001 he taught typography and corporate design at the Ontario College of Art and Design and was also a visiting lecturer at several international universities. In 1993 he turned to painting, producing work characterized by brightly colored geometric shapes, and in 2001 he retired from the design business, handing the agency over to his son Jeremy. Since then Kramer has devoted himself exclusively to abstract painting, continuing to experiment with the Modernist designs that were the hallmark of many of his commercial commissions.

Burton Kramer wurde 1932 im New Yorker Stadtteil Bronx geboren. Er studierte zwischen 1954 und 1957
am Institute of Design in Chicago, an der Yale University School of Arts & Architecture und ein Jahr am
Royal College of Art in London. Seine berufliche Laufbahn begann er zunächst als Assistent im Atelier von
Will Burtin in New York sowie als Gestalter für verschiedene Unternehmen wie dem Medikamentenher-
steller Geigy. 1961 zog er in die Schweiz, arbeitete für
die Werbeagentur Erwin Halpern und erhielt erste
Auszeichnungen für seine Arbeiten. Nach vier Jahren
in Zürich ging er nach Toronto, wo er bei Paul Arthur
Associates an Designelementen und Leitsystemen
für die Expo '67 arbeitete. Unter dem Namen Burton
Kramer & Associates (später Kramer Design Associates) gründete er 1967 sein eigenes Studio, das in den
folgenden Jahren zu einem der bekanntesten Designbüros des Landes aufstieg. Die Entwicklung von kom-
plexen Erscheinungsbildern wurde zum Schwerpunkt
des Studios. In den 1970er-Jahren entwickelte Kramer
international beachtete Identitäten für Auftraggeber
wie das Royal Ontario Museum oder die Canadian
Broadcasting Corporation. Er wurde 1974 kanadischer
Staatsbürger und im gleichen Jahr als eines der ersten
kanadischen Mitglieder in den renommierten Design-
verband Alliance Graphique Internationale aufgenommen. Zwischen 1980 und 2001 unterrichtete er
Typografie und Corporate Design am Ontario College
of Art and Design und war als Gastdozent an mehreren internationalen Hochschulen tätig. Seine Be-
schäftigung mit freier, auf geometrischen Formen
basierender Malerei begann 1993. Mit dem Jahr 2001
zog er sich ganz aus dem Agenturgeschäft zurück
und übergab die Leitung des Designbüros an seinen
Sohn Jeremy. Seither beschäftigt er sich ausschließlich mit abstrakter Malerei. Sein modernistischer
Gestaltungsansatz, der sich bereits in sämtlichen
seiner auftragsgebundenen Arbeiten zeigte, wird hier
experimentell fortgeführt.

Ytong
Paper
1961 · Burton Kramer · CA

Clairtone Sound Corporation
Audio electronics
1967 · Burton Kramer · CA

Children's Playgrounds
Toys
1969 · Burton Kramer · CA

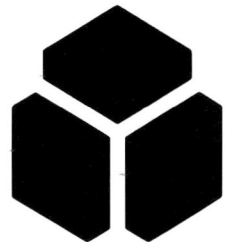

York Construction
1972 · Burton Kramer · CA

Pinestone Inn and Country Club
Resort and golf club
1972 · Burton Kramer · CA

Aerographics
Printing
1975 · Burton Kramer · CA

Hallmark Hotels
Hotel chain
1977 · Burton Kramer · CA

Glassworks
Art glass
1980 · Burton Kramer · CA

Burton Kramer est né en 1932 à New York dans le quartier du Bronx. De 1954 à 1957, il étudie à l'Institute of Design à Chicago, à la Yale University School of Arts and Architecture et pendant un an au Royal College of Art à Londres. Il commence sa carrière professionnelle comme assistant dans le studio new-yorkais de Will Burtin et comme designer pour différentes entreprises comme le fabricant de produits pharmaceutiques Geigy. En 1961, il s'installe en Suisse, où il travaille pour le compte de l'agence publicitaire Erwin Halpern et reçoit les premières distinctions pour ses réalisations. Après quatre années passées à Zurich, il s'installe à Toronto et travaille chez Paul Arthur Associates sur des éléments de design et des systèmes signalétiques pour l'Exposition universelle de 1967. En 1967, il fonde son propre studio Burton Kramer & Associates (futur Kramer Design Associates), qui devient au cours des années suivantes un des bureaux de design les plus célèbres du pays. La conception de systèmes visuels complexes devient le cœur de métier du studio. Dans les années 1970, Kramer conçoit les identités visuelles de commanditaires internationalement respectés comme le Musée royal de l'Ontario ou la Canadian Broadcasting Corporation. En 1974, il devient citoyen canadien. La même année, il est un des premiers Canadiens à intégrer la célèbre association de designers Alliance graphique internationale. Entre 1980 et 2001, il enseigne la typographie et le corporate design à l'Ontario College of Art and Design et travaille comme professeur invité dans plusieurs écoles internationales. Son intérêt pour la peinture indépendante basée sur des formes géométrique commence en 1993. En 2001, il se retire des affaires et confie la direction de l'agence de design à son fils Jeremy. Depuis, il se consacre exclusivement à la peinture abstraite. Son approche créative moderniste, déjà visible dans tous ses travaux appliqués, y trouve son prolongement expérimental.

In the early 1970s, the Canadian state television company was seeking a new corporate identity. In the competition to design a new logo, Burton Kramer's image of radio waves spreading from the central letter "C" was declared the winner. The logo was first used in 1974 as part of an overall visual design strategy. It remained in service, unchanged, until 1992 and is still one of Canada's best-known trademarks.

Das kanadische Staatsfernsehen suchte Anfang der 1970er-Jahre nach einer neuen visuellen Identität. Burton Kramers Konzept des Buchstabens „C" im Zentrum, um den herum sich Sendewellen ausbreiten, setzte sich im internationalen Wettbewerb durch. Eingebettet in ein umfangreiches visuelles Gesamtkonzept wurde es 1974 erstmals verwendet. Das Logo war unverändert bis 1992 im Einsatz und gehört zu den bekanntesten Markenzeichen Kanadas.

Au début des années 1970, la télévision nationale canadienne cherchait une nouvelle identité visuelle. Le concept de Burton Kramer – la lettre «C» centrale autour de laquelle se répandent les ondes radiodiffusées – s'imposa dans le cadre d'un concours international. Inséré dans un vaste concept général, le logo fut utilisé pour la première fois en 1974. Il resta inchangé jusqu'en 1992 et fait partie des sigles les plus connus du Canada.

Storwal
Office equipment
1977 · Burton Kramer · CA

Hornepayne Hallmark Town Centre
Shopping center
1978 · Burton Kramer · CA

International Sculpture Symposium
1982 · Burton Kramer · CA

Teknion
Office furniture
1984 · Burton Kramer · CA

Onex
Packaging
1980 · Burton Kramer · CA

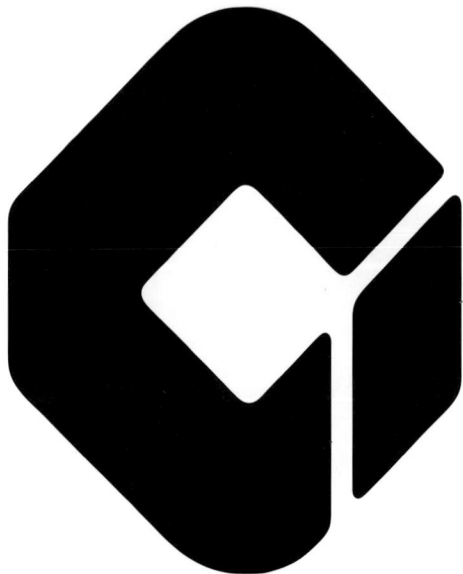

Centre Inn
Hotel
1984 · Burton Kramer · CA

Science North
Museum
1985 · Burton Kramer · CA

ZoomIt
Computer software
1988 · Burton Kramer · CA

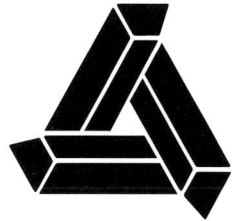

Amblin Resources
Gold mining
1988 · Burton Kramer · CA

Energy Corporation
1990 · Burton Kramer · CA

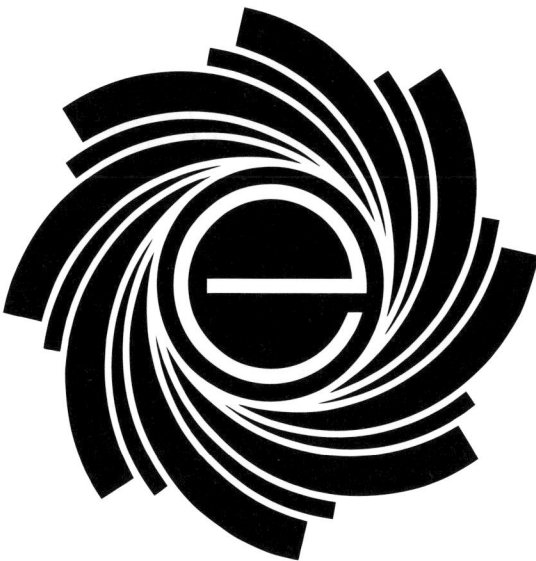

Silver Nightingale Lounge
Bar
1991 · Burton Kramer · CA

Paul Rand

1914–1996 · US

Paul Rand was born in Brooklyn in 1914. From 1929 to 1934 he studied in New York, first at the Pratt Institute, then at the Parsons School of Design, and finally at the Art Students League of New York. He then began his career as an illustrator and art director for magazines, including *Esquire*. Rand first achieved recognition on the design scene between 1938 and 1945 with his extraordinary cover designs for *Direction* magazine. At the same time, he took up his first teaching posts, while also designing book jackets and creating images for advertising campaigns. In 1954 he was named one of New York's ten best art directors. He began designing for IBM in 1956, completely revamping the company's corporate identity, and continued to fine-tune its logos until the early 1990s. Also in 1956 he became professor of graphic design at Yale University, a post he held, apart from some minor interruptions, until 1993. As an educator Rand influenced entire generations of American designers. In the early 1960s he created some of the USA's best-known trademarks, including logos for Westinghouse, ABC and UPS. He published a number of books, some of which are still regarded as standard works, and by participating in countless exhibitions he gradually became one of the 20th century's most important design pioneers. In collaboration with his first wife, Ann, he wrote and illustrated several successful books for children which, like all his other work, were examples of his playful, Modernist style. Developing complex designs and creating eye-catching logos were still his favorite occupations until well into old age. Paul Rand died in 1996 at the age of 82 in Norwalk, Connecticut.

Paul Rand wurde 1914 im New Yorker Stadtteil Brooklyn geboren. Er studierte zwischen 1929 und 1934 am Pratt Institute, an der Parsons School of Design sowie bei der Art Students League in New York. Im Anschluss begann seine Laufbahn als angestellter Illustrator und Art Director, u. a. für das *Esquire* Magazine. Mit außergewöhnlichen Cover-Entwürfen für das *Direction* Magazine erhielt Rand zwischen 1938 und 1945 erste Aufmerksamkeit in der Design-szene. Zur gleichen Zeit trat er erste Lehraufträge an, realisierte Buchumschläge und Werbekampagnen. Im Jahr 1954 wurde er zu einem der zehn besten New Yorker Art Directors gewählt. Seine Arbeit für das Unternehmen IBM begann 1956, dessen visuelle Identität er grundlegend überarbeitete und bis in die frühen 1990er-Jahre bestimmte. Im gleichen Jahr trat er eine Professur an der Yale University an, die er mit kurzer Unterbrechung bis 1993 innehatte. In dieser Funktion prägte Rand ganze Generationen amerika-nischer Designer. Anfang der 1960er-Jahre entwarf er einige der bis heute bekanntesten amerikanischen Markenzeichen – darunter die Logos für Westinghouse, ABC und UPS. Durch mehrere Buchveröffentlichungen, von denen viele bis heute als Standardwerke gelten, sowie durch zahlreiche Ausstellungen wurde er über die Jahre zu einer der wegweisenden Gestalterper-sönlichkeiten des 20. Jahrhunderts. Gemeinsam mit seiner ersten Frau Ann schrieb und illustrierte Paul Rand mehrere erfolgreiche Kinderbücher, die wie fast alle seine Arbeiten von einem spielerisch-moder-nistischen Stil geprägt sind. Bis ins hohe Alter blieb die Entwicklung komplexer Designsysteme und der Entwurf prägnanter Zeichen seine bevorzugte Auf-gabe. Paul Rand starb 1996 im Alter von 82 Jahren in Norwalk, Connecticut.

Smith, Kline and French
Pharmaceuticals
1945 · Paul Rand · US

Consolidated Cigar Corporation
1959 · Paul Rand · US

Colorforms
Toys
1959 · Paul Rand · US

United Parcel Service of America
Courier service
1961 · Paul Rand · US

American Broadcasting Company
Television network
1962 · Paul Rand · US

Atlas Corporation
Crankshaft drives
1964 · Paul Rand · US

Ford Motor Company
Automobiles (proposed design)
1966 · Paul Rand · US

US Bureau of Indian Affairs
Office for American Indian welfare
1968 · Paul Rand · US

Paul Rand naît en 1914 dans le quartier de Brooklyn, à New York. De 1929 à 1934, il étudie au Pratt Institute, à la Parsons School of Design et à l'Art Students League à New York. Après ses études, il se lance dans une carrière d'illustrateur et directeur artistique, notamment pour le magazine *Esquire*. Entre 1938 et 1945, il se fait remarquer par les pages de couverture inhabituelles qu'il crée pour le magazine *Direction*. À la même époque, il accepte ses premiers postes d'enseignement, réalise des couvertures de livres et des campagnes publicitaires. En 1954, il est élu parmi les dix meilleurs directeurs artistiques de New York. C'est en 1956 que Rand commence son travail pour IBM : il redéfinit entièrement l'identité visuelle de l'entreprise et continuera de le faire jusqu'au début des années 1990. Toujours en 1956, il accepte à l'Université Yale une chaire qu'il occupera jusqu'en 1993 avec une courte interruption. C'est à ce poste qu'il marquera des générations entières de designers américains. Au début des années 1960, il conçoit quelques-uns des logos américains les plus célèbres jusqu'à ce jour – notamment ceux de Westinghouse, ABC et UPS. Grâce à plusieurs ouvrages, dont beaucoup font aujourd'hui encore référence, mais aussi a de nombreuses expositions, Rand est devenu au fil des années une des personnalités du monde du design les plus influentes du XXe siècle. En collaboration avec sa première femme Ann, Paul Rand a aussi écrit et illustré plusieurs livres pour enfants couronnés de succès ; comme presque tous ses travaux, ils sont marqués par un style ludique et moderniste. Le développement de systèmes graphiques complexes et la conception de signes marquants sont restés son cœur de métier. Paul Rand s'est éteint en 1996 à Norwalk, Connecticut, à l'âge de 82 ans.

Westinghouse Electric
Energy supplier
1960 · Paul Rand · US

American Institute of Graphic Arts
(proposed design)
1982 · Paul Rand · US

Yale University
1985 · Paul Rand · US

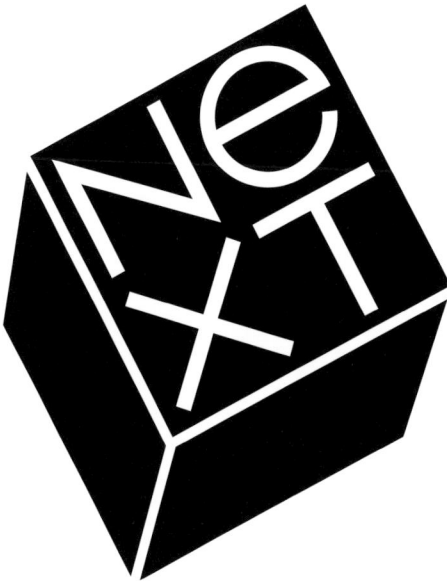

Next
Computers
1986 · Paul Rand · US

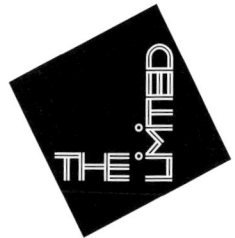

The Limited
Clothing store
1988 · Paul Rand · US

Okasan Securites Inc.
Finance
1991 · Paul Rand · US

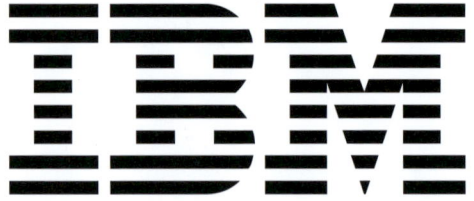

International Business Machines
Technology and computing solutions
1956/1967 · Paul Rand · US

In 1956, Paul Rand was asked if he
could develop a corporate identity for
the business-machine developer IBM.
Although he had never before been
offered such a mammoth assignment,
he said he could. He began by designing
a new logo and an entire alphabet in a
new, custom-made typeface. A whole
series of other applications, such as
packaging, would follow later. He also
laid down a set of rules for how the
corporation should be represented
internationally. The logo in use today
was designed by Rand in 1967.

Paul Rand wurde 1956 gefragt, ob er für
den Büromaschinenhersteller IBM ein
Designsystem entwickeln könne. Obwohl
er einen Auftrag dieser Größe noch nicht
bearbeitet hatte, sagte er zu und entwickelte zunächst ein neues Logo samt
vollständigem Alphabet. Später folgten
zahlreiche weitere Anwendungsmöglich-
keiten, etwa für Verpackungen, sowie
Regeln für das internationale Auftreten
des Unternehmens. Das Logo in seiner
heute verwendeten Form gestaltete
Rand 1967.

En 1956, on demanda à Paul Rand s'il
pouvait développer un système graphique
pour le fabricant de machines de bureau
IBM. Bien qu'il n'eût encore jamais
traité de commande de cette envergure,
il accepta et créa d'abord un nouveau
logo et un alphabet complet. Plus tard
suivirent de nombreuses autres possibilités d'utilisation, notamment pour des
emballages, ainsi que des règles pour
l'identité visuelle internationale de
l'entreprise. Dans sa forme actuelle,
le logo d'IBM a été développé par Rand
en 1967.

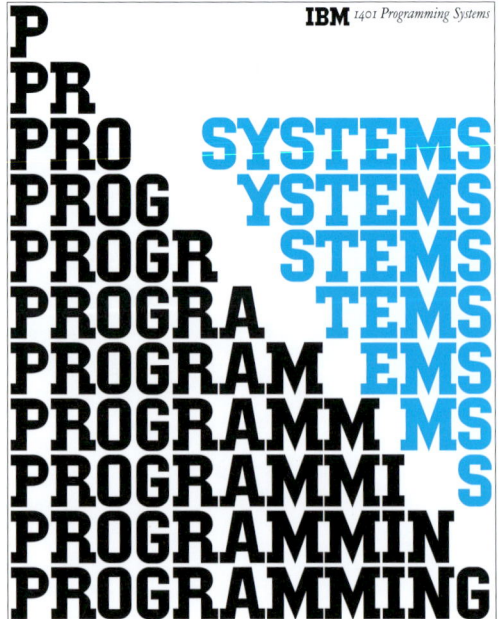

Enron
Energy supplier
1996 · Paul Rand · US

Pastore DePamphilis Rampone
Computer graphics
1987 · Paul Rand · US

Morningstar
Investment research
1991 · Paul Rand · US

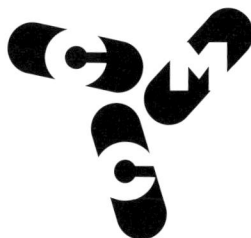

Creative Media Center
Design
1994 · Paul Rand · US

English First
Language schools
1993 · Paul Rand · US

Hub TV
Broadcasting
1995 · Paul Rand · US

Karol Śliwka was born in 1932 in the village of Harbutowice in Silesia. In 1946, when he was only 14, he began studying painting, sculpture and graphics at night school in the city of Bielsko-Biała. Moving on to the state-run school of art in the early 1950s, he gained a diploma in sculpture and stonemasonry. After completing his studies at the Academy of Fine Arts in Warsaw in 1959, Śliwka decided to make a career in graphic design and opened his own studio in Warsaw. Before long he had successfully completed a large number of assignments. At the same time he competed for and was awarded contracts to create new trademarks. He went on to design postage stamps, posters, packaging and prospectuses for a wide variety of clients in commerce, industry and the cultural sector, and to win awards in national and international competitions. The logo he originally intended for a 1969 poster advertising the Polish bank PKO is still one of the country's best-known trademarks. Śliwka's poster designs won the international competition to design the graphics for the 1980 Moscow Olympics and, four years later, his was also the winning entry in the poster competition for the Olympic Games in Los Angeles. Over the years, he has concentrated more and more on logos. Karol Śliwka lived in Warsaw up to his death in 2018.

Karol Śliwka

1932–2018 · PL

Karol Śliwka wurde 1932 in dem schlesischen Dorf Harbutowice geboren. Im Alter von nur 14 Jahren begann er 1946 eine Ausbildung an der Abendschule für Malerei, Bildhauerei und Graphik in Bielsko-Biała. Anfang der 1950er-Jahre wechselte er zur nationalen Kunstschule und erwarb sich dort ein Diplom als Skulpteur und Steinmetz. Schließlich beendete er 1959 sein Studium an der Akademie der Bildenden Künste in Warschau. Śliwka entschloss sich auf dem Feld der angewandten Grafik aktiv zu werden und eröffnete ein eigenes Atelier in Warschau. Bereits nach kurzer Zeit stellte sich der Erfolg ein und zahlreiche Aufträge wurden realisiert. Zudem setzte er sich bei mehreren Wettbewerben durch und gewann zahlreiche Ausschreibungen für neue Markenzeichen. In den folgenden Jahren gestaltete er Briefmarken, Plakate, Verpackungen und Prospekte für unterschiedlichste Auftraggeber aus Wirtschaft, Kultur und Industrie. Auszeichnungen in nationalen und internationalen Wettbewerben folgten. Das eigentlich nur für einen Plakatentwurf angelegte Logo der polnischen Bank PKO entstand 1969 und ist noch heute eines der bekanntesten Signets des Landes. Seine Plakatentwürfe von 1980 setzten sich im internationalen Wettbewerb um Motive für die Olympischen Spiele in Moskau durch, vier Jahre später konnte er diesen Erfolg bei dem Plakatwettbewerb der Spiele von Los Angeles wiederholen. Der Entwurf von Logos blieb über die Jahre Schwerpunkt seines grafischen Schaffens. Karol Śliwka lebte bis zum Tod im Jahr 2018 in Warschau.

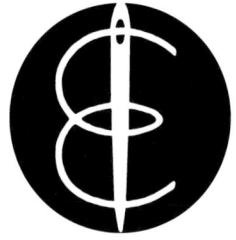

Elegancja
Fashion
1964 · Karol Śliwka · PL

Zakłady Artystyczne Z.P.A.P.
Artists association
1964 · Karol Śliwka · PL

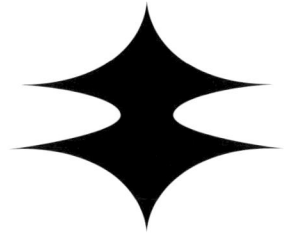

Exhibition of Polish Trademarks
1968 · Karol Śliwka · PL

Mysiadlo
State farm
1971 · Karol Śliwka · PL

S.P. Powisle
Interior design
1965 · Karol Śliwka · PL

Chelmec
Footwear
1967 · Karol Śliwka · PL

Zakład Obuwniczy Kobra
Footwear
1967 · Karol Śliwka · PL

Cosmetics
1969 · Karol Śliwka · PL

Karol Śliwka est né en 1932 à Harbutowice, un village de Silésie. En 1946, tout juste âgé de quatorze ans, il commence une formation de peintre, sculpteur et graphiste à Bielsko-Biała dans le cadre de cours du soir. Au début des années 1950, il entre à l'École nationale d'Art, d'où il sort avec un diplôme de sculpteur et tailleur de pierre. En 1959, il complète finalement ses études à l'École des Beaux-Arts de Varsovie. Śliwka décide ensuite de travailler dans le domaine du graphisme appliqué et ouvre son propre studio à Varsovie. Il connaît rapidement le succès et reçoit de nombreuses commandes, mais s'impose aussi dans plusieurs concours et gagne de nombreux appels d'offres pour la création de nouveaux logos. Au cours des années suivantes, il réalise des timbres, affiches, emballages et brochures pour différents commanditaires issus de l'économie, de la culture et de l'industrie. Suivent alors des distinctions dans des concours nationaux et internationaux. Le logo de la banque polonaise PKO, initialement conçu pour un projet d'affiche, a vu le jour en 1969 et est aujourd'hui encore un des sigles les plus connus du pays. En 1980, les projets d'affiches de Śliwka se sont imposés dans le cadre du concours international lancé autour de motifs pour les jeux Olympiques de Moscou, succès que le designer réitérera quatre ans plus tard à l'occasion du concours d'affiches des jeux Olympiques de Los Angeles. Pendant toutes ces années, la création de logos n'en est pas moins restée le noyau de son travail graphique. Karol Śliwka a vécu a Varsovie jusqu'à sa mort en 2018.

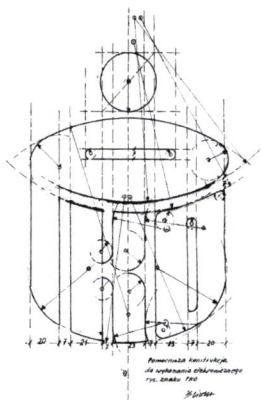

PKO
Bank
1969 · Karol Śliwka · PL

Every year Poland's PKO bank commissioned a different graphic designer to create a new poster to celebrate World Savings Day in October. Karol Śliwka designed this distinctive poster in 1969 in which he played with the bank's initials to produce a money box into which a coin is being dropped. Awarded the gold medal at the Polish Poster Biennale, the image so delighted PKO management that the bank has used it to this day.

Zum Weltspartag im Oktober gab die polnische Bank PKO jedes Jahr ein neues Werbeplakat bei jeweils einem anderen Grafiker in Auftrag. Karol Śliwka entwarf dieses markante Plakat 1969, bei dem das Buchstabenkürzel der Bank zu einer Spardose wird, in die eine Münze fällt. Die Arbeit erhielt die Goldmedaille der polnischen Plakatbiennale und gefiel auch den Verantwortlichen der Bank so gut, dass daraus das bis heute verwendete Logo des Unternehmens wurde.

Chaque année en octobre, à l'occasion de la Journée mondiale de l'épargne, la banque polonaise PKO commandait une nouvelle affiche publicitaire à un autre graphiste. En 1969, Karol Śliwka dessina cette affiche mémorable qui transformait le sigle de la banque en tirelire. Ce travail reçut la médaille d'or de la Biennale polonaise de l'affiche et plut tellement à la direction qu'elle devint le logo de la banque, qui l'a conservé jusqu'à aujourd'hui.

**Council for Mutual
Economic Assistance**
1970s · Karol Śliwka · PL

Zorza
Photographic services
1971 · Karol Śliwka · PL

Pollena
Cosmetics
1973 · Karol Śliwka · PL

Elektryków Polskich
Electrical engineers association
1976 · Karol Śliwka · PL

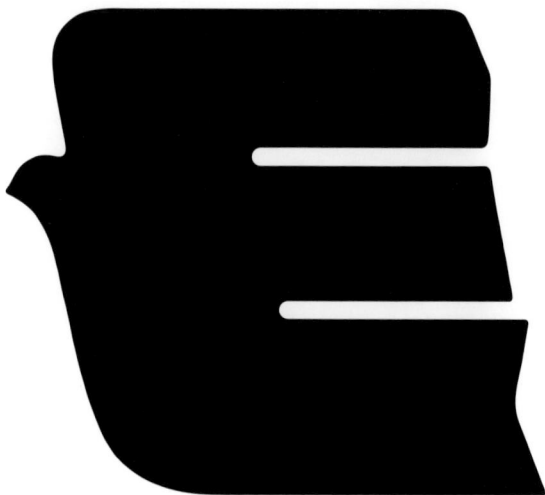

Europejskie Zgromadzenie Studentów
Students association
1974 · Karol Śliwka · PL

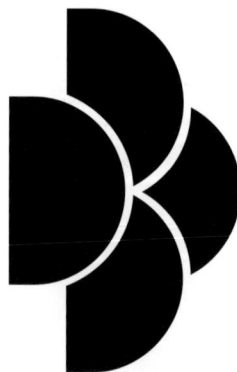

Dika
Import-export
1989 · Karol Śliwka · PL

Urbanistyki Miasta
Urban planning
1979 · Karol Śliwka · PL

Polton
Record label
1984 · Karol Śliwka · PL

Spółdzielnia Mieszkaniowa
Housing association
1987 · Karol Śliwka · PL

Alfa
Chemicals
1990 · Karol Śliwka · PL

Biocom
Pharmaceuticals
1996 · Karol Śliwka · PL

Anton Stankowski was born in 1906 in Gelsenkirchen. He served an apprenticeship as a painter of stage sets before becoming a journeyman in a church painter's studio. From 1927 to 1929 he attended the Folkwang School of Art in Essen, where his tutors included Max Burchartz, a pioneer of German graphic design. In 1929 Stankowski moved to Zurich to work in an advertising studio where he first came into contact with Constructivist artists such as Richard Paul Lohse, Herbert Matter and Max Bill. In 1938 he returned to Germany and two years later was drafted for military service, but was soon taken prisoner by Soviet forces and was not released from the PoW camp until 1948. He then spent four years as an editor, graphic artist and photographer for the magazine Stuttgarter Illustrierte before finally setting up his own studio in Stuttgart in 1951. He quickly made a name for himself, especially as a designer of trademarks for industrial corporations, and rapidly built up a solid customer base. Within a few years he had to hire more designers and assistants, and his studio became one of Germany's premier addresses for graphic design. Alongside graphic design, Stankowski pursued his interest in Constructivist art, and often the boundaries between his commissioned work and his own artistic projects became blurred. For example, on a number of occasions he used experimental works as illustrations for promotional calendars. He was also commissioned as an interior designer for corporate buildings. His Deutsche Bank logo, designed in 1974 for a competition to create a new brand for the bank, is one of the world's best-known trademarks. When Karl Duschek became a partner in the practice in 1980, Stankowski was able to devote more time to painting. Ever since, the work he did for his own pleasure rather than for clients has been admired in several solo and group exhibitions. Until his death in 1998 Stankowski remained true to his role as an artist who successfully straddled the boundary between working to order and self-expression. His motto continued to be: "Whether it's art or design, it has to be good."

Anton Stankowski

1906–1998 · DE

Anton Stankowski wurde 1906 in Gelsenkirchen geboren. Seine Ausbildung begann er bei einem Dekorationsmaler und als Geselle bei einem Atelier für Kirchenkunst. Zwischen 1927 und 1929 studierte er an der Folkwangschule in Essen, u. a. bei Max Burchartz, einem Pionier des deutschen Grafikdesigns. Der Umzug nach Zürich erfolgte 1929, wo er in einem Reklameatelier tätig war und erste Kontakte zu konstruktivistischen Künstlern wie Richard Paul Lohse, Herbert Matter oder Max Bill knüpfen konnte. Er musste 1938 nach Deutschland zurückkehren und wurde zwei Jahre später zum Kriegsdienst eingezogen. Bald darauf geriet Stankowski in russische Kriegsgefangenschaft und kam erst 1948 wieder frei. Danach arbeitete er vier Jahre lang als Schriftleiter, Grafiker und Fotograf bei der Stuttgarter Illustrierten und gründete schließlich 1951 ein eigenes Atelier in Stuttgart. Besonders als Entwickler von Markenzeichen für Industrieunternehmen machte er sich schnell einen Namen und konnte einen veritablen Kundenstamm aufbauen. Sein Atelier, in dem er bereits nach wenigen Jahren mehrere Mitarbeiter und Assistenten beschäftigte, wurde zu einer der ersten Adressen für Grafikdesign in Deutschland. Parallel arbeitete Stankowski immer an konstruktivistisch-künstlerischen Arbeiten. Nicht selten war die Grenze zwischen Auftragsarbeit und künstlerischem Projekt fließend. So publizierte er beispielsweise seine experimentellen Arbeiten mehrfach als Werbekalender oder wurde mit künstlerischen Arbeiten für die Gestaltung von Firmengebäuden beauftragt. Mit seinem Logo für die Deutsche Bank, das sich in einem internen Wettbewerb durchsetzte, schuf er 1974 eines der bestbekannten internationalen Markenzeichen. Der Gestalter Karl Duschek wurde 1980 Partner des Ateliers. Stankowski konnte sich nun verstärkt der Malerei widmen. Seine freien Arbeiten wurden spätestens seit dieser Zeit in zahllosen Einzel- und Gruppenausstellungen gewürdigt. Bis zu seinem Tod im Jahr 1998 blieb Stankowski seiner Rolle als Grenzgänger zwischen freien und angewandten Arbeiten treu, gemäß des von ihm selber formulierten Leitspruchs: „Ob Kunst oder Design ist egal – nur gut muss es sein."

Canis Lehrfilme
Educational films
1938 · Anton Stankowski · DE

Berga
Curtains
1949 · Anton Stankowski · DE

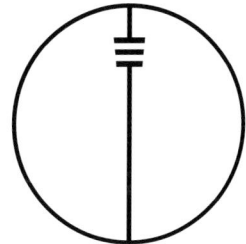

Süddeutscher Rundfunk
Broadcasting
1954 · Anton Stankowski · DE

Dr. O. S. Rechenauer
Management consultancy
1956 · Anton Stankowski · DE

Animal Feed
1950 · Anton Stankowski · DE

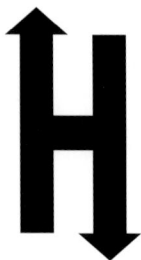

Haushahn Aufzugfabrik
Elevators
1950s · Anton Stankowski · DE

Savag Versicherung
Insurance
1959 · Anton Stankowski · DE

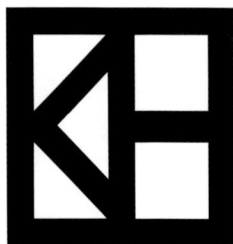

Kornhaus
Textiles
1960s · Anton Stankowski · DE

Anton Stankowski naît en 1906 à Gelsenkirchen, en Allemagne. Il commence sa formation chez un peintre décorateur, puis comme apprenti dans un atelier d'art d'église. De 1927 à 1929, il suit des études à la Folkwangschule, à Essen, notamment avec Max Burchartz, pionnier du design graphique allemand. En 1929, il s'installe à Zurich, où il travaille dans un atelier de réclames et noue ses premiers liens avec des artistes constructivistes comme Richard Paul Lohse, Herbert Matter ou Max Bill. Contraint de rentrer en Allemagne en 1938, il est mobilisé deux ans plus tard pour le service de guerre. Peu après, il est fait prisonnier de guerre en Russie et ne sera libéré qu'en 1948. À son retour, Stankowski travaille pendant quatre ans comme rédacteur en chef, graphiste et photographe à la Stuttgarter Illustrierte avant de fonder finalement son propre atelier en 1951 à Stuttgart. Il se fait rapidement un nom, principalement comme développeur de marques commerciales pour des entreprises industrielles, et parvient à se constituer une véritable clientèle fixe. Son studio, dans lequel il emploie plusieurs collaborateurs et assistants après seulement quelques années, devient une des premières adresses de design graphique en Allemagne. Parallèlement, Stankowski travaille régulièrement à des œuvres artistiques constructivistes, et il n'est pas rare que la frontière entre travail de commande et projet artistique soit perméable : c'est ainsi qu'il publie à plusieurs reprises ses travaux expérimentaux sous forme de calendriers publicitaires ou qu'on lui passe commande d'œuvres artistiques pour décorer des bâtiments industriels. Avec le logo conçu pour la Deutsche Bank, qui s'impose dans le cadre d'un concours interne, il crée en 1974 un des signes les mieux connus au niveau international. En 1980, le graphiste Karl Duschek devient associé de son studio. Stankowski peut alors consacrer davantage de temps à la peinture. À partir de cette époque, son travail indépendant est présenté dans de nombreuses expositions de groupe ou personnelles. Jusqu'à sa mort en 1998, Stankowski est resté fidèle à son rôle de frontalier entre les domaines appliqué et indépendant, conformément à sa devise «Art ou design, peu importe – pourvu que ce soit bon.»

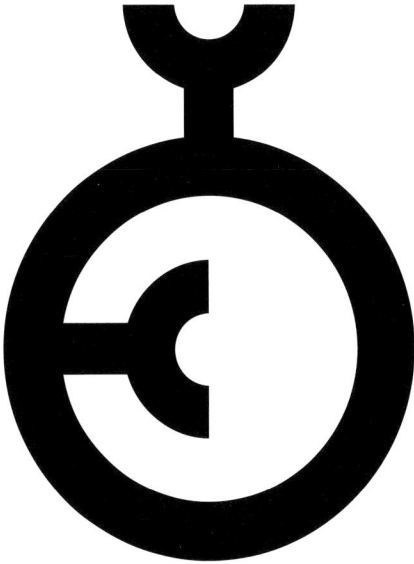

Rat für Formgebung
Design council
1960 · Anton Stankowski · DE

LTG Lufttechnische Gesellschaft
Air-conditioning
1962 · Anton Stankowski · DE

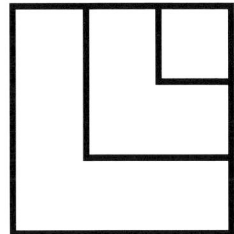

VIESSMANN

Viessmann
Heating technology
1960 · Anton Stankowski · DE

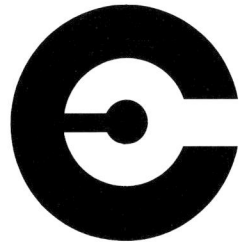

Reproduktionsmaschinen AG
Reprographics
1960s · Anton Stankowski · DE

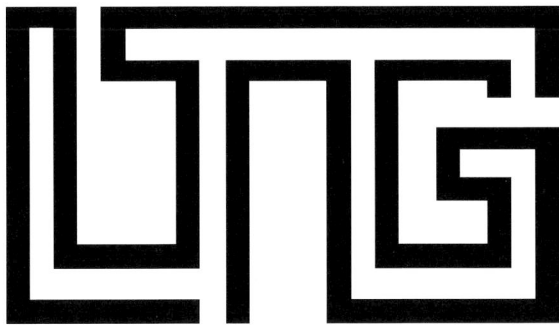

**Rationalisierungskuratorium
der Deutschen Wirtschaft**
Trade organization
1968 · Anton Stankowski · DE

**Internationale Messe für
Sanitär Heizung und Klima**
Heating and sanitation trade fair
1974 · Anton Stankowski · DE

The Deutsche Werkbund is an association of artists, architects, designers and industrialists that was founded in 1907. When Stankowski was commissioned to design a new logo in 1963, the organization had 14 independent regional branches. His design solution consisted of the words "Werk" and "Bund," which could be changed through color variations and different positioning of the two syllables. The image reflected the centralized as well as the decentralized nature of the association. The logo is still in use today.

Der Deutsche Werkbund ist eine wirtschaftskulturelle Vereinigung von Künstlern, Architekten, Unternehmern und Sachverständigen, die bereits 1907 gegründet wurde. Als Stankowski 1963 mit dem Entwurf eines neuen Signets beauftragt wurde, hatte der Werkbund 14 unabhängige Landesverbände. Seine Lösung bestand in einer kombinierten Wortmarke, die sich durch unterschiedliche Platzierung und Farbigkeit verändern ließ. Als visuelle Synthese wurde Zentralisation und Dezentralisation des Vereins widergespiegelt. Bis heute ist sein Logo in Verwendung.

Le Deutscher Werkbund, regroupement économique et culturel d'artistes, architectes, entrepreneurs et experts a été fondé dès 1907. En 1963, au moment où Stankowski est chargé d'en concevoir le nouveau signet, le Werkbund compte déjà 14 associations indépendantes œuvrant chacune dans le cadre d'un Land. Sa solution graphique fut une marque combinée pouvant être modulée en termes de disposition et de couleurs. La synthèse visuelle traduisait le caractère centralisé et décentralisé du Werkbund.

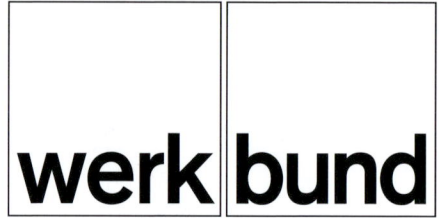

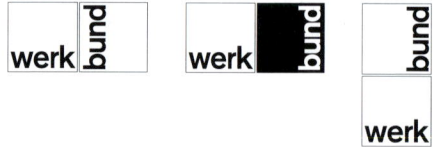

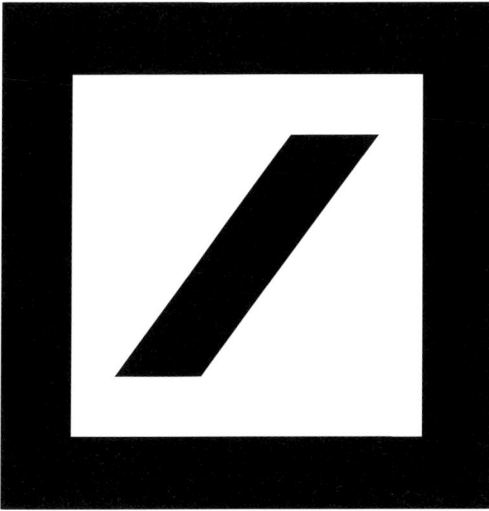

Deutsche Bank
1973 · Anton Stankowski · DE

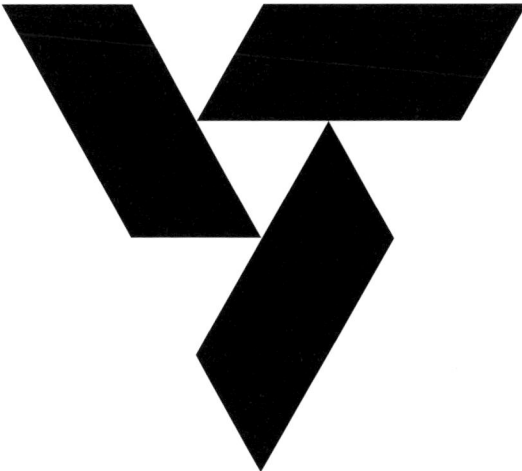

Vereinte Versicherung
Insurance
1986 · Anton Stankowski · DE

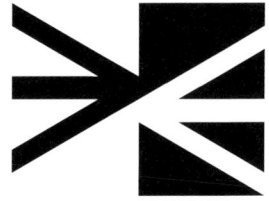

Moeckl Dialog Funkgeräte
Radio equipment
1979 · Anton Stankowski · DE

Hatje Verlag
Publishing
1980 · Anton Stankowski · DE

**BKK Bundesverband der
Betriebskrankenkassen**
Union of company health insurance funds
1988 · Anton Stankowski · DE

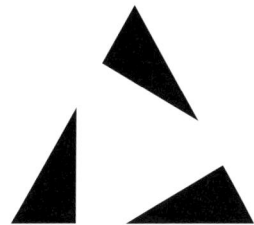

Altana AG
Chemicals
1990 · Anton Stankowski · DE

507

EACH AND EVERY TASCHEN BOOK PLANTS A SEED!
Each year, we offset our annual carbon emissions with carbon credits at the Instituto Terra, a reforestation program in Minas Gerais, Brazil, founded by Lélia and Sebastião Salgado. To find out more about this ecological partnership, please check: www.taschen.com/institutoterra. Inspiration: unlimited. Carbon footprint: (almost) zero.

Want to see more? Visit taschen.com to view our current publications, browse our latest magazine, and subscribe to our newsletter.

© 2025 TASCHEN GmbH
Hohenzollernring 53
D-50672 Köln
www.taschen.com

Original edition © 2015 / 2022
TASCHEN GmbH

Picture Credits
p. 252: SLUB Dresden/
Deutsche Fotothek
© Sabine F. Bloch for the work
of F. H. Ehmcke

Design
Jens Müller/vista
www.studiovista.de

Editor
Julius Wiedemann

English Translation
Logo Beginnings: Hayley Haupt, Brussels
Logo Modernism: Isabel Varea Riley for
Grapevine Publishing Services, London

German Translation
Logo Modernism: Ursula Wulfekamp for
Grapevine Publishing Services, London

French Translation
Logo Beginnings: Claire Debard, Freiburg
Logo Modernism: Wolf Fruhtrunk

Printed in Bosnia-Herzegovina
ISBN 978-3-7544-0137-8